DB2® SQL PL, Second Edition

ON DEMAND COMPUTING BOOKS

On Demand Computing: Technologies and Strategies
Fellenstein

Grid Computing
Joseph and Fellenstein

Autonomic Computing
Murch

Business Intelligence for the Enterprise
Biere

DB2 BOOKS

DB2 Express: Easy Development and Administration
Yip, Cheung, Gartner, Liu, and O'Connell

DB2 Universal Database V8.1 Certification Exam 700 Study Guide
Sanders

DB2 Universal Database V8.1 Certification Exams 701 and 706 Study Guide
Sanders

DB2 Universal Database V8.1 Certification Exam 703 Study Guide
Sanders

High Availability Guide for DB2
Eaton and Cialini

DB2 for Solaris: The Official Guide
Bauch and Wilding

DB2 Universal Database V8 for Linux, UNIX, and Windows DBA Certification Guide, Fifth Edition
Baklarz and Wong

Advanced DBA Certification Guide for DB2 Universal Database V8 for Linux, UNIX, and Windows
Snow and Phan

DB2 Universal Database V8 Application Development Certification Guide, Second Edition
Martineau, Sanyal, Gashyna, and Kyprianou

DB2 Version 8: The Official Guide
Zikopoulos, Baklarz, deRoos, and Melnyk

DB2 for z/OS Version 8 DBA Certification Guide
Lawson

DB2 Universal Database V8 Handbook for Windows, UNIX, and Linux
Gunning

Integrated Solutions with DB2
Cutlip and Medicke

The Official Introduction to DB2 for z/OS
Sloan

MORE BOOKS FROM IBM PRESS

IBM WebSphere: Deployment and Advanced Configuration
Barcia, Hines, Alcott, and Botzum

Enterprise Java Programming with IBM WebSphere, Second Edition
Brown, Craig, Hester, Pitt, Stinehour, Weitzel, Amsden, Jakab, and Berg

The Inventor's Guide to Trademarks and Patents
Fellenstein, Vassallo, and Ralston

Developing Quality Technical Information, Second Edition
Hargis, Carey, Hernandez, Hughes, Longo, Rouiller, and Wilde

IBM WebSphere and Lotus: Implementing Collaborative Solutions
Lamb, Laskey, and Indurkhya

IBM WebSphere System Administration
Williamson, Chan, Cundiff, Lauzon, and Mitchell

Enterprise Messaging Using JMS and IBM WebSphere
Yusuf

DB2® SQL PL, Second Edition

Essential Guide for DB2® UDB on Linux™, UNIX®, Windows®, i5/OS™, z/OS®

DB2® Information Management Systems

Zamil Janmohamed, Clara Liu, Drew Bradstock,
Raul Chong, Michael Gao, Fraser McArthur, Paul Yip

An Imprint of PEARSON EDUCATION
Upper Saddle River, NJ • New York • San Francisco
Toronto • London • Munich • Paris • Madrid
Capetown • Sydney • Tokyo • Singapore • Mexico City
www.phptr.com

Library of Congress Publication in Data: 2004109908

IBM Consulting Editor: *Susan Visser*
Acquisitions Editor: *Jeff Pepper*
Marketing Manager: *Robin O'Brien*
Managing Editor: *Gina Kanouse*
Project Management: *Michael Thurston*
Editorial/Production Supervision: *Specialized Composition, Inc.*
Cover Design: *IBM Corporation*
Manufacturing Buyer: *Dan Uhrig*

Published by Pearson Education, Inc.
Publishing as IBM Press
Upper Saddle River, New Jersey 07458

Pearson Education offers excellent discounts on this book when ordered in quantity for bulk purchases or special sales. For more information, please contact U.S. Corporate and Government Sales, 1-800-382-3419, corpsales@pearsontechgroup.com. For sales outside the U.S., please contact International Sales at international@pearsoned.com.

The following terms are trademarks or registered trademarks of International Business Machines Corporation in the United States, other countries, or both: DB2, Lotus, Tivoli, WebSphere, Rational, IBM, the IBM logo, and IBM Press.

Java and all Java-based trademarks are trademarks of Sun Microsystems, Inc. in the United States, other countries, or both.

Microsoft, Windows, Windows NT, and the Windows logo are trademarks of the Microsoft Corporation in the United States, other countries, or both.

Intel, Intel Inside (logo), MMX, and Pentium are trademarks of Intel Corporation in the United States, other countries, or both.

UNIX is a registered trademark of The Open Group in the United States and other countries.

Other company, product, or service names may be trademarks or service marks of others.

Printed in the United States of America
First Printing: November 2004
ISBN 0-13-147700-5

Pearson Education LTD.
Pearson Education Australia PTY, Limited.
Pearson Education Singapore, Pte. Ltd.
Pearson Education North Asia, Ltd.
Pearson Education Canada, Ltd.
Pearson Educatión de Mexico, S.A. de C.V.
Pearson Education—Japan
Pearson Education Malaysia, Pte. Ltd.

CONTENTS

Chapter 4 Using Flow of Control Statements

CONTRIBUTORS

This book is a result of many people's efforts and we would like to thank the following individuals for their contributions.

Serge Rielau and Gustavo Arocena from DB2 development provided tremendous support and technical guidance on almost every topic we covered in the book. Their continuous support since the first edition of this book greatly helped us in verifying the content and providing insight to SQL PL.

Without the encouragement of Susan Visser, we might still be "thinking" about updating the first edition of this book. She has once again provided guidance to help us complete the book smoothly.

A book that is technical in nature and filled with as many code samples as this book has, cannot be published without engaging technical reviewers to both read and test the samples. Providing coverage for multiple platforms with this edition means that we had even more eyes looking at this book. We would like to thank the following people who helped us with this process:

From the iSeries organization:

Scott Forstie

Kent Milligan

Kathy Passe

Jarek Miszczyk

Through the publisher:

George Baklaz

Graham Milne

James Campbell

Acknowledgments

It was great working with my "old" team again on a project. Many of us have moved on to different roles, and it was nice to have an excuse to work together again. I can't forget the many weekends spent on the group edit sessions! Incorporating the additional platforms provided us with a few challenges and a rewrite, which meant more time to write the book and more time away from our families.

For Zarin and Amal, thanks for your love and understanding; I know you felt my stress through this. And for Sherdil, thank you is not nearly enough. Your love, patience, understanding, and support were invaluable. —Zamil

First of all, I am grateful to have the opportunity to work with this book team. Not only that they are all good people to work with, they are also fun people to hang out with. Without their dedication to this project (our second one!!), we wouldn't have gone this far. Adding iSeries and zSeries materials—whose idea was that?

I would also like to thank my family—Louis, Christina, and Esther—for their endless love and support. Most of all, I want to thank my husband, Heison, for his patience and understanding when I spent numerous late nights and weekends writing the chapters. —Clara

I would like to thank my former teammates Clara, Zamil, Paul, Fraser, Raul, and Michael for giving me the opportunity to work with them again. I think I saw all of you more this past winter than my own family. I also want to thank Lisa for being so understanding and putting up with me throughout the creation of this book. She was always there for me, and it meant a lot. —Drew

I would like to thank this great team for inviting me to be a co-author of this book. It certainly has been a demanding experience, but after all the effort I only feel satisfaction and would do it all over again if needed! I would like to thank my family: Elias, Olga, Alberto, David, Patricia, and Nancy. Through their example, I have learned you need to work hard to achieve your goals. I thank them for their understanding, support, and love. —Raul

To my buddies Clara, Drew, Fraser, Paul, Raul, and Zamil: it has been great fun, and you guys are the best! It has been many late nights and missing Saturdays. The book is impossible without the great support from my family. To my wife Lili, for the love and understanding. To my daughters Alyssa and Marissa, for all the missing trips to the play parks. —Michael

I couldn't have asked for a better group of people to work with on this book. Their dedication, professionalism, and drive were unparalleled. Thanks for making this another great experience! Also, thanks to my family—Larry, Carole, Leanne, and Jez—and all my friends for their constant understanding and support. To summarize with a Canadian colloquialism, I guess I owe you all a beer, eh? —Fraser

I am grateful to the entire book team for their tremendous work on this second edition. Spending weekends and weeknights together, sometimes in 12-hour edit marathons, will always be remembered. I would like to thank Susan Visser for her encouragement and follow-through, never doubting that we could pull this off. Thanks to the IBM DB2 Partner Enablement managers, Bridget Reid and Peter Crocker, for creating a great work atmosphere that allows us to publish books like this. Finally, thanks to my parents and friends, for their patience and support. I promise—no more books for at least a year. Now, where is my beer? —Paul

ABOUT THE AUTHORS

Zamil Janmohamed is a Websphere Commerce Development Manager at the IBM Toronto Lab. He manages a team focused on developer productivity and tooling for Websphere Commerce practitioners. In his 16 years of experience in information technology, he has held various positions such as a services consultant for Websphere Commerce and DB2, an application developer, a database administrator, and an engagement manager, to name a few. Zamil has had an extensive background working with relational databases, not only as they relate to developing applications but also designing, implementing, and supporting databases. He was a co-author of the first edition of this book.

Clara Liu works for the IBM Toronto Laboratory as a database consultant. In the past five years, Clara has been working with a wide variety of IBM partners and customers on projects utilizing DB2 Universal Database. She specializes in database application development and integration of new technologies with DB2. She is also the co-author two other books, *DB2 Express: Easy Development* and *Administration and DB2 UDB for Mere Mortals*. Besides working with DB2, Clara has several ongoing projects, such as "Scuba Diving 101" and "Karaoke in the Basement."

Drew Bradstock is an Engagement Manager with the IBM Data Management Competitive Migrations team. He manages teams that migrate a customer's infrastructure and databases to DB2 from other relational databases. Previously, he was a database consultant in the IBM Toronto lab and specialized in DB2 performance tuning and EEE. He helped write DB2 Certification exams and has also worked on previous books such as the *IBM Redbook Scaling DB2 UDB on Windows Server 2003* and the earlier edition of this book.

Raul F. Chong is a database consultant from the IBM Toronto Lab and works primarily with IBM Business Partners. Raul has worked for six years at IBM—three of them in DB2 Technical Support helping customers with problems on the OS/390, z/OS, Linux, UNIX, and Windows platforms; and three of them as a consultant specializing in database application development and migrations from other RDBMSs to DB2.

Michael X. Gao is a DB2 consultant from the IBM Toronto Lab. He specialized in DB2 UDB performance tuning, application development, porting, and customized education. Michael has presented at several international conferences. He was the author of several published DB2 technical articles and was a co-author of the first edition of this book. In his spare time, Michael tries to spend as much time as possible with his wife Lili and their two lovely daughters, Alyssa and Marissa.

Fraser McArthur is a DB2 Technical Consultant with the Information Management Partner Enablement organization at the IBM Toronto Lab, where he has worked for the last four years. He focuses on assisting IBM Business Partners performing application migrations and performance tuning. He also conducts DB2 technical workshops and publishes the occasional article to the IBM Developer Domain for the DB2 community. He spends his spare time volunteering around Toronto, backpacking around the world, and trying to keep his cat under control. Fraser is a DB2 Certified Solutions Expert in both DB2 Administration and Application Development, was a co-author of the first version of this book, and also contributed to the DB2 Certification exams.

Paul Yip is part of the DB2 Business Partner Enablement Team helping companies build or port solutions from competitive databases to DB2 UDB. He wears many hats in DB2 land, including database consultant, troubleshooter, instructor, and author. His newest hobbies include eating healthy, exercising regularly, focusing on the important things in life, and pondering why these are just hobbies rather than a way of life.

FOREWORD

The more things change, the more they stay the same.

Last year, when the first edition of this book was released, IBM had just released an updated version of DB2 on the Linux, UNIX, and Windows platforms—a version that was the most significant release to date, and one that provided new capabilities to reflect advances in the technology of both database systems and IT in general.

As I write this only a year later, IBM has once again just released an updated versions of the DB2 UDB product family; DB2 UDB for Linux, UNIX, and Windows, DB2 UDB for iSeries and DB2 UDB for zSeries—significant new releases that include many new features and enhancements that make this the most advanced set of database products IBM has ever offered—and we believe the most advanced in the industry.

Unlike the first edition of the book, which covered only the Linux, UNIX, and Windows platforms, the second edition of this book covers SQL Procedural Language for the entire DB2 family—those platforms covered in the first edition, and now including DB2 for z-Series (OS/390) and i-Series (i5/OS) platforms. Additionally, this edition introduces a method for resolving performance issues—how to monitor and identify bottlenecks, and how to provide alternatives for resolution.

DB2 UDB is evolving to reflect the changing needs of the development community. Many of the new features in DB2 UDB are designed to significantly improve ease of use for the development community, including new autonomic capabilities than will help to change the role of the DBA. There have been many other areas of technical leadership that have been introduced in technical support; all have helped to propel DB2 into the leadership position in the database market.

Another such developer-oriented feature is the subject of the original edition of this publication; this updated second edition focuses on the updates and improvements for SQL PL in updated versions of DB2 UDB.

SQL PL for DB2 provides a high-level language to build portable application logic that has the potential for better performance and scalability, by virtue of exploiting server-side resources and eliminating client bottlenecks. Exploiting SQL PL can also serve to improve the manageability and security of applications by providing a more modular structure. The latest version of DB2 UDB on all platforms includes enhancements for stored procedure development that significantly increases usability, allowing more developers to experiment with writing these stored procedures. This updated edition discusses this enhancement in detail.

An important feature in the updated versions of DB2 is that SQL PL is now native in all versions—DB2 UDB is no longer dependent upon translation into C stored procedures. For you as a developer, you'll see increased productivity and faster performance from your applications. And, you'll see reduced costs of ownership—no more additional expenses from compilers or run-times.

Knowing how and when to exploit the many capabilities of SQL PL for DB2 is an important skill to develop—and the authors of this book are experts on the subject, as certified DB2 specialists.

They have done a very nice job in efficiently laying out the many benefits in an easy to understand fashion. They've covered all language elements of DB2 SQL PL, with a large number of examples and detailed explanations. They offer expert tips and best practices derived from experiences with real customers. Nowhere else will the reader find such a vast array of experience-driven tips; this book is the ultimate developer's resource for writing SQL procedures.

We at IBM are very proud of the success that we've seen with DB2, and we're grateful to our many partners, developers and customers who have chosen to build and run their solutions with our database product. Working together, we've built the industry's premiere database product and the broadest set of applications and solutions in the market.

We continue to listen intently to your needs and requirements, and have focused on addressing many of these requirements as DB2 continues to evolve. I know that the skills that you are about to learn or hone for SQL PL for DB2 will serve you well; on behalf of IBM, I look forward to a continuing relationship of delivering the industry's best solutions and applications.

Janet Perna
General Manager, Information Management
IBM Software Group

IBMers Value
Dedication to every client's success.
Innovation that matters—for our company and for the world.
Trust and personal responsibility in all relationships.

Introduction

The **DB2 Universal Database** (DB2 UDB) refers to a family of database products:

- DB2 for Linux, UNIX, and Windows (distributed platforms, also referred to as **DB2 LUW**)
- DB2 for iSeries
- DB2 for z/OS (also referred to as **DB2 zSeries**)

Although each of these products have their own code base (which has been highly optimized for its intended hardware), application development and SQL support is fairly consistent across the platforms. All of these database products also support the DB2 SQL Procedural Language (SQL PL) but to varying degrees.

In the first edition of this book, we focused only on distributed platforms and have received very positive feedback on the approach we took to teach the SQL PL language. In this second edition, we expand our focus to include the rest of the DB2 family.

You can appreciate the difficulties of discussing a language in the context of three different development environments. Each platform has unique optimizations, and calling out the subtle (but important) differences can make it difficult to keep the discussion concise. We've worked hard to make this text an easy and enjoyable read. To that end, the approach we take is to describe each SQL PL feature as supported on DB2 for Linux, UNIX, and Windows platforms, and highlight the differences that may exist on the other platforms.

Before we begin, let's set up an SQL PL development environment.

Installing DB2

The CD included with this book includes a trial version of DB2 UDB Enterprise Server Edition version 8.2 for Windows.

The install program is located in <CDROM>:\db2\setup.exe.

If you are new to DB2, start by reading through Appendix A, "Getting Started with DB2." After you install DB2, create the DB2 SAMPLE database (also explained in Appendix A) because the examples presented in this book will make use of it. The SAMPLE database is provided as part of the DB2 (Linux, UNIX, and Windows) installation. For DB2 iSeries and DB2 zSeries, the CD contains scripts to create the SAMPLE database so that all examples can be demonstrated in a consistent environment.

The CD also provides all code samples listed in this book in directories associated with each platform by chapter. For example, the code snippets for DB2 LUW for Chapter 4 are located in the file <CDROM>:\samples\LUW\LUWchpt4CD.sql.

Now that you've installed the necessary files, lean back, and read on to begin your journey...

History of Stored Procedures

The use of databases has progressed rapidly in the last 20 years. As the amount of data collected by companies has increased, so have the demands on application developers to make use of it.

When databases were originally used, all the processing was performed on large mainframes with the output being sent to dumb terminals. There was no concern about where the application processed the data, because the data always resided on the server. This process changed when databases began to appear on mid-range UNIX machines, where the client and server were often separate. **Stored procedures** were created to allow data processing to occur on the much faster servers, to reduce the workload and CPU bottlenecks on the slower clients, and to reduce the amount of data sent across the network.

In those days, DB2 stored procedures were primarily developed using the C programming language, which gave developers greater flexibility in how they could manipulate data. This flexibility, however, came with a price—writing C procedures was a complicated and error-prone process. Developers had to be highly knowledgeable in both C and embedded SQL, which was often a difficult combination to find.

This issue created a demand for an easier method to write stored procedures and led to the creation of a new third-generation (3GL) programming language. The language was based on the existing SQL syntax and used a simple structured programming language very similar to early BASIC. **DB2 SQL Procedural Language** (DB2 SQL PL) was born. This new language enabled programmers to quickly develop and build stored procedures without having to know any complex programming languages or data structures. The ease of development led to an explosion in the use of stored procedures, as both developers and database administrators quickly learned how to work with this new simplified programming language.

DB2 SQL PL for stored procedures was originally available on DB2 for AS/400, which is now referred to as **DB2 UDB for iSeries**. From there, DB2 for mainframe (now called **z/OS** or **zSeries**) and DB2 for Linux, UNIX, and Windows adopted the language as well.

A Brief Introduction to Stored Procedures, Triggers, and Functions

SQL PL is usually associated with stored procedures and incorrectly referred to as "DB2 Stored Procedure Language." The proper meaning of DB2 SQL PL is "DB2 SQL Procedural Language." Furthermore, SQL PL is not used just for stored procedures. Database triggers, user-defined functions (UDFs), and dynamic compound SQL are also developed using this language, and this book will show you how.

Stored procedures, triggers, and functions are a class of objects called **database application objects**. Application objects encapsulate application logic at the database server rather than in application-level code. Use of application objects help reduce network traffic. In the case of stored procedures, for example, only the original request and the final output need to be transmitted between the client and the server.

Triggers are useful for enforcing business rules consistently and automatically across many applications that share a database.

Functions are useful for simplifying application development by encapsulating commonly used calculations or data lookups.

All of these objects help improve application runtime performance and can take advantage of the larger number of CPUs and disks that typically reside on a database server.

Use of database application objects is very popular because of their many benefits:

- **Improved manageability.** Application objects are modular and can be moved from database to database.

- **Clear division of roles between DBA and application developer.** The DBA knows the data model best. The application developer knows application interfaces best. Complex business logic can be encapsulated in database application objects. Application developers only need to know which procedures or functions to call.

- **Increased performance.** Keeping business logic in stored procedures residing on the server will help improve the performance of most data-driven applications. Instead of an application having to send data back and forth across a network for every SQL statement and cursor, a single call can be made with results returned at the end just once.

There are almost always opportunities to improve application performance using database application objects. Newer applications using three-tier or (n-tier) architectures were designed to reduce the cost of creating and maintaining applications. Practical experience, however, has shown that the performance of keeping all business logic in the application-server tier can have a large performance impact.

We have consistently witnessed that applications can benefit significantly by moving data-intensive logic from the middle tier back into the database tier. Application developers have discovered that while moving all business logic to the middle tier makes for very clean design, some classes of data processing should remain at the database tier for even reasonable performance. Use of SQL procedures, functions, and triggers has therefore continued to gain popularity in modern applications.

What's New in the Second Edition

If you are familiar with IBM Press books, your first question may have appropriately been, "Where was the first edition?" *DB2 SQL PL, Second Edition: Essential Guide for DB2 UDB on Linux, UNIX, Windows, i5/OS*, and z/OS is actually based on the book *DB2 SQL Procedural Language for Linux, UNIX, and Windows* (©2002). The change of book title was motivated by the need to create greater awareness of the DB2 SQL Procedural Language by using the term DB2 SQL PL, and deliver value to a broader audience by increasing the scope of the content to cover SQL PL for the entire DB2 family—not just Linux, UNIX, and Windows. Hence, the second edition builds on content from DB2 SQL Procedural Language for Linux, UNIX, and Windows.

Since the first edition, significant enhancements have been delivered in DB2 UDB version 8.2 for LUW (or DB2 UDB version 8.1 with FixPak 7) and have warranted an updated book. Following is a summary of the new features on DB2 UDB 8.2 for LUW:

- Native support for SQL procedures on Linux, UNIX, and Windows (the C compiler is no longer required)
- Enhanced SQL for greater application efficiency and performance
- Enhanced SQL Table function support to allow SQL PL logic as well as UPDATE, INSERT, DELETE, and MERGE statements
- Ability to call stored procedures from inline SQL PL blocks, functions, and triggers
- Support for nested save points
- Session-based locking (SET LOCK WAIT and SET LOCK NO WAIT)
- A new SQL procedure REOPT option, which causes a procedure to re-optimize with the latest available statistics at runtime
- Increased length of SQL procedure statements from 64KB to 2MB
- Ability to change procedure building prepare options using utility procedures SET_ROUTINE_OPTS and GET_ROUTINE_OPTS
- Enhanced GET ROUTINE and PUT ROUTINE commands for easier deployment

New versions of other DB2 products have also been released. Our previous edition of this book did not discuss these platforms.

```
p_parameterName: SQL procedure input and output parameters
v_parameterName: SQL variables
c_cursorName: Cursors
```

Meanings of Style

A number of different styles are used to indicate items of interest throughout the guide.

Code

```
CREATE PROCEDURE intro1 (OUT p_output INT)
LANGUAGE SQL
BEGIN
    SET p_output = 1;
END
```

TIP

This sidebar indicates a useful tip in the context of the current topic.

NOTE

This sidebar indicates a note to draw attention to important information.

Book Structure

Each successive chapter in the book is designed to be a prerequisite for the chapters that follow it. At the beginning of every chapter is a summary of the terms and subjects that will be covered. The summary allows experienced users to check whether they already understand the material that will be covered in the chapter.

Contacting the Authors

We are always looking for any feedback that you have both about this book and about DB2 SQL procedures. Please contact us with your opinions and inquiries at

```
db2sqlpl@ca.ibm.com
```

Depending on the volume of inquires, we may be unable to respond to every technical question but we'll do our best.

The DB2 newsgroup at `comp.databases.ibm-db2` is another great way to get assistance from IBM employees and the DB2 user community.

Finally, for the latest information on this book, including updates and errata, be sure to visit

`www.chak.ca/publications/sqlpl`

Have fun!

CHAPTER 2

Basic SQL Procedure Structure

In this chapter, you will learn

- The fundamental structure of an SQL procedure
- The various clauses for the CREATE PROCEDURE statement
- The structure of the procedure body
- The statements that can be coded in the procedure body

Stored procedures are used to encapsulate multiple SQL statements with flow logic. They are database objects that serve as sub-routines to applications. SQL procedures are defined in a database using the CREATE PROCEDURE statement. This chapter introduces the syntax of the CREATE PROCEDURE statement and uses examples to illustrate how to create simple SQL procedures.

The *CREATE PROCEDURE* Statement

The CREATE PROCEDURE statement defines a procedure in the database. The clauses define the name and parameters as well as the procedure body consisting of one or more SQL PL statements. Figure 2.1 describes the syntax of the CREATE PROCEDURE statement and the clauses that apply to SQL procedures.

NOTE

We discuss the differences in the CREATE PROCEDURE statement for iSeries and zSeries platforms at the end of this chapter.

Many clauses are available for the CREATE PROCEDURE statement; however, it is often appropriate to just use the defaults.

11

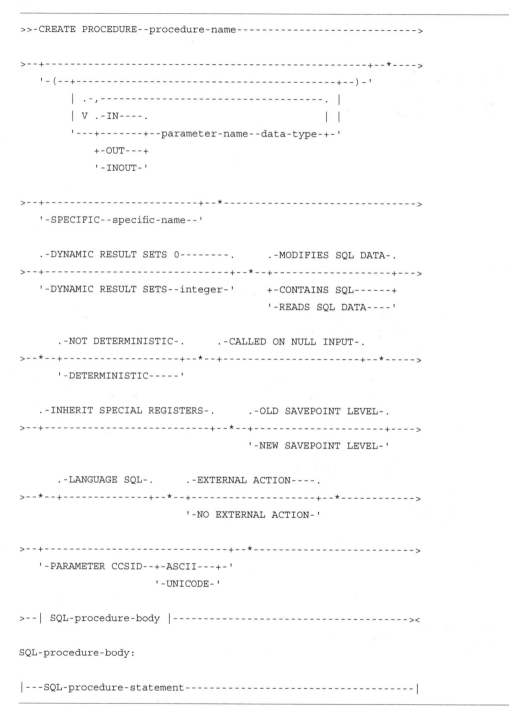

```
>>-CREATE PROCEDURE--procedure-name---------------------------->

>--+-------------------------------------------------+--*---->
   '-(--+-------------------------------------+--)-'
        | .-,-----------------------------------. |
        | V .-IN----.                           | |
        '---+-------+--parameter-name--data-type-+-'
            +-OUT---+
            '-INOUT-'

>--+---------------------+--*------------------------------->
   '-SPECIFIC--specific-name--'

   .-DYNAMIC RESULT SETS 0--------.      .-MODIFIES SQL DATA-.
>--+-----------------------------+--*--+-------------------+--->
   '-DYNAMIC RESULT SETS--integer-'     +-CONTAINS SQL------+
                                        '-READS SQL DATA----'

     .-NOT DETERMINISTIC-.      .-CALLED ON NULL INPUT-.
>--*--+------------------+--*--+----------------------+--*----->
      '-DETERMINISTIC-----'

   .-INHERIT SPECIAL REGISTERS-.      .-OLD SAVEPOINT LEVEL-.
>--+--------------------------+--*--+--------------------+---->
                                     '-NEW SAVEPOINT LEVEL-'

     .-LANGUAGE SQL-.      .-EXTERNAL ACTION----.
>--*--+-------------+--*--+-------------------+--*----------->
                          '-NO EXTERNAL ACTION-'

>--+-----------------------------+--*------------------------>
   '-PARAMETER CCSID--+-ASCII---+-'
                      '-UNICODE-'

>--| SQL-procedure-body |-------------------------------------><

SQL-procedure-body:

|---SQL-procedure-statement----------------------------------|
```

Figure 2.1   *CREATE PROCEDURE* statement syntax for DB2 UDB LUW.

When you issue the CREATE PROCEDURE statement, DB2 defines the procedure in the database and makes entries in the catalog tables to record the existence of the procedure.

Procedure Name

The **procedure name** specifies the procedure being defined. The name is an SQL identifier that can be a maximum of 128 characters. It must begin with a letter and may be followed by additional letters, digits, or the underscore character "_".

These are examples of valid procedure names:

```
UPDATE_EMPLOYEE_SALARY
READEMP
```

These examples are of unqualified procedure names. When a procedure name is unqualified, the procedure schema is determined by the CURRENT SCHEMA special register. The DB2 special register will be discussed later in this chapter. By default, the CURRENT SCHEMA is the authorization ID of the current user. Procedure names may also be qualified by a schema name explicitly. These are examples of valid qualified procedure names:

```
HRAPP.UPDATE_EMPLOYEE_SALARY
DB2ADMIN.READEMP
```

Similar to the procedure name, the **schema name** is an SQL identifier with a maximum of 128 characters or 10 characters on iSeries. The schema name cannot begin with sys.

> **NOTE**
> On iSeries, the schema name actually can start with sys, but as a best practice you should not start a schema name with sys or Q. These types of schema names are typically used for system schemas.

The **qualified procedure name** does not necessarily need to be unique in the database. The combination of qualified procedure name and number of parameters (procedure signature), however, must uniquely identify a procedure. This topic will be discussed in more detail in the following section.

The SPECIFIC clause is important when there is a requirement to define procedures with the same name but with a different number of parameters. To fully understand the purpose of this clause, we must discuss parameters.

Parameters

The **parameters** for a procedure are defined in the CREATE PROCEDURE statement. The definition of each parameter consists of three parts:

- **Mode** defines whether the parameter is an input (IN), output (OUT), or both (INOUT).
- **Parameter name** specifies the name of the parameter. It is recommended that all parameter variables be prefixed with p_. This is discussed in detail in the "Variables" section of this chapter.
- **Data type** is the SQL data type and size, if applicable, for this parameter.

The list of parameters is enclosed in parentheses "( )", and each parameter definition is delimited by a comma ",".

Figure 2.2 is an example of a partial CREATE PROCEDURE statement that defines the procedure and its parameters.

```
CREATE PROCEDURE update_employee_salary ( IN  P_EMPID INTEGER
                                        , IN  P_PERCENTINCR DECIMAL(4,2)
                                        , INOUT P_EMPCOUNT INTEGER
                                        , OUT P_UPDATED_SALARY DECIMAL(5,2))
    . . .
```

Figure 2.2   Defining procedure parameters.

A procedure may be defined without any parameters, and the parentheses can be omitted, as in this example:

```
CREATE PROCEDURE increase_salary LANGUAGE SQL BEGIN . . .
```

To allow back-level DB2 support, parentheses may be coded in the CREATE PROCEDURE statement.

```
CREATE PROCEDURE increase_salary() LANGUAGE SQL BEGIN . . .
```

On LUW and iSeries, it is possible to define multiple procedures with the same qualified name but different numbers of parameters. This is called **overloading**, and the procedures are referred to as **overloaded procedures**. Figures 2.3 and 2.4 show examples of overloaded procedures. zSeries does not support overloaded procedures. Therefore, examples run in zSeries have to be created with different procedure names.

> **NOTE**
> DB2 does not allow you to define two procedures with the same schema name, same procedure name, and same number of parameters even if the parameters are of different types. However, DB2 (including zSeries) does support User-Defined Functions (UDFs) overloaded with the same schema, same name, and same number of parameters, given that the data types of the parameters are different. For more information about UDFs, refer to Chapter 9, "User-Defined Functions and Triggers".

```
CREATE PROCEDURE sum( IN   p_a INTEGER
                    , IN   p_b INTEGER
                    , OUT  p_s INTEGER)
    LANGUAGE SQL
    SPECIFIC sum_ab                       -- applies to LUW and iSeries
 -- WLM ENVIRONMENT <env>                 -- applies to zSeries
BEGIN
    SET p_s = p_a + p_b;
END
```

Figure 2.3   Procedure sum with three parameters.

```
CREATE PROCEDURE sum( IN   p_a INTEGER
                    , IN   p_b INTEGER
                    , IN   p_c INTEGER
                    , OUT  p_s INTEGER)
    LANGUAGE SQL
    SPECIFIC sum_abc                      -- applies to LUW and iSeries
 -- WLM ENVIRONMENT <env>                 -- applies to zSeries
BEGIN
    SET p_s = p_a + p_b + p_c;
END
```

Figure 2.4   Procedure sum with four parameters.

In the examples, two procedures have the same name, sum. The first procedure has three parameters, and the second has four parameters. When sum is called, DB2 determines which version of the procedure to execute based on the number of parameters. Note that each procedure is defined with a unique specific name. Specific names will be discussed in the next section.

> **NOTE**
> To invoke SQL procedures, use the Command-Line Processor (CLP) for LUW and zSeries
> or the iSeries Navigator.

The following statement can be used to invoke the SQL procedure:

```
CALL sum(100,200,?)
```

This call results in the `sum` procedure in Figure 2.3 to be executed because there are three parameters. Note that because the third parameter is an output parameter, a "?" must be specified in its place.

Executing the following statement invokes the `sum` procedure in Figure 2.4 because there are four parameters.

```
CALL sum(100,200,300,?)
```

If you attempt to call a procedure where there is no procedure defined in the database with the same number of parameters, an error occurs, as in this example:

```
CALL sum(100,200,300,400,?)
```

This call fails because a procedure named `sum` with five parameters does not exist.

Specific Name

`SPECIFIC` is an optional clause that defines a unique name for a procedure. Specific names are particularly useful when there are multiple procedures defined with the same name but have a different number of parameters (also known as overloaded procedures, as discussed in the previous section). In this case, each procedure would be given a different specific name which would be used to drop or comment on the stored procedure. Attempting to drop an overloaded procedure using only the procedure name would result in ambiguity and error.

> **TIP**
> We recommend that you use a specific name for a procedure for easier management.
> However, this option is not supported on zSeries for SQL procedures because overloaded
> procedures are not supported.

The following example illustrates the use of `SPECIFIC` name when two procedures with the same name are defined. Consider the two `sum` procedures defined in Figures 2.3 and 2.4.

To drop the procedure `sum`, issue the following `DROP PROCEDURE` statement:

```
DROP PROCEDURE sum
```

This statement fails with SQLCODE -476 (SQLSTATE 42725) because the procedure is ambiguous. DB2 cannot determine which of the two procedures called sum should be dropped. To drop a particular version of the sum procedure, you must either specify the procedure parameters with the DROP PROCEDURE statement or use the DROP SPECIFIC PROCEDURE statement. These valid statements drop the procedure:

```
DROP PROCEDURE sum(INTEGER,INTEGER,INTEGER)
DROP SPECIFIC PROCEDURE sum_ab
```

> **NOTE**
> On zSeries, these two DROP statements are not supported.

By using DROP SPECIFIC PROCEDURE, DB2 knows that it should drop the procedure with the specific name sum_ab. The specific name can also be used with the COMMENT ON statement, as in this example:

```
COMMENT ON SPECIFIC PROCEDURE sum_abc IS 'THIS IS THE 3 PARM VERSION OF THE
PROCEDURE'
```

The **specific name** is an SQL identifier with a maximum length of 18 characters on LUW and 128 characters on iSeries. The name can be unqualified or qualified by a schema name. If it is qualified, it must use the same schema name as the procedure name. The specific name can be the same name as its procedure name. The qualified specific name must be unique among specific procedure names.

In LUW, if the specific name is not explicitly specified when creating a procedure, DB2 generates a unique name for the procedure. The generated unique name consists of SQL and a character timestamp:

```
SQLyymmddhhmmsshhn
```

On iSeries, if the specific name is not specified, DB2 uses the procedure name as the specific name. If a procedure already exists with that specific name, a unique name is generated using a portion of the procedure name and a sequence number.

DYNAMIC RESULT SETS

The DYNAMIC RESULT SETS clause specifies the maximum number of result sets you are returning. Handling result sets is explained in detail in Chapter 5, "Understanding and Using Cursors and Result Sets," and Chapter 8, "Nested SQL Procedures."

CONTAINS SQL, READS SQL DATA, MODIFIES SQL DATA

The SQL data access indication clause restricts the type of SQL statements that can be executed by the procedure. The default, MODIFIES SQL DATA, is the least restrictive and indicates that any supported SQL statements can be executed.

When CONTAINS SQL is specified, then only statements that do not read or modify data are allowed in the procedure. Examples of such statements are PREPARE, the SET special register, and SQL control statements.

READS SQL DATA can be specified if the procedure contains only statements that do not modify SQL data. Refer to the SQL Reference of the corresponding platform for statements allowed in the SQL procedure for each access indicator.

DETERMINISTIC or NOT DETERMINISTIC

This clause allows you to specify the procedure as DETERMINISTIC if it returns the same results for each invocation of identical input parameters. You can also specify NOT DETERMINISTIC, the default, if the results depend on the input values and/or other values which may change, such as the current date or time. Identifying a procedure as DETERMINISTIC allows DB2 to perform additional optimizations to improve performance because DB2 can just call it once, cache the result, and reuse it.

CALLED ON NULL INPUT

This clause indicates that the procedure will always be called even if its input parameters are null. This behavior is the default, and is the only value that can be specified. This clause is optional and is usually left out.

INHERIT SPECIAL REGISTERS

Special registers are memory registers that allow DB2 to provide information to an application about its environment. Refer to the section "DB2 Special Registers" for more information.

INHERIT SPECIAL REGISTERS is an optional clause and indicates that updateable special registers in the procedure will inherit their initial values from the environment of the invoking statement. Special register inheritance is the default behavior on all platforms.

NOTE

On zSeries, some special registers inherit their initial values from different sources. Refer to the zSeries SQL Reference for details.

OLD SAVEPOINT LEVEL, NEW SAVEPOINT LEVEL

This clause is available only in LUW and iSeries. A **save point level** refers to the scope of reference for any save point related statements. All save point names in the same save point level must be unique.

The OLD SAVEPOINT LEVEL means that any SAVEPOINT statements issued within the procedure are created in the same save point level as the caller of the procedure. Thus, any save point created inside the stored procedure must not have the same name as those defined at the caller. This is the default behavior.

The NEW SAVEPOINT LEVEL, on the other hand, creates a new save point level when the stored procedure is called. Any save points set within the procedure are created at a level that is nested deeper than the level at which this procedure was invoked. Therefore, names of any new save point set within the procedure will not conflict with any existing save points.

You can also make stored procedure calls from inline SQL such as SQL functions, triggers, and stand-alone code. Such a procedure will be executed as if it were created in the NEW SAVEPOINT LEVEL mode even if the OLD SAVEPOINT LEVEL was specified.

Save points are discussed in more detail in Chapter 10, "Leveraging DB2 Application Development Features."

LANGUAGE SQL

LANGUAGE SQL identifies this procedure as an SQL procedure, and indicates that the body of the procedure will be specified in the CREATE PROCEDURE statement body. LANGUAGE SQL is an optional clause for LUW. For iSeries and zSeries, LANGUAGE SQL must be specified. Furthermore, on iSeries, it must be specified as the first clause.

The LANGUAGE keyword is required when creating procedures in other languages such as Java or C.

NOTE
To increase portability, always use the LANGUAGE SQL clause and ensure it is the first clause.

EXTERNAL ACTION or NO EXTERNAL ACTION

This clause is only available on LUW. If the SQL procedure takes some action that changes the state of an object not managed by DB2, specify the EXTERNAL ACTION. Otherwise, use NO EXTERNAL ACTION so that DB2 can use certain optimizations that assume the procedure has no external impact.

PARAMETER CCSID

CCSID stands for **Coded Character Set ID**. This clause specifies the encoding scheme used for all string data passed into and out of the stored procedure for LUW and zSeries. Possible values are ASCII, UNICODE, and EBCDIC (for zSeries only).

On iSeries, the specification of the CCSID is at a more granular level. You specify the CCSID for each string parameter of the procedure (CHAR, VARCHAR, CLOB, GRAPHIC, VARGRAPHIC, and DBCLOB). There are numerous options for specifying CCSID on iSeries. Refer to the iSeries

SQL Reference for a listing of valid CCSIDs and the allowed conversions between these CCSIDs.

On zSeries, the CCSID can be specified at either the parameter level, the subsystem level in the field DEF ENCODING SCHEME on installation panel DSNTIPF, or at the SQL procedure level. The default is the value specified at the parameter level or the subsystem level. If specified at both the parameter level and the SQL procedure, they must be the same CCSID value for all parameters.

TIP

In practice, this clause is rarely used. It can be used to overwrite the default character set as specified by the code page of the database.

SQL Procedure Body

For SQL procedures, the logic of the procedure is contained in the SQL procedure body of the CREATE PROCEDURE statement. The SQL procedure body can consist of a single SQL statement or several SQL statements in the form of a compound SQL statement. The next section explains the details of writing the SQL procedure body.

The SQL Procedure Body Structure

The SQL procedure body can consist of a single SQL statement or, more typically, a compound SQL statement consisting of a BEGIN/END block with multiple statements within it. The compound statement consists of various declarations followed by SQL procedure statements. All declarations must be specified first followed by SQL procedural statements. The syntax diagram in Figure 2.5 shows the required order of declarations.

```
                                 .-NOT ATOMIC--.
>>-+----------+--BEGIN----+-------------+-----------------------><
   '-label:--'           '-ATOMIC------'


>-----+------------------------------------------------+-------->
      |   .------------------------------------------.  |
      |   V                                          |  |
      '-----+-| SQL-variable-declaration |-+---;---+--'
            +-| condition-declaration |----+
            '-| return-codes-declaration |-'


>--+---------------------------------+-----------------------><
   |   .---------------------------.  |
   |   V                           |  |
   '---| statement-declaration |--;-+-'
```

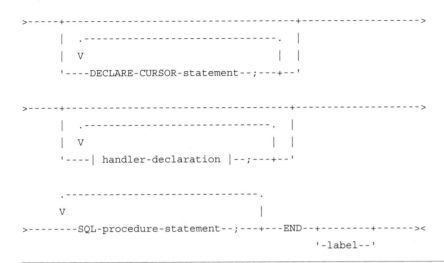

```
>-----+-------------------------------------+------------------->
      |   .-----------------------------.   |
      |   V                             |   |
      '----DECLARE-CURSOR-statement--;---+--'


>-----+-------------------------------------+------------------->
      |   .---------------------------.     |
      |   V                           |     |
      '----| handler-declaration |--;---+--'


      .-----------------------------.
      V                             |
>--------SQL-procedure-statement--;---+---END--+--------+------><
                                              '-label--'
```

Figure 2.5   Compound statement syntax diagram.

Variable declarations are discussed later in this chapter. Compound statements are discussed in Chapter 4, "Using Flow of Control Statements." Cursor declarations are discussed in Chapter 5, "Understanding and Using Cursors and Result Sets." Condition handlers are discussed in Chapter 6, "Condition Handling." Statement declarations, available in LUW, are discussed in Chapter 7, "Working with Dynamic SQL."

Comments

It is always good practice to include comments in programs. DB2 allows two styles of comments:

- When two dashes are specified, any text following them is treated as a comment. This style is typically used to comment on a specific variable declaration or statement. It can be used on any line of the CREATE PROCEDURE statement and terminates with the newline character.
- /* */ are C-style comments. The /* begins a comment and */ ends the comment. There may be multiple lines of comments between the delimiters. This style can be used in the body of an SQL procedure only.

Figure 2.6 are examples of comments used in an SQL procedure.

```
CREATE PROCEDURE proc_with_comments ( IN aaa INTEGER
                                    , OUT bbb INTEGER )
    LANGUAGE SQL
    SPECIFIC proc_with_comments                 -- applies to LUW and iSeries
 -- WLM ENVIRONMENT <env>                       -- applies to zSeries
```

```
BEGIN
    /*
      Variables
    */
    DECLARE v_total INTEGER DEFAULT 0;
    SELECT 1 INTO v_total FROM SYSIBM.SYSDUMMY1;
END
```

Figure 2.6   Sample comments.

Variables

The DECLARE statement is used to define variables within a compound SQL statement (see Figure 2.7). Each variable declaration consists of a name for the variable, a DB2 data type, and optionally a default value.

Variable declarations must be specified at the beginning of a BEGIN/END block before any SQL procedural statements are defined. The CREATE PROCEDURE statement will fail if a DECLARE is found anywhere else.

You should ensure that the variables defined in your procedure are different from column names of tables that will be referenced in the procedure. Such a declaration is allowed but only causes confusion. It is recommended that you define a naming convention for your procedures that clearly differentiates variables and columns. In this book, the convention is to precede variables with a prefix of v_ and precede procedures parameters with a prefix of p_ to differentiate them from possible column names.

```
CREATE PROCEDURE proc_with_variables (IN p_empno VARCHAR(6))
    LANGUAGE SQL
    SPECIFIC proc_with_vars                    -- applies to LUW and iSeries
    -- WLM ENVIRONMENT <env>                   -- applies to zSeries
BEGIN
    DECLARE v_empno VARCHAR(6);
    DECLARE v_total, v_count INTEGER DEFAULT 0;
    SELECT empno INTO v_empno FROM employee WHERE empno = p_empno ;
END
```

Figure 2.7   Defining variables.

When variables are declared, they are initialized as NULL unless the DEFAULT clause is used to initialize the variable to a value. In Figure 2.7 the value of v_empno is null until it is set within the procedure body. The integer variables v_total and v_count are initialized to zero in the declaration.

Setting Variables

As in any programming language, you can initialize or set variables. There are several ways to set variables in SQL procedures, and they are demonstrated in Figure 2.8.

```
CREATE PROCEDURE set_variables ()
    LANGUAGE SQL
    SPECIFIC set_variables                  -- applies to LUW and iSeries
    -- WLM ENVIRONMENT <env>                -- applies to zSeries


BEGIN
    DECLARE v_rcount INTEGER;
    DECLARE v_max DECIMAL(9,2);
    DECLARE v_adate,v_another DATE;
    DECLARE v_total INTEGER DEFAULT 0;          -- (1)
    SET v_total = v_total + 1;                  -- (2)
    SELECT MAX(salary) INTO v_max FROM employee;  -- (3)
    VALUES CURRENT DATE INTO v_adate;           -- (4)
    SELECT CURRENT DATE, CURRENT DATE
      INTO v_adate, v_another
      FROM SYSIBM.SYSDUMMY1;                     -- (5)
END
```

Figure 2.8 Setting variables.

When declaring a variable, you can specify a default value using the DEFAULT clause as in Line (1).

Line (2) shows that a SET can be used to set a single variable.

Variables can also be set by executing a SELECT or FETCH statement in combination with INTO as shown in (3). Details on using FETCH can be found in Chapter 4, "Understanding and Using Cursors and Result Sets."

Lines (4) and (5) show how the VALUES INTO statement can be used to evaluate a function or special register and assign the value to a variable. Special registers are discussed in more detail in the next section.

DB2 Special Registers

Recall that special registers are memory registers that allow DB2 to provide information to an application about its environment. They can be referenced in SQL statements. The most commonly used special registers are

- CURRENT DATE. A date based on the time-of-day clock at the database server. If this register is referenced more than once in a single statement, the value returned will be the same for all references. This is a non-updateable register.

- CURRENT ISOLATION (LUW only). Identifies the isolation level for any dynamic SQL statements issued within the current session.

- CURRENT LOCK TIMEOUT (LUW only). Specifies the number of seconds that an application will wait to obtain a lock. This is an updateable register.

- CURRENT PATH. Identifies the SQL path used to resolve procedure, functions, and data type references for dynamically prepared SQL statements. The value of the CURRENT PATH special register is a list of one or more schema names. This is an updateable register.

- CURRENT PACKAGE PATH (LUW and zSeries only). Identifies the path to be used when resolving references to packages. This is an updateable register.

- CURRENT SCHEMA. Identifies the schema name used to qualify unqualified database objects in dynamic SQL statements. The default value is the authorization ID of the current user or the value of CURRENT SQLID on zSeries. This special register can be modified using the SET CURRENT SCHEMA statement. This is an updateable register.

- CURRENT TIME. A time based on the time-of-day clock at the database server. If this register is referenced more than once in a single statement, the value returned will be the same for all references. This is a non-updateable register.

- CURRENT TIMESTAMP. A timestamp based on the time-of-day clock at the database server. If this register is referenced more than once in a single statement, the value returned will be the same for all references. This is a non-updateable register.

- USER. Specifies the runtime authorization ID used to connect to the database. This is a non-updateable register.

- SESSION_USER (LUW only). Specifies the authorization ID to be used for the current session. This is a synonym for the USER special register. This is a non-updateable register.

- SYSTEM_USER (LUW only). Specifies the authorization ID of the user who connected to the database. This is a non-updateable register.

Special registers can be categorized as updateable and non-updateable. For example, CURRENT SCHEMA and CURRENT PATH are both updateable registers. CURRENT TIMESTAMP is an example of a non-updateable register. To obtain the value of the register, use the SELECT statement as shown:

```
SELECT CURRENT SCHEMA FROM SYSIBM.SYSDUMMY1;
```

Use the SET command to update the updateable registers such as the current schema:

```
SET CURRENT SCHEMA = DB2ADMIN
```

When invoking SQL procedures with unqualified names, the CURRENT PATH special register is used to resolve the requested SQL procedure. The path is a list of schemas which DB2 searches to locate a procedure. To obtain the CURRENT PATH special register, connect to the database and simply issue this command

```
SELECT CURRENT PATH FROM SYSIBM.SYSDUMMY1;
```

The default setting for the PATH register in LUW looks like

```
"SYSIBM","SYSFUN","SYSPROC","DB2ADMIN"
```

The default PATH is made up of system schemas followed by the current user connected to the database. On LUW, SYSIBM, SYSFUN, and SYSPROC are the system schemas. With the previously shown PATH, DB2 first searches for the procedure in schema SYSIBM, then SYSFUN, then SYSPROC, and lastly DB2ADMIN. If there are overloaded procedures in both SYSPROC and DB2ADMIN, the SYSPROC one will be used. Sometimes you might want to use the DB2ADMIN procedure instead. In that case, set the CURRENT PATH to customize the search order of the schemas:

```
SET CURRENT PATH = DB2ADMIN,SYSIBM,SYSFUN,SYSPROC
```

Figure 2.9 shows the use of several special registers.

```
CREATE PROCEDURE registersample ( OUT p_start TIMESTAMP
                                , OUT p_end   TIMESTAMP
                                , OUT p_c1    TIMESTAMP
                                , OUT p_c2    TIME
                                , OUT p_user  CHAR(20))
      LANGUAGE SQL
      SPECIFIC registersample                 -- applies to LUW and iSeries
 -- WLM ENVIRONMENT <env>                      -- applies to zSeries
BEGIN
```

```
   CREATE TABLE datetab (c1 TIMESTAMP,c2 TIME,c3 DATE);

   VALUES CURRENT TIMESTAMP INTO p_start;                    -- (1)
   INSERT INTO datetab VALUES( CURRENT TIMESTAMP
                             , CURRENT TIME
                             , CURRENT DATE + 3 DAYS); -- (2)
   SELECT c1,c2 INTO p_c1,p_c2 FROM datetab;
   VALUES CURRENT TIMESTAMP INTO p_end;
   SET p_user = USER;                                        -- (3)
   DROP TABLE datetab;
END
```

Figure 2.9   Using special registers.

The procedure `registersample` creates a table, `datetab`, to demonstrate how special registers are used with SQL statements. This table is dropped at the end so that the procedure can be run repeatedly.

On Line (1), the values statement is used to set the variable `p_start` to the current timestamp.

Line (2) shows several special registers being used within a single SQL statement to retrieve the date or time. Here, the time portion of the CURRENT TIMESTAMP special register will be the same as the value of the CURRENT TIME special register, and date portion of the CURRENT TIMESTAMP special register will be the same as the value of CURRENT DATE. This statement also demonstrates the use of built-in functions. Column `c3` will receive a date that is three days from the current date. You can find more details on using built-in functions such as DATE, TIME, and TIMESTAMP in the DB2 SQL Reference.

The `p_user` variable is set to the authorization ID of the currently connected user on Line (3).

The following list includes other special registers that are available. More information about them can be found in the DB2 SQL Reference for the corresponding platform.

- CURRENT APPLICATION ENCODING SCHEME (zSeries only). Specifies which encoding scheme is to be used for dynamic statements. It allows an application to indicate the encoding scheme that is used to process data. This is an updatable register.

- CURRENT DBPARTITIONNUM (LUW only). Specifies an INTEGER value that identifies the coordinator node number for the statement. This is a non-updateable register.

- CURRENT DEFAULT TRANSFORM GROUP (LUW only). Identifies the name of a transform group used by dynamic SQL statements for exchanging user-defined structured type values with host programs. This is an updateable register.

- CURRENT DEGREE (LUW and zSeries only). Specifies the degree of intra-partition parallelism for the execution of dynamic SQL statements. This is an updateable register.

- CURRENT EXPLAIN MODE (LUW only). Holds a value that controls the behavior of the Explain facility. This is an updateable register.

- CURRENT EXPLAIN SNAPSHOT (LUW only). Holds a value that controls behavior of the Explain Snapshot facility. This is an updateable register.

- CURRENT LOCALE LC_CTYPE (zSeries only). Specifies the LC_CTYPE locale that will be used to execute SQL statements which use a built-in function that references a locale. This is an updatable register.

- CURRENT MAINTAINED TABLE TYPES FOR OPTIMIZATION (LUW and zSeries only). Specifies the types of tables that can be considered for optimization when dynamic SQL queries are processed. This is an updateable register.

- CURRENT MEMBER (zSeries only). Specifies the member name of a current DB2 data sharing member on which a statement is executing. This is a non-updatable register.

- CURRENT OPTIMIZATION HINT (zSeries only). Specifies the user-defined optimization hint that DB2 should use to generate the access path for dynamic statements. This is an updateable register.

- CURRENT PRECISION (zSeries only). Specifies the rules to be used when both operands in a decimal operation have precisions of 15 or less. This is an updatable register.

- CURRENT QUERY OPTIMIZATION (LUW only). Specifies the query optimization level used when binding dynamic SQL statements. This is an updateable register.

- CURRENT REFRESH AGE (LUW and zSeries only). Specifies the maximum duration that a cached data object, such as a materialized query table, can be used for dynamic queries before it must be refreshed. This is an updateable register.

- CURRENT RULES (zSeries only). Specifies whether certain SQL statements are executed in accordance with DB2 rules or the rules of the SQL standard. This is an updatable register.

- CURRENT SERVER. Specifies the name of the database to which the application is connected. This is a non-updateable register.

- CURRENT TIMEZONE. Specifies the difference between UTC (Coordinated Universal Time) and local time at the application server. This is a non-updatable register.

- CLIENT ACCTNG (LUW and zSeries only). Specifies the accounting string for the client connection. On zSeries, use CURRENT CLIENT_ACCTNG. This is an updateable register.

- CLIENT APPLNAME (LUW and zSeries only). Specifies the client application name. On zSeries, use CURRENT CLIENT_APPLNAME. This is an updateable register.

- CLIENT USERID (LUW and zSeries only). Specifies the client user ID. On zSeries, use CURRENT CLIENT_USERID. This is an updateable register.

- CLIENT WRKSTNNAME (LUW and zSeries only). Specifies the client workstation name. On zSeries, use CURRENT CLIENT_WRKSTNNAME. This is an updateable register.

Bringing It All Together Example

A detailed example is presented in this section to demonstrate all the basic features discussed thus far. The procedure in Figure 2.10 inserts a row into the employee table of the SAMPLE database. If you have not created the SAMPLE database, see Appendix A, "Getting Started with DB2." We recommend that you create this database because most examples in this book make use of it to demonstrate concepts.

```
CREATE PROCEDURE add_new_employee ( IN   p_empno    VARCHAR(6)     -- (1)
                                  , IN   p_firstnme CHAR(12)
                                  , IN   p_midinit  CHAR(1)
                                  , IN   p_lastname VARCHAR(15)
                                  , IN   p_deptname VARCHAR(30)
                                  , IN   p_edlevel  SMALLINT
                                  , OUT  p_status   VARCHAR(100)
                                  , OUT  p_ts       TIMESTAMP)
     LANGUAGE SQL
     SPECIFIC add_new_employee                      -- applies to LUW and iSeries
     -- WLM ENVIRONMENT <env>                       -- applies to zSeries

BEGIN
     DECLARE v_deptno CHAR(3) DEFAULT '   ';                    -- (2)
     DECLARE v_create_ts TIMESTAMP;                             -- (3)
     SET v_create_ts = CURRENT TIMESTAMP;
     /* Get the corresponding department number */
     SELECT deptno
       INTO v_deptno                                            -- (4)
       FROM department
      WHERE deptname = p_deptname;

     /* Insert new employee into table */                       -- (5)
     INSERT INTO employee ( empno
                          , firstnme
                          , midinit
```

```
                         , lastname
                         , workdept
                         , hiredate
                         , edlevel)
      VALUES ( p_empno
             , p_firstnme
             , p_midinit
             , p_lastname
             , v_deptno
             , DATE(v_create_ts)
             , p_edlevel );
      SET p_status = 'Employee added';                            -- (6)
      SET p_ts = v_create_ts;                                     -- (7)
END
```

Figure 2.10   add_new_employee procedure

The parameter list shown in Line (1) defines input and output variables to the procedures. The **input parameters** represent column values that will be inserted into the Employee table. Note that the p_ prefix is used for each variable to differentiate variables from column names. The **output parameters** are used to return a status and the TIMESTAMP of the execution of the procedure.

Line (2) declares the v_deptno variable to hold the department number retrieved from the Department table. v_deptno is initialized to ''.

Line (3) declares the v_create_ts variable to hold the TIMESTAMP of execution of the procedure. To ensure that the same value of hiredate is used to insert into the Employee table, the CURRENT TIMESTAMP register is retrieved only once in the procedure.

To look up the department number in the Department table, a SELECT statement shown in Line (4) is used to retrieve deptno and saved in v_deptno.

Line (5) inserts into the Employee table using parameter values v_deptno and v_create_ts. The value of v_create_ts, which is of type TIMESTAMP, must be cast to DATE using the DATE casting function.

On Lines (6) and (7), the output parameters p_status and p_ts are set.

To execute the add_new_employee procedure on LUW, enter the following in CLP:

```
CALL add_new_employee('123456','ROBERT','K','ALEXANDER','PLANNING',1,?,?)
```

The output of this call is

```
P_STATUS: Employee added
P_TS: 2002-09-29 17:19:10.927001


"ADD_NEW_EMPLOYEE" RETURN_STATUS: "0"
```

The results of many examples in the book are shown using the CLP on LUW. The output will vary based on the operating system. For example, if you are using the Run an SQL Script window of the iSeries Navigator, the output from the call above would be

```
Output Parameter #7 = Employee added
Output Parameter #8 = 2002-09-29 17:19:10.927001


Statement ran successfully    (591 ms)
```

DB2 UDB for iSeries Considerations

The CREATE PROCEDURE statement syntax for DB2 UDB for iSeries is very similar to the CREATE PROCEDURE statement syntax for DB2 UDB for distributed platforms shown in Figure 2.1. In iSeries, the following is true:

- The LANGUAGE SQL clause is mandatory and must be listed right after the parameter declaration in the procedure.
- The PARAMETER CCSID clause is not supported, but specification of the encoding scheme can be specified with the data type of the parameters.
- The EXTERNAL ACTION clause is not part of the syntax.
- An option to specify whether the procedure runs FENCED or NOT FENCED is supported for compatibility with other products in the DB2 family.
- A COMMIT ON RETURN clause can be specified to commit a transaction when returning from a SQL procedure.
- An optional SET OPTION clause is supported to specify precompile options.

For completeness, Figure 2.11 shows the syntax diagram for the iSeries CREATE PROCEDURE statement, followed by a more detailed explanation of some of the clauses.

```
>>-CREATE PROCEDURE---procedure-name ---------------------------->


>--+----------------------------------------------------------+->
   '-- (--+----------------------------------------------+--)--'->
          |   .-,----------------------------------------. |
          |   V .-IN----.                                | |
          '----+-------+---parameter-name--data-type---+-'
               +-OUT---+
               '-INOUT-'


>--LANGUAGE SQL----------------------------------------------+->


   .-NOT DETERMINISTIC--.     .-MODIFIES SQL DATA--.
>--+-------------------+-----+-------------------+------------>
   '-DETERMINISTIC------'     +-CONTAINS SQL-------+
                              '-READS SQL DATA-----'


   .-CALLED ON NULL INPUT-.
>--+---------------------+-----+-------------------------+---->
                               '-SPECIFIC--specific-name--'


   .-DYNAMIC RESULT SETS 0---------.     .-FENCED-----.
>--+----------------------------+-----+------------+--------->
   '-DYNAMIC RESULT SETS--integer--'     '-NOT FENCED-'


   .-COMMIT ON RETURN NO--.     .-OLD SAVEPOINT LEVEL-.
>--+--------------------+-----+-------------------+--------->
   '-COMMIT ON RETURN YES-'     '-NEW SAVEPOINT LEVEL-'


   .-INHERIT SPECIAL RESGISTERS-.
>--+---------------------------+----------------------------->


>--+--------------------+---SQL-routine-body----------------><
   '-SET OPTION-statement-'
```

Figure 2.11   CREATE PROCEDURE statement syntax for DB2 UDB for iSeries.

FENCED and *NOT FENCED*

This option is provided only for compatibility with other products in the DB2 family and is not
used by SQL procedures in DB2 UDB for iSeries.

COMMIT ON RETURN

This clause can be specified to tell the database manager to commit the transaction when returning from the SQL procedure call. The default value is NO. If a value of YES is specified, the transaction is committed only upon successful completion of the procedure. If an error is encountered, a COMMIT is not issued.

> **NOTE**
> If you specify YES for this clause, then any cursors that are opened in the SQL procedure for the purpose of returning a result set must be declared using the WITH HOLD option. For more details on cursors, refer to Chapter 5., "Understanding and Using Cursors and Result Sets."

SET OPTION Statement

The SET OPTION statement is used to specify processing options that will be used to create the procedure. For example, a procedure can be created for debug by specifying the following:

```
SET OPTION DBGVIEW = *SOURCE
```

DBGVIEW identifies that debug information is to be provided by the compiler. The *SOURCE specifies that the compiled object is to be debugged using the program source code.

Chapter 12, "Performance Tuning," discusses the SET OPTION statement in more detail. For a complete list of options, refer to the SET OPTION statement information found in the Statements chapter of the DB2 UDB for iSeries SQL Reference.

DB2 UDB for zSeries Considerations

In DB2 UDB for zSeries, the CREATE PROCEDURE statement defines a procedure in the DB2 subsystem. Figure 2.12 shows the syntax diagram of such a statement. It is very similar to the syntax shown in Figure 2.1 for DB2 for LUW. In zSeries, the following is true:

- The LANGUAGE SQL clause is mandatory.
- The SPECIFIC, SAVEPOINT LEVEL, and EXTERNAL ACTION clauses are not part of the syntax.
- PARAMETER CCSID has an extra possible value of EBCDIC. In addition, the CCSID clause can be included with each stored procedure parameter.
- The FENCED clause is the default value and an optional clause. There is no NOT FENCED option.
- A COMMIT ON RETURN clause can be specified to commit a transaction when returning from an SQL procedure.

```
>>-CREATE PROCEDURE--------------------------------------------->

>----procedure-name--(--+--------------------------------------------+---)->
                        |   .-,-------------------------------------. |
                        |   V .-IN----.                             | |
                        '----+-------+---parameter-name--data-type---+-'
                             +-OUT---+
                             '-INOUT-'


   .-DYNAMIC RESULT SETS 0--------.      .-MODIFIES SQL DATA-.
>--+----------------------------+--*--+------------------+--->
   '-DYNAMIC RESULT SETS--integer-'    +-CONTAINS SQL------+
                                       '-READS SQL DATA----'


     .-NOT DETERMINISTIC-.      .-CALLED ON NULL INPUT-.
>--*--+------------------+--*--+----------------------+--*----->
      '-DETERMINISTIC-----'


   .-INHERIT SPECIAL REGISTERS-.
>--+-------------------------+---*-------LANGUAGE SQL---------->
   '-DEFAULT SPECIAL REGISTERS-'


                                  .-FENCED-.   .-NO DBINFO-.
>--+----------------------------+---+--------+---+-----------+-->
   '-PARAMETER CCSID--+-ASCII---+-'
                      '-EBCDIC -'
                      '-UNICODE-'


   .-NO COLLID ------------.
>--+----------------------+---+------------------------------+-->
   '-COLLID Collection-Id -'   '-WLM ENVIRONMENT--+--name----+-'
                                                  '-(name,*)-'


   .-ASUTIME NO LIMIT ------.     .-STAY RESIDENT NO--.
>--+----------------------+----+------------------+----------->
   '-ASUTIME LIMIT integer--'     +-STAY RESIDENT YES-'


   .-PROGRAM TYPE MAIN--.    .-SECURITY DB2-----.
```

```
>--+-------------------+----+-----------------+---------------->
   '-PROGRAM TYPE SUB---'    +-SECURITY USER ---+
                             '-SECURITY DEFINER-'



                                            .-COMMIT ON RETURN NO---.
>--+----------------------------+----+----------------------+->
   '-RUN OPTIONS run time options--'   '-COMMIT ON RETURN YES--'



   .-STOP AFTER SYSTEM DEFAULT FAILURES --.
>--+----------------------------------------+--------------------->
   +-STOP AFTER integer FAILURES ---------+
   '-CONTINUE AFTER FAILURE--------------'


>-----| SQL-procedure-body |------------------------------------><

SQL-procedure-body:

 |---SQL-procedure-statement------------------------------------|
```

Figure 2.12   *CREATE PROCEDURE* statement syntax in DB2 UDB for zSeries.

FENCED

This option specifies that the SQL procedure runs in an external address space to prevent user programs from corrupting the DB2 engine storage. This clause is optional and is the default value in DB2 UDB for zSeries. There is no NOT FENCED option. Note that SQL procedures created in DB2 UDB for LUW are all UNFENCED; this is the default and the only behavior.

NO DBINFO

NO DBINFO indicates that specific internal information known to DB2 will not be passed to the SQL procedure. NO DBINFO is the default for SQL procedures.

NO COLLID or *Collid collection-id*

NO COLLID indicates that the package collection for the SQL procedure is the same as the package collection of the calling program. COLLID collection-id provides the collection ID to be used for the SQL procedure.

WLM ENVIRONMENT

This option identifies the Workload Manager (WLM) environment where the SQL procedure is to run if defined as a WLM-established SQL procedure. If WLM ENVIRONMENT is not specified, the default WLM environment specified at installation time is used.

ASUTIME

This option indicates whether the SQL procedure will use unlimited processor time for a single invocation of an SQL procedure (NOLIMIT) or a specific amount of processor time (LIMIT integer).

STAY RESIDENT

This option indicates the SQL procedure will remain in memory when it ends (YES) or not (NO).

PROGRAM TYPE

This option specifies whether the SQL procedure will run as a subroutine (SUB) or as a main program (MAIN).

SECURITY

This option indicates how the SQL procedure interacts with an external security product to control access to non-SQL resources. Possible values include the following:

- DB2. The SQL procedure does not require a special external security environment. If it accesses resources that an external security product protects, the access is performed using the authorization ID associated with the SQL procedure address space. DB2 is the default.

- USER. An external security environment should be established for the SQL procedure. If the SQL procedure accesses resources that the external security product protects, the access is performed using the authorization ID of the user who invoked the SQL procedure.

- DEFINER. An external security environment should be established for the SQL procedure. If the SQL procedure accesses resources that the external security product protects, the access is performed using the authorization ID of the owner of the SQL procedure.

RUN OPTIONS

This option indicates the Language Environment runtime options that are to be used for the SQL procedure.

COMMIT ON RETURN

This option indicates whether a COMMIT is automatically issued upon return from the SQL procedure, regardless of whether a COMMIT or ROLLBACK is explicitly coded in the SQL procedure. NO is the default.

STOP AFTER SYSTEM DEFAULT FAILURES or CONTINUE AFTER FAILURE

This option indicates whether the SQL procedure is to be put in a stopped state after some number of failures. Possible values include the following:

- STOP AFTER SYSTEM DEFAULT FAILURES. The value of field MAX ABEND COUNT on installation panel DSNTIPX is used to determine the number of failures allowed before placing the SQL procedure in stopped state. This is the default.

- STOP AFTER nn FAILURES. Indicates that after nn failures, the SQL procedure should be placed in a stopped state. The value nn can be an integer from 1 to 32767.

- CONTINUE AFTER FAILURE. Specifies that this SQL procedure should not be placed in a stopped state after any failure.

Summary

SQL procedures are defined using the CREATE PROCEDURE statement. The statement defines the name, the parameters, and several other properties of the procedure.

The SQL procedure logic is defined in the procedure body of the CREATE PROCEDURE statement. The body is typically a compound statement consisting of declarations followed by procedural statements. The DECLARE statement is used to declare variables, their data type, and optionally, a default value. Statements such as SET, SELECT...INTO, and VALUES can also be used to assign values to variables.

This chapter demonstrated creation of simple procedures with some basic procedural statements. Other SQL PL statements will be discussed in detail in the rest of this book.

Overview of SQL PL Language Elements

In this chapter, you will learn

- DB2 data types and the range of their values
- How to work with large objects
- How to choose proper data types
- How to work with user-defined data types (UDTs)
- How to manipulate date, time, and string data
- How to use generated columns
- How to work with SEQUENCE objects and IDENTITY columns

Now that you have learned the basic DB2 SQL procedure structure, it is time for an overview of the DB2 SQL PL language elements and their usage before discussing any of the more advanced features of the language. Many decisions on the topics covered in this chapter—such as the choices of the proper data types and the usages of SEQUENCE objects, IDENTITY columns, and generated columns—are generally the tasks performed during database setup and table creation. Choices of the data types for parameters and local variables in the SQL procedures, User-Defined Functions (UDFs) and triggers, which are covered extensively in the rest of the book, mostly need to match the column definition in your underlying tables.

DB2 Data Types

A **data type** tells you what kind of data can be saved in a column or in a variable, and how large the value may be. There are two categories of data types in DB2:

- Built-in data types
- User-defined data types

Valid DB2 Built-In Data Types and Their Value Ranges

The built-in data types are provided with DB2. DB2 supports a wide range of data types for your business need. A summary of DB2 built-in data types are shown in Figure 3.1.

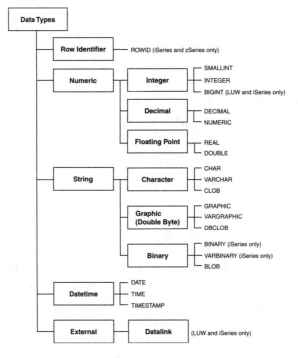

Figure 3.1   DB2 built-in data types.

> **NOTE**
> LONG VARCHAR and LONG VARGRAPHIC data types are supported in DB2 for LUW for backward compatibility only. They are being deprecated, which means that these data types will not be supported in the future. Use VARCHAR and VARGRAPHIC instead.

DB2 for iSeries and zSeries supports the ROWID data type. A ROWID data type is one that uniquely identifies a row. A query that uses ROWID navigates directly to the row because the column implicitly contains the location of the row. When a row is inserted into a table, DB2 generates a value for the ROWID column, unless one is supplied. If it is supplied, it must be a value that was previously generated. The value of ROWID cannot be updated and does not change, even after table space reorganizations. There can only be one ROWID column in a table.

There are six numeric data types in DB2. Their precisions and value ranges are listed in Table 3.1.

Table 3.1 DB2 Built-In Numeric Data Types

Data Type	Precision (Digits)	Data Value Range
SMALLINT	5	−32,768 to 32,767
INTEGER	10	−2,147,483,648 to 2,147,483,647
BIGINT	19	−9,223,372,036,854,775,808 to 9,223,372,036,854,775,807
DECIMAL/NUMERIC	LUW, zSeries: 31 iSeries: 63	LUW, zSeries: Any value with 31 digits or less. iSeries: Any value with 63 digits or less.
REAL	LUW, iSeries: 24 zSeries: 21	LUW: Smallest REAL value −3.402E+38 Largest REAL value +3.402E+38 Smallest positive REAL value +1.175E-37 Largest negative REAL value −1.175E-37 iSeries: Smallest REAL value −3.4E+38 Largest REAL value +3.4E+38 Smallest positive REAL value +1.18E-38 Largest negative REAL value −1.18E-38 zSeries: Smallest REAL value −7.2E+75 Largest REAL value +7.2E+75 Smallest positive REAL value +5.4E−79 Largest negative REAL value −5.4E−79
DOUBLE	53	LUW: Smallest DOUBLE value −1.79769E+308 Largest DOUBLE value +1.79769E+308 Smallest positive DOUBLE value +2.225E−307 Largest negative DOUBLE value −2.225E−307 iSeries: Smallest DOUBLE value −1.79E+308 Largest DOUBLE value +1.79E+308 Smallest positive DOUBLE value +2.23E−308 Largest negative DOUBLE value −2.23E−308

Table 3.1   DB2 Built-In Numeric Data Types (continued)

Data Type	Precision (Digits)	Data Value Range
		zSeries: Smallest REAL value −7.2E+75 Largest REAL value +7.2E+75 Smallest positive REAL value +5.4E−79 Largest negative REAL value −5.4E−79

DB2 supports both single-byte and double-byte character strings. DB2 uses 2 bytes to represent each character in double-byte strings. Their maximum lengths are listed in Table 3.2.

Table 3.2   DB2 Built-In String Data Types

Data Type	Maximum Length
CHAR	LUW: 254 bytes iSeries: 32,766 bytes zSeries: 255 bytes
VARCHAR	LUW: 32,672 bytes iSeries: 32,740 bytes zSeries: 32,704 bytes
LONG VARCHAR (LUW only)	32,700 bytes
CLOB	2,147,483,647 bytes
GRAPHIC	LUW: 127 characters iSeries: 16,383 characters zSeries: 127 characters
VARGRAPHIC	LUW: 16,336 characters iSeries: 16,370 characters zSeries: 16,352 characters
DBCLOB	1,073,741,823 characters
BINARY (iSeries only)	32,766 bytes
VARBINARY (iSeries only)	32,740 bytes
BLOB	2,147,483,647 bytes

You can also specify a subtype for string data types. For example, CHAR and VARCHAR columns can be defined as FOR BIT DATA to store binary data. On iSeries, other subtypes can be specified such as FOR SBCS DATA, FOR DBCS DATA, and CCSID. On zSeries, other subtypes that can be specified are FOR SBCS DATA and FOR MIXED DATA.

DB2 date and time data types include DATE, TIME, and TIMESTAMP. The TIMESTAMP data type consists of both the date part and the time part, while DATE and TIME data types only deal with the date and the time component, respectively. Their limits are listed in Table 3.3.

Table 3.3   DB2 Built-In Date Time Data Types

Description	Limits
Smallest DATE value	0001-01-01
Largest DATE value	9999-12-31
Smallest TIME value	00:00:00
Largest TIME value	24:00:00
Smallest TIMESTAMP value	0001-01-01-00.00.00.000000
Largest TIMESTAMP value	9999-12-31-24.00.00.000000

The last data type in Figure 3.1, DATALINK, is used to work with files stored outside the database. It is not covered in this book.

Large Objects

Large Object (LOB) data types are used to store data greater than 32KB, such as long XML documents, audio files, or pictures (up to 2GB). Three kinds of LOB data types are provided by DB2:

- Binary Large Objects (BLOBs)
- Single-byte Character Large Objects (CLOBs)
- Double-Byte Character Large Objects (DBCLOBs)

You will need to take into account some performance considerations when dealing with LOBs. Refer to Chapter 12, "Performance Tuning," for more details.

LOBs can be used as parameters and local variables of SQL procedures. Figure 3.2 demonstrates a very simple usage of LOBs and returns a CLOB to the stored procedure caller.

```
CREATE PROCEDURE staffresume ( IN p_empno CHAR(6)
                             , OUT p_resume CLOB(1M) )
    LANGUAGE SQL
    SPECIFIC staffresume                         -- applies to LUW and iSeries
 -- WLM ENVIRONMENT <env>                        -- applies to zSeries
BEGIN
    SELECT resume INTO p_resume
        FROM emp_resume
        WHERE empno=p_empno AND resume_format = 'ascii';

    INSERT INTO emp_resume ( empno
                           , resume_format
```

```
                              , resume )
        VALUES                ( p_empno
                              , 'backupcopy'
                              , p_resume );
END
```

Figure 3.2   SQL procedure *STAFFRESUME.*

Choosing Proper Data Types

Choosing the correct data type is a simple and yet important task. Specifying the wrong data type may result in not only wasted disk space but also poor performance. To choose the correct data type, you need to fully understand your data and their possible values and usage. Table 3.4 offers a checklist for data type selection.

Table 3.4   Simple Data Type Checklist

Question	Data Type
Is the string data variable in length?	VARCHAR
If the string data is variable in length, what is the maximum length?	VARCHAR
Do you need to sort (order) the data?	CHAR, VARCHAR,NUMERIC
Is the data going to be used in arithmetic operations?	DECIMAL, NUMERIC,REAL, DOUBLE,BIGINT, INTEGER,SMALLINT
Does the data element contain decimals?	DECIMAL, NUMERIC,REAL, DOUBLE
Is the data fixed in length?	CHAR
Does the data have a specific meaning (beyond DB2 base data types)?	USER DEFINED TYPE
Is the data larger than what a character string can store, or do you need to store non-traditional data?	CLOB, BLOB, DBCLOB

TIP

Unnecessary casting can cost performance. Try to define the variables in the SQL procedures with the same data types as the underlining table columns.

REAL, FLOAT, and DOUBLE are imprecise data types where rounding may occur. You should not use these data types for storing precise data, such as primary key values or currency data.

Working with User-Defined Distinct Types

User-defined distinct types are simple user-defined data types (UDTs) which are defined on existing DB2 data types. DB2 also supports other kinds of UDTs, which are beyond the scope of this book. In this book, UDT is only used to refer to the user-defined distinct type.

UDTs can be used to give your data semantic meaning. The syntax of creating UDTs is shown in Figure 3.3.

```
>>-CREATE DISTINCT TYPE--distinct-type-name--AS----------------->

>--| source-data-type |--WITH COMPARISONS--------------------->< 
```

Figure 3.3 *CREATE DISTINCT TYPE* syntax.

The `source-data-type` can be any DB2 built-in data type discussed in this chapter. The WITH COMPARISONS clause allows you to use system-provided operators for source data types on your UDTs. The WITH COMPARISONS clause is not allowed with BLOB, CLOB, DBCLOB, LONG VARCHAR, LONG VARGRAPHIC, or DATALINK source data types.

> **NOTE**
> In DB2 UDB for iSeries and zSeries, the WITH COMPARISON clause is optional. Comparison operator functions will be created for all allowed source data types except for the DATALINK.

You can use the UDTs to enforce your business rules and prevent different data from being used improperly because DB2 SQL PL enforces strong data typing. Strong data typing requires more explicit casting when comparing different data types because the data types are not implicitly cast.

To show you an example, suppose you define the two following variables:

```
DECLARE v_in_mile      DOUBLE;
DECLARE v_in_kilometer DOUBLE;
```

Nothing will prevent you from performing incorrect operations such as

```
IF (v_in_mile > v_in_kilometer)
```

This operation is meaningless because you cannot compare miles with kilometers without converting one of them first. But DB2 is unable to tell this. To DB2, both variables are floating-point numbers. It is perfectly normal to add them or directly compare them. UDTs can be used to prevent such mistakes.

You can create two new data types: `miles` and `kilometers`.

```
CREATE DISTINCT TYPE miles AS DOUBLE WITH COMPARISONS;
CREATE DISTINCT TYPE kilometers AS DOUBLE WITH COMPARISONS;
```

Then you can declare your variables using the UDTs instead:

```
DECLARE v_in_mile        miles;
DECLARE v_in_kilometer   kilometers;
```

Now you will receive an SQL error

```
SQL0401N  The data types of the operands for the operation ">" are not
compatible.  LINE NUMBER=7.  SQLSTATE=42818
```

if you try to execute the same statement:

```
IF (v_in_mile > v_in_kilometer)
```

If this error is somewhat expected, you might be surprised to learn that the following statement will also result in the same SQL error:

```
IF (v_in_mile > 30.0)
```

What is happening here? The answer is that DB2 requires you to explicitly cast both DOUBLE and `kilometers` data type to `miles` data type.

When you create one user-defined distinct data type, DB2 generates two casting functions for you: one to cast from UDT to the source data type and another to cast back.

In this example, for `miles` UDT, you have these two functions:

```
MILES (DOUBLE)
DOUBLE (MILES)
```

Similarly, you have these two functions for `kilometers` UDT:

```
KILOMETERS (DOUBLE)
DOUBLE (KILOMETERS)
```

In order for these two statements to work, they need to be rewritten using the casting functions:

```
IF (v_in_mile > MILES(DOUBLE(v_in_kilometer)/1.6))
IF (v_in_mile > miles(30.0))
```

You have to cast the `v_in_kilometers` twice because there is no casting function between `miles` and `kilometers` unless you create it manually. The factor of 1.6 is added to convert kilometers into miles.

Data Manipulation

DB2 provides many built-in supports for data manipulation. Because of the complexity involved with manipulating date, time, and string data, it is particularly important to understand how to use system-provided features on these data types.

Working with Dates and Times

Dates and times are the data types that differ the most among Database Management Systems (DBMSs). This section shows you examples of some of the basic date and time manipulations.

You can get the current date, time, and timestamp by using the appropriate DB2 special registers:

```
SELECT CURRENT DATE      FROM SYSIBM.SYSDUMMY1;
SELECT CURRENT TIME      FROM SYSIBM.SYSDUMMY1;
SELECT CURRENT TIMESTAMP FROM SYSIBM.SYSDUMMY1;
```

`CURRENT DATE`, `CURRENT TIME`, and `CURRENT TIMESTAMP` are three DB2 special registers. Another useful DB2 special register for date and time operation is `CURRENT TIMEZONE`. You can use it to get the `CURRENT TIME` or `CURRENT TIMESTAMP` adjusted to GMT/CUT. All you need to do is to subtract the `CURRENT TIMEZONE` register from the `CURRENT TIME` or `CURRENT TIMESTAMP`:

```
SELECT CURRENT TIME - CURRENT TIMEZONE      FROM SYSIBM.SYSDUMMY1;
SELECT CURRENT TIMESTAMP - CURRENT TIMEZONE FROM SYSIBM.SYSDUMMY1;
```

Given a date, time, or timestamp, you can extract (where applicable) the year, month, day, hour, minutes, seconds, and microseconds portions independently using the appropriate function:

```
SELECT YEAR (CURRENT TIMESTAMP)        FROM SYSIBM.SYSDUMMY1;
SELECT MONTH (CURRENT TIMESTAMP)       FROM SYSIBM.SYSDUMMY1;
SELECT DAY (CURRENT TIMESTAMP)         FROM SYSIBM.SYSDUMMY1;
SELECT HOUR (CURRENT TIMESTAMP)        FROM SYSIBM.SYSDUMMY1;
SELECT MINUTE (CURRENT TIMESTAMP)      FROM SYSIBM.SYSDUMMY1;
SELECT SECOND (CURRENT TIMESTAMP)      FROM SYSIBM.SYSDUMMY1;
SELECT MICROSECOND (CURRENT TIMESTAMP) FROM SYSIBM.SYSDUMMY1;
```

You can also extract the date and time independently from a timestamp:

```
SELECT DATE (CURRENT TIMESTAMP) FROM SYSIBM.SYSDUMMY1;
SELECT TIME (CURRENT TIMESTAMP) FROM SYSIBM.SYSDUMMY1;
```

The date and time calculations are very straightforward:

```
SELECT CURRENT DATE + 1 YEAR                              FROM SYSIBM.SYSDUMMY1;
SELECT CURRENT DATE + 3 YEARS + 2 MONTHS + 15 DAYS       FROM SYSIBM.SYSDUMMY1;
SELECT CURRENT TIME + 5 HOURS - 3 MINUTES + 10 SECONDS FROM SYSIBM.SYSDUMMY1;
```

DB2 also provides many date and time functions for easy date and time data manipulation. For a complete list, refer to the SQL Reference corresponding to your platform.

A few date and time functions are used here as examples to show you how you can work with date and time data in DB2. To calculate how many days there are between two dates, you can subtract dates as in the following:

```
SELECT DAYS (CURRENT DATE) - DAYS (DATE('2000-01-01'))
  FROM SYSIBM.SYSDUMMY1;
```

If you want to concatenate date or time values with other text, you need to convert the value into a character string first. To do this, you can simply use the CHAR function:

```
SELECT CHAR(CURRENT DATE)             FROM SYSIBM.SYSDUMMY1;
SELECT CHAR(CURRENT TIME)             FROM SYSIBM.SYSDUMMY1;
SELECT CHAR(CURRENT TIME + 12 HOURS) FROM SYSIBM.SYSDUMMY1;
```

To convert a character string to a date or time value, you can use:

```
SELECT TIMESTAMP ('2002-10-20-12.00.00.000000') FROM SYSIBM.SYSDUMMY1;
SELECT TIMESTAMP ('2002-10-20 12:00:00')
  FROM SYSIBM.SYSDUMMY1; -- For LUW, zSeries
--SELECT TIMESTAMP '2002-10-20 12:00:00'
    FROM SYSIBM.SYSDUMMY1; -- For iSeries
SELECT DATE ('2002-10-20')                       FROM SYSIBM.SYSDUMMY1;
SELECT DATE ('10/20/2002')                       FROM SYSIBM.SYSDUMMY1;
SELECT TIME ('12:00:00')                         FROM SYSIBM.SYSDUMMY1;
SELECT TIME ('12.00.00')                         FROM SYSIBM.SYSDUMMY1;
```

Working with Strings

String manipulation is relatively easy compared with date and timestamps. Again, DB2 built-in functions are heavily used. A few of them are used in this section to show you how DB2 string operations work. For a complete list, refer to the SQL Reference corresponding to your platform.

You can use either the CONCAT function or the || operator for string concatenation. The following two statements are exactly the same:

```
SELECT CONCAT('ABC', 'DEF') FROM SYSIBM.SYSDUMMY1;
SELECT 'ABC' || 'DEF' FROM SYSIBM.SYSDUMMY1;
```

However, when you have more than two strings to concatenate, the ‖ operator is much easier to use.

You might have to use UPPER or LOWER function in string comparisons if you want the comparison to be case-insensitive. DB2 string comparison is case-sensitive.

COALESCE is another frequently used string function. It returns the first argument that is not null. In your application, if you have the following query SELECT coalesce(c1, c2, 'ABC') FROM t1;

assuming the c1 and c2 columns of table T1 are both nullable character strings, you will receive the value of c1 if it is not null. If c1 is null, you will receive the value of c2 if it is not null. If both c1 and c2 contain null values, you will receive the string ''ABC'' instead.

Working with Generated Columns

LUW allows a column to be declared as a generated column. It is a column that derives the values for each row from an expression, and is used to embed your business logic into the table definition. The syntax for generated columns is shown in Figure 3.4. Generated columns have to be defined with either the CREATE TABLE or ALTER TABLE statements.

```
|---column-name----+--------------------+----------------------------------->
                   |                    |
                   '-| data-type |-------'

|--+-GENERATED--+-ALWAYS-----+--AS--+-(--generation-expression--)------------|
               '-BY DEFAULT-'
```

Figure 3.4   Generated column syntax for LUW.

Values will be generated for the column when a row is inserted into the table. Two options are supported, namely GENERATED ALWAYS and GENERATED BY DEFAULT. For a GENERATED ALWAYS identity column, DB2 has full control over the values generated, and uniqueness is guaranteed. An error will be raised if an explicit value is specified. On the other hand, the GENERATED BY DEFAULT option does not guarantee uniqueness. DB2 will only generate a value for the column when no value is specified at the time of insert.

Figure 3.5 shows an example of a table using a generated column.

```
CREATE TABLE payroll
( employee_id INT NOT NULL
, base_salary DOUBLE
, bonus DOUBLE
, commission DOUBLE
, total_pay DOUBLE GENERATED ALWAYS AS
          (base_salary*(1+bonus) + commission)
)
```

Figure 3.5   An example of generated columns using a simple expression for LUW.

In this example, there is a table named `payroll` in the department. Three columns are related to an employee's total pay, namely `base_salary`, `bonus`, and `commission`. The `base_salary` and `commission` are in dollars, and the `bonus` is a percentage of the `base_salary`. The `total_pay` is calculated from these three numbers. The benefit of using a generated column here is to perform pre-calculation before the query time and to save the calculated value in the column. If your application has to use the value frequently, using the generated column will obviously improve the performance.

NOTE

An alternative to using generated columns (applicable to all platforms) is presented in Figures 3.21 and 3.22 toward the end of this chapter.

To insert a record into the `payroll` table, you can either use the `DEFAULT` keyword, as in

```
INSERT INTO payroll VALUES (1, 100, 0.1, 20, DEFAULT);
```

You could also not enumerate the column:

```
INSERT INTO payroll (employee_id, base_salary, bonus, commission)
VALUES (1, 100, 0.1, 20);
```

Both will generate the same result. Because the column is always defined as generated, you cannot supply a real value for the `total_pay` column. If not all identity columns are specified in the `INSERT` statement, DB2 will automatically substitute them with default values according to the column definitions.

It is a good practice to specify all the columns defined in the table and the associated values. This allows you to easily identify if there is a mismatch or missing column names and values. Notice how the reserved word `DEFAULT` is used so that DB2 will supply the default value for the generated column.

NOTE

`DEFAULT` is a DB2 reserved word. It is mandatory if a `GENERATED ALWAYS` column name is specified in an `INSERT` statement. Specifying all values for the columns in the `VALUES` clause of an `INSERT` statement is a good practice because it gives a clear view of what values are being inserted.

The generation expression in Figure 3.5 is a very simple arithmetic formula. More logic could be built into it by using a `CASE` statement. The `CASE` statement will be discussed in detail in Chapter 4, "Using Flow of Control Statements." For now, it is sufficient to know that a `CASE` statement checks conditions and chooses which statement to execute depending on the result. In the next example, the company has decided that each employee will be either a bonus employee or a commission employee, but not both. A bonus employee receives a base salary and a bonus. A commission employee receives a base salary and a commission. A more complex table definition is shown in Figure 3.6.

```
CREATE TABLE payroll2
( employee_id INT NOT NULL
, employee_type CHAR(1) NOT NULL
, base_salary DOUBLE
, bonus DOUBLE
, commission DOUBLE
, total_pay DOUBLE GENERATED ALWAYS AS
    ( CASE employee_type
      WHEN 'B' THEN base_salary*(1+bonus)
      WHEN 'C' THEN (base_salary + commission)
      ELSE 0
      END
    )
)
```

Figure 3.6   An example of generated columns using a CASE expression for LUW.

When the total pay is calculated, the employee type is checked first. If the type is 'B', indicating a bonus employee, the total pay is the total of the base salary and the bonus. If the type is 'C', indicating a commission employee, the total pay is calculated by adding the base salary and the commission. If a wrong employee type is entered, the total pay is set to 0, indicating a problem.

Working with Identity Columns and Sequence Objects

Numeric generation is a very common requirement for many types of applications, such as the generation of new employee numbers, order purchase numbers, ticket numbers, and so on. In a heavy online transaction processing (OLTP) environment with a high number of concurrent users, use of database tables and user-defined programmatic increment methods usually degrade performance. The reason is that the database system has to lock a table row when a value is requested to guarantee no duplicated values are used. The locks are discussed more in detail in Chapter 5, "Understanding and Using Cursors and Result Sets." Instead of relying on your own methods for generating unique IDs, you can make use of facilities provided by DB2.

DB2 provides two mechanisms to implement such sets of numbers: identity columns and sequence objects. As you explore the usage of identity columns and sequence objects, you will see that both of them achieve basically the same goal: automatically generating numeric values. Their behaviors can be tailored by using different options to meet specific application needs. Although they are created and used differently, DB2 treats both of them as sequences. An identity column is a system-defined sequence, and a sequence object is a user-defined sequence.

A few SQL procedure examples will be used to demonstrate how to work with automatic numbering in DB2. In order to better illustrate the usage, some of the procedures use DB2 SQL PL features covered in the following chapters.

Identity Column

An **identity column** is a numeric column defined in a table for which the column values can be generated automatically by DB2. The definition of an identity column is specified at table creation time. Existing tables cannot be altered to add or drop an identity column. Figure 3.7 shows the syntax of an identity column clause used in a CREATE TABLE statement. Only one column in a table can be defined to be an identity column.

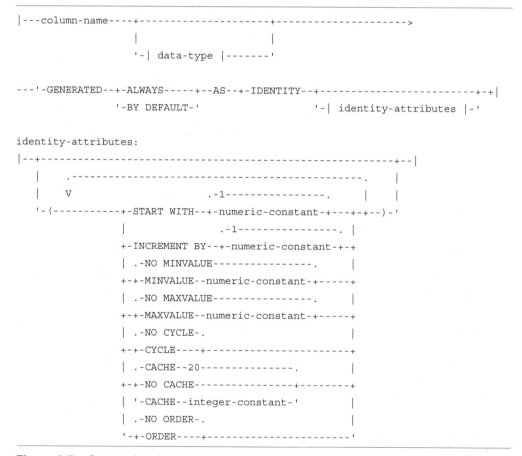

```
|---column-name----+--------------------+--------------------->
                   |                    |
                   '-| data-type |-------'


---'-GENERATED--+-ALWAYS-----+---AS--+-IDENTITY--+------------------------+-+|
                '-BY DEFAULT-'                   '-| identity-attributes |-'


identity-attributes:
|--+---------------------------------------------------------+--|
   |     .-------------------------------------------------.   |
   |     V                        .-1---------------.      |   |
   '-(-----------+-START WITH--+-numeric-constant-+---+-+--)-'
                 |                      .-1---------------.  |
                 +-INCREMENT BY--+-numeric-constant-+-+
                 | .-NO MINVALUE---------------.       |
                 +-+-MINVALUE--numeric-constant-+-----+
                 | .-NO MAXVALUE---------------.       |
                 +-+-MAXVALUE--numeric-constant-+-----+
                 | .-NO CYCLE-.                        |
                 +-+-CYCLE----+----------------------+
                 | .-CACHE--20--------------.         |
                 +-+-NO CACHE----------------+--------+
                 | '-CACHE--integer-constant-'        |
                 | .-NO ORDER-.                       |
                 '-+-ORDER----+----------------------'
```

Figure 3.7   Syntax of the identity column clause.

Data types for identity columns can be any exact numeric data type with a scale of zero such as SMALLINT, INTEGER, BIGINT, or DECIMAL. Single and double precision floating-point data types are considered to be approximate numeric data types, and they cannot be used as identity columns.

NOTE

In zSeries, any column defined with the ROWID data type will default to GENERATED ALWAYS.

Within the IDENTITY clause, you can set a number of options to customize the behavior of an identity column. Before discussing these options, let's look at Figure 3.8 to see how a table can be created with an identity column.

```
CREATE TABLE service_rq
    ( rqid SMALLINT NOT NULL
        CONSTRAINT rqid_pk
        PRIMARY KEY                                          -- (1)
    , status VARCHAR(10) NOT NULL
        WITH DEFAULT 'NEW'
        CHECK ( status IN ( 'NEW', 'ASSIGNED', 'PENDING',
        'CANCELLED' ) )                                      -- (2)
    , rq_desktop CHAR(1) NOT NULL
        WITH DEFAULT 'N'
        CHECK ( rq_desktop IN ( 'Y', 'N' ) )                -- (3)
    , rq_ipaddress CHAR(1) NOT NULL
        WITH DEFAULT 'N'
        CHECK ( rq_ipaddress IN ( 'Y', 'N' ) )              -- (4)
    , rq_unixid CHAR(1) NOT NULL
        WITH DEFAULT 'N'
        CHECK ( rq_unixid IN ( 'Y', 'N' ) )                 -- (5)
    , staffid INTEGER NOT NULL
    , techid INTEGER
    , accum_rqnum INTEGER NOT NULL                          -- (6)
        GENERATED ALWAYS AS IDENTITY
        ( START WITH 1
        , INCREMENT BY 1
        , CACHE 10 )
    , comment VARCHAR(100))
```

Figure 3.8   Example of a table definition with an identity column

Figure 3.8 is the definition of a table called service_rq, which will be used in a later sample. The service_rq table contains an identity column called accum_rqnum, shown in Line (6). Note that the GENERATED ALWAYS option is specified, and therefore DB2 will always generate a unique integer. The value of accum_rqnum will start at 1 and increment by 1.

From examining the other column definitions (2, 3, 4, and 5), you will see that some are defined with a CHECK constraint so that only the specified values are allowed as column values. A primary key is also defined for this table, as shown in Line (1).

NOTE

For LUW and iSeries, a unique index is automatically created when a primary key is defined, if one does not exist already. On zSeries, you need to explicitly create the unique index associated with a primary key declaration.

In DB2 for zSeries, explicitly create a unique index on the primary key column:

```
CREATE UNIQUE INDEX rqid_pk ON service_rq (rqid);  -- zSeries only
```

Figures 3.9 and 3.10 show two different ways to insert a record into the service_rq table.

```
INSERT INTO service_rq
    ( rqid
    , rq_desktop
    , rq_ipaddress
    , rq_unixid
    , staffid
    , comment )
VALUES
    ( 1
    , 'Y'
    , 'Y'
    , 'Y'
    , 10
    , 'First request for staff id 10' )
```

Figure 3.9   First method of inserting into a table with an identity column.

```
INSERT INTO service_rq
    ( rqid
    , status
    , rq_desktop
    , rq_ipaddress
    , rq_unixid
    , staffid
    , techid
    , accum_rqnum
    , comment )
```

```
VALUES
    ( 2
    , DEFAULT                -- (1)
    , 'Y'
    , 'Y'
    , 'Y'
    , 10
    , NULL
    , DEFAULT                -- (2)
    , 'Second request for staff id 10' )
```

Figure 3.10 Second method of inserting into a table with an identity column.

The use of the DEFAULT keyword in Figure 3.10 is the same as what has been discussed in the generated columns section.

As shown in Figure 3.7, a few other options are available when defining the identity attribute. The START WITH option indicates the first value of the identity column and can be a positive or negative value. Identity values can be generated in ascending or descending order, and can be controlled by the INCREMENT BY clause. The default behavior is to auto-increment by 1 (and therefore, it is ascending). Options MINVALUE and MAXVALUE allow you to specify the lower and upper limit of the generated values. These values must be within the limit of the data type. If the minimum or maximum limit has been reached, you can use CYCLE to recycle the generated values from the minimum or maximum value governed by the MINVALUE and MAXVALUE option.

The CACHE option can be used to provide better performance. Without caching, (by using option NO CACHE), DB2 will issue a database access request every time the next value is requested. Performance can be degraded if the insert rate of a table with an identity column is heavy. To minimize this synchronous effect, specify the CACHE option so that a block of values is obtained and stored in memory to serve subsequent identity value generation requests. When all the cached values in memory are used, the next block of values will be obtained. In the example shown in Figure 3.8, 10 values are generated and stored in the memory cache. When applications request a value, it will be obtained from the cache rather than from the system tables that are stored on disk. If DB2 is stopped before all cached values are used, any unused cached values will be discarded. After DB2 is restarted, the next block of values is generated and cached, introducing gaps between values. If your application does not allow value gaps, use the NO CACHE option instead of the default value of CACHE 20.

Generate Value Retrieval

It is often useful to be able to use the identity value previously generated by DB2 in subsequent application logic. The generated value can be obtained by executing the function IDENTITY_VAL_LOCAL within the same session of the INSERT statement; otherwise NULL is returned. The function does not take any parameters. Figure 3.11 demonstrates two different ways to use the IDENTITY_VAL_LOCAL function.

```
CREATE PROCEDURE addnewrq ( IN p_rqid SMALLINT
                          , IN p_staffid INTEGER
                          , IN p_comment VARCHAR(100)
                          , OUT p_accum_rqnum INTEGER )
    LANGUAGE SQL
    SPECIFIC addnewrq                         -- applies to LUW and iSeries
 -- WLM ENVIRONMENT <env>                     -- applies to zSeries
BEGIN
    INSERT INTO service_rq
        ( rqid, status, rq_desktop
        , rq_ipaddress, rq_unixid, staffid
        , techid, accum_rqnum, comment )
    VALUES
        ( p_rqid, DEFAULT, 'Y'
        , 'Y', 'Y', p_staffid
        , NULL, DEFAULT, p_comment ) ;

    SELECT                        -- (1)
        identity_val_local()
    INTO
        p_accum_rqnum
    FROM
        sysibm.sysdummy1;

    VALUES                        -- (2)
        identity_val_local()
    INTO
        p_accum_rqnum;
END
```

Figure 3.11   Example of using *IDENTITY_VAL_LOCAL*.

In Figure 3.11, procedure addnewrq uses two ways to obtain the value just inserted into service_rq. On Line (1), it uses the SYSIBM.SYSDUMMY1 table. Another method is to instead use the VALUES clause shown in Line (2). If you call the procedure multiple times with the same rqid value, as in

```
CALL addnewrq(3, 1050, 'New Request', ?)
```

you receive an error with SQLSTATE 23505 indicating a unique constraint was violated because the rqid column is defined as a primary key in Figure 3.8. Note that the result of IDENTITY_VAL_LOCAL keeps increasing even though the INSERT statement fails. This indicates that once an identity value is assigned by DB2, it will not be reused regardless of the success or failure of the previous INSERT statement.

Notice that the example in Figure 3.11 only involves a single row insert. If the statement inserts multiple rows prior to execution of IDENTITY_VAL_LOCAL, it will not return the last value generated—it will return NULL.

NOTE

In DB2 UDB for iSeries, the IDENTITY_VAL_LOCAL function does not return a null value after multi-row inserts. It will return the last value that was generated.

Consider the example in Figure 3.12.

```
CREATE PROCEDURE insert_multirow
    ( OUT p_id_generated INTEGER )
    LANGUAGE SQL
    SPECIFIC insrt_multirow                      -- applies to LUW and iSeries
BEGIN
    INSERT INTO service_rq                    -- (1)
        ( rqid
        , staffid
        , accum_rqnum
        , comment )
    VALUES
        ( 30000, 1050, DEFAULT, 'INSERT1')    -- (2)
        ,( 30001, 1050, DEFAULT, 'INSERT2')   -- (3)
    ;
    VALUES                                    -- (4)
        identity_val_local()
    INTO
        p_id_generated;

    -- For clean up purpose
    DELETE FROM service_rq
        WHERE rqid = 30000 or rqid = 30001;

END
```

Figure 3.12 Example of a multi-row insert before *IDENTITY_VAL_LOCAL* for LUW and iSeries.

Two sets of values on Lines (2) and (3) are being inserted with a single INSERT statement separated by a comma. The output parameter p_id_generated is assigned to the result of the IDENTITY_VAL_LOCAL function at Line (4). Successfully calling insert_multirow will give you the following on LUW:

```
P_ID_GENERATED: NULL
"INSERT_MULTIROW" RETURN_STATUS: "0"
```

On iSeries, the result would be something similar to

```
Output Parameter #1 = 5
Statement ran successfully    (761 ms)
```

> **NOTE**
> In DB2 for zSeries, the example shown in Figure 3.12 will not work because inserting two rows with one INSERT statement as shown is not supported. To insert multiple rows with one statement, use the INSERT INTO <table1> (<columns>) SELECT <columns> FROM <table2> statement; however, the IDENTITY_VAL_LOCAL function is not supported with this statement. Another alternative to insert multiple rows in zSeries is using Dynamic SQL and host variable arrays.

Change of Identity Column Characteristics

Because an identity column is part of a table definition, to reset or change a characteristic of an identity column you need to issue an ALTER TABLE statement as shown in Figure 3.13.

```
                              .-COLUMN-.
>>-ALTER TABLE--table-name---ALTER--+--------+--column-name------>

           .----------------------------------------.
           V                                        |
|----------+-SET INCREMENT BY--numeric-constant--+-+-+---------->< 
           +-SET--+-NO MINVALUE----------------+-+
           |      '-MINVALUE--numeric-constant-' |
           +-SET--+-NO MAXVALUE----------------+-+
           |      '-MAXVALUE--numeric-constant-' |
           +-SET--+-NO CYCLE-+------------------+
           |      '-CYCLE----'                  |
           +-SET--+-NO CACHE--------------+----+
           |      '-CACHE--integer-constant-'   |
```

```
                      +-SET--+-NO ORDER-+-------------------+
                      |      '-ORDER----'                   |
                      '-RESTART--+-----------------------+-'
                                  '-WITH--numeric-constant-'
```

Figure 3.13 Syntax and example of altering identity column characteristics.

Except for the RESTART option (which has not been introduced), the options listed in Figure 3.13 behave exactly the same as they were described earlier in this chapter. If you want the identity column to be restarted at a specific value at any time, you will find the RESTART option very useful. Simply alter the table, provide the RESTART WITH clause, and explicitly specify a numeric constant.

Sequence Object

A **sequence** is a database object that allows automatic generation of values. Unlike an identity column that is bound to a specific table, a sequence is a global and stand-alone object that can be used by any table in the same database. The same sequence object can be used for one or more tables. Figure 3.14 lists the syntax for creating a sequence object.

```
                                       .-AS INTEGER-----.
>>-CREATE SEQUENCE--sequence-name---*----+---------------+--*-->
                                       '-AS--data-type--'
>-----+------------------------------+--*--------------------->
      '-START WITH--numeric-constant--'
      .-INCREMENT BY 1-----------------.
>-----+------------------------------+--*------------------->
      '-INCREMENT BY--numeric-constant--'
      .-NO MINVALUE----------------.
>-----+------------------------------+--*----------------------->
      '-MINVALUE--numeric-constant--'
      .-NO MAXVALUE----------------.        .-NO CYCLE--.
>-----+------------------------------+--*----+-----------+--*---->
      '-MAXVALUE--numeric-constant--'        '-CYCLE-----'
      .-CACHE 20----------------.        .-NO ORDER--.
>-----+------------------------+--*----+-----------+--*------><
      +-CACHE--integer-constant--+        '-ORDER-----'
      '-NO CACHE----------------'
```

Figure 3.14 Syntax of the *CREATE SEQUENCE* statement.

As with identity columns, any exact numeric data type with a scale of zero can be used for the sequence value. These include SMALLINT, INTEGER, BIGINT, or DECIMAL. In addition, any user-defined distinct type based on of these data types can hold sequence values. This extends the usage of user-defined distinct types in an application. You may already notice that options supported for sequence objects are the same as the ones for identity columns. Refer to the previous subsection for their descriptions.

```
CREATE SEQUENCE staff_seq AS INTEGER
    START WITH 360
    INCREMENT BY 10
    NO MAXVALUE
    NO CYCLE
    NO CACHE
```

Figure 3.15   Example of sequence *staff_seq*.

```
CREATE SEQUENCE service_rq_seq AS SMALLINT
    START WITH 1
    INCREMENT BY 1
    MAXVALUE 5000
    NO CYCLE
    CACHE 50
```

Figure 3.16   Example of sequence *service_rq_seq*.

Figure 3.15 and Figure 3.16 show the creation of two sequence objects. For example, the sequence staff_seq is used to provide a numeric ID for each staff member. It is declared as an INTEGER, starts at 360, is incremented by 10, and no maximum value is explicitly specified. It is implicitly bound by the limit of the data type. In this example, values generated are within the limit of an INTEGER data type. The NO CYCLE option indicates that if the maximum value is reached, SQLSTATE 23522 will be returned, which means that the values for the sequence have been exhausted. The second sequence object, shown in Figure 3.16, is defined as SMALLINT and used to generate ticket numbers for service requests. This sequence object will start at 1 and increment by 1. Because NO CYCLE is specified, the maximum value generated will be 5000. The CACHE 50 option indicates that DB2 will acquire and cache 50 values at a time for application use. Like identity columns, if DB2 is stopped and sequence values were cached, gaps in sequence values may result.

Change of Sequence Object Characteristics

At any time, you can either drop and re-create the sequence object or alter the sequence to change its behavior. Figures 3.17 and 3.18 show the syntax of the ALTER SEQUENCE and DROP SEQUENCE statements, respectively.

```
>>-ALTER SEQUENCE--sequence-name---------------------------------->
   .--------------------------------------------.
       V                                        |
   >-------+-RESTART--+----------------------+-+--+------------><
           |              '-WITH--numeric-constant--' |
           +-INCREMENT BY--numeric-constant-------+
           +-+-MINVALUE--numeric-constant--+------+
           | '-NO MINVALUE----------------'       |
           +-+-MAXVALUE--numeric-constant--+------+
           | '-NO MAXVALUE----------------'       |
           +-+-CYCLE----+------------------------+
           | '-NO CYCLE-'                        |
           +-+-CACHE--integer-constant--+--------+
           | '-NO CACHE---------------'          |
           '-+-ORDER----+----------------------'
             '-NO ORDER-'
```

Figure 3.17   Syntax of the *ALTER SEQUENCE* statement.

> **NOTE**
> In DB2 UDB for iSeries, the ALTER SEQUENCE statement also allows you to change the data type of the sequence in addition to the options listed in the syntax diagram in Figure 3.17.

```
                              .-RESTRICT-.
--DROP--+-SEQUENCE--sequence-name--+----------+----------------------------+<
```

Figure 3.18   Syntax of the *DROP SEQUENCE* statement.

Privileges Required for Using Sequence Objects

Just like other database objects in DB2, manipulation of sequence objects is controlled by privileges. By default, only the sequence creator or a user with administrative authorities (such as SYSADM and DBADM on LUW), hold the ALTER and USAGE privileges of the object. If you want other users to be able to use the sequence, you need to issue the following:

```
GRANT USAGE ON SEQUENCE <sequence_object_name> TO PUBLIC
```

The USAGE and ALTER privileges can be granted to PUBLIC or any individual user or group.

Generated Value Retrieval

Two expressions, NEXT VALUE and PREVIOUS VALUE, are provided to generate and retrieve a sequence value. Figure 3.19 is an example of their usage. Two alternate expressions, NEXTVAL and PREVVAL, can be used interchangeably with NEXT VALUE and PREVIOUS VALUE, respectively, for backward compatibility reasons.

```
CREATE PROCEDURE seqexp ( out p_prevval1 int
                        , out p_nextval1 int
                        , out p_nextval2 int
                        , out p_prevval2 int )
    LANGUAGE SQL
    SPECIFIC seqexp                              -- applies to LUW and iSeries
 -- WLM ENVIRONMENT <env>                        -- applies to zSeries
BEGIN

    -- DECLARE host variables
    DECLARE v_prevstaffno INT;

    -- Procedure logic
    INSERT INTO staff
        ( id, name, dept
        , job, years, salary
        , comm )
    VALUES
        ( NEXT VALUE FOR staff_seq, 'Bush', 55
        , 'Mgr', 30, NULL
        , NULL);

    UPDATE staff
       SET id = ( NEXT VALUE FOR staff_seq )
     WHERE name='Bush';

    VALUES PREVIOUS VALUE FOR staff_seq INTO v_prevstaffno;    -- (1)

    DELETE FROM staff WHERE id = v_prevstaffno;                -- (2)

    VALUES                                                     -- (3)
        ( PREVIOUS VALUE FOR staff_seq
```

```
    , NEXT VALUE FOR staff_seq
    , NEXT VALUE FOR staff_seq
    , PREVIOUS VALUE FOR staff_seq )
  INTO p_prevval1, p_nextval1, p_nextval2, p_prevval2;
END
```

Figure 3.19   Usage of the *NEXT VALUE* and *PREVIOUS VALUE* expressions.

You can use the NEXT VALUE and PREVIOUS VALUE expressions in SELECT, VALUES, INSERT, and UPDATE statements. In Figure 3.19 on Line (2), the DELETE statement needs to reference the value just generated in the WHERE clause. Because NEXT VALUE and PREVIOUS VALUE cannot be used in a WHERE clause, you need to use two separate SQL statements. You can use a VALUES INTO statement to obtain and store the generated value in a variable, v_prevstaffno. The DELETE statement can then specify the variable in the WHERE clause.

The last VALUES statement on Line (3) in the example shows that if more than one sequence expression for a single sequence object is used in a statement, DB2 will execute NEXT VALUE and PREVIOUS VALUE only once. In the example, assuming the value last generated is 500, the statement on Line (3) will have the result 500, 510, 510, 500.

For more examples on how to use sequence objects in your stored procedures, refer to Chapter 10, "Leveraging DB2 Application Development Features."

Platform Portability Considerations

Database triggers can be used to achieve the same results as generated columns. Triggers are discussed in greater detail in Chapter 9, "User-Defined Functions and Triggers." This section presents an alternative to the generated column example show in Figure 3.5.

Figure 3.20 shows the alternate table creation script.

```
CREATE TABLE payroll
( employee_id INT NOT NULL,
  base_salary DOUBLE,
  bonus DOUBLE,
  commission DOUBLE,
  total_pay DOUBLE
);
```

Figure 3.20   Table creation for an alternative to a generated column.

The column `total_pay` needs to be generated based on the values in the `base_salary`, `bonus`, and `commission` columns. Figure 3.21 shows the two triggers required to support this.

```
CREATE TRIGGER bi_genpayroll
    NO CASCADE BEFORE INSERT ON payroll
    REFERENCING NEW AS n
    FOR EACH ROW MODE DB2SQL
        SET n.total_pay=n.base_salary*(1+n.bonus) + n.commission;

CREATE TRIGGER bu_genpayroll
    NO CASCADE BEFORE UPDATE OF base_salary, bonus, commission ON payroll
    REFERENCING NEW AS n
    FOR EACH ROW MODE DB2SQL
        SET n.total_pay=n.base_salary*(1+n.bonus) + n.commission;
```

Figure 3.21   Triggers for generated column logic.

Summary

In this chapter, DB2 data types were discussed. You learned all DB2 built-in data types and their valid values, which enable you to choose the right data type for your SQL procedure development. LOB data, date and time data, and string data and their manipulations were further demonstrated with examples.

The DB2 user-defined distinct data type UDT was also introduced. You can use the UDT to have better control over the use of your data.

Generated columns (for LUW), identity columns, and sequence objects were also covered. The values of generated columns are calculated and generated for you automatically by DB2. DB2 sequence object and identity columns are used to implement auto-incremental sequential numbers. Even though these features are normally defined at database setup time, you still may have to work with them in SQL procedures.

Using Flow of Control Statements

In this chapter, you will learn how to

- Use the compound statement
- Use labels in both compound statements and loops
- Work with the two conditional statements (IF and CASE)
- Implement the four looping statements (FOR, WHILE, REPEAT, and LOOP)
- Implement the four transfer of control statements (GOTO, LEAVE, ITERATE, and RETURN)

Sequential execution is the most basic path that program execution can take. With this method, the program starts execution at the first line of the code, followed by the next, and continues until the final statement in the code has been executed. This approach works fine for very simple tasks but tends to lack usefulness because it can only handle one situation. Programs often need to be able to decide what to do in response to changing circumstances. By controlling a code's execution path, a specific piece of code can then be used to intelligently handle more than one situation.

Flow of control statements are used to control the sequence of statement execution. Statements such as IF and CASE are used to conditionally execute blocks of SQL PL statements, while other statements, such as WHILE and REPEAT, are typically used to execute a set of statements repetitively until a task is complete.

Although there are many flow of control statements to be discussed in this chapter, there are three main categories: conditional statements, loop statements, and transfer of control statements. Before jumping into a discussion on flow of control statements, it is important to first understand the use of compound statements.

Compound Statements

Of all the SQL control statements, the compound statement is the easiest to work with and understand. **Compound statements** are used to group a set of related lines of code. You can declare variables, cursors, and condition handlers, and use flow of control statements within a compound statement. Cursors and condition handlers are discussed in Chapter 5, "Understanding and Using Cursors and Result Sets" and Chapter 6, "Condition Handling," respectively.

BEGIN and END are keywords that define a compound statement. The BEGIN keyword defines the starting line of code for the compound statement, while the END keyword defines the final line of code. Compound statements are used to control variable scoping and for executing more than a single statement where a single statement is expected, such as within a condition handler (this topic is explored more fully in Chapter 6, "Condition Handling").

On LUW and iSeries, for nested compound statements, each compound statement has its own scope. Only variables and the like that have been declared within the same compound statement or within enclosing compound statements can be seen. That is, statements within one compound statement may not be able to refer to variables and values that are declared within another compound statement, even if both compound statements are part of the same SQL procedure body.

NOTE
Compound statements in DB2 for zSeries cannot be nested.

It is perfectly logical and, in most cases, completely valid to define as many compound statements as needed within an SQL procedure. These compound statements are typically used to introduce scoping and a logical separation of related statements.

There is a specific order for declaring variables, conditions, cursors, and handlers within a compound statement. Specifically, the order of declarations must proceed as follows:

```
BEGIN
variable declarations
condition declarations
cursor declarations
handler declarations
assignment, flow of control, SQL statements, and other compound statements
END
```

On iSeries and zSeries, variable and condition declarations can be mixed, but for portability of procedures, you should follow the order specified.

Don't worry if you are not familiar with some of these terms; they are discussed in greater detail later in the book. Also, notice that one or many compound statements can be nested within other compound statements. In such cases, the same order of declarations continues to apply at each level.

It is important to understand the type of variable scoping (or visibility) that occurs when a compound statement has been defined. Specifically:

- Outer compound statements cannot see variables declared within inner compound statements.

- Inner compound statements can see variables that have been declared in outer compound statements.

Scoping is illustrated in Figure 4.1.

```
CREATE PROCEDURE nested_compound ()
    LANGUAGE SQL
    SPECIFIC nested_compound              -- applies to LUW and iSeries
BEGIN                                     -- (1)
    DECLARE v_outer1 INT;
    DECLARE v_outer2 INT;

    BEGIN                                 -- (2)
        DECLARE v_inner1 INT;
        DECLARE v_inner2 INT;

        SET v_outer1 = 100;               -- (3)
        SET v_inner1 = 200;               -- (4)
    END;                                  -- (5)

    SET v_outer2 = 300;                   -- (6)
    SET v_inner2 = 400;                   -- (7)
END                                       -- (8)
```

Figure 4.1   Variable scoping example for LUW and iSeries.

In the previous figure, Lines (1) and (8) define the outer compound statement, while Lines (2) and (5) define the inner compound statement.

On LUW, all statements, except the statement shown in Line (7), will succeed. This statement fails because an outer compound statement cannot see a variable declared within an inner compound statement. You will receive an SQLSTATE 42703 error with the message 'V_INNER2' is not valid in the context where it is used.

On iSeries, the error is caught at procedure create time, and the CREATE PROCEDURE statement fails with SQLSTATE 42618 with the message Variable V_INNER2 not defined or not usable.

Scoping can be especially useful in the case of looping and exception handling, allowing the program flow to jump from one compound statement to another.

The next few sections describe two distinct types of compound statements, each of which serve a different purpose.

NOT ATOMIC Compound Statement

The previous example illustrated a NOT ATOMIC compound statement and is the default type used in SQL procedures. If an unhandled error (that is, no condition handler has been declared for the SQLSTATE raised) occurs within the compound statement, any work that is completed before the error will not be rolled back, but will not be committed either. The group of statements can only be rolled back if the unit of work is explicitly rolled back using ROLLBACK or ROLLBACK TO SAVEPOINT. You can also COMMIT successful statements if it makes sense to do so.

The syntax for a NOT ATOMIC compound statement is shown in Figure 4.2.

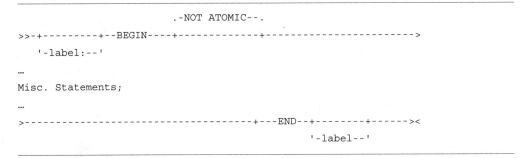

Figure 4.2   The *NOT ATOMIC* compound statement syntax diagram.

The optional label is used to define a name for the code block. The label can be used to qualify SQL variables declared within the compound statement. If the ending label is used, it must be the same as the beginning label. You will learn more about labels in section, "Using Labels," in this chapter.

TIP

The use of the NOT ATOMIC keywords is optional, but usually suggested because it reduces ambiguity of the code.

The SQL procedure illustrated in Figure 4.3 demonstrates the non-atomicity of NOT ATOMIC compound statements.

```
CREATE PROCEDURE not_atomic_proc ()
    LANGUAGE SQL
    SPECIFIC not_atomic_proc                     -- applies to LUW and iSeries
 -- WLM ENVIRONMENT <env>                        -- applies to zSeries
nap: BEGIN NOT ATOMIC
    -- Procedure logic
    INSERT INTO cl_sched (class_code, day)
       VALUES ('R11:TAA', 1);
    SIGNAL SQLSTATE '70000';                          -- (1)
    INSERT INTO cl_sched (class_code, day)
       VALUES ('R22:TBB', 2);
END nap
```

Figure 4.3   An example of a *NOT ATOMIC* compound statement.

Although the SIGNAL statement on Line (1) has not been introduced, it is sufficient to understand that the statement is used to explicitly raise an error. Additionally, because this error is unhandled, the procedure will exit right after the error. More information can be found in Chapter 6, "Condition Handling".

After calling this procedure, you will see that although an error has been raised halfway through execution, the first INSERT successfully inserted a row into the atomic_test table. You need to realize, however, that the procedure itself does not issue either COMMIT or ROLLBACK implicitly.

ATOMIC Compound Statement

ATOMIC compound statements are supported in DB2 for LUW and iSeries only. In DB2 zSeries, the NOT ATOMIC compound statement is the default and the only type used in SQL procedures.

The ATOMIC compound statement, as the name suggests, can be thought of as a singular whole. If any unhandled error conditions arise within it, all statements that have executed up to that point are considered to have failed as well and are therefore rolled back.

On LUW, ATOMIC compound statements cannot be nested inside other ATOMIC compound statements. iSeries does not have this restriction.

In addition, you cannot use SAVEPOINTS or issue explicit COMMITS or ROLLBACKS from within an ATOMIC compound statement.

NOTE

On LUW, COMMIT, ROLLBACK, SAVEPOINTS, and nested ATOMIC compound statements are not allowed within an ATOMIC compound statement.

On iSeries, COMMIT, ROLLBACK, and SAVEPOINTS are not allowed within an ATOMIC compound statement, although ROLLBACK TO SAVEPOINT may be specified.

The syntax to declare an ATOMIC compound statement is shown in Figure 4.4.

```
>>-+---------+--BEGIN ATOMIC------------------------------------->
   '-label:--'

...

Misc. Statements;

...

>--------------------------------------+---END--+--------+------><
                                                 '-label--'
```

Figure 4.4   *ATOMIC* compound statement syntax diagram.

A label is used in the same way as with a NOT ATOMIC compound statement.

The example in Figure 4.5 illustrates the behavior of an ATOMIC compound statement. It is quite similar to the NOT ATOMIC example shown in Figure 4.4, and only differs in name and in the fact that it uses an ATOMIC compound statement.

```
CREATE PROCEDURE atomic_proc ()
    LANGUAGE SQL
    SPECIFIC atomic_proc                          -- applies to LUW and iSeries
ap: BEGIN ATOMIC
   -- Procedure logic
   INSERT INTO cl_sched (class_code, day)
      VALUES ('R33:TCC', 3);
   SIGNAL SQLSTATE '70000';                       -- (1)
   INSERT INTO cl_sched (class_code, day)
      VALUES ('R44:TDD', 4);
END ap
```

Figure 4.5   *ATOMIC* compound statement example for LUW and iSeries.

When the error condition of SQLSTATE 70000 is raised on Line (1), the unhandled error causes procedure execution to stop. Unlike the NOT ATOMIC example in Figure 4.3, the first INSERT statement will be rolled back, resulting in a table with no inserted rows from this procedure.

Using Labels

Labels can be used to name any executable statement, which includes compound statements and loops. By using labels, you can have the flow of execution either jump out of a compound statement or loop, or jump to the beginning of a compound statement or loop.

Optionally, you may supply a corresponding label for the END of a compound statement. If an ending label is supplied, it must be the same as the label used at its beginning.

Each label must be unique within the body of an SQL procedure.

TIP

Labels also help increase the readability of code. Try to label based on purpose of the statement or code block.

From this point on, all examples in the book use labels.

A label can also be used to avoid ambiguity if a variable with the same name has been declared in more than one compound statement of the stored procedure. A label can be used to qualify the name of an SQL variable.

Figure 4.6 shows the use of a label to name a compound statement and also how to avoid ambiguous references to similarly named variables. It uses two variables of the same name (v_ID) defined in two differently labeled compound statements.

```
-- Example applies to LUW and iSeries only
--     because nested compound statements are used
CREATE PROCEDURE show_label (OUT p_WorkerID INT)
    LANGUAGE SQL
    SPECIFIC show_label                          -- applies to LUW and iSeries
sl1: BEGIN
    -- Declare variables
    DECLARE v_ID INT;                            -- (1)

    -- New compound statement
    sl2: BEGIN
        -- Declare variables
        DECLARE v_ID INT;                        -- (2)

        -- Procedure logic
        SET sl1.v_ID = 1;                        -- (3)
        SET sl2.v_ID = 2;                        -- (4)
        SET v_ID = 3;                            -- (5)
        SET p_WorkerID = sl2.v_ID;               -- (6)
    END sl2;
END sl1
```

Figure 4.6   A labeled compound statement example for LUW and iSeries.

You can see that, to avoid ambiguity, the two v_ID variables defined in Lines (1) and (2) are qualified with the label of the compound statement in which they were defined at Lines (3), (4), and (6). When qualification is not used, as in Line (5), the variable will be qualified with the label of the compound statement from which it is being referenced. So the value assignment at Line (5) will actually assign a value of 3 to sl2.v_ID, which means that p_WorkerID in Line (6) will also be assigned a value of 3.

> **TIP**
>
> It is good programming practice not to declare multiple variables of the same name, regardless of the fact that they can be referenced as label.variable_name.

Additionally, the label of the compound statement or loop can be used with the LEAVE statement to exit the labeled compound statement or loop. Labels can also be used with the ITERATE statement to jump back to the labeled beginning of a LOOP. These SQL PL statements are covered in greater detail later on in this chapter.

Conditional Statements

Conditional statements allow stored procedures to make decisions. They are used to define multiple branches of execution based on whether or not a condition was met.

A commonly used conditional statement is the IF statement, where a branch of execution can be taken if a specific condition is satisfied. IF statements can also define a branch of execution for when a condition is not met.

Another conditional statement in SQL PL is the CASE statement, which is similar to an IF statement, but the branching decision is more flexible.

The *IF* Statement

The most commonly used approach for conditional execution is the IF statement. There are essentially three different types of IF statements.

The simplest form of the IF statement does something if a condition is true, and nothing otherwise.

But what happens if you want to do one thing if a condition is true and something else if it is false? This is where the ELSE clause comes in handy. When used in conjunction with an IF statement, you can do something IF a condition is true and something ELSE if the condition is false.

Thirdly, ELSEIF is used to branch to multiple code paths based on mutually exclusive conditions in the same manner as an IF statement. You can make use of an ELSEIF statement to rewrite a ladder of nested IF ... ELSE statements for readability. Your procedure can specify an unlimited number of ELSEIF statements.

The syntax of an IF statement is depicted in Figure 4.7.

```
>>-IF--search-condition--THEN----------------------------------->


      .------------------------------.
      V                              |
>---------SQL-procedure-statement--;---+------------------------->


      .------------------------------------------------------------
      V
  |
>----+----------------------------------------------------------------+--+>
     |                                                                 |
    ·|                           .------------------------------.      |  |
     '-ELSEIF--search-condition--THEN-----SQL-procedure-statement--;---+--'


>-----+-----------------------------------------+--END IF-----><
      |            .------------------------------.   |
      |            V                              |   |
      '-ELSE-----SQL-procedure-statement--;---+--'
```

Figure 4.7   An *IF* syntax diagram.

The search-condition specifies the condition for which an SQL statement should be invoked. If the condition is false, processing continues to the next search-condition, until either a condition is true or processing reaches the ELSE clause.

SQL-procedure-statement specifies the statements to be invoked if the preceding search-condition is true. If no search-condition evaluates to true, then the SQL-procedure-statement following the ELSE keyword is invoked.

The snippet of an SQL procedure shown in Figure 4.8 demonstrates how the rating of an employee determines the raise in salary and bonus that he or she will receive.

```
CREATE PROCEDURE demo_if ( IN p_rating INT
                         , IN p_employee_number char(6) )
    LANGUAGE SQL
    SPECIFIC demo_if                             -- applies to LUW and iSeries
 -- WLM ENVIRONMENT <env>                        -- applies to zSeries
di: BEGIN
    -- Procedure logic
```

```
   IF p_rating = 1 THEN                            -- (1)
      UPDATE employee
         SET salary = salary * 1.10, bonus = 1000
       WHERE empno = p_employee_number;
   ELSEIF p_rating = 2 THEN                         -- (2)
      UPDATE employee
         SET salary = salary * 1.05, bonus = 500
       WHERE empno = p_employee_number;
   ELSE                                             -- (3)
      UPDATE employee
         SET salary = salary * 1.03, bonus = 0
       WHERE empno = p_employee_number;
   END IF;
END di
```

Figure 4.8   An *IF* statement example.

NOTE

SQL PL does not require the use of a compound statement to execute more than one statement in a branch of a conditional statement.

TIP

Indent statements within the body of IF, ELSEIF, and ELSE statements, in order to improve readability. If there are several levels of nesting, indent code at each level to reflect their level of nesting.

On Line (1), an employee with a 1 rating can expect a raise of 10 percent and a bonus of $1,000. On Line (2), an employee with a 2 rating earns a 5 percent raise with a $500 bonus. On Line (3), all other employees can expect a 3 percent pay hike with no bonus.

You are not simply limited to mathematical operators such as equals (=) and greater than (>). You can also use the SQL keywords NOT, AND, and OR to build conditions in your IF statements.

NOTE

An IF or ELSEIF condition must involve an operator. It is not sufficient to merely specify a variable (as can be done in some other programming languages), because SQL PL does not support the notion of a negative value meaning false and a positive value meaning true.

> **NOTE**
> Your SQL procedure can also make use of nested IF statements. There is no limit imposed by DB2 on the number of nested levels, though it is best not to get too carried away as it takes away from the readability of your code. Now if that's not enough, you can also nest IF statements inside of loops and loops inside of IF statements.

> **TIP**
> When nesting IFs, a common problem is inadvertently matching an ELSE with the wrong IF. Beware.

The *CASE* Statement

The CASE statement provides the ability to evaluate a list of options based on the value of a single variable. You would most likely choose to use a CASE statement if you have a large decision tree and all branches depend on the value of the same variable. Otherwise, you would be better off using a series of IF, ELSEIF, and ELSE statements. The syntax diagram for the CASE statement is shown in Figure 4.9.

```
>>-CASE----+-| searched-case-statement-when-clause |-+---------->
           '-| simple-case-statement-when-clause |---'

>----END CASE----------------------------------------------><

simple-case-statement-when-clause

|---expression------------------------------------------------>

        .----------------------------------------------------------.
        |                       .------------------------------.    |
        V                       V                              |    |
>--------WHEN--expression--THEN-----SQL-procedure-statement--;---+--+>

>-----+------------------------------------------+-------------|
      |              .-----------------------------.   |
      |     V                              |    |
      '-ELSE-----SQL-procedure-statement--;---+--'

searched-case-statement-when-clause
```

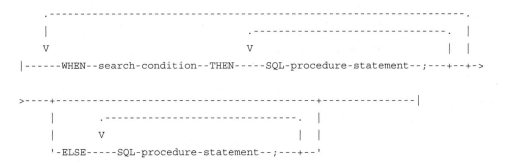

Figure 4.9   A *CASE* statement syntax diagram.

The CASE statement has two general forms: one that uses a simple-case-statement-when-clause, and another that uses a searched-case-statement-when-clause.

In the simple-case-statement-when-clause, the expression prior to the first WHEN keyword is tested for equality with the value of each expression that follows the WHEN keyword. If the expression results in the same value, the SQL-procedure-statement following the THEN keyword is executed. Otherwise, comparisons are continued between the first expression and the expression following the next WHEN clause. If the result does not match any of the search conditions and an ELSE clause is present, the statements in the ELSE clause are processed.

In a searched-case-statement-when-clause, the search-condition following each WHEN keyword is evaluated. If search-condition evaluates to true, the statements in the associated THEN clause are processed. If it evaluates to false, the next search-condition is evaluated. If no search-condition evaluates to true and an ELSE clause is present, the statements in the ELSE clause are processed.

Both forms of the CASE statement require END CASE to denote the end of the statement.

NOTE
It is possible to use a CASE statement without an ELSE clause. However, if none of the conditions specified in the WHEN clause are true at runtime, an error will result (SQLSTATE 20000).

The example that you have already seen in Figure 4.8 could be rewritten as shown in Figure 4.10 using the simple-case-statement-when-clause.

```
CREATE PROCEDURE demo_simple_case ( IN p_rating INT
                                    , IN p_employee_number char(6) )

    LANGUAGE SQL
    SPECIFIC demo_simple_case                    -- applies to LUW and iSeries
 -- WLM ENVIRONMENT <env>                        -- applies to zSeries
```

```
dsc: BEGIN
   -- Procedure logic
   CASE p_rating
      WHEN 1 THEN                                          -- (1)
Note: WHEN argument is a value
         UPDATE EMPLOYEE
            SET SALARY = SALARY *1.10, BONUS = 1000
          WHERE EMPNO = p_employee_number;
      WHEN 2 THEN                                          -- (2)
         UPDATE EMPLOYEE
            SET SALARY = SALARY *1.05, BONUS = 500
          WHERE EMPNO = p_employee_number;
      ELSE
         UPDATE EMPLOYEE                                   -- (3)
            SET SALARY = SALARY *1.03, BONUS = 0
          WHERE EMPNO = p_employee_number;
   END CASE;
END dsc
```

Figure 4.10 A simple *CASE* example.

Once again, on Line (1) an employee with a rating of 1 can expect a raise of 10 percent and a bonus of $1,000. On Line (2), an employee with a rating of 2 earns a 5 percent raise and a bonus of $500, while on Line (3), all other employees can simply expect a raise of 3 percent and no bonus.

Perhaps there have been some recent changes to the rating system, where there is now a wider range of ratings that employees can receive. Now, two employees with slightly different ratings can earn the same raise and bonus. Obviously, the code needs to be updated.

Figure 4.11 reflects the changes to the rating system and shows how to handle this using a searched-case-statement-when-clause. Note that the WHEN clause now contains a condition.

```
CREATE PROCEDURE demo_searched_case ( IN p_rating INT
                              , IN p_employee_number char(6) )

   LANGUAGE SQL
   SPECIFIC demo_searched_case               -- applies to LUW and iSeries
 -- WLM ENVIRONMENT <env>                    -- applies to zSeries
dsc: BEGIN
```

```
   -- Procedure logic
   CASE
      WHEN p_rating >= 1 AND p_rating < 4 THEN              -- (1)
         UPDATE EMPLOYEE
            SET SALARY = SALARY *1.10, BONUS = 1000
          WHERE EMPNO = p_employee_number;
      WHEN p_rating >= 4 AND p_rating < 8 THEN
         UPDATE EMPLOYEE
            SET SALARY = SALARY *1.05, BONUS = 500
          WHERE EMPNO = p_employee_number;
      ELSE
         UPDATE EMPLOYEE
            SET SALARY = SALARY *1.03, BONUS = 0
          WHERE EMPNO = p_employee_number;
   END CASE;
END dsc
```

Figure 4.11   A searched *CASE* example.

As you can see, the code now handles a range of ratings for each condition of the CASE statement. For example, on Line (1), an employee with a rating that falls between 1 and 3 inclusive will receive a raise of 10 percent and a bonus of $1,000.

Looping Statements

Loops allow you to execute a set of statements repeatedly until a certain condition is reached. The loop-terminating condition may be defined at the beginning, in the middle, or at the end of the loop using the WHILE LOOP, and REPEAT statements, respectively. Also, a FOR loop is available for iterating over a read-only result set and its terminating condition is when no more rows are left to read. Once the loop-terminating condition has been met, looping ceases and the flow of control continues on the line directly following the loop.

NOTE
Variables cannot be declared within loops.

TIP
For readability, it is best to indent the loop body relative to the loop statement.

The WHILE and REPEAT loops are typically used when you do not know how many times to iterate through the loop prior to entering it. You should use the WHILE loop when you may not want to execute the loop even once, and the REPEAT loop when you want to ensure that the statements within the loop are executed at least once. The FOR loop is used for situations where you need to iterate over a read-only result set, using result set values for some purpose such as defining the value of a variable. LOOP is generally used if you have multiple exit conditions for the loop, perhaps at various possible locations.

FOR Loop

The FOR loop statement is supported on DB2 for LUW and iSeries only. It is used to iterate over a read-only result set that is defined by its select-statement. Looping will cease when there are no rows left in the result set. You can easily use a WHILE loop to achieve the same result in DB2 for zSeries.

NOTE
Positioned updates and deletes are not supported in the FOR loop. However, searched updates and deletes are allowed.

The syntax is depicted in Figure 4.12.

```
>>-+--------+--FOR--for-loop-name--AS------------------------->
   '-label:-'


>--+-------------------------------------------------+-------------->
   |                                                  |
   '-cursor-name--CURSOR--+-----------+--FOR------'
                          '-WITH HOLD-'


                          .----------------------------.
                          V                            |
>--select-statement--DO----SQL-procedure-statement--;-+--------->

>--END FOR--+-------+-------------------------------------------><
            '-label-'
```

Figure 4.12   A *FOR* statement syntax diagram.

The for-loop-name specifies a label for the implicit compound statement generated to implement the FOR statement. It follows the rules for the label of a compound statement. The for-loop-name can used to qualify the column names in the result set as returned by the select-statement.

The *cursor-name* simply names the cursor that is used to select rows from the result set. If not specified, DB2 will automatically generate a unique cursor name internally.

The WITH HOLD option dictates the behavior of cursors across multiple units of work. It is described in detail in Chapter 5, "Understanding and Using Cursors and Result Sets."

The column names of the *select-statement* must be unique, and a FROM clause specifying a table (or multiple tables if doing some kind of JOIN or UNION) is required. The table(s) and column(s) referenced must exist prior to the loop being executed. This allows you to iterate over result sets that are formed from tables which exist prior to invoking the stored procedure, or tables that have been created by a previous SQL PL statement (such as declared user-temporary tables, which are discussed in Chapter 10, "Leveraging DB2 Application Development Features").

The FOR loop is essentially a CURSOR defined by the *select-statement*. This CURSOR cannot be referenced outside of the FOR loop, however, so OPEN, FETCH, and CLOSE statements will result in error.

In Figure 4.13, the FOR loop is used to iterate over all rows of the employee table (because no WHERE clause is being used). For each row, it generates a full name from the values out of three columns—last name, first name, and middle name initial.

```
-- Example applies to LUW and iSeries only
--     because of the usage of FOR loops.
CREATE PROCEDURE demo_for_loop (  )
    LANGUAGE SQL
    SPECIFIC demo_for_loop                         -- applies to LUW and iSeries
dfl: BEGIN
    -- Declare variables
    DECLARE v_fullname VARCHAR(50);

    -- Procedure logic
    FOR v_row AS SELECT firstnme, midinit, lastname            -- (1)
                 FROM employee
      DO
      SET v_fullname = v_row.lastname || ', ' ||
                      v_row.firstnme || ' '  || v_row.midinit;   -- (2)
      INSERT INTO tname VALUES (v_fullname);                    -- (3)
    END FOR;
END dfl
```

Figure 4.13   A *FOR* loop example.

You can see the defining `select-statement` on Line (1) and where the columns of the result set are being concatenated together to form the `v_fullname` on Line (2). Finally, this newly formed `v_fullname` is inserted into a table called `tname` on Line (3).

To test the procedure in Figure 4.13, you need to have a table created as

```
CREATE TABLE tname ( fullname VARCHAR(50) )
```

> **NOTE**
> Please note that the simple example in Figure 4.13 is only used to show an example on how to use the FOR loop to go through a result set from a SELECT statement. The logic of the example is so simple that you can easily accomplish the same with one SQL statement instead. However, you should realize that the FOR loop can accommodate more complex programming logic than a simple SQL statement can, and that is when you should consider using the FOR loop in your own applications.

WHILE Loop

The defining feature of a WHILE loop is that its looping condition is evaluated prior to initial loop execution and all following loop iterations. The WHILE loop will continue to execute until the looping condition evaluates to false.

> **NOTE**
> Be sure not to define a condition that always evaluates to true, or you will become caught in an infinite loop.

When defining the looping condition, be sure to specify a full conditional statement (that includes operators). Otherwise, your SQL procedure will not build. For example,

```
WHILE (variable) DO
        statement1;
        statement2;
END WHILE;
```

is not enough. You need to use an operator, as in

```
WHILE (variable = 1) DO
        statement1;
        statement2;
END WHILE;
```

The syntax for the WHILE loop is illustrated in Figure 4.14.

```
>>-+---------+--WHILE--search-condition--DO-------------------->
   '-:label--'


      .-----------------------------.
      V                             |
>--------SQL-procedure-statement--;---+--END WHILE-------------->

>-----+--------+----------------------------------------------><
      '-label--'
```

Figure 4.14   A *WHILE* loop syntax diagram.

The *search-condition* specifies a condition that is evaluated before each execution of the loop. If the condition is true, the *SQL-procedure-statements* in the loop are processed.

Figure 4.15 illustrates how to use a WHILE loop to sum all integer values between n and m (which are assumed to be positive and provided by input parameters to the procedure).

```
CREATE PROCEDURE sum_mn ( IN p_start INT
                        , IN p_end INT
                        , OUT p_sum INT )
   LANGUAGE SQL
   SPECIFIC sum_mn                            -- applies to LUW and iSeries
 -- WLM ENVIRONMENT <env>                     -- applies to zSeries
smn: BEGIN
   DECLARE v_temp INTEGER DEFAULT 0;
   DECLARE v_current INTEGER;

   SET v_current = p_start;

   WHILE (v_current <= p_end) DO
      SET v_temp = v_temp + v_current;        -- (1)
      SET v_current = v_current + 1;
   END WHILE;

   SET p_sum = v_temp;
END smn
```

Figure 4.15   A simple WHILE loop example.

This example is fairly simple and is intended to show you how the WHILE loop works using as little code as possible. More commonly, however, a WHILE loop is used to repeatedly perform SQL procedure statements, such as FETCH (for retrieving row values from a cursor). For examples of using WHILE loops with cursor operations such as OPEN, FETCH and CLOSE, see Chapter 5, "Understanding and Using Cursors and Result Sets."

REPEAT Loop

In the WHILE loop, you saw that the looping condition is evaluated at the very beginning of the loop. If the looping condition evaluates to false at this first examination, then the loop body will not execute at all.

In some cases, however, it may be necessary that the loop be executed at least once. This is where the REPEAT loop is useful. A REPEAT loop ensures that at least one iteration of the loop is completed. This is the case because the looping condition is not evaluated until the final line of code in the loop.

The syntax for the REPEAT loop is shown in Figure 4.16.

```
                          .------------------------------.
                          V                              |
>>-+----------+--REPEAT-------SQL-procedure-statement--;---+----->
   '-label:--'


>----UNTIL--search-condition---END REPEAT----+--------+-------->< 
                                             '-label--'
```

Figure 4.16   A *REPEAT* loop syntax diagram.

In Figure 4.17, the procedure in Figure 4.15 is re-implemented using REPEAT.

```
CREATE PROCEDURE sum_mn2 ( IN p_start INT
                         , IN p_end INT
                         , OUT p_sum INT )
    LANGUAGE SQL
    SPECIFIC sum_mn2                            -- applies to LUW and iSeries
 -- WLM ENVIRONMENT <env>                       -- applies to zSeries
smn2: BEGIN
    DECLARE v_temp INTEGER DEFAULT 0;
    DECLARE v_current INTEGER;

    SET v_current = p_start;
```

```
REPEAT
   SET v_temp = v_temp + v_current;                          -- (1)
   SET v_current = v_current + 1;
UNTIL (v_current > p_end)
END REPEAT;

   SET p_sum = v_temp;
END smn2
```

Figure 4.17   A *REPEAT* loop example.

If you execute both the WHILE loop example in Figure 4.15 and the REPEAT loop example in Figure 4.17 with p_start smaller than p_end, you will see the difference between the two. The WHILE loop example in Figure 4.15 generates p_sum with 0. The statement on Line (1) in Figure 4.15 is never executed because the condition in the WHILE clause is not met. The REPEAT loop example generates p_sum with the value of p_start instead because the statement on Line (1) in Figure 4.17 is always executed once.

LOOP

The LOOP statement is somewhat different from the other types of loops that you have seen thus far. The LOOP does not have a terminating condition clause that is part of its declaration statement. It will continue to loop until some other piece of code inside it explicitly forces the flow of control to jump to some point outside of the loop.

LOOP will commonly have some logic that eventually branches to a LEAVE statement. You can also use a GOTO statement instead of a LEAVE, but the use of GOTO is discouraged.

NOTE
Ensure that some action within the loop eventually invokes a LEAVE or GOTO statement. Otherwise, your code can become caught in an infinite loop.

The LOOP syntax is illustrated in Figure 4.18.

```
                        .-------------------------------.
                        V                               |
>>-+---------+--LOOP-------SQL-procedure-statement--;---+------->
   '-label:--'


>----END LOOP----+--------+------------------------------------><
                 '-label--'
```

Figure 4.18   A *LOOP* syntax diagram.

> **NOTE**
> There is no terminating condition defined within the LOOP syntax itself.

An example of using LOOP is deferred until the discussion on LEAVE in the next section.

Transfer of Control Statements

Transfer of control statements are used to tell the SQL procedure where to continue execution. This unconditional branching can be used to cause the flow of control to jump from one point to another point, which can either precede or follow the transfer of control statement.

SQL PL supports four such statements: GOTO, LEAVE, ITERATE, and RETURN. Each will be discussed in detail in the following sections.

ROLLBACK and COMMIT statements can also be used within the procedure body. These two are introduced here for completeness, even though they are more transaction control statements than flow of control statements.

GOTO

GOTO is a straightforward and basic flow of control statement that causes an unconditional change in the flow of control. It is used to branch to a specific user-defined location using labels defined in the procedure.

Usage of the GOTO statement is generally considered to be poor programming practice and is not recommended. Extensive use of GOTO tends to lead to unreadable code especially when procedures grow long. Besides, GOTO is not necessary because there are better statements available to control the execution path. There are no specific situations that require the use of GOTO; instead, it is more often used for convenience (or lack of effort).

The GOTO syntax is shown in Figure 4.19.

```
>>-GOTO--label-------------------------------------------------><
```

Figure 4.19 The *GOTO* syntax diagram.

You should be aware of a few additional scope considerations:

- If the GOTO statement is defined in a FOR statement, the label must be defined inside the same FOR statement, unless it is in a nested FOR statement or nested compound statement.
- If the GOTO statement is defined in a compound statement, *label* must be defined inside the same compound statement, unless it is in a nested FOR statement or nested compound statement.
- If the GOTO statement is defined in a handler, *label* must be defined in the same handler, following the other scope rules.

- If the GOTO statement is defined outside of a handler, *label* must not be defined within a handler.

- If *label* is not defined within a scope that the GOTO statement can reach, an error is returned (SQLSTATE 42736).

Good programming practice should limit the use of the GOTO statement in your SQL procedure. The use of GOTO decreases the readability of your code since it causes execution to jump to a new line contained anywhere within the procedure body. This spaghetti code can be difficult to understand, debug, and maintain.

TIP

If you must use GOTO, then try to use it to skip to the end of the SQL procedure or loop.

The GOTO statement is local to the SQL procedure which declares it. The label that a GOTO statement could jump to must be defined within the same SQL procedure as the GOTO statement, and don't forget that scoping rules still apply.

In Figure 4.20, an SQL procedure is used to increase the salary of those employees who have been with the company for more than one year. The employee's serial number and rating are passed into the stored procedure, which then returns an output parameter of the newly calculated salary. The employee's salary is increased based on his or her rating.

This SQL procedure makes use of the GOTO statement on Line (1) to avoid increasing the salary of those employees who have not yet been with the company for more than a year.

```
CREATE PROCEDURE adjust_salary ( IN  p_empno CHAR(6)
                               , IN  p_rating INTEGER
                               , OUT p_adjusted_salary DECIMAL (8,2) )
    LANGUAGE SQL
    SPECIFIC adjust_salary                    -- applies to LUW and iSeries
 -- WLM ENVIRONMENT <env>                     -- applies to zSeries
ads: BEGIN
   -- Declare variables
   DECLARE v_new_salary DECIMAL (9,2);
   DECLARE v_service DATE;
   -- Procedure logic
   SELECT salary, hiredate
     INTO v_new_salary, v_service
     FROM employee
    WHERE empno = p_empno;
```

```
    IF v_service > (CURRENT DATE - 1 year) THEN
        GOTO bye;                                                    -- (1)
    END IF;


    IF p_rating = 1 THEN
        SET v_new_salary = v_new_salary + (v_new_salary * .10);      -- (2)
    ELSEIF p_rating = 2 THEN
        SET v_new_salary = v_new_salary + (v_new_salary * .05);      -- (3)
    END IF;


    UPDATE employee                                                  -- (4)
        SET salary = v_new_salary
      WHERE empno = p_empno;


  bye:                                                               -- (5)
    SET p_adjusted_salary = v_new_salary;
END ads
```

Figure 4.20   Another *GOTO* example.

To try the example on your own, use any valid employee number from the EMPNO column in the EMPLOYEE table as p_empno. Use either 1 or 2 for p_rating.

```
CALL adjust_salary('000010', 2, ?)
```

If the employee has worked for the company for more than a year, he or she is given a 5 or 10 percent raise if he or she received a rating of 2 or 1, respectively, on Lines (1) and (3). The EMPLOYEE table is updated to reflect the new salary on Line (4).

If it is discovered that the employee has not yet worked with the company for at least one year, the GOTO exit statement causes execution to jump to the second-last line of code on Line (5) in the procedure. The p_adjusted_salary is simply set to the original salary, and no changes are made to the EMPLOYEE table.

LEAVE

The LEAVE statement is used to transfer the flow of control out of a loop or compound statement. The syntax for the command, shown in Figure 4.21, is trivial.

```
>>-LEAVE--label-------------------------------------------------><
```

Figure 4.21   The *LEAVE* syntax diagram.

Figure 4.22 illustrates how to use LOOP and LEAVE.

```
CREATE PROCEDURE verify_ids ( IN p_id_list VARCHAR(100)
                            , OUT p_status INT )
   LANGUAGE SQL
   SPECIFIC verify_ids                          -- applies to LUW and iSeries
 -- WLM ENVIRONMENT <env>                       -- applies to zSeries
vid: BEGIN
   DECLARE v_current_id VARCHAR(10);
   DECLARE v_position INT;
   DECLARE v_remaining_ids VARCHAR(100);
   DECLARE v_tmp INT;
   DECLARE SQLCODE INT DEFAULT 0;

   SET v_remaining_ids = p_id_list;
   SET p_status = 0;

   L1: LOOP
       SET v_position = LOCATE (':',v_remaining_ids);               --(1)

       -- take off the first id from the list
       SET v_current_id = SUBSTR (v_remaining_ids, 1, v_position);    --(2)

       IF LENGTH(v_remaining_ids) - v_position > 0 THEN              --(3)
             SET v_remaining_ids = SUBSTR (v_remaining_ids, v_position+1);
       ELSE
          SET v_remaining_ids = '';
       END IF;

       -- take off the colon in last position of the current token
       SET v_current_id = SUBSTR (v_current_id, 1, v_position-1);     --(4)

          -- determine if employee exists
       SELECT 1 INTO v_tmp FROM employee where empno = v_current_id;   --(5)
```

```
        IF (SQLCODE <> 0) THEN
            -- employee id does not exist
                SET p_status=-1;
                  LEAVE L1;                                      --(6)
        END IF;



        IF length(v_remaining_ids) = 0 THEN
                LEAVE L1;
        END IF;


    END LOOP;
END vid
```

Figure 4.22   An example of *LOOP* and *LEAVE*.

The SQL procedure in Figure 4.22 takes a colon-separated list of employee IDs as input. For example, this input might look like:

```
000310:000320:000330:
```

The list is then parsed—in Lines (1) through (4)—to determine if all employee IDs are valid by verifying if the employee exists on Line (5). If any IDs in the list are not valid, the LOOP immediately exits using LEAVE on Line (6). If all employee IDs in the list are valid, the result of p_status is 0. Otherwise, the result of p_status is -1 to indicate an error.

ITERATE

The ITERATE statement is used to cause the flow of control to return to the beginning of a labeled LOOP. The syntax for ITERATE, depicted in Figure 4.23, is simple.

```
>>-ITERATE--label---------------------------------------------><
```

Figure 4.23   An *ITERATE* syntax diagram.

The example in Figure 4.24 is similar to the example in Figure 4.22, except that instead of exiting on the first invalid employee ID, the procedure returns the number of valid IDs found. ITERATE at Line (1) is used to return to the top of the LOOP whenever an invalid ID is encountered so that it is not counted.

```
CREATE PROCEDURE verify_ids2 ( IN p_id_list VARCHAR(100)
                             , OUT p_status INT )
    LANGUAGE SQL
    SPECIFIC verify_ids2                        -- applies to LUW and iSeries
 -- WLM ENVIRONMENT <env>                       -- applies to zSeries
vid: BEGIN
    DECLARE v_current_id VARCHAR(10);
    DECLARE v_position INT;
    DECLARE v_remaining_ids VARCHAR(100);
    DECLARE v_tmp INT;
    DECLARE SQLCODE INT DEFAULT 0;

    SET v_remaining_ids = p_id_list;
    SET p_status = 0;

    L1: LOOP
        SET v_position = LOCATE (':',v_remaining_ids);

        -- take off the first id from the list
        SET v_current_id = SUBSTR (v_remaining_ids, 1, v_position);

        IF LENGTH(v_remaining_ids) - v_position > 0 THEN
            SET v_remaining_ids = SUBSTR (v_remaining_ids, v_position+1);
        ELSE
            SET v_remaining_ids = '';
        END IF;

        -- take off the colon in last position of the current token
        SET v_current_id = SUBSTR (v_current_id, 1, v_position-1);

        -- determine if employee exists
        SELECT 1 INTO v_tmp FROM employee where empno = v_current_id;

        IF (SQLCODE <> 0) THEN
            -- employee id does not exist
            IF length(v_remaining_ids) > 0 THEN
                ITERATE L1;                         --(1)
            ELSE
                LEAVE L1;
```

```
            END IF;
        END IF;

        SET p_status = p_status + 1;
            IF length(v_remaining_ids) = 0 THEN
                LEAVE L1;
            END IF;
    END LOOP;
END vid
```

Figure 4.24 An *ITERATE* example.

RETURN

RETURN is used to unconditionally and immediately terminate an SQL procedure by returning the flow of control to the caller of the stored procedure.

It is mandatory that when RETURN statement is issued, it returns an integer value. If the return value is not provided, the default is 0. The value returned is typically used to indicate success or failure of the stored procedure's execution. This value can be a literal, variable, or an expression as long as it is an integer or evaluates to an integer.

> **NOTE**
> In order for an OUT parameter to return a value, it must be set prior to the RETURN statement being invoked.

You can make use of more than one RETURN statement in a stored procedure. RETURN can be used anywhere after the declaration blocks within the SQL procedure body.

The partial syntax for RETURN in the SQL procedure is illustrated in Figure 4.25.

```
>>-RETURN--+------------+--------------------------------------->< 
           '-expression-'
```

Figure 4.25 The *RETURN* syntax diagram.

The following example uses the employee serial number (p_empno) to check if an employee's last name, as stored in the database, matches the last name passed in as an input parameter (p_emplastname).

```
CREATE PROCEDURE return_test ( IN p_empno CHAR(6)
                              , IN p_emplastname VARCHAR(15) )

    LANGUAGE SQL
```

```
     SPECIFIC return_test                          -- applies to LUW and iSeries
  -- WLM ENVIRONMENT <env>                          -- applies to zSeries
rt: BEGIN
   -- Declare variables
   DECLARE v_lastname VARCHAR(15);
   -- Procedure logic
   SELECT lastname
     INTO v_lastname
     FROM EMPLOYEE
WHERE empno = p_empno;
   IF v_lastname = p_emplastname THEN             -- (1)
      RETURN 1;                                    -- (2)
   ELSE                                            -- (3)
      RETURN -1;                                   -- (4)
   END IF;
END rt
```

Figure 4.26   A *RETURN* example.

This procedure receives two input parameters: p_emplastname and p_empno. If p_emplastname matches the lastname in the employee table identified by the employee number (p_empno) at Line (1), then the procedure exits with a return value of 1 at Line (2) implying success. If there is no match as shown in Line (3), then the SQL procedure returns with a failure indicated by a -1 return code on Line (4).

TIP

Only use the RETURN statement to return integers as status indicators.

COMMIT

The COMMIT statement is used to complete the current unit of work, and to permanently record any of the changes made inside it to the database.

The syntax is trivial (see Figure 4.27).

```
              .-WORK--.
>>-COMMIT----+-------+----------------------------------------------><
```

Figure 4.27   *COMMIT* statement syntax.

A HOLD option is also provided for the COMMIT clause in DB2 for iSeries. If the COMMIT is invoked with the HOLD option, any open cursors are not closed, and any resources (except locks on table rows) acquired during the unit of work are held. The similar behavior in DB2 for LUW and zSeries is defined at the cursor declaration time. Refer to the FOR loop discussion in this chapter and Chapter 5, "Understanding and Using Cursors and Result Sets," for more details.

> **NOTE**
> On zSeries, the CREATE PROCEDURE statement provides the COMMIT ON RETURN clause to automatically issue a COMMIT after the SQL procedure returns to the caller.

ROLLBACK

The ROLLBACK statement is used to explicitly back out of any database changes that were made within the current unit of work (UOW). A **unit of work** is a sequence of SQL statements that are atomic for the purposes of recovery. Once the changes have been rolled back, a new unit of work is initiated.

DB2 also supports transaction save points and ROLLBACK TO SAVEPOINT. A ROLLBACK will cause the flow of control in your application to return to the previous save point declared within your unit of work.

> **NOTE**
> You cannot issue a ROLLBACK or COMMIT from within an ATOMIC compound statement, although on iSeries you can issue a ROLLBACK TO SAVEPOINT in an ATOMIC compound statement.

The syntax for the ROLLBACK statement is shown in Figure 4.28.

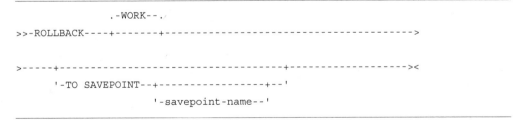

```
                   .-WORK--.
>>-ROLLBACK----+-------+---------------------------------------->

>-----+---------------------------------------+------------------><
      '-TO SAVEPOINT--+-----------------+--'
                      '-savepoint-name--'
```

Figure 4.28   *ROLLBACK statement syntax.*

ROLLBACK TO SAVEPOINT indicates that a partial rollback is to be performed. If no save point is active, an SQL error is returned (SQLSTATE 3B001).

The save point name indicates which save point to rollback to. After a successful ROLLBACK TO SAVEPOINT, the save point defined by save point name continues to exist. If the save point name does not exist, an error is returned (SQLSTATE 3B001). Data and schema changes made since the save point was set are undone.

To rollback the entire transaction, use the ROLLBACK WORK statement. All save points within the transaction are also released. For more information about save points, refer to Chapter 10, "Leveraging DB2 Application Development Features."

In addition to the WORK and TO SAVEPOINT options of the ROLLBACK statement, DB2 UDB for iSeries also supports the HOLD option. When the ROLLBACK statement is issued with this option, any open cursors are not closed, and any resources (except locks on table rows) acquired during the unit of work are held.

Summary

This chapter discussed all SQL PL elements related to flow of control. This included discussions and examples of the following:

- Compound statements and scope, which can be defined as ATOMIC or NOT ATOMIC to suit your needs
- Labels and the various ways in which they are used
- IF and CASE conditional statements (and their various forms) for more intelligent SQL procedures
- Looping statements FOR, WHILE, REPEAT, and LOOP to perform repetitive sets of SQL statements
- GOTO, LEAVE, ITERATE, and RETURN transfer of control statements
- COMMIT and ROLLBACK transaction control statements

With these flow of control statements at your disposal, you can write powerful and robust SQL stored procedures.

Understanding and Using Cursors and Result Sets

In this chapter, you will learn

- What a cursor is
- How to use cursors inside SQL procedures
- How to perform positioned deletes and positioned updates
- How cursors affect locking
- About cursor behavior on commit and rollback
- How to use nested save points
- How cursors are used to return result sets to applications.

In previous chapters, you have seen how SQL procedures can manipulate table data by directly executing INSERT, UPDATE, and DELETE statements. Using SQL in this manner, however, means that operations must be applied to the entire set of data defined by the WHERE clause of the statement. In SQL procedures, it is possible to define a set of data rows (which will be called a **result set** from here on) and then perform complex logic on a row-by-row basis. By using the same mechanics, an SQL procedure can also define a result set and return it directly to another program for further processing.

To take advantage of these features, you need to know about cursors. A **cursor** can be viewed as a pointer to one row in a set of rows. The cursor can reference only one row at any given time, but can move to other rows of the result set as needed. For example, consider a cursor that is defined with this SELECT statement:

```
SELECT * FROM employees WHERE sex='M'
```

The result set will contain a list of male employees. The cursor will be positioned just before the first row of the result set initially. To position the cursor onto the first row, you execute a FETCH operation. Once the cursor is positioned onto a row, the data can be processed. To retrieve the next row, FETCH can be executed again. The FETCH operation can be repeated until all rows of the result set have been exhausted.

This chapter covers only returning result sets from SQL procedures. Chapter 8, "Nested SQL Procedures," tells you how to receive result sets from another SQL procedure. Examples of receiving result sets in Java or C client programs will be presented in Appendix H, "Sample Application Code."

Using Cursors in SQL Procedures

In order to use cursors inside SQL procedures, you need to do the following:

- Declare the cursor
- Open the cursor to establish the result set
- Fetch the data into local variables as needed from the cursor, one row at a time
- Close the cursor when finished

The simplified syntax of the DECLARE CURSOR and FETCH statements is shown in Figures 5.1 and 5.2, respectively. The complete syntax of the DECLARE CURSOR statement is covered in Chapter 8, "Nested SQL Procedures" where returning nested results are discussed. The syntax of the OPEN cursor and CLOSE cursor statements is very straightforward, and no syntax diagram is presented here. They are illustrated in the following examples.

```
>>-DECLARE--cursor-name--CURSOR--------------------------------->
>----FOR----select-statement---------------------------------><
```

Figure 5.1   A simplified *DECLARE CURSOR* syntax.

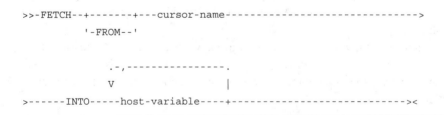

```
>>-FETCH--+-------+---cursor-name------------------------------->
          '-FROM--'

                  .-,----------------.
                  V                  |
>------INTO-----host-variable----+---------------------------><
```

Figure 5.2   A simplified *FETCH* syntax.

The FETCH statement positions the cursor at the next row of the result set and assigns values of the current cursor position to the specified procedure variables.

Figure 5.3 demonstrates the use of a cursor inside a SQL procedure to access data one row at a time. The procedure calculates the cost of giving raises to the employees of a company based on the following rules:

- The company has decided that everyone in the company except for the president will receive at least the minimum raise, which is defined by the input parameter `p_min`.

- Any employee with a bonus greater than $600 will receive an extra 4 percent raise.

- Employees with higher commissions will receive a smaller raise. Employees with commissions of less than $2,000 will receive an extra 3 percent raise, while those with commissions between $2,000 and $3,000 will receive an extra 2 percent raise.

- Anyone with commissions greater than $3,000 will receive an extra 1 percent raise.

- Finally, no matter how much of a raise an employee might receive, the total amount cannot be higher than a maximum limit, which is provided by the other input parameter `p_max`.

Given the complexity of these rules, a cursor can be used here to simplify the programming logic.

```
CREATE PROCEDURE total_raise ( IN   p_min    DEC(4,2)
                             , IN   p_max    DEC(4,2)
                             , OUT  p_total DEC(9,2) )
    LANGUAGE SQL
    SPECIFIC total_raise                    -- applies to LUW and iSeries
 -- WLM ENVIRONMENT <env>                   -- applies to zSeries
tr: BEGIN
    -- Declare variables
    DECLARE v_salary DEC(9,2);
    DECLARE v_bonus  DEC(9,2);
    DECLARE v_comm   DEC(9,2);
    DECLARE v_raise  DEC(4,2);
    DECLARE v_job    VARCHAR(15) DEFAULT 'PRES';
    -- Declare returncode
    DECLARE SQLSTATE CHAR(5);

    -- Procedure logic
    DECLARE c_emp CURSOR FOR
        SELECT salary, bonus, comm
        FROM   employee
        WHERE  job != v_job;                        -- (1)
```

```
    OPEN c_emp;                                           -- (2)

    SET p_total = 0;

    FETCH FROM c_emp INTO v_salary, v_bonus, v_comm;      -- (3)

    WHILE ( SQLSTATE = '00000' ) DO
        SET v_raise = p_min;

        IF ( v_bonus >= 600 ) THEN
            SET v_raise = v_raise + 0.04;
        END IF;

        IF ( v_comm < 2000 ) THEN
            SET v_raise = v_raise + 0.03;
        ELSEIF ( v_comm < 3000 ) THEN
            SET v_raise = v_raise + 0.02;
        ELSE
            SET v_raise = v_raise + 0.01;
        END IF;

        IF ( v_raise > p_max ) THEN
            SET v_raise = p_max;
        END IF;

        SET p_total = p_total + v_salary * v_raise;
        FETCH FROM c_emp INTO v_salary, v_bonus, v_comm;   -- (4)
    END WHILE;

    CLOSE c_emp;                                          -- (5)
END tr
```

Figure 5.3   An example of simple cursor usage.

This procedure shown in Figure 5.3 works on the employee table. The SELECT statement in Line (1) within the DECLARE CURSOR statement defines the columns and rows that make up of the result set. Once the cursor is declared, it needs to be opened using the OPEN cursor statement shown in Line (2) so that you can then later fetch data from the resulting table. The FETCH cursor statement shown in Line (3) retrieves data from a row and assigns the values into local variables. The second FETCH cursor statement on Line (4) is used to retrieve more data as the processing repeats in the WHILE loop. As a good programming practice, the CLOSE cursor statement on Line (5) should be issued once the cursor is no longer needed.

Normally the FETCH cursor statements are used in conjunction with loops to step through all rows of the result set. The SQLSTATE can be used to check if the last line is reached. The SQLCODE value is also commonly used to determine when the end of the result set has been reached. For detailed discussions on SQLCODE, SQLSTATE, and error handling, refer to Chapter 6, "Condition Handling."

TIP

If the SELECT statement of the cursor declaration contains multiple occurrences of CURRENT DATE, CURRENT TIME, and CURRENT TIMESTAMP, all FETCH statements will return the same date, time, and timestamp value. This is because the value for these special registers is determined at the time of OPEN CURSOR.

In SQL procedures, the SET parameter statement shown in the following example will fail if more than one row is returned. DB2 will not simply assign the first value to the local variable.

```
SET v_c1 = (SELECT c1 FROM t1);
```

A **scalar fullselect** is a fullselect, enclosed in parentheses, that returns a single row consisting of a single column. A scalar fullselect can be used wherever expressions are allowed.

Creating a cursor solely for the purpose of fetching the first value to a local variable (as shown in Figure 5.4) is highly inefficient and is not recommended because opening a cursor is an expensive operation for a database.

```
DECLARE c_tmp CURSOR FOR
       SELECT c1
       FROM t1;

OPEN c_emp;
FETCH FROM c_emp INTO v_c1;
CLOSE c_emp;
```

Figure 5.4   Improper use of cursor to fetch only one row.

The proper way of handling this situation is to use the FETCH FIRST 1 ROW ONLY clause.

```
SELECT c1 INTO v_c1 FROM t1 FETCH FIRST 1 ROW ONLY;
```

This statement will set the local variable to the value in the first row should more than one row be returned. It is important to realize, however, that if multiple rows are returned, there is no guarantee that the same row being returned with FETCH FIRST 1 ROW ONLY will always be the same row unless an ORDER BY clause is used.

DB2 for zSeries limits the use of the FETCH FIRST 1 ROW ONLY clause; it is not allowed in a scalar fullselect. The statement

```
SET v_c1 = (SELECT c1 FROM t1 FETCH FIRST 1 ROW ONLY);
```

can be rewritten without a scalar fullselect to work on all platforms:

```
SELECT c1 INTO v_c1 FROM t1 FETCH FIRST 1 ROW ONLY;
```

Positioned Delete

The previous example demonstrated a read-only cursor. Cursors can also be used to delete data at the current cursor position as long as it is deletable. Here are some of the characteristics of a deletable cursor:

- Each FROM clause of the outer fullselect references only one table.
- The outer fullselect does not include a VALUES, GROUP BY, or HAVING clause and does not include column functions.
- The select list of the outer fullselect does not include DISTINCT.
- The select-statement does not include an ORDER BY or FOR READ ONLY clause.
- The cursor is statically defined, or the FOR UPDATE clause is specified.

The definition for what constitutes a deletable cursor is quite similar for each of the platforms, but there are some minor differences. Refer to the individual SQL references for the complete requirements.

Using a cursor to delete the row on which it is currently positioned is known as a **positioned delete**. The syntax diagram for positioned delete is shown in Figure 5.5.

```
>>-DELETE FROM-|----table-name---------|---------------------->
               +----view-name----------+


>----WHERE CURRENT OF--cursor-name------------------------------><
```

Figure 5.5   A simplified positioned *DELETE* syntax.

The example in Figure 5.6 demonstrates how to use a cursor for positioned delete.

```
CREATE PROCEDURE cleanup_act ( IN   p_date    DATE
                             , OUT p_deleted INT )
    LANGUAGE SQL
    SPECIFIC cleanup_act                    -- applies to LUW and iSeries
 -- WLM ENVIRONMENT <env>                   -- applies to zSeries
ca: BEGIN
    -- Declare variable
    DECLARE v_date  DATE;
    -- Declare returncode
    DECLARE SQLSTATE CHAR(5);

    -- Procedure logic

    DECLARE c_emp CURSOR FOR                 -- (1)
        SELECT emendate
        FROM   emp_act
    FOR UPDATE;

    OPEN c_emp;

    FETCH FROM c_emp INTO v_date;
    SET p_deleted = 0;

    WHILE ( SQLSTATE = '00000' ) DO

        IF ( v_date < p_date ) THEN
            DELETE FROM emp_act
            WHERE CURRENT OF c_emp;          -- (2)

            SET p_deleted = p_deleted + 1;
        END IF;

        FETCH FROM c_emp INTO v_date;
    END WHILE;

    CLOSE c_emp;
END ca
```

Figure 5.6   An example of a positioned delete.

This procedure removes old records from the `emp_act` table. It takes a cut-off date as the input parameter. All records prior to this date are deleted from the `emp_act`, and the total number of deleted records is returned as an output parameter once the entire result set has been processed. This is a simple example to show how to use positioned delete. In the real world, a **searched delete** (that is, a direct `DELETE` statement without using a cursor) would perform much better for a simple operation like this. However, with positioned delete, you are able to implement much more complicated logic on the data retrieved before you decide if you want to delete the current row.

The `DECLARE CURSOR` statement in Line (1) is similar to the read-only cursor except that it has the `FOR UPDATE` clause. This clause is not required if you intend to perform positioned deletes, but it is good practice to use it so that DB2 can place more granular locks on the affected rows.

The `WHERE CURRENT OF` clause in the `DELETE` statement on Line (2) indicates that the row to be deleted is the row where the cursor is currently positioned. When the positioned delete is executed, the cursor must be positioned on a row. That is, if you want to delete the first row in a result set, you must execute `FETCH` to properly position the cursor.

Positioned Update

Positioned update works similar to a positioned delete, except that the cursor has to meet requirements for being updatable. A cursor is **updatable** if all of the following are true:

- The cursor is deletable (as previously defined).
- A column being updated resolves to a column of the base table.
- Any columns being updated must be specified explicitly or implicitly in the `FOR UPDATE` clause.

Similar to deletable cursors, the definition for updatable cursors is not identical across all platforms. Refer to the individual SQL references for the complete requirements.

The syntax diagram for positioned update is shown in Figure 5.7.

```
>>-UPDATE----+-table-name-----------------+------------------->
             +-view-name------------------+
>-----SET--| assignment-clause |------------------------------>
>-----WHERE CURRENT OF--cursor-name-------------------------><
```

Figure 5.7   A simplified positioned UPDATE syntax.

The example in Figure 5.8 is similar to the `total_raise` procedure in Figure 5.3. Instead of calculating the total cost of issuing a raise, the `upd_raise` procedure applies the raise directly by updating the salary field of the employee record.

```
CREATE PROCEDURE upd_raise ( IN   p_min    DEC(4,2)
                           , IN   p_max    DEC(4,2) )
LANGUAGE SQL
    SPECIFIC upd_raise                          -- applies to LUW and iSeries
 -- WLM ENVIRONMENT <env>                       -- applies to zSeries

ur: BEGIN
    -- Declare variables
    DECLARE v_salary DEC(9,2);
    DECLARE v_bonus  DEC(9,2);
    DECLARE v_comm   DEC(9,2);
    DECLARE v_raise  DEC(4,2);
    -- Declare returncode
    DECLARE SQLSTATE CHAR(5);

    -- Procedure logic
    DECLARE c_emp CURSOR FOR
        SELECT salary, bonus, comm
        FROM    employee
        WHERE   job!='PRES'
    FOR UPDATE OF salary;

    OPEN c_emp;

    FETCH FROM c_emp INTO v_salary, v_bonus, v_comm;

    WHILE ( SQLSTATE = '00000' ) DO
        SET v_raise = p_min;

        IF ( v_bonus >= 600 ) THEN
            SET v_raise = v_raise + 0.04;
        END IF;

        IF ( v_comm < 2000 ) THEN
            SET v_raise = v_raise + 0.03;
```

```
        ELSEIF ( v_comm < 3000 ) THEN
            SET v_raise = v_raise + 0.02;
        ELSE
            SET v_raise = v_raise + 0.01;
        END IF;


        IF ( v_raise > p_max ) THEN
            SET v_raise = p_max;
        END IF;


        UPDATE employee                                    -- (1)
           SET salary = v_salary * (1 + v_raise)
         WHERE CURRENT OF c_emp;

        FETCH FROM c_emp INTO v_salary, v_bonus, v_comm;
    END WHILE;


    CLOSE c_emp;
END ur
```

Figure 5.8   An example of a positioned update.

The logic used to determine the appropriate raise amount is the same as in the `total_raise` procedure of Figure 5.3. After the raise amount is calculated for the current employee, the salary is
updated immediately using a positioned update on Line (1) before the cursor moves forward. The
`WHERE CURRENT OF` clause indicates that the update should occur on the row where the cursor is
currently positioned. In our case, the cursor is still positioned at the employee whose information
was just fetched.

     If you are going to be updating only a few columns for a table, then you can use the `FOR`
`UPDATE OF <column list>`. This will improve performance because the DB2 engine will know
that only certain columns are going to be updated.

Selecting Data from *UPDATE*, *INSERT*, or *DELETE* Statements

When you are working with complex data manipulation, it can be useful to know how much of an
impact the changes have had. In earlier versions of DB2 LUW, you had to issue two separate SQL
statements. The first statement would be used to determine what the impact of the `INSERT`,
`UPDATE`, or `DELETE` would be, and the second would actually execute the command. This was
tedious and required extra code and execution time. You are now able to issue one command
where both the data alterations are executed and changes just made can be retrieved.

An INSERT, UPDATE, or DELETE (IUD) statement can now be used as the input for a subselect statement by using the NEW_TABLE table function. The NEW_TABLE function allows your SELECT statements to work with the changes made by the IUD statement as if it were a temporary data table.

```
SELECT empid, job, salary
FROM NEW_TABLE(UPDATE employee
              WHERE salary > 100000
              SET salary = salary * .9)
ORDER BY salary
```

Figure 5.9   An example of a *SELECT* against an *UPDATE* on LUW.

The simple example in Figure 5.9 will return the list of all employees, their jobs, and their new salary after all employees with a salary greater than $100,000 receive a pay cut. A more complex example is given in Figure 5.10.

```
CREATE PROCEDURE upd_raise2
    ( IN  p_paychange   DEC(4,2)
     ,OUT p_littleCount INTEGER)
LANGUAGE SQL
SPECIFIC upd_raise2
DYNAMIC RESULT SETS 1
ur2: BEGIN
    -- Declare variables
    -- Declare returncode
    DECLARE SQLSTATE CHAR(5);

    -- Procedure logic
    DECLARE c_big CURSOR FOR
        SELECT empno, salary
        FROM FINAL TABLE(UPDATE employee
    SET salary = salary * (1 + 10 * p_paychange)
    WHERE salary >= 1000000);

  DECLARE c_little CURSOR FOR
        SELECT COUNT(*)
        FROM FINAL TABLE(UPDATE employee
                        SET salary = salary * (1 - p_paychange)
                        WHERE salary < 1000000);
```

```
    OPEN c_little;                                    --   (1)
    FETCH c_little into p_littleCount;                --   (2)
    CLOSE c_little;

    OPEN c_big;                                       --   (3)
END ur2
```

Figure 5.10   An example of a *SELECT* against an *UPDATE* on LUW.

The example opens two cursors. Both of them update the table and count the number of rows that were affected. The first cursor, c_big, gives a raise to all employees who earn $1 million or more. The second cursor, c_little, reduces the salaries of all the remaining employees. When the first cursor is opened on Line (1), the UPDATE statement is applied to the employee table. The UPDATE statement occurs before the SELECT statement and before a single row is fetched. The 'FINAL TABLE' component of the SQL statement obtains the updated results after all triggers and referential constraints have been applied. It is important to remember that even if you do not fetch any rows, the UPDATE statement (or DELETE or INSERT, depending on the query) will have already occurred. The use of the 'FINAL TABLE' command can be quite powerful because it allows you to work with the results of SQL that manipulates your data without having to create multiple cursors. More information on the use of the NEW TABLE clause can be found in the online help under 'FINAL TABLE'.

The FETCH statement on Line (2) will return the number of employees who received a pay cut. The SELECT is taken against the result set of the UPDATE statement in the FINAL TABLE clause. If no rows had been updated, then the SELECT would have been applied against an empty transition table.

When the second cursor is opened on Line (3), the second UPDATE statement will occur. Even though the stored procedure did not fetch any rows but instead passed the cursor back to the calling program, the UPDATE would have already taken place. It is not encouraged that you pass cursors like this back to other procedures or programs because the caller may not fully understand the impact the cursor may have had. The second UPDATE statement will be applied to the table when the c_big cursor is opened on Line (3).

DB2 for iSeries does not allow INSERT or UPDATE statements in the FROM clause of a query.

DB2 for zSeries allows a SELECT statement to include an INSERT statement as part of the FROM clause. This works similarly to DB2 for LUW, and the FINAL TABLE clause is also required. At this time, only INSERT statements are supported with the FINAL TABLE clause.

Because of these restrictions, the example procedure upd_raise2 in Figure 5.10 will not work on iSeries or zSeries; however, it can be re-written using the GET DIAGNOSTICS statement (discussed in Chapter 6, "Condition Handling") as shown in Figure 5.11.

```
CREATE PROCEDURE upd_raise2iz
    ( IN  p_paychange   DEC(4,2)
     ,OUT p_littleCount INTEGER)
LANGUAGE SQL
    SPECIFIC upd_raise2iz                          -- applies to iSeries
 -- WLM ENVIRONMENT <env>                          -- applies to zSeries
    DYNAMIC RESULT SETS 1

ur2iz: BEGIN
 -- Declare variables
    DECLARE v_rows INT DEFAULT 0;

 -- Declare returncode
    DECLARE SQLSTATE CHAR(5);

 -- Procedure logic
    DECLARE c_big CURSOR FOR
        SELECT empno, salary
          FROM employee
         WHERE salary >= 1000000;

    UPDATE employee
       SET salary = salary * (1 + 10 * p_paychange)
      WHERE salary >= 1000000;                     -- (1)

    UPDATE employee
       SET salary = salary * (1 - p_paychange)
      WHERE salary < 1000000;                      -- (2)

    GET DIAGNOSTICS v_rows = ROW_COUNT;            -- (3)
    SET p_littleCount = v_rows;

    OPEN c_big;                                    -- (4)
END ur2iz
```

Figure 5.11   The procedure *upd_raise2* rewritten for iSeries and zSeries.

The UPDATE statements on Lines (1) and (2) apply the updates to the database. The GET DIAGNOS-TICS statement on Line (3) returns the number of rows affected by the previous statement, and the OPEN statement on Line (4) will open a cursor with rows that were updated by the first update.

Cursor Behavior with *COMMIT/ROLLBACK*

One of the most important concepts in database programming is the **transaction** or the **unit of work** (UOW), a set of one or more SQL statements that execute as a single operation. In order for the transaction to complete properly, all SQL statements in it must execute without errors. If even one part of an atomic transaction fails, then the entire transaction must fail. Proper transaction control using COMMIT and/or ROLLBACK is critical for guaranteeing data integrity.

In DB2, the COMMIT and ROLLBACK statements are supported inside SQL procedures. When you use COMMIT or ROLLBACK statements with cursors, the behavior of the cursor depends on whether or not it is declared using the WITH HOLD clause. Figure 5.12 is an enhanced version of the syntax diagram presented in Figure 5.1 for DECLARE CURSOR that includes the WITH HOLD clause. The WITH RETURN clause is used to pass the result set defined by the cursor to an application or another procedure. The TO CALLER and TO CLIENT clauses are meaningful only in the context of nested SQL procedures that will be discussed in Chapter 8, "Nested SQL Procedures."

NOTE

Differences in the DECLARE CURSOR statement for iSeries are discussed at the end of the chapter.

```
>>-DECLARE--cursor-name--CURSOR----+-----------+--------------->
                                   '-WITH HOLD--'


>-----+----------------------------+------------------------->
      |                  .-TO CALLER--.  |
      '-WITH RETURN--+------------+--'
                     '-TO CLIENT--'


>----FOR--+-select-statement-+------------------------------><
          '-statement-name---'
```

Figure 5.12   A syntax diagram for *DECLARE CURSOR*.

The simplified syntax diagram for DECLARE CURSOR is shown in Figure 5.12. If the cursor is not declared using the WITH HOLD clause, all of its resources (cursor, locks, and large-object datatype, or LOB, locators) are released upon either COMMIT or ROLLBACK. Therefore, if you need to use the cursor after completing a transaction, you will have to re-open the cursor and traverse it again from the first row. Defining a cursor using WITH HOLD will cause the cursor to maintain its position and some locks across transactions. You should understand that only locks which are used to protect the current cursor position are held.

DB2 for iSeries has additional cursor functionality that is described in more detail at the end of the chapter.

A **lock** is a database object that is used to control how multiple applications can access the same resource. A **LOB locator** is a 4-byte value stored in a host variable that a program can use to refer to a LOB value held in the database system.

For cursors defined WITH HOLD after COMMIT:

- The cursor will remain open.
- The cursor will be positioned before the next logical row.
- The only permitted operations on cursors immediately after the COMMIT statement are FETCH and CLOSE.
- Positioned delete and positioned update are valid only for rows that are fetched within the same UOW.
- All LOB locators will be released.
- All locks are released, except locks protecting the current cursor position of open WITH HOLD cursors. The locks held include the locks on the table and, for parallel environments, the locks on the rows where the cursors are currently positioned. Locks on packages and dynamic SQL sections (if any) are held.
- The set of rows modified by
    - A data change statement
    - Routines that modify SQL data embedded within open WITH HOLD cursors are committed

For cursors defined WITH HOLD after ROLLBACK:

- All open cursors will be closed.
- All locks acquired during the UOW will be released.
- All LOB locators are freed.

To better explain behavior of a WITH HOLD cursor, let's look at the example in Figure 5.13.

```
CREATE PROCEDURE update_department (  )
    LANGUAGE SQL
    SPECIFIC upd_dept                        -- applies to LUW and iSeries
 -- WLM ENVIRONMENT <env>                     -- applies to zSeries

ud: BEGIN
    -- Declare variable
    DECLARE v_deptno CHAR(3);
    -- Declare returncode
```

```
DECLARE SQLSTATE CHAR(5);

DECLARE c_dept CURSOR WITH HOLD FOR
    SELECT deptno
    FROM    department
FOR UPDATE OF location;

-- Declare condition handler
DECLARE CONTINUE HANDLER FOR SQLSTATE '24504', SQLSTATE '24501'
  L1: LOOP                                                          -- (1)
     LEAVE L1;
  END LOOP;

-- Procedure logic
OPEN c_dept;

FETCH FROM c_dept INTO v_deptno;                                    -- (2)
UPDATE department SET location='FLOOR1' WHERE CURRENT OF c_dept;    -- (3)
COMMIT;                                                             -- (4)

FETCH FROM c_dept INTO v_deptno;                                    -- (5)
COMMIT;                                                             -- (6)
UPDATE department SET location='FLOOR2' WHERE CURRENT OF c_dept;    -- (7)

FETCH FROM c_dept INTO v_deptno;                                    -- (8)
UPDATE department SET location='FLOOR3' WHERE CURRENT OF c_dept;    -- (9)
COMMIT;                                                             -- (10)

FETCH FROM c_dept INTO v_deptno;                                    -- (11)
UPDATE department SET location='FLOOR4' WHERE CURRENT OF c_dept;    -- (12)
ROLLBACK;                                                           -- (13)

FETCH FROM c_dept INTO v_deptno;                                    -- (14)
UPDATE department SET location='FLOOR5' WHERE CURRENT OF c_dept;    -- (15)

CLOSE c_dept;

RETURN 0;
END ud
```

Figure 5.13   An example of the cursor behavior on *COMMIT/ROLLBACK*.

For platform compatibility, the LEAVE control statement has been placed in the condition handler on Line (1). DB2 for iSeries and DB2 for zSeries cannot have empty condition handlers. The handler is not doing anything but allowing the procedure to continue.

The update_department procedure mixes five FETCH/UPDATE blocks with COMMIT and ROLLBACK statements to show their effect on transactions. It queries and updates the department table. Figure 5.14 shows the first five rows of the two relevant columns in the department table, before the execution of the procedure.

```
DEPTNO LOCATION
------ --------
A00    -
B01    -
C01    -
D01    -
D11    -
```

Figure 5.14   A partial table *DEPARTMENT* before the execution of *update_department*.

Figure 5.15 shows the same five rows after the update_department procedure is invoked. Only two rows are updated.

```
DEPTNO LOCATION
------ --------
A00    FLOOR1
B01    -
C01    FLOOR3
D01    -
D11    -
```

Figure 5.15   A partial table *DEPARTMENT* after the execution of *update_department*.

Here is an analysis of the sequence of execution. After the cursor was declared with the FOR UPDATE clause, it was opened so that the cursor was positioned before the first row. The first block of FETCH and UPDATE on Lines (2) and (3) ran without a problem. Line (4) includes a COMMIT statement. Because the cursor was declared using the WITH HOLD clause, it remained open and was positioned before the second row for the next UOW, Lines (5) and line (6). The lock on the first row has been released, and the location field in the first row has been updated to *"FLOOR1"*.

The FETCH statement on Line (5) was successful. However, because of the COMMIT statement on Line (6), the cursor was no longer positioned at the second row, it was positioned before the third row, which has not been fetched at this point. The UPDATE statement on Line (7) failed because the cursor was not positioned on any rows. The cursor was between the second and third rows. It would have generated the following SQL error if the error handling is not in place:

```
SQL0508N  The cursor specified in the UPDATE or DELETE statement is not
positioned on a row. SQLSTATE=24504
```

Even though error handling has not yet been covered, (see Chapter 6, "Condition Handling"), the example uses it to allow all the procedure to run through to the end. If the handler did not exist, the procedure would terminate at the first error and roll back changes up to the last COMMIT point.

The next two sets of FETCH and UPDATE statements on Lines (8), (9), (11), and (12) ran successfully, and the third and fourth rows were updated.

Line (13) is a ROLLBACK statement. It can only roll back changes made since the last COMMIT statement. So the change made to the location field on the fourth row was set back to the original null value. But the change to the third row was not affected because of the COMMIT statement on Line (10).

After the ROLLBACK statement, the cursor was closed and all locks were released. The FETCH statement on Line (14) would have caused the following error, which was also caught by the error-handling block. The UPDATE statement on Line (15) failed as well.

```
SQL0501N  The cursor specified in a FETCH or CLOSE statement is not open.
SQLSTATE=24501
```

If the cursor had not been declared using the WITH HOLD clause, all the FETCH and UPDATE statements from Line (5) through (15) would have failed with the previous SQL error because the cursor would be closed implicitly by either a COMMIT or ROLLBACK statement.

Save Points Within Procedures

As the SQL PL has become more robust, developers have increased the amount of program logic they execute at the database level. This has led to very large stored procedures and transactions. With a very large transaction, it is likely that if one part of the stored procedure fails, you don't want to have the entire unit of work rolled back. Save points can be used to save interval points where the transaction can be rolled back to.

A **save point** is an indicator in a stored procedure that marks a point within a transaction. You can then use the save point to control how locking and transactions are handled if a rollback occurs. The syntax of a save point is shown in Figure 5.16.

```
>>- SAVEPOINT--savepoint-name----+--------+----------------------->
                                 '-UNIQUE-'
>---ON ROLLBACK RETAIN CURSORS--+---------------------------+------><
                                '-ON ROLLBACK RETAIN LOCKS-'
```

Figure 5.16   A SAVEPOINT syntax diagram.

The *savepoint-name* field cannot begin with 'SYS' or you will receive a SQLSTATE 42939 error. The UNIQUE option indicates that the save point name will not be reused while the save point is active. The ON ROLLBACK RETAIN CURSORS clause in the statement causes your cursors to be retained after a rollback occurs. An additional option, ON ROLLBACK RETAIN LOCKS, is needed to keep from losing your locks on ROLLBACK.

When you are using save points, they will be implicitly released when a SQL statement, utility, or DB2 command issues a COMMIT statement. Save points will also affect the use of buffered inserts. The insert buffer will be implicitly flushed when a SAVEPOINT, ROLLBACK, or RELEASE TO SAVEPOINT command is issued.

You can use more than one save point within your transaction. Each save point can be placed after another save point by using a different name. This allows you to nest save points within each other and have more flexibility regarding from where you would like the rollback to continue. A pseudo-code example of using save points is shown in Figure 5.17.

```
savepoint A;
Do program logic;
savepoint B;
Do more program logic;
savepoint C;
Do even more program logic;
```

Figure 5.17 A *SAVEPOINT* example.

Once you have set one or more save points, you can now have the option of rolling back to a specific save point. You can think of the nested save points as different levels. If you roll back to a save point at the bottom level, which is the one that was issued last, then all of the save points which are before it are still active. You can still roll back to the earlier save points even after issuing the ROLLBACK statement. The syntax is given in Figure 5.18.

```
ROLLBACK TO SAVEPOINT savepoint-name
```

Figure 5.18 The *ROLLBACK TO SAVEPOINT* syntax.

The example in Figure 5.19 illustrates how multiple save points can be rolled back. The first ROLLBACK command on Line (1) will return the transaction data to the point at save point c. The second ROLLBACK command on Line (2) will then return the data to how it was in the transaction at save point a. The third ROLLBACK on Line (3) will fail since save point b will no longer exist. This is because it was created after the transaction point marked by save point a. Because it was at a later nested level, the save point has been lost.

```
savepoint a;

Do program logic;

savepoint b;

Do more program logic;

savepoint c;

Do even more program logic;

ROLLBACK TO SAVEPOINT c;              (1)

Do some new logic;

ROLLBACK TO SAVEPOINT a;              (2)

Do some more logic;

ROLLBACK TO SAVEPOINT b;              (3)
```

Figure 5.19   A *ROLLBACK TO SAVEPOINT* example.

With large transactions, nested save points can give you more flexibility in how you handle program or data errors. It is not recommended to use very complex nested save point logic because it makes the flow of your procedures difficult to understand. It can also lead to some unexpected behavior if someone else modifies your code and does not fully understand how you are using the nested save points. A detailed discussion and example of save points can be found in Chapter 10, "Leveraging DB2 Application Development Features."

Using Cursors to Return Result Sets

Besides using cursors to process data within the SQL procedure, you can also use cursors to return result sets to the calling program for processing. To contrast these two cursor usage scenarios, the total_raise procedure in Figure 5.3 is rewritten as an SQL procedure which returns all qualifying employees' salary, bonus, and commission fields as a result set. The total raise is then calculated at the client. The SQL procedure called read_emp is shown in Figure 5.20.

The result sets can be received by either SQL procedures or client programs developed in programming languages such as Java or C. Receiving result sets from another SQL procedure is covered in Chapter 8, "Nested SQL Procedures." The Java and C client program used to receive this result set is provided in Appendix H, "Sample Application Code."

```
CREATE PROCEDURE read_emp  (   )

    LANGUAGE SQL

    SPECIFIC read_emp                       -- applies to LUW and iSeries

  -- WLM ENVIRONMENT <env>                  -- applies to zSeries

DYNAMIC RESULT SETS 1                       --(1)

re: BEGIN

    -- Procedure logic

    DECLARE c_emp CURSOR WITH RETURN FOR     --(2)
```

```
    SELECT salary, bonus, comm
    FROM    employee
    WHERE   job!='PRES';

  OPEN c_emp;                                          -- (3)
END re
```

Figure 5.20 An example of using a cursor to return a single result set.

When using a cursor to return the result set to a calling application, you need to

- Specify DYNAMIC RESULT SETS clause in CREATE PROCEDURE statement on Line (1).
- Declare the cursor using the WITH RETURN clause on Line (2).
- Keep the cursor open for the client application on Line (3).

If you do not follow the steps outlined above the cursor will not return the results out of procedure. The DYNAMIC RESULT SETS clause is optional on DB2 for LUW and iSeries. Refer to Chapter 2, "Basic SQL Procedure Structure," for a further discussion on this clause. In the example shown in Figure 5.22, the cursor has been defined and then opened. The result set will be passed back to the calling procedure or program where the results can be processed. This example is quite straightforward.

In SQL procedures, besides Data Manipulation Language (DML) statements such as SELECT, DELETE, and UPDATE, Data Definition Language (DDL) statements (such as the CREATE TABLE statement) are also supported. You can create a table, populate it, and then use a cursor to return the result set from the same table. The tricky part is that the DECLARE CURSOR statement has to be at the beginning of the BEGIN ... END block. The table creation has to be in the body of the block. If you put the DECLARE CURSOR statement at the beginning, the table is not created yet. On LUW, you will receive a compile-time error complaining the table is not found. If you put the CURSOR statement after the CREATE TABLE statement, you will run into another compile-time error indicating your DECLARE CURSOR statement is not supposed to be there. What should you do now?

The solution to this requires understanding the concept of scope. In DB2, the BEGIN ... END blocks can be nested. The scope of any declarations within a BEGIN ... END block is the block itself. The DECLARE CURSOR statement is required to be at the beginning of a BEGIN ... END block, before any SELECT, DELETE, UPDATE, or CREATE TABLE statements in that block. Hence, you can use a nested BEGIN ... END block to declare a cursor at the end of procedure. Figure 5.21 illustrates this.

TIP

In order to return result sets from a table created in the same BEGIN ... END block, you need to declare cursors inside a nested BEGIN ... END block.

```
CREATE PROCEDURE create_and_return (  )
    LANGUAGE SQL
    SPECIFIC create_and_return                    -- applies to LUW and iSeries
DYNAMIC RESULT SETS 1
cr: BEGIN
    -- Procedure logic
    CREATE TABLE mytable (sid INT);

    INSERT INTO mytable VALUES (1);
    INSERT INTO mytable VALUES (2);

    BEGIN                                         --(1)
    DECLARE c_cur CURSOR WITH RETURN
        FOR SELECT *
            FROM mytable;
    OPEN c_cur;                                   --(2)
    END;                                          --(3)
END cr
```

Figure 5.21   An example of using cursor on newly created table for LUW and iSeries.

You can see from the example in Figure 5.21 how a new BEGIN ... END block from Lines (1) to (3) allows cursor declaration for the table created in the same procedure. The OPEN CURSOR statement at Line (2) must also be inside the new BEGIN ... END block because the cursor c_cur is only valid in the inner BEGIN ... END block. It is not visible outside the block.

A very practical usage of this scheme is when you need to create and use a temporary table in your SQL procedure. For more information on DB2 user temporary tables, refer to Chapter 10, "Leveraging DB2 Application Development Features."

Another approach is to use dynamic SQL, which will be covered in Chapter 7, "Working with Dynamic SQL."

The example in Figure 5.21 will not work on zSeries because the example exploits the use of nested compound statements which are not supported on DB2 for zSeries. Nonetheless, the problem the example is trying to resolve may not happen on zSeries. DB2 for zSeries has the VALIDATE bind parameter set to RUN by default. This means that any dependency error like 'object not found' or 'not authorized' will not stop the bind process, and the procedures can be built regardless of dependency issues. Specifically for the example, on zSeries a cursor can be declared even if it references a table that is to be created later in the procedure. This is also discussed in Chapter 10, "Leveraging DB2 Application Development Features."

Returning Multiple Result Sets

So far, the examples presented have returned a single result set to the calling application. It is also possible to define multiple cursors and return multiple result sets to the caller. To do this, the following are required:

- Specify DYNAMIC RESULT SETS clause in the CREATE PROCEDURE statement corresponding to the number of result sets you intend to return.
- Declare the cursors for each result set using the WITH RETURN clause.
- Keep all cursors to be returned open for the client application.

Figure 5.22 shows a procedure that returns multiple result sets. To demonstrate the use of multiple result sets, the procedure read_emp from Figure 5.20 is rewritten to return each of the columns via three separate cursors, instead of one cursor with three columns. An example of a Java and C program used to receive multiple result sets has been provided in Appendix H, "Sample Application Code."

```
CREATE PROCEDURE read_emp_multi    (   )
     LANGUAGE SQL
     SPECIFIC read_emp_multi                     -- applies to LUW and iSeries
  -- WLM ENVIRONMENT <env>                       -- applies to zSeries
     DYNAMIC RESULT SETS 3                        --(1)
re: BEGIN
     -- Procedure logic
     DECLARE c_salary CURSOR WITH RETURN FOR
         SELECT salary
           FROM employee;

     DECLARE c_bonus CURSOR WITH RETURN FOR
         SELECT bonus
           FROM employee;

     DECLARE c_comm CURSOR WITH RETURN FOR
         SELECT comm
           FROM employee;

     OPEN c_salary;
     OPEN c_bonus;
     OPEN c_comm;
END re
```

Figure 5.22   An example of returning multiple result sets.

Because three result sets are returned, the DYNAMIC RESULT SETS value is set to 3 in Line (1).
Each cursor is declared and left open for the client application. The order in which the cursors are
opened reflects the order in which the result sets are returned to the client. In this example, the
first result set your client code can access is the salary result set, followed by the bonus and then
the commission result sets.

Cursors and Locking

It is important to understand that using cursors in your stored procedures can affect other applications or people using the database. Whenever you access data, DB2 puts a lock on the row or table
where it is stored. Locks in DB2 vary in severity from those that will prevent anyone from reading any data in a table to a row on a row that only lasts for as long as you are reading it. The type
of lock that DB2 uses depends on the type of cursor being used and the DB2 isolation level. Both
factors are summarized in the following sections.

Lock Modes

DB2 has different lock modes, and each has its own specific attributes. The common locks that
can be held on rows are listed in Table 5.1. A complete list of all the lock modes and their behaviors can be found in the DB2 documentation under "Lock Attributes."

Table 5.1   Row Lock Descriptions

Lock Mode	Applicable Object Type	Description
S (Share)	Rows, blocks, tables	The lock owner and all concurrent applications can read, but not update, the locked data.
U (Update)	Rows, blocks, tables	The lock owner can update data. Other UOW can read the data in the locked object, but cannot attempt to update it.
X (Exclusive)	Rows, blocks, tables, bufferpools	The lock owner can both read and update data in the locked object. Only uncommitted read appli-cations can access the locked object.

Isolation Levels

Isolation levels are used by DB2 to control the level of protection you provide to the data you are
reading. Increasing the isolation level will reduce the ability to access the data by the other applications. This makes your queries more consistent, but it can also greatly reduce concurrency of
your application as more lock contention can occur. The four isolation levels in order from least
severe to most severe are Uncommitted Read, Cursor Stability (the default), Read Stability, and
Repeatable Read. In addition to the four isolation levels supported by all three platforms, DB2 for
iSeries supports a fifth isolation level No Commit which is less severe than Uncommitted Read.

Uncommitted Read (UR)

This isolation level is the lowest level and is often referred to as *Dirty Read* because it ignores all locks on rows in a table and will return the data regardless. With this isolation level, any row read during a unit of work can be read and changed by any other application. The application can also read any uncommitted changes made by other application. Uncommitted changes are also known as *dirty* data. The values could be rolled back, and you would never know that you have read incorrect data. This isolation level is normally only used in read-only databases, such as data warehouses, or where data integrity is not an issue.

No Commit (NC)—iSeries Only

This isolation level behaves the same as the UR isolation level, with the exception that COMMIT and ROLLBACK operations have no effect on the SQL statements. What this means is that when a COMMIT or ROLLBACK is issued, cursors are not closed and locks held are not released (even those acquired with the LOCK TABLE statement). Additionally, any updates to the database are applied immediately and visible to other applications. With this isolation level, no locks are acquired for READ operations. For UPDATE operations, the duration of the lock is minimized—for example, a row is locked only while it is being updated.

Cursor Stability (CS)

This is the default isolation level and it will keep the row currently being read or updated locked and protected from changes by other applications. You will also not be able to read data altered by other processes until the data has been committed.

A share lock will be placed on any rows being read, while an X lock will be used for deleted rows. An X lock will also be placed for updated rows.

Read Stability (RS)

Read Stability is similar to Cursor Stability but instead of locking the current row that is being processed, it will apply the appropriate locks to all rows that are in the result set. This will ensure that within the same transaction, rows that have been previously read by a cursor cannot be altered by other applications.

Repeatable Read (RR)

Repeatable Read is the strongest isolation level. DB2 will lock all the rows in the result set as well as rows that are used to build the result set. If a row is read by the application using this isolation level, no other application can alter it until the transaction is completed. This will ensure that your result set is consistent. However, it can greatly reduce concurrency because of the large number of locks may be held.

The example in Figure 5.23 uses the data in the department table to demonstrate how the rows would be locked by each ISOLATION level as a cursor runs against it.

```
DEPTNO LOCATION

------ --------

A00    A

B01    B0

C01    B1

D01    D

D11    E
```

Figure 5.23   Partial table for *DEPARTMENT*.

```
SELECT deptno, location
FROM department
WHERE location LIKE 'B%'
```

Figure 5.24   *SELECT* statement for the example.

The example in Figure 5.24 demonstrates the locks that will he held on the different rows in the department table when the cursor is first opened. Figure 5.25 demonstrates which locks will be held during the second fetch.

Deptno	Location	UR/NC	CS	RS	RR
A00	A				S
B01	B0		S	S	S
C01	B1			S	S
D01	D				S
E01	E				S

Figure 5.25   Lock types on each row at first fetch of row (B01,B0).

Deptno	Location	UR/NC	CS	RS	RR
A00	A				S
B01	B0			S	S
C01	B1		S	S	S
D01	D				S
E01	E				S

Figure 5.26   Lock types on each row at second fetch of row (C01,B1).

As you can see in the example, the locking behavior on each row is the same with RR, RS, and UR/NC during the first and second fetch. The row that is locked does vary with CS because when a row is fetched, the lock on the previous row is released. You should use the isolation level that gives you the data integrity you need in your queries but also causes the minimal amount of contention. Cursor Stability and Read Stability are most often used to achieve these goals.

Controlling Locking in DB2 LUW

Database applications can sometimes result in concurrency issues when two different applications both try to access the same row. By default, DB2 will lock all rows that it scans until it determines if the row will be used in the result set. This is normally the desired behavior, but it may cause unnecessary locks if there is lock contention on a row that will end up not even being in the result set. You have the ability to change this behavior for CS and RS. DB2 can evaluate the row first before it tries to lock it.

The DB2 registry variable DB2_EVALUNCOMMITTED must first be turned on before this will take effect. The registry variable can be set by following command by a user with DB2 System Administrator authority. The example in Figure 5.27 demonstrates how the DB2_EVALUNCOMMITTED registry variable can be set.

```
Set:
db2set DB2_EVALUNCOMMITTED=YES


Unset
db2set DB2_EVALUNCOMMITTED=
```

Figure 5.27   Turning on the *DB2_EVALUNCOMMITTED* behavior.

The following example illustrates the new uncommitted evaluation behavior.

The table in Figure 5.28 illustrates the new uncommitted evaluation behavior on the department table.

DEPTNO	DEPTNAME	MGRNO	ADMRDEPT	LOCATION
A00	SPIFFY COMPUTER SERVICE DIV.	000010	A00	-
B01	PLANNING	000020	A00	-
C01	INFORMATION CENTER	000030	A00	-
D01	DEVELOPMENT CENTER	-	A00	-
D11	MANUFACTURING SYSTEMS	000060	D01	-
D21	ADMINISTRATION SYSTEMS	000070	D01	-
E01	SUPPORT SERVICES	000050	A00	-
E11	OPERATIONS	000090	E01	-
E21	SOFTWARE SUPPORT	000100	E01	-

Figure 5.28   *DEPARTMENT* table data.

The following two transactions in Figure 5.29 are acting against the same data table.

```
Application 1            |    Application 2
-----------------------------------------------------------------------------
CONNECT TO sample        |    CONNECT TO sample (+c)
-----------------------------------------------------------------------------
UPDATE                   |
department               |
SET mgrno = 005000       |
WHERE deptno = B01       |
-----------------------------------------------------------------------------
                         |    SELECT deptname, mgrno
                         |    FROM department
                         |    WHERE mgrno > 00050
-----------------------------------------------------------------------------
```

Figure 5.29   *department* table data.

The first application updates a row in the table without committing the change. This is controlled by the command-line option (+c) to turn off autocommit. The update stops Application 2 from returning any rows because it waits to obtain a lock on the second row before the application can continue processing the remainder of the rows. The second application waits even though the row it is waiting on will not be part of its final result set. Unless the first application commits or rolls back the transaction to release the lock, the second application would not be able to complete its update.

This problem could be avoided if the evaluate uncommitted feature was used. With the feature turned on, the second application would have first checked to see if the second row is part of the final result set. Because it would not be, the application will not lock the row and no lock contention would occur. Application 2 could then continue processing the other rows. Using the feature can help you minimize concurrency issues that can occur with data that is updated, and also has reports run against it.

No Wait and Lock Wait

The amount of time an application will wait for a lock before returning an error is set at the database level using the LOCKTIMEOUT parameter. This controls the number of seconds that an application should wait for a lock. However, there are times when you do not want your application to ever wait on a lock. You may want to know immediately if there is any lock contention for certain processes or applications.

You can directly control how long an individual application will wait for a lock using the SET CURRENT LOCK TIMEOUT command. This command will override the default wait time for the particular application. This would be useful in a system where there is a mixed work load of large long running reports and update batch sessions. The reports would be willing to wait indefinitely until the locks were freed, but the update sessions may want to return immediately. You could then determine why there is lock contention occurring and fix the problem.

The syntax of the command is given in Figure 5.30.

```
        .-CURRENT-.                    .-=-.
>>-SET--+----------+--LOCK TIMEOUT--+----+------------------------->

>--+-WAIT-------------------------+-----------------------------><
   +-NOT WAIT------------------+
   +-NULL---------------------+
   |  .-WAIT-.                |
   +-+------+--integer-constant-+
            '---host-variable---'
```

Figure 5.30   The *SET LOCK MODE* syntax.

Figure 5.31 demonstrates how you can use the SET LOCK TIMEOUT command.

```
Setting lock waiting to 0
SET CURRENT LOCK TIMEOUT NOT WAIT


Setting the application for up to 30 seconds on a lock
SET CURRENT LOCK TIMEOUT WAIT 30


Return the lock timeout value to the database LOCKTIMEOUT value
SET CURRENT LOCK TIMEOUT NULL
```

Figure 5.31   *SET CURRENT LOCK TIMEOUT* examples.

Controlling Locking in DB2 UDB for iSeries

DB2 UDB for iSeries is tightly integrated with the operating system. As such, 'its locking algorithms are the same as the i5/OS object locking algorithms.

For DML statements, the record (row) wait time can be modified using the WAITRCD parameter of the create (CRTPF, CRTLF) or change (CHGPF, CHGLF) file commands or the override database file command (OVRDBF). The default is 60 seconds. Similarly, the file (table) wait time can be modified using the WAITFILE parameter of the create or change file commands, or the override database file command. The default is 0 seconds.

For DDL statements and the LOCK TABLE statements, the lock-wait time is defined by the job default wait time (DFTWAIT), and can be changed with the change job (CHGJOB) or class (CHG-CLS) commands.

Controlling Locking in DB2 UDB for zSeries

DB2 for zSeries uses two bind parameters to control lock duration:

- ACQUIRE. Determines when the table, table space, or partition locks are taken. If the value of this parameter is set to ALLOCATE, when the first SQL statement is issued, the maximum required lock is taken on all the objects in the plan or package. If the value of this parameter is set to USE, when a SQL statement is issued, the required lock is taken on the involved object at this time.

- RELEASE. This parameter determines when the table, table space, or partition locks are released. If RELEASE DEALLOCATE is used, the locks will be released at the end of the program; when RELEASE COMMIT is used, the locks will be released at commit time.

Evaluate Uncommitted and Avoiding Locks

zSeries has a parameter called EVALUATE UNCOMMITTED that is the equivalent to the registry variable DB2_EVALUNCOMMITTED used in LUW. This parameter can be found in installation panel DSNTIP8. In addition, zSeries has mechanisms to avoid locking on rows and pages for committed data. A small instruction is used to test if a row or page contains committed data. If it does, zSeries will avoid using locks on that row or page at all. Lock avoidance is normally the default for most use; however, a combination of settings and events need to occur for zSeries to avoid using locks:

- It will only occur when dealing with read-only or ambiguous cursors.
- The proper isolation level needs to be set; CS allows for the most lock avoidance.
- The proper value for the CURRENTDATA bind parameter needs to be set; a value of NO provides for the most lock avoidance.

Using isolation level UR by itself will also provide for lock avoidance.

Lock Timeout and Deadlock Detection

zSeries does not have controls available at the statement level to manage lock timeouts or deadlock detection. The parameters that are used for these at the subsystem level are

- **Resource Timeout (IRLMRWT)**. The number of seconds a transaction will wait for a lock before a timeout is detected. The default value is 60 seconds.

- **Deadlock Time (DEADLOK)**. Specifies the time, in seconds or milliseconds, of the local deadlock detection cycle. One second is the default.

DB2 UDB for iSeries Considerations

This section covers specific iSeries issues related to cursors.

DECLARE CURSOR Statement in DB2 UDB for iSeries

The DECLARE CURSOR statement in DB2 UDB for iSeries allows for additional options:

- Specifying cursor sensitivity
- Specifying cursor scrollability
- Explicit specification for not returning a cursor

Figure 5.32 shows the complete syntax diagram for the statement in iSeries.

```
                              .--ASENSITIVE----------------.      .--NO SCROLL--.
>>-DECLARE--cursor-name---+----------------------------+----+-------------+---->
                          +--INSENSITIVE--------------+      '--SCROLL-----'
                          |               .--DYNAMIC--.  |
                          '--SENSITIVE--+-----------+--'


           .--WITHOUT HOLD--.      .-WITHOUT RETURN---------------.
>--CURSOR----+---------------+----+-----------------------------------+---------->
             '--WITH HOLD-----'   |                 .--TO CALLER--.  |
                                  '-WITH RETURN--+-------------+--'
                                                 '--TO CLIENT--'

>----FOR--+-select-statement-+------------------------------------------------><
          '-statement-name---'
```

Figure 5.32   The DECLARE CURSOR statement in DB2 UDB for iSeries.

The sensitivity specification indicates whether the cursor is sensitive to changes made to the data after the cursor is opened.

- ASENSITIVE implies that if a cursor is read-only it will be INSENSITIVE; otherwise it could be SENSITIVE or INSENSITIVE.
- INSENSITIVE implies that if changes are made to the data after the cursor is opened, they will not be visible in the cursor. The cursor is read-only in this case.
- SENSITIVE implies that if changes are made to the data (by this, or other applications) after the cursor is opened, they will be visible in the cursor.

The scrollable specification indicates whether the cursor is scrollable.

- SCROLL implies that the cursor is scrollable.
- NO SCROLL implies that the cursor is not scrollable.

The WITHOUT RETURN clause is also available to explicitly state that the cursor will not be returned to the CALLER and CLIENT. This is the default behavior on iSeries.

Summary

In this chapter, you have seen the usage of the cursors in SQL procedures. Cursors allow you to access and process data one row at a time, giving you the opportunity to implement much more complex logic that would otherwise be impossible or difficult to carry out. When using cursors to process data, you can perform reads and positioned deletes/updates. You can use the cursor either to process the data within the SQL procedure, or to return result sets to the client program.

Condition Handling

In this chapter, you will learn

- What SQLCODE and SQLSTATE are and their differences
- What a condition handler is, how and when to best use it, its range and scope, and how to work with multiple handlers
- How to force an application or user-defined exception, and set the appropriate message tag to go along with it
- Various ways of returning errors, and how to check the success and/or failure of a stored procedure call

Any textbook that deals with the subject of writing code is not complete without a discussion on how to process errors and other conditions. Anticipating and handling conditions is part and parcel of good, robust programming style. With DB2 SQL procedures, this is accomplished through the use of condition handlers. In fact, it is often desirable to also be able to check for and act on warnings that may be encountered. With DB2 SQL procedures, warnings are also a type of condition, and thus warnings and errors are handled in a very similar fashion. This chapter will describe the various types of condition handlers and techniques of how and when to use them.

Basic Error Checking: *SQLCODE* and *SQLSTATE*

A stored procedure can be written without any error checking at all. In this case, if an error is encountered, execution stops and the procedure terminates. In order to write SQL procedures responsibly, you need to learn how errors can be best handled within procedures.

SQLSTATE and SQLCODE are two values within DB2's communications area that are populated each time an SQL statement is executed. These values can be accessed within a stored procedure to determine the state, such as success or failure, of the previously executed statement. They are identifiers that can be used to get more detailed information about the state of the statement.

SQLSTATE is a five-digit numeric string that conforms to the ISO/ANSI SQL92 standard. This is a code that is common across the DB2 family of products. For example, if you were trying to drop a table that did not exist, you would get an SQLSTATE 42704, which would be the same SQLSTATE regardless of which product in the DB2 family the statement was issued against. The first two characters of SQLSTATE are known as the **SQLSTATE class code**. A class code of 00 means successful completion. Thus, an SQLSTATE beginning with 00 implies a successful completion of the previous statement. Similarly, a class code of 01 implies a warning, and a class code of 02 implies a "not found" condition. All other class codes are considered errors. Messages associated with SQLSTATES are general in nature. For example, the message associated with SQLSTATE 42704 is, 'An undefined object or constraint name was detected'.

SQLCODE is an integer status code. It is a database vendor-specific code. Some SQLCODES are common across database vendors, such as +100 (which means NOT FOUND), but the vast majority of codes do not overlap across the various database products. You can follow some simple rules when working with SQLCODES. A value of 0 for SQLCODE means that the statement executed successfully, a positive value implies successful completion but with a warning message, and a negative value indicates an error. Messages associated with an SQLCODE are specific in nature. By using the same example of dropping a table that does not exist, the SQLCODE returned is -204 and the associated message is '<name> is an undefined name', where <name> would be the name of the table.

So how are SQLSTATE and SQLCODE used in a DB2 SQL procedure? Each statement in an SQL procedure is an SQL statement. Therefore, after the execution of each statement, the value of SQLCODE and SQLSTATE are implicitly set. To access these values, you need to explicitly declare the variables SQLCODE and SQLSTATE.

TIP

SQLCODE and SQLSTATE are reserved variable names and can only be declared at the outermost scope of a procedure, meaning they can only be declared at the start of the procedure.

SQLCODE and SQLSTATE can only be accessed in the first statement after a statement has been executed, because they are set after every statement execution.

To make your code more portable, use SQLSTATE for exception handling instead of SQLCODE. In addition to being standard across the DB2 family of products, a large proportion of SQLSTATES are also standard across database vendors.

It's probably a good time to look at some code snippets to elaborate on what has been presented so far. Consider the example in Figure 6.1.

```
CREATE PROCEDURE simple_error1 ( IN p_midinit CHAR
                               ,IN p_empno   CHAR(6) )
   LANGUAGE SQL
   SPECIFIC simple_error1                        -- applies to LUW and iSeries
 -- WLM ENVIRONMENT <env>                         -- applies to zSeries
se: BEGIN
   DECLARE SQLSTATE CHAR(5) DEFAULT '00000';
   DECLARE SQLCODE INT DEFAULT 0;
   UPDATE employee                                        -- (1)
      SET midinit = p_midinit
    WHERE empno = p_empno;
   IF SUBSTR(SQLSTATE,1,2) NOT IN ('00','01','02') THEN  -- (2)
      . . . ;
   END IF;
END se
```

Figure 6.1   An incorrect example of simple error checking.

The IF statement on Line (2) will evaluate to true if an error condition exists. Recall that SQL-STATES not beginning with 00, 01, or 02 are considered errors. We could have also checked for SQLCODE being less than zero.

   At first glance, you may think that this is a reasonable example of exception handling but it will not perform as expected. If the UPDATE statement on Line (1) is successful, the procedure will run as expected. If the UPDATE statement is unsuccessful, however, it will never reach the IF on Line (2). Remember that whenever an error is encountered, the stored procedure terminates and control is transferred to the calling application.

   So, is this a Catch-22? Not really. This is where we introduce the concept of condition handlers—the subject of the next section.

Condition Handlers

A **condition handler** is basically an SQL statement that is executed when a specified condition is encountered by a statement within the procedure body. The handler is declared within a compound statement, and its scope is limited to the compound statement in which it is declared. The body of an SQL procedure is always enclosed within a BEGIN and END block and hence, by definition, an SQL procedure is a compound statement. The scope for a handler declared at the start of a procedure is the entire SQL procedure.

You must include two things when declaring a condition handler:

- You need to determine under which condition the handler will be invoked.
- You need to decide which type of handler to declare.

The type of handler is used to indicate where control is passed after the handler completes execution.

DB2 SQL PL provides some general conditions: SQLEXCEPTION, SQLWARNING, and NOT FOUND. SQLEXCEPTION covers all conditions where the execution of an SQL procedure body statement results in an error, represented by an SQLSTATE value whose first two characters are not 00, 01, or 02, or an SQLCODE whose value is a negative integer. SQLWARNING and NOT FOUND will be discussed later in this section.

You can declare EXIT and CONTINUE handlers. In LUW and iSeries, UNDO handlers are also supported. An EXIT handler will execute the SQL statement in the handler, and continue execution at the end of the compound statement in which it was declared. Thus, an EXIT handler declared at the start of a procedure would EXIT the procedure upon completion. In contrast, a CONTINUE handler will continue execution at the statement following the one that raised the exception.

UNDO handlers (supported in LUW and iSeries only) are similar to EXIT handlers in that execution will continue at the end of the compound statement in which it was declared. Any statements that were successfully executed within the compound statement will be rolled back with an UNDO handler, however. UNDO handlers can only be declared within ATOMIC compound statements.

Figure 6.2 shows the syntax diagram for declaring handlers.

```
---DECLARE----+-CONTINUE-+---HANDLER--FOR-----condition-------->
              +-EXIT-----+
              '-UNDO-----'


>----SQL-procedure-statement----------------------------------|
```

Figure 6.2 An abbreviated syntax diagram for condition handler declaration.

You can see from the syntax diagram that the handler declaration is very simple. The variable condition refers to a specific condition described using a keyword for a general condition, an SQLSTATE, or a previously declared condition. The examples in the next few sections will explain handler declarations in detail.

Note that within compound statements, a condition handler declaration follows all other types of declarations, such as variable declarations and cursor declarations.

> **TIP**
>
> In LUW and iSeries, if you require multiple statements to be executed within a condition handler, use a compound statement (BEGIN and END block). To execute multiple statements within a condition handler on zSeries, refer to the examples presented in the section "DB2 UDB for zSeries Considerations" of this chapter.

Figure 6.3 expands on the example presented earlier and shows how it can be corrected using a condition handler.

```
CREATE PROCEDURE simple_error2 ( IN p_midinit CHAR
                              , IN p_empno   CHAR(6) )
    LANGUAGE SQL
    SPECIFIC simple_error2                         -- applies to LUW and iSeries
 -- WLM ENVIRONMENT <env>                          -- applies to zSeries
se: BEGIN
    -- Declare variables
    DECLARE v_sqlstate_test CHAR(5);                          -- (1)
    DECLARE v_sqlcode_test INT;                               -- (2)
    -- Declare return codes
    DECLARE SQLSTATE CHAR(5) DEFAULT '00000';
    DECLARE SQLCODE INT DEFAULT 0;
    -- Declare condition handlers
    DECLARE CONTINUE HANDLER FOR SQLEXCEPTION                 -- (3)
         SELECT SQLSTATE
               ,SQLCODE
           INTO v_sqlstate_test
               ,v_sqlcode_test
           FROM sysibm.sysdummy1;
    -- Procedure logic
    UPDATE employee                                           -- (4)
       SET midinit = p_midinit
     WHERE empno = p_empno;
    IF SUBSTR(v_sqlstate_test,1,2) NOT IN ('00','01','02') THEN -- (5)
       . . . ;
    END IF;
END se
```

Figure 6.3 An example of simple error checking.

As you can see, two variables, v_sqlstate_test and v_sqlcode_test, have been added on Lines (1) and (2), as well as a CONTINUE handler on Line (3). The handler sets the values of SQLCODE and SQLSTATE raised by the error condition to the variables v_sqlcode_test and v_sqlstate_test. The other change made was the test condition on Line (5) to test for the variable set in the handler as opposed to the actual SQLSTATE.

Note that SQLCODE and SQLSTATE from the statement that raised the condition are only accessible in the first statement of the handler. That is the reason why a SELECT INTO statement is used to capture both simultaneously so that both variables (v_sqlcode_test and v_sqlstate_test) can be assigned properly. The table, sysibm.sysdummy1, referenced in the FROM clause is a DB2 special built-in catalog view that contains one row only.

The previous example works, but it seems like a very cumbersome way to perform any error checking. It forces you to check for an error after each and every execution of a statement. In fact, it was only presented for demonstration purposes. Creating a handler just to set SQLCODE and SQLSTATE defeats its intended purpose. The real value in creating handlers is to group errors into classes for which similar action can be taken.

To elaborate, if you were to rethink this example, what you would really want to do is to return SQLCODE and SQLSTATE as output parameters to the calling application. This can be accomplished by writing an EXIT handler instead of a CONTINUE handler. Figure 6.4 shows the previous example rewritten with a more appropriate use of the condition handler.

```
CREATE PROCEDURE simple_error3 ( IN p_midinit       CHAR
                               , IN p_empno         CHAR(6)
                               ,OUT p_sqlstate_out CHAR(5)
                               ,OUT p_sqlcode_out  INT )
    LANGUAGE SQL
    SPECIFIC simple_error3                      -- applies to LUW and iSeries
 -- WLM ENVIRONMENT <env>                       -- applies to zSeries
se: BEGIN
   -- Declare return codes
   DECLARE SQLSTATE CHAR(5) DEFAULT '00000';
   DECLARE SQLCODE INT DEFAULT 0;
   -- Declare condition handlers
   DECLARE EXIT HANDLER FOR SQLEXCEPTION
        SELECT SQLSTATE
              ,SQLCODE
           INTO p_sqlstate_out
               ,p_sqlcode_out
           FROM sysibm.sysdummy1;
   -- Procedure logic
```

```
   -- Initialize output parameters with defaults
   VALUES (SQLSTATE, SQLCODE)
     INTO p_sqlstate_out
         ,p_sqlcode_out;
   UPDATE employee                              -- (1)
     SET midinit = p_midinit
   WHERE empno = p_empno;
END se
```

Figure 6.4   A revised example of simple error checking.

As soon as an error is encountered, the handler is invoked. It sets the values for the output parameters p_sqlcode and p_sqlstate. After the handler completes, the procedure exits. Because the procedure terminates on error, there is no need to check for an error condition after the UPDATE statement on Line (1).

In addition to SQLEXCEPTION, two other general conditions exist for handlers—SQLWARNING and NOT FOUND. SQLWARNING covers all conditions where the execution of an SQL statement completed successfully, but a warning was issued—that is, an SQLSTATE value whose first two characters are 01, or an SQLCODE value that is a positive integer, not including +100. The NOT FOUND condition represents the case where the execution of an SQL statement returns an SQLSTATE value whose first two characters are 02, or an SQLCODE value of +100.

It is also possible to declare handlers for specific conditions, rather than one of the general conditions, by declaring a handler for a specific SQLSTATE. This can be done in two ways. One is through the declaration of the condition handler, as in

```
DECLARE EXIT HANDLER FOR SQLSTATE '23503' ...;
```

Although this statement will work, it does not make the code in the procedure very readable or intuitive. The SQL PL allows you to declare condition names for specific SQLSTATEs to make the code clearer. Consider the following code snippet:

```
DECLARE FOREIGN_KEY_VIOLATION CONDITION FOR SQLSTATE '23503';
DECLARE EXIT HANDLER FOR FOREIGN_KEY_VIOLATION ...;
```

This makes your code more readable and easier to understand. Following are two syntax diagrams, one for the condition declaration (see Figure 6.5), and the other for the more complete handler declaration (see Figure 6.6).

```
|---DECLARE--condition-name--CONDITION--FOR-------------------->

                      .-VALUE-.
       .-SQLSTATE--+-------+---.
>----+----------------------+---string-constant---------------|
```

Figure 6.5   A syntax diagram for condition declaration.

```
---DECLARE----+-CONTINUE-+----HANDLER--FOR-------------------->
              +-EXIT-----+
              '-UNDO-----'


      .-,-----------------------------------.
      V                  .-VALUE-.          |
>---------+-SQLSTATE--+-------+---string--+--+------------------>
          +-condition-name--------------+
          +-SQLEXCEPTION----------------+
          +-SQLWARNING------------------+
          '-NOT FOUND-------------------'

>----SQL-procedure-statement----------------------------------|
```

Figure 6.6   A complete syntax diagram for condition handler declaration.

For any given procedure, you can declare multiple handlers for different conditions. For example, you can declare an EXIT handler for SQLEXCEPTION and another EXIT handler for SQLSTATE 23503. This can introduce some ambiguity because SQLSTATE 23503 is also an SQLEXCEPTION. In cases where more than one condition handler might fit the bill, the handler for the more specific condition is invoked. So in an example where handlers for both SQLEXCEPTION and SQLSTATE 23503 are declared, a statement that results in a foreign key violation would invoke the condition handler declared for SQLSTATE 23503, and the SQLEXCEPTION condition handler is ignored.

Several concepts have been introduced in the last section. It's time now to look at a more comprehensive example, with multiple handlers, to bring some of these ideas together.

The example in Figure 6.7 is a procedure that inserts into the department table. If the insert fails because of a duplicate row error, then an update is performed. It takes the column values for department as input and returns SQLCODE and SQLSTATE as output parameters.

```
CREATE PROCEDURE insert_update_department1 ( IN  p_deptno         CHAR(3)
                                            ,IN  p_deptname       VARCHAR(29)
                                            ,IN  p_mgrno          CHAR(6)
                                            ,IN  p_admrdept       CHAR(3)
                                            ,IN  p_location       CHAR(16)
                                            ,OUT p_sqlstate_out   CHAR(5)
                                            ,OUT p_sqlcode_out    INT )
    LANGUAGE SQL
    SPECIFIC ins_upd_dept1                        -- applies to LUW and iSeries
 -- WLM ENVIRONMENT <env>                         -- applies to zSeries
iud: BEGIN
    -- Declare variables
    DECLARE SQLSTATE CHAR(5) DEFAULT '00000';
    DECLARE SQLCODE INT DEFAULT 0;
    DECLARE v_duplicate INT DEFAULT 0;
    -- Declare condition
    DECLARE c_duplicate CONDITION FOR SQLSTATE '23505';            -- (1)
    -- Declare handlers
    DECLARE EXIT HANDLER FOR SQLEXCEPTION
        SELECT SQLSTATE                                            -- (2)
              ,SQLCODE
          INTO p_sqlstate_out
              ,p_sqlcode_out
          FROM sysibm.sysdummy1;
    -- Handler for duplicate condition
    DECLARE CONTINUE HANDLER FOR c_duplicate                       -- (3)
        SET v_duplicate = 1;

    -- Initialize output parms
    VALUES (SQLSTATE, SQLCODE)                                     -- (4)
      INTO p_sqlstate_out
          ,p_sqlcode_out;
    -- Try insert, if duplicate, then update
    INSERT INTO department ( deptno
                            ,deptname
                            ,mgrno
                            ,admrdept
                            ,location )
                   VALUES ( p_deptno
                           ,p_deptname
```

```
                        ,p_mgrno
                        ,p_admrdept
                        ,p_location ) ;
    IF v_duplicate = 1 THEN
        -- only update if non-null value provided as input parameter
        UPDATE department
           SET deptname = coalesce(p_deptname, deptname)
              ,mgrno    = coalesce(p_mgrno, mgrno)
              ,admrdept = coalesce(p_admrdept, admrdept)
              ,location = coalesce(p_location, location)
         WHERE deptno = p_deptno;
    END IF;
END iud
```

Figure 6.7   An example of a named condition and multiple handlers.

A condition is declared on Line (1) for SQLSTATE 23505, which is the SQLSTATE for duplicate rows. A handler is then declared on Line (3) for the specific condition that sets the variable indicating a duplicate condition.

Take a look at the VALUES statement on Line (4). This is an alternative to issuing two SET statements or a statement such as SELECT ... FROM sysibm.sysdummy1 as seen on Line (2). The VALUES INTO statement is more efficient than two SET statements because the variables are assigned in parallel. Additionally, each statement has some overhead associated with it—for example, condition checking at the end of each statement. Therefore, reducing the number of statements also reduces the processing cost.

Custom Errors and Error Messages

So far, you've only seen examples where condition handlers are automatically invoked for a specific SQLSTATE. What if you want to force the invocation of a handler? For example, a column value returned from a select statement may indicate an application error for which you may want to invoke a handler. This section shows you various ways to customize errors and error messages.

Using *SIGNAL* to Force the Invocation of a Handler

The SIGNAL statement allows you to force an error or warning through the SQLSTATE setting. You also have the option of customizing a message associated with the SQLSTATE. If a handler is declared for that SQLSTATE, it will be invoked. If no handler is declared for that SQLSTATE, then the handler for SQLEXCEPTION or SQLWARNING is invoked as necessary. If no handlers are declared at all, the exception is returned to the application as a database exception.

SQLSTATES beginning with the characters 01 or 02 are warnings and "not found" conditions, respectively. All other SQLSTATES (not beginning with the characters 00) are considered exceptions. Any warnings and "not found" conditions issued via a SIGNAL statement will be assigned an SQLCODE of +438, and any exceptions will be assigned an SQLCODE of -438.

In fact, the SIGNAL statement even allows you to issue a customized condition or SQLSTATE. If a condition for an SQLSTATE—customized or otherwise—is declared, then it can be referenced in a SIGNAL statement. Figure 6.8 shows the syntax diagram for the SIGNAL statement in LUW.

> **NOTE**
> A SIGNAL statement in iSeries does not support the variable name to be used as the SQL-STATE value; a string constant must be used. On the other hand, you can obtain a much richer set of condition information items from the SIGNAL statement in iSeries. A complete syntax diagram of the SIGNAL statement for DB2 UDB for iSeries is captured in the section "DB2 UDB for iSeries Consideration" of this chapter.

```
>>-SIGNAL-------------------------------------------------------->

                 .-VALUE-.
>--+-SQLSTATE--+-------+--+-sqlstate-string-constant-+-+--------->
   |                        '-variable-name------------' |
   '-condition-name-----------------------------------'


>--+----------------------+-----------------------------------><
   '-| signal-information |-'

signal-information:

|--+-SET MESSAGE_TEXT-- = --diagnostic-string-expression-+------|
   '-(--diagnostic-string-expression--)-----------------'
```

Figure 6.8   The syntax diagram for the *SIGNAL* statement for DB2 UDB for LUW and zSeries.

To raise an SQLSTATE, you can explicitly specify it with the SQLSTATE value such as 90000. Alternatively, the use of a variable containing an SQLSTATE is also allowed. Some rules need to be followed when defining your own SQLSTATE. The following excerpt is from the DB2 SQL Reference pertaining to custom SQLSTATES:

> SQLSTATE values are comprised of a two-character class code value, followed by a three-character subclass code value. Class code values represent classes of successful and unsuccessful execution conditions. Any valid SQLSTATE value can be used in the SIGNAL statement. However, it is recommended that programmers define new SQLSTATES based on ranges reserved for applications. This prevents the unintentional use of an SQLSTATE value that might be defined by the database manager in a future release.

- SQLSTATE classes that begin with the characters '7' through '9', or 'I' through 'Z' may be defined. Within these classes, any subclass may be defined.

- SQLSTATE classes that begin with the characters '0' through '6', or 'A' through 'H' are reserved for the database manager. Within these classes, subclasses that begin with the characters '0' through 'H' are reserved for the database manager. Subclasses that begin with the characters 'I' through 'Z' may be defined.

As shown in the syntax diagram of Figure 6.8, you can also specify the message text for the particular SQLSTATE or condition being raised. If message text is provided, it must be enclosed by two single quotation marks. However, you should note that for LUW and zSeries the diagnostic text must be fewer than 70 characters.

Figure 6.9 shows an example that employs the SIGNAL statement. To illustrate, the previous example from Figure 6.7 is expanded to declare a condition for a customized SQLSTATE. The logic is changed such that if more than 10 rows are found in the department table, an exception is raised.

```
CREATE PROCEDURE insert_update_department2 ( IN p_deptno        CHAR(3)
                                            ,IN p_deptname      VARCHAR(29)
                                            ,IN p_mgrno         CHAR(6)
                                            ,IN p_admrdept      CHAR(3)
                                            ,IN p_location      CHAR(16)
                                            ,OUT p_sqlstate_out CHAR(5)
                                            ,OUT p_sqlcode_out  INT )
    LANGUAGE SQL
    SPECIFIC ins_upd_dept2                      -- applies to LUW and iSeries
 -- WLM ENVIRONMENT <env>                       -- applies to zSeries
iud: BEGIN
    -- Declare variables
    DECLARE SQLSTATE CHAR(5) DEFAULT '00000';
    DECLARE SQLCODE INT DEFAULT 0;
    DECLARE v_duplicate INT DEFAULT 0;
    DECLARE v_num_rows INT DEFAULT 0;
    -- Declare condition
    DECLARE c_duplicate CONDITION FOR SQLSTATE '23505';
    DECLARE c_too_many_rows CONDITION FOR SQLSTATE '99001';
    -- Declare handlers
    DECLARE EXIT HANDLER FOR SQLEXCEPTION
        SELECT SQLSTATE
              ,SQLCODE
          INTO p_sqlstate_out
              ,p_sqlcode_out
          FROM sysibm.sysdummy1;
```

```
DECLARE CONTINUE HANDLER FOR c_duplicate
    SET v_duplicate = 1;

-- Initialize output parms
VALUES (SQLSTATE, SQLCODE)
  INTO p_sqlstate_out
      ,p_sqlcode_out;

-- See how many rows are already in the DEPARTMENT table
SELECT COUNT(1)
  INTO v_num_rows
  FROM department;

-- Signal an error if more than 10 rows exist
IF v_num_rows > 10 THEN
    SIGNAL c_too_many_rows SET MESSAGE_TEXT =
    'Too many rows in table DEPARTMENT'; -- (1)
END IF;

-- Try insert, if duplicate, then update
INSERT INTO department ( deptno
                        ,deptname
                        ,mgrno
                        ,admrdept
                        ,location )
              VALUES ( p_deptno
                        ,p_deptname
                        ,p_mgrno
                        ,p_admrdept
                        ,p_location);
IF v_duplicate = 1 THEN
    -- only update if non-null value provided as input parameter
    UPDATE department
      SET deptname = coalesce(p_deptname, deptname)
         ,mgrno    = coalesce(p_mgrno, mgrno)
         ,admrdept = coalesce(p_admrdept, admrdept)
         ,location = coalesce(p_location, location)
      WHERE deptno = p_deptno;
END IF;
END iud
```

Figure 6.9   An example of the *SIGNAL* statement.

If you examine Figure 6.9, you will see that if fewer than 11 rows exist in the department table, the SQL procedure will function as it did in Figure 6.7. However, if more than 10 rows are encountered, an exception with an SQLSTATE of 99001 is raised by the SIGNAL statement on Line (1). Because there is no specific handler for the specified SQLSTATE, the EXIT handler for the SQLEXCEPTION is invoked. The control returns to the caller after the handler finishes execution. In this case, 99001 will be returned as the SQLSTATE value, and -438 will be returned as the SQLCODE.

Using *RESIGNAL* to Force the Invocation of a Handler

Along the same lines of the SIGNAL statement, a similar statement—RESIGNAL—warrants some discussion. The RESIGNAL statement can only be invoked from inside a condition handler. It is used for one of two things:

- It can be used to issue a warning or error in the same way as the SIGNAL statement but from within a handler. The SQLSTATE and SQLCODE that caused the handler to be invoked are overridden.

- It can be used to reissue the same condition that caused the handler to be invoked. The reason for this case will become more apparent in the next section.

Figure 6.10 shows the syntax diagram for the RESIGNAL statement in LUW.

> **NOTE**
> The RESIGNAL statement syntax in iSeries is different from what is presented in Figure 6.10. Refer to the section "DB2 UDB for iSeries Considerations" toward the end this chapter for its syntax diagram.
> The RESIGNAL statement syntax in zSeries is the same as shown in Figure 6.10 with the exception that the MESSAGE_TEXT can only be set to a diagnostic string expression.

```
>>-RESIGNAL-------------------------------------------------------------->

>--+-------------------------------------------------------------------+-><
   |                .-VALUE-.                                           |
   '-+-SQLSTATE--+-------+---+-sqlstate-string-constant-+-+-+-------------+-'
     |                         '-variable-name------------' | '-|signal-info|-'
     '-condition-name-----------------------------------'

signal-information:

|--SET--MESSAGE_TEXT-- = --+-variable-name--------------+---------------|
                           '-diagnostic-string-constant-'
```

Figure 6.10   The syntax diagram for the *RESIGNAL* statement in LUW and zSeries.

The syntax diagram shows that the SQLSTATE value and signal-information specifications are optional. If they are omitted, the statement will reissue the same SQLSTATE and SQLCODE that caused the handler to be invoked.

This is a good time for another example. Again, this example is for illustration purposes only to show a crude way to override the SQLSTATE that invoked the handler. The example in Figure 6.9 is expanded to contain a handler for the condition forced by the SIGNAL statement. The handler in turn issues a RESIGNAL statement.

```
CREATE PROCEDURE insert_update_department3 ( IN   p_deptno          CHAR(3)
                                           , IN   p_deptname        VARCHAR(29)
                                           , IN   p_mgrno           CHAR(6)
                                           , IN   p_admrdept        CHAR(3)
                                           , IN   p_location        CHAR(16)
                                           , OUT  p_sqlstate_out    CHAR(5)
                                           , OUT  p_sqlcode_out     INT )
    LANGUAGE SQL
    SPECIFIC ins_upd_dept3                         -- applies to LUW and iSeries
 -- WLM ENVIRONMENT <env>                          -- applies to zSeries
iud: BEGIN
    -- Declare variables
    DECLARE SQLSTATE CHAR(5) DEFAULT '00000';
    DECLARE SQLCODE INT DEFAULT 0;
    DECLARE v_duplicate INT DEFAULT 0;
    DECLARE v_num_rows INT DEFAULT 0;
    -- Declare condition
    DECLARE c_duplicate CONDITION FOR SQLSTATE '23505';
    DECLARE c_too_many_rows CONDITION FOR SQLSTATE '99001';
    DECLARE c_error CONDITION FOR SQLSTATE '99999';
    -- Declare handlers
    DECLARE EXIT HANDLER FOR SQLEXCEPTION
        SELECT SQLSTATE, SQLCODE
          INTO p_sqlstate_out
              ,p_sqlcode_out
          FROM sysibm.sysdummy1;
    -- Handler with RESIGNAL
    DECLARE EXIT HANDLER FOR c_too_many_rows      -- (1)
        RESIGNAL c_error SET MESSAGE_TEXT = 'Too many rows in table
DEPARTMENT';
    DECLARE CONTINUE HANDLER FOR c_duplicate
        SET v_duplicate = 1;
    -- Initialize output parms
    VALUES (SQLSTATE, SQLCODE)
```

```
     INTO p_sqlstate_out
         ,p_sqlcode_out;


  -- See how many rows are already in the DEPARTMENT table
  SELECT COUNT(1)
    INTO v_num_rows
    FROM department;
  -- Signal an error if more than 10 rows exist
  IF v_num_rows > 10 THEN
      SIGNAL c_too_many_rows;
  END IF;


  -- Try insert, if duplicate, then update
  INSERT INTO department ( deptno
                          ,deptname
                          ,mgrno
                          ,admrdept
                          ,location )
              VALUES ( p_deptno
                      ,p_deptname
                      ,p_mgrno
                      ,p_admrdept
                      ,p_location);
  IF v_duplicate = 1 THEN
      -- only update if non-null value provided as input parameter
      UPDATE department
         SET deptname = coalesce(p_deptname, deptname)
            ,mgrno    = coalesce(p_mgrno, mgrno)
            ,admrdept = coalesce(p_admrdept, admrdept)
            ,location = coalesce(p_location, location)
       WHERE deptno = p_deptno;
  END IF;
END iud
```

Figure 6.11   An example of a *RESIGNAL* statement.

The example shows that when more than 10 rows exist in the department table, an error is SIG-NALed with an SQLSTATE of 99001. The condition handler for this condition RESIGNALS with an SQLSTATE of 99999. Thus, when there are too many rows in the department table, the calling application will receive an SQLSTATE of 99999, not 99001 as in the example from Figure 6.9.

The real value of the RESIGNAL statement is shown when you have multiple handlers with multiple levels of compound statements, which you will see in the next section.

Scope of Handlers

Recall that condition handlers are declared within a compound statement. In LUW and iSeries, an SQL procedure by definition is a compound statement, which can contain other compound statements, and so on. Hence, it follows that each of these nested compound statements can contain condition handlers as well. What is the behavior of the stored procedure when nested compound statements with multiple handlers are used?

> **TIP**
> Nested compound statements are not currently supported in zSeries, Figure 6.12 does not apply to this platform. Therefore, the scope of the handlers will always be for the entire stored procedure.

Figure 6.12 shows some pseudo-code to help paint a scenario for discussion.

```
CREATE PROCEDURE
s: BEGIN
    s1: DECLARE EXIT HANDLER FOR SQLEXCEPTION RESIGNAL
    s2: SQL Procedure Statement
    s3: SQL Procedure Statement
    s4: BEGIN
        s4-1: DECLARE EXIT HANDLER FOR SQLEXCEPTION RESIGNAL
        s4-2: DECLARE EXIT HANDLER FOR '99999' BEGIN END
        s4-3: SQL Procedure Statement
        s4-4: SQL Procedure Statement
        s4-5: BEGIN
            s4-5-1: DECLARE EXIT HANDLER FOR SQLSTATE '23503'
            RESIGNAL SQLSTATE '99999'
            s4-5-2: SQL Procedure Statement
            s4-5-3: SQL Procedure Statement
            s4-5-4: IF <cond> THEN SIGNAL SQLSTATE '23503' END IF
        END s4-5
        s4-6:  BEGIN ATOMIC
            s4-6-1: DECLARE UNDO HANDLER FOR SQLSTATE '23503'
            RESIGNAL SQLSTATE '99998'
            s4-6-2: SQL Procedure Statement
            s4-6-3: SQL Procedure Statement
            s4-6-4: IF <cond> THEN SIGNAL SQLSTATE '23503' END IF
```

```
        END s4-6
        s4-7: IF <cond> THEN SIGNAL SQLSTATE '23503' END IF
    END s4
    s5: SQL Procedure Statement
END s
```

Figure 6.12   Pseudo-code for nested handlers.

Based on the previous example, the scope of each of the handlers is the compound statement in which they are declared, specifically

- The scope of the handler declared in line s1 is the s compound statement (lines s1 through s5).

- The scope of the handler declared in line s4-1 is the s4 compound statement (lines s4-1 through s4-7).

- The scope of the handler declared in line s4-2 is also the s4 compound statement (lines s4-1 through s4-7).

- The scope of the handler declared in line s4-5-1 is the s4-5 compound statement (lines s4-5-2 through s4-5-4).

- The scope of the handler declared in line s4-6-1 is the s4-6 compound statement (lines s4-6-2 through s4-6-4).

So it follows that if an exception is encountered or SIGNALed in line:

- s4-5-4, then the procedure continues execution after executing a few handlers. First, the EXIT handler declared at line s4-5-1 is invoked with SQLSTATE 23503 and SQLCODE -438. It RESIGNALS an exception with SQLSTATE 99999 and SQLCODE -438 and EXITS the s4-5 compound statement. At this point, the EXIT handler declared at line s4-2 is invoked. This handler executes and EXITS the s4 compound statement upon completion and continues to execute line s5. Note that compound statement s4-6 is skipped. Because the EXIT handler s4-2 did not RESIGNAL a condition, the s1 handler was not invoked upon EXIT of the s4 compound statement.

- s4-6-4, then the procedure continues execution after executing a few handlers. First, the UNDO handler declared at line s4-6-1 is invoked with SQLSTATE 23503 and SQLCODE -438. Any statements within the s4-6 compound statement are rolled back. Thus, statements s4-6-2 and s4-6-3 are rolled back. The UNDO handler RESIGNALS an exception with SQLSTATE 99998 and SQLCODE -438 and EXITS the s4-6 compound statement. At this point, the EXIT handler declared at line s4-1 is invoked, because there is no specific handler declared for SQLSTATE 99998. This handler RESIGNALS with the same SQLSTATE and SQLCODE and EXITS the s4 compound statement. Here the handler declared at line s1 takes over, and the handler RESIGNALS the same SQLSTATE and SQLCODE, and EXITS the procedure.

- s4-7, then SQLSTATE 23503 and SQLCODE -438 are returned to the calling application. First, the EXIT handler declared at line s4-1 is invoked with SQLSTATE 23503 and SQLCODE -438. This handler RESIGNALS with the same SQLSTATE and SQLCODE, and EXITS the s4 compound statement. Here, the handler declared at line s1 takes over, and this handler RESIGNALS the same SQLSTATE and SQLCODE, and EXITS the procedure.

- s4-5-3, then the SQLSTATE and SQLCODE causing the exception is returned to the calling program. In this case, there is no handler within the s4-5 compound statement to handle this exception, so a handler in the outer scope is invoked—namely, the handler declared at line s4-1. This handler RESIGNALS with the same SQLSTATE and SQLCODE, and EXITS the s4 compound statement. Here, the handler declared at line s1 takes over, and this handler RESIGNALS the same SQLSTATE and SQLCODE, and EXITS the procedure.

Note the use of the RESIGNAL statement in the scenario described. It is sometimes useful to have a handler that executes some SQL statements, and then reissue the same condition. This is especially useful when nested scoping is used. In Figure 6.12, the handler in line s4-5-1 could easily be modified to contain one or more SQL statements prior to the RESIGNAL statement (as long as they are enclosed with a BEGIN and END).

The pseudo-code in Figure 6.12 is not a working example, but does serve to show you the flow of logic under some of the more complex situations. The "Bringing It All Together" section will build a working example of such a scenario.

RAISE_ERROR Function

Besides the SIGNAL and RESIGNAL statements, DB2 UDB for LUW and zSeries also provide a built-in function, RAISE_ERROR, which causes a statement to return an error. The function contains two arguments that specify the SQLSTATE and error message to be returned. Figure 6.13 shows the syntax diagram of the function.

```
>>-RAISE_ERROR--(--sqlstate--,--diagnostic-string--)-----------><
```

Figure 6.13   The syntax diagram for the *RAISE_ERROR* function.

When defining your own SQLSTATE, the same rules discussed for the SIGNAL statement in the "Using *SIGNAL* to Force the Invocation of a Handler" section also apply here. SQLCODE -438 is returned after executing the statement that includes the RAISE_ERROR. The error message text or diagnostic string as indicated in Figure 6.13 is a string that's 70 bytes long. If the message is longer than 70 bytes, it will be truncated.

The RAISE_ERROR function is found to be most useful in a CASE expression. Refer to Figure 6.14 for an example.

```
CREATE PROCEDURE app_raise_error ( IN p_admrdept      CHAR(3)
                                   ,OUT p_sqlstate_out CHAR(5)
                                   ,OUT p_sqlcode_out  INT )
    LANGUAGE SQL
    SPECIFIC app_raise_eror                      -- applies to LUW and iSeries
 -- WLM ENVIRONMENT <env>                        -- applies to zSeries
ae: BEGIN
    -- Declare variables
    DECLARE SQLSTATE CHAR(5) DEFAULT '00000';
    DECLARE SQLCODE INT DEFAULT 0;
    -- Declare handlers
    DECLARE EXIT HANDLER FOR SQLEXCEPTION                          -- (1)
       SELECT SQLSTATE, SQLCODE
         INTO p_sqlstate_out
            ,p_sqlcode_out
          FROM sysibm.sysdummy1;


    UPDATE department
       SET LOCATION =
           (CASE WHEN p_admrdept = 'A00' THEN 'Boston'          -- (2)
                 WHEN p_admrdept = 'B01' THEN 'Chicago'
                 WHEN p_admrdept = 'C01' THEN 'Dallas'
                 WHEN p_admrdept = 'D01' THEN 'San Mateo'
                 ELSE RAISE_ERROR('70001', 'ADMRDEPT does not exist') -- (3)
           END);
END ae
```

Figure 6.14   An example of the *RAISE_ERROR* function for LUW and zSeries.

This example accepts an input parameter that is evaluated in the CASE expression on Line (2). If the input does not match any value specified, an error is raised. On Line (3), SQLSTATE 70001 and an error message ADMRDEPT does not exist are raised. This error will be captured by the EXIT handler declared on Line (1) and handled in the exact same fashion as discussed in the previous sections.

> **NOTE**
> Although the RAISE_ERROR function is not supported in iSeries, most applications of the function can be handled by the SIGNAL or RESIGNAL statement. An example showing how to use the SIGNAL statement in iSeries is presented in the "DB2 UDB for iSeries Considerations" section in this chapter.

GET DIAGNOSTICS

When presenting scenarios for condition handling, it is necessary to introduce the use of the GET DIAGNOSTICS statement. The GET DIAGNOSTICS statement is used to obtain information relating to the statement that was just executed. For example, many tests for error conditions rely on knowing how many rows are affected as a result of an INSERT, UPDATE, or DELETE statement. The GET DIAGNOSTICS statement helps you get this information. The syntax diagram for this statement in LUW is shown in Figure 6.15.

> **NOTE**
> DB2 UDB for iSeries and zSeries offer a more comprehensive set of information than what is available in LUW shown in Figure 6.15. Refer to the considerations section in the chapter for detailed discussions and examples.

```
>>-GET DIAGNOSTICS-+-SQL-variable-name--=-----+-ROW_COUNT-----+--+->< 
                   |                           '-RETURN_STATUS-' |
                   '-condition-information---------------------'


condition-information
            .-,-----------------------------------------------.
            V                                                 |
|-EXCEPTION-1-+--SQL-variable-name--=---+--MESSAGE_TEXT-------+--+---|
                                        '--DB2_MESSAGE_STRING--'
```

Figure 6.15   The syntax diagram for the *GET DIAGNOSTICS* statement in LUW.

You will notice that it has three alternatives. When invoked as the first statement after an INSERT, UPDATE, or DELETE statement, ROW_COUNT will retrieve the number of rows that were affected by the previous statement. If this statement follows a PREPARE statement, then ROW_COUNT will return the number of estimated rows expected as a result of the PREPAREd statement. Note that it is a common misconception that the GET DIAGNOSTICS statement will also give the number of rows retrieved by a SELECT. This is not true.

Figure 6.16 shows a simple example of using the statement with the ROW_COUNT keyword. It deletes from the employee table rows that have values of empno beginning with the parameter value passed in, and returns the number of rows deleted.

```
CREATE PROCEDURE get_diag ( IN p_empno VARCHAR(6)
                           ,OUT p_rows INT )

    LANGUAGE SQL
    SPECIFIC get_diag                    -- applies to LUW and iSeries
 -- WLM ENVIRONMENT <env>                -- applies to zSeries
```

```
gd: BEGIN
     DECLARE v_rows INT DEFAULT -1;
     DELETE FROM employee
      WHERE empno like p_empno || '%';
     GET DIAGNOSTICS v_rows = ROW_COUNT;
     SET p_rows = v_rows;
END gd
```

Figure 6.16   An example of *GET DIAGNOSTICS* with *ROW_COUNT*.

GET DIAGNOSTICS supports another option called RETURN_STATUS that is used after a CALL statement to another procedure. It returns the value specified in the RETURN statement of the called procedure. The RETURN statement and working with results from called procedures is the subject of the next section, "Processing Results from Called Procedures."

The condition-information clause allows the retrieval of error or warning information related to the SQL statement that just executed. The MESSAGE_TEXT keyword will retrieve the actual error or warning message associated with the SQL statement, or a blank or empty string if the statement completed successfully without warnings. This is useful in cases where you would like to return an error message from the procedure instead of just the SQLSTATE and/or SQLCODE.

The example in Figure 6.17 shows the simple_error procedure from Figure 6.4 that's been changed to return a message instead of SQLCODE and SQLSTATE.

```
CREATE PROCEDURE simple_error_message ( IN p_midinit       CHAR
                                       , IN p_empno         CHAR(6)
                                       , OUT p_error_message VARCHAR(300) )
    LANGUAGE SQL
    SPECIFIC simple_error_msg                    -- applies to LUW and iSeries
-- WLM ENVIRONMENT <env>                         -- applies to zSeries
sem: BEGIN
    -- Declare condition handlers
    DECLARE EXIT HANDLER FOR SQLEXCEPTION
        GET DIAGNOSTICS EXCEPTION 1 p_error_message = MESSAGE_TEXT;
    -- Procedure logic
    SET p_error_message = '';
    UPDATE employee                              -- (1)
        SET midinit = p_midinit
      WHERE empno = p_empno;
END sem
```

Figure 6.17   A revised example of simple error checking with *MESSAGE_TEXT*.

The procedure in Figure 6.17 will return a message when an exception occurs, instead of SQLCODE and SQLSTATE, as shown in Figure 6.4. On LUW, the error message will contain both the SQLCODE and SQLSTATE inside it. Note that the MESSAGE_TEXT is not bound by 70 bytes as in the customized error messages.

To see an example of an error message, assume that the employee table is dropped after the procedure in Figure 6.17 is created. A subsequent execution of the stored procedure would result in the following message being passed in the output parameter:

```
On LUW:


SQL0727N  An error occurred during implicit system action type "1".
Information returned for the error includes SQLCODE "-204", SQLSTATE "42704"
and message tokens "DB2ADMIN.EMPLOYEE".  SQLSTATE=56098


On iSeries:


EMPLOYEE in DB2ADMIN type *FILE not found.


On zSeries:


DB2ADMIN.EMPLOYEE is an undefined name.
```

Figure 6.18   Examples of an error message.

On LUW, the message starts with a message identifier and ends with the SQLSTATE. The message identifier for SQL messages begins with a prefix (SQL) followed by a message number. The message number can be easily translated to an SQLCODE. It contains an unsigned number representing the SQLCODE and one of three letters: N, W, or C, indicating notifications, warnings or critical errors, respectively. For the SQLCODE translation, warnings imply that the sign of the SQLCODE is positive, and notifications and critical errors imply the sign of the SQLCODE is negative. The rest of the message is informative and may contain one or more tokens which are enclosed in double quotes ("). Not all messages will contain tokens.

On iSeries and zSeries, the value returned is just the informative message and may contain one or more tokens which are enclosed in double quotes ("). Similar to LUW, not all messages will contain tokens.

The DB2_TOKEN_STRING keyword of the condition-information clause in the GET DIAGNOSTICS statement of LUW and iSeries can be used to retrieve just the string of tokens without the error message. Why would you want to do this? In some cases, you may know what the message is and the action you need to take in a handler is based on the value of one of the tokens. Thus getting just the tokens would be sufficient. Alternatively, you may just want to return the SQLCODE or SQLSTATE and the string of tokens to your calling application and have your calling application's

error-handling process use the DB2 APIs (`sqlaintp()`, `sqlogstt()`) to receive the error message. In this case, when the calling application retrieves the error message, the message will have
placeholders for the tokens because the context of the original message is no longer known. This
is where the string of tokens can be used for a manual substitution. This second approach seems
like a lot of work for the calling application, but is often desired to limit the size of the parameter
being passed back.

NOTE

The mechanism for obtaining the DB2 error token string is not the same in zSeries. Instead
of using the `DB2_TOKEN_STRING` keyword, other keywords such as `DB2_RETURNED_SQLCODE`
and `RETURNED_SQLSTATE` can be used to obtain the same information. To see this in an SQL
procedure example, refer to the section "DB2 UDB for zSeries Considerations."

It may not be obvious, but being able to return both the `SQLCODE` or `SQLSTATE` and the
`DB2_TOKEN_STRING` presents a dilemma. Recall that if you want to retrieve the `SQLCODE` or `SQL-
STATE`, it needs to be accessed on the first statement after an SQL statement is executed, or be the
first statement in a handler. The same rules apply for the `GET DIAGNOSTICS` statement. So how can
we have both values related to a single statement? For LUW and iSeries, the answer is to use
nested handlers and the `RESIGNAL` statement. As for zSeries (and as an alternate solution on
iSeries), you can simply access `SQLCODE`, `SQLSTATE`, and `MESSAGE_TEXT` using a single `GET DIAG-
NOSTICS` statement. Refer to Figure 6.30 for an example.

The example in Figure 6.19 will show the procedure from Figure 6.17 rewritten to return
`SQLCODE`, `SQLSTATE`, and the string of message tokens.

```
CREATE PROCEDURE simple_error_token ( IN p_midinit      CHAR
                                     ,IN p_empno        CHAR(6)
                                     ,OUT p_sqlcode_out  INT
                                     ,OUT p_sqlstate_out CHAR(5)
                                     ,OUT p_token_string VARCHAR(100) )
    LANGUAGE SQL
    SPECIFIC simple_error_token                    -- applies to LUW and iSeries
setk: BEGIN
    -- Declare variables
    DECLARE SQLSTATE CHAR(5) DEFAULT '00000';
    DECLARE SQLCODE INT DEFAULT 0;
    -- Declare condition handlers
    DECLARE EXIT HANDLER FOR SQLEXCEPTION                              -- (1)
        BEGIN
            DECLARE CONTINUE HANDLER FOR SQLEXCEPTION                  -- (4)
                GET DIAGNOSTICS EXCEPTION 1 p_token_string = DB2_TOKEN_STRING;
            SELECT SQLCODE                                            -- (2)
```

```
              ,SQLSTATE
          INTO p_sqlcode_out
              ,p_sqlstate_out
          FROM sysibm.sysdummy1;
        RESIGNAL;                                              -- (3)
      END;
   -- Procedure logic
   SET p_token_string = '';
   VALUES (SQLCODE, SQLSTATE)
     INTO p_sqlcode_out
          ,p_sqlstate_out;
   UPDATE employee
      SET midinit = p_midinit
    WHERE empno = p_empno;
END setk
```

Figure 6.19   An example of simple error checking with *DB2_TOKEN_STRING* and nested handlers for LUW and iSeries.

Notice the EXIT handler on Line (1) contains a CONTINUE handler within it. If an error occurred, the first statement to execute within the handler—on Line (2)—will receive the SQLCODE and SQL-STATE values. The next statement to execute, on Line (3), will reissue the same error. At this point, the nested handler on Line (4) will kick in to retrieve the DB2_TOKEN_STRING. Because this handler is a CONTINUE handler, execution will continue after the RESIGNAL statement on Line (3), which is the end of the EXIT handler; thus control is returned to the calling program.

Again, to see an example of DB2_TOKEN_STRING, assume that the EMPLOYEE table is dropped after the procedure in Figure 6.19 is created. A subsequent execution of the procedure would result in the following string being passed in the p_token_string parameter:

```
LUW: 1ÿ-204ÿ42704ÿDB2ADMIN.EMPLOYEE
iSeries: DB2ADMIN.EMPLOYEEÿTABLE
```

The tokens in the string are delimited by the 'ÿ' character, 0xFF in hexadecimal, or ASCII character code 255. The LUW string contains four tokens that are substitution values for the corresponding message. The actual message was shown in Figure 6.17 with the tokens substituted. Note the order of the tokens is the substitution order.

Processing Results from Called Procedures

So far you've seen examples of passing values back to the calling program through OUT parameters in the SQL procedure declaration. You can also return values using the RETURN statement. Figure 6.20 shows the syntax diagram for the RETURN statement within a procedure.

```
>>-RETURN--+------------+-------------------------------------->< 
           '-expression-'
```

Figure 6.20   The syntax diagram for a *RETURN* statement.

It is optional to specify an expression in the RETURN statement. If an expression is provided, it must be an INTEGER, and therefore you are quite limited in what you can RETURN through this statement. The calling procedure issues GET DIAGNOSTICS with RETURN_STATUS to obtain the returned value. GET DIAGNOSTICS must be issued immediately after the CALL to a procedure.

You must be very careful when using this method for returning parameters. Typical use for this statement would be to RETURN 0 upon success and -1 on failure. In order to ensure -1 on failure, you can write a handler to catch exceptions and issue a RETURN -1 from the handler. However, this is only allowed in iSeries and zSeries. In LUW, RETURN statements are not allowed within handlers. To get around such situations, you would have to use a nested compound statement, as shown in Figure 6.21. Figure 6.31 in the section "DB2 UDB for zSeries Considerations" demonstrates an SQL procedure with the equivalent behavior for iSeries and zSeries.

```
CREATE PROCEDURE ret_value ( )
    LANGUAGE SQL
    SPECIFIC ret_value                          -- applies to LUW and iSeries
rv: BEGIN
    DECLARE v_ret_value INT DEFAULT 0;

    body: BEGIN
        DECLARE EXIT HANDLER FOR SQLEXCEPTION
            SET v_ret_value = -1;
        -- <body of procedure>;
    END body;
    RETURN v_ret_value;
END rv
```

Figure 6.21   An example of *RETURN* with a compound statement in LUW.

TIP

It is often not enough for an application to just see a return value. The application may need more information if an error occurred. The additional information can be passed back using an OUT parameter. This is shown in Figure 6.23.

The body of the procedure is within a compound statement that has a handler which sets the return value on an exception. Note that there are limitations even with this solution. For example, if you wanted to RESIGNAL an SQLSTATE to the calling program, you would not be able to do so because you cannot have a handler declared at the outermost compound statement in the procedure and still RETURN a value.

The alternative to the RETURN statement is the passing of OUT parameters in the procedure declaration, for which you've already seen many examples. What you haven't seen is an example of a CALL to another procedure, and checking the output parameters and/or return codes, as in Figure 6.22.

```
CREATE PROCEDURE call_procs (  )
    LANGUAGE SQL
    SPECIFIC call_procs                    -- applies to LUW and iSeries
 -- WLM ENVIRONMENT <env>                  -- applies to zSeries
cp: BEGIN

    DECLARE v_empno CHAR(6) DEFAULT 'A';   -- Input to get_diag()
    DECLARE v_num_rows INT;                -- Output from get_diag()
    DECLARE v_ret_value INT;               -- Return value from
ret_value()

    -- Example of a call to a procedure where a parameter is passed back in the
    --   argument list as an OUT parameter
    CALL get_diag( v_empno, v_num_rows );
    IF v_num_rows = 0 THEN
        -- <some statements>
    END IF;

    -- Example of a call to a procedure where the RETURN statement is used to
    --   return the value to the caller
    CALL ret_value();
    GET DIAGNOSTICS v_ret_value = RETURN_STATUS;
    RETURN v_ret_value;
END cp
```

Figure 6.22   An example of a stored procedure call with checking for parameters.

This example makes two calls to other procedures. The first CALL statement is a call to the get_diag procedure (shown in Figure 6.16), which passes back return values in the argument list. The second call is a call to the ret_value procedure (shown in Figure 6.21), which uses a RETURN statement to pass back a value to the calling program.

Bringing It All Together

To summarize the concepts that have been introduced in this chapter, this section presents an example that incorporates many of these concepts.

The sample procedure in Figure 6.23 shows an example of a procedure that is used to delete a row from the department table. It takes the department number to be deleted as an input parameter and returns a message as an output parameter. The row is only deleted if none of the child tables beneath it contain the department number that is to be deleted. A return value of -1 is returned if an error is encountered, 0 upon successful completion, and 1 if successful but no rows were deleted because none existed.

> **NOTE**
> Because DB2 UDB for zSeries does not support nested compound statements, the example shown in Figure 6.23 is rewritten in Figure 6.32 for zSeries.

```
CREATE PROCEDURE delete_dept ( IN p_deptno CHAR(3)
                              ,OUT p_message VARCHAR(100) )
     LANGUAGE SQL
     SPECIFIC delete_dept                          -- applies to LUW and iSeries
-----------------------------------------------------------------------
-- Procedure Description
--
-- Deletes a department, as long as there are no rows with the input
--     department number in any child tables (EMPLOYEE and PROJECT).
--
-- RETURNS:  1 if successful, but now rows existed for deletion
--           0 on successful completion
--          -1 on un-successful complete
--     SETS: Appropriate message in output parameter 'p_message'
-----------------------------------------------------------------------
dd: BEGIN
    -- Declare variables
    DECLARE SQLCODE INT DEFAULT 0;                                 -- (1)
    DECLARE SQLSTATE CHAR(5) DEFAULT '00000';
    DECLARE v_ret_value INT DEFAULT 0;
    -- In order to return a value to the calling program, the value
    --    to be returned is set in the compound statement, and possibly
    --    in a handler within the compound statement.
    body:BEGIN                                                     -- (2)
        -- Declare variables within compound statement
```

```
DECLARE v_num_rows INT DEFAULT 0;
-- Declare conditions                                          -- (3)
DECLARE c_EMP_child_rows_exist  CONDITION FOR SQLSTATE '99001';
DECLARE c_PROJ_child_rows_exist CONDITION FOR SQLSTATE '99002';
-- Declare handlers
DECLARE EXIT HANDLER FOR SQLEXCEPTION
BEGIN
    SET p_message = 'Unknown error, SQLSTATE: "' || SQLSTATE ||
                    '", SQLCODE=' || CHAR(SQLCODE);               -- (4)
    SET v_ret_value = -1;
END;
-- Declare handlers for custom conditions                      -- (5)
DECLARE EXIT HANDLER FOR c_EMP_child_rows_exist
BEGIN
    SET p_message = 'Cannot delete, child EMPLOYEE rows exist.';
    SET v_ret_value = -1;
END;
DECLARE EXIT HANDLER FOR c_PROJ_child_rows_exist
BEGIN
    SET p_message = 'Cannot delete, child PROJECT rows exist.';
    SET v_ret_value = -1;
END;

-- Child table: EMPLOYEE
SELECT COUNT(1)
  INTO v_num_rows
  FROM employee
 WHERE workdept = p_deptno;
IF v_num_rows <> 0 THEN
    SIGNAL c_EMP_child_rows_exist;                              -- (6)
END IF;

--Child table: PROJECT
SELECT COUNT(1)
  INTO v_num_rows
  FROM project
 WHERE deptno = p_deptno;
IF v_num_rows <> 0 THEN
    SIGNAL c_PROJ_child_rows_exist;                            -- (7)
END IF;
```

```
    -- No rows in dependant tables, delete department
    DELETE FROM department
     WHERE deptno = p_deptno;
    GET DIAGNOSTICS v_num_rows = ROW_COUNT;                        -- (8)


    -- Set the appropriate return message
    IF v_num_rows = 0 THEN
    BEGIN
        SET v_ret_value = 1;
        SET p_message = 'No rows exist for deletion of department '
        || p_deptno || '.';
    END;
    ELSE
        SET p_message = 'Department ' || p_deptno
        || ' successfully deleted.';
    END IF;
END body;


    RETURN v_ret_value;                                           -- (9)
END dd
```

Figure 6.23   An example for the Delete Department for LUW and iSeries.

The following notes correspond to the location numbers shown in Figure 6.23:

1. SQLCODE and SQLSTATE need to be declared, because they will be accessed in the EXIT handler on Line (4).

2. Because the SQL procedure returns a return value (in addition to an output parameter), the main logic of the procedure lies within a nested compound statement. This way, the nested statement can set the appropriate return value in an EXIT handler. The EXIT handler will continue execution at the end of the compound statement. This will then execute the RETURN statement with the appropriate value.

3. Conditions are named for customized SQLSTATES. These conditions will be used to set the appropriate error message within the handler declared on Line (5).

4. The message for non-handled conditions is constructed using SQLCODE and SQLSTATE, so the calling program can have access to it.

5. Handlers for the named conditions SET the appropriate message for the output parameter.

6. The SIGNAL statement is used to invoke the handler if child rows in the employee table are found.

7. The SIGNAL statement is used to invoke the handler if child rows in the project table are found.

8. The GET DIAGNOSTICS statement is used to determine if any rows were deleted. If no rows were deleted, then an appropriate message is sent back to the calling application.

9. The RETURN statement is used to send the return value to the calling application. At this point, the appropriate return value has been set, along with the output parameter, so all that is required is to execute the RETURN statement.

On iSeries, you can have a RETURN statement from within the handler. The example in Figure 6.23 can be changed to replace all the

```
SET v_ret_value = -1;
```

in the handlers to

```
RETURN -1;
```

Hence, the body of the procedure does not need to be nested in a BEGIN and END block as described in the second point.

DB2 UDB for iSeries Considerations

DB2 UDB for iSeries supports all of the condition handling techniques discussed in this chapter except for the RAISE_ERROR built-in function. Some other statements—namely SIGNAL, RESIGNAL, and GET DIAGNOSTICS—offer a much richer set of functionality.

SIGNAL and RESIGNAL Statements

Figure 6.24 shows the syntax diagrams for the SIGNAL and RESIGNAL statements in DB2 UDB for iSeries.

```
                      .-VALUE-.
>>-SIGNAL----+-SQLSTATE--+-------+--sqlstate-string-constant--+------------->
             '-condition-name-------------------------------'


        .-,---------------------------------------------------.
        V                                                     |
>---+-SET----+--MESSAGE_TEXT-------+-- = --+-SQL-variable-name---+-+-+------><
    |        |--CONSTRAINT CATALOG-|       | SQL-parameter-name--|   |
    |        |--CONSTRAINT SCHEMA--|       '-diagnostic-str-const'   |
    |        |--CONSTRAINT NAME----|                                |
    |        |--CATALOG NAME-------|                                |
```

```
         |              |--SCHEMA NAME--------|                    |
         |              |--TABLE NAME---------|                    |
         |              |--COLUMN NAME--------|                    |
         |              |--CURSOR NAME--------|                    |
         |              |--CLASS ORIGIN-------|                    |
         |              '--SUBCLASS ORIGIN----'                    |
         |                                                         |
         '-(--diagnostic-string-constant--)-------------------------------'

                          .-VALUE-.
>>-RESIGNAL--+-SQLSTATE--+-------+--sqlstate-string-constant--+------------->
             '-condition-name-------------------------------'


         .-,-----------------------------------------------------.
         V                                                       |
>---+-SET----+---MESSAGE_TEXT-------+-- = --+-SQL-variable-name--+-+--------><
             |--CONSTRAINT CATALOG-|        | SQL-parameter-name---|
             |--CONSTRAINT SCHEMA--|        '-diagnostic-str-const-'
             |--CONSTRAINT NAME----|
             |--CATALOG NAME-------|
             |--SCHEMA NAME--------|
             |--TABLE NAME---------|
             |--COLUMN NAME--------|
             |--CURSOR NAME--------|
             |--CLASS ORIGIN-------|
             '--SUBCLASS ORIGIN----'
```

Figure 6.24   Syntax diagrams for *SIGNAL* and *RESIGNAL* statements in DB2 UDB for iSeries.

As you can see, the SET clause allows you to assign several values related to the condition. All of these values can be accessed by the richer iSeries GET DIAGNOSTICS statement. Table 6.1, taken from the DB2 UDB for iSeries SQL Reference, gives a brief explanation for each condition information value that can be used in the GET DIAGNOSTICS statement.

The *(diagnostic string constant)* option of the SIGNAL statement is used in the CREATE TRIGGER statement only, and is provided for compatibility with other products. As a best practice, this syntax should not be used, because it does not conform to ANSI and ISO standards.

Table 6.1   Explanation of Condition Information Items

Condition Information Item	Description
MESSAGE_TEXT	Specifies a string that describes the error or warning. If an SQLCA is used, the string is returned in the SQLERRMC field of the SQLCA; if the actual length of the string is longer than 70 bytes, it is truncated without a warning.
CONSTRAINT_CATALOG	Specifies a string that indicates the name of the database that contains a constraint related to the signaled error or warning.
CONSTRAINT_SCHEMA	Specifies a string that indicates the name of the schema that contains a constraint related to the signaled error or warning.
CONSTRAINT_NAME	Specifies a string that indicates the name of a constraint related to the signaled error or warning.
CATALOG_NAME	Specifies a string that indicates the name of the database that contains a table or view related to the signaled error or warning.
SCHEMA_NAME	Specifies a string that indicates the name of the schema that contains a table or view related to the signaled error or warning.
TABLE_NAME	Specifies a string that indicates the name of a table or view related to the signaled error or warning.
COLUMN_NAME	Specifies a string that indicates the name of a column in the table or view related to the signaled error or warning.
CURSOR_NAME	Specifies a string that indicates the name of a cursor related to the signaled error or warning.
CLASS ORIGIN	Specifies a string that indicates the origin of the SQLSTATE class related to the signaled error or warning.
SUBCLASS ORIGIN	Specifies a string that indicates the origin of the SQLSTATE subclass related to the signaled error or warning.

RAISE_ERROR Function

Recall that the RAISE_ERROR function is not supported in DB2 UDB for iSeries. Figure 6.25 demonstrates how you can rewrite the SQL procedure in Figure 6.14 by using the SIGNAL statement to provide the same behavior.

```
CREATE PROCEDURE app_raise_error2 ( IN p_admrdept      CHAR(3)
                                   ,OUT p_sqlstate_out CHAR(5)
                                   ,OUT p_sqlcode_out  INT )
        LANGUAGE SQL
```

```
   SPECIFIC app_raise_error
ae: BEGIN
   -- Declare variables
   DECLARE SQLSTATE CHAR(5) DEFAULT '00000';
   DECLARE SQLCODE INT DEFAULT 0;
   -- Declare handlers
   DECLARE EXIT HANDLER FOR SQLEXCEPTION                               -- (1)
      SELECT SQLSTATE, SQLCODE
        INTO p_sqlstate_out
            ,p_sqlcode_out
         FROM sysibm.sysdummy1;

   IF p_admrdept NOT IN ('A00', 'B01', 'C01', 'D01') THEN
     SIGNAL SQLSTATE '70001' SET MESSAGE_TEXT = 'ADMRDEPT does not exist';
   END IF;

   UPDATE department
     SET LOCATION =
           (CASE WHEN p_admrdept = 'A00' THEN 'Boston'                 -- (2)
                 WHEN p_admrdept = 'B01' THEN 'Chicago'
                 WHEN p_admrdept = 'C01' THEN 'Dallas'
                 WHEN p_admrdept = 'D01' THEN 'San Mateo'              -- (3)
           END);
END ae
```

Figure 6.25   An example of an alternative in iSeries to the *RAISE_ERROR* function.

The main difference is that RAISE_ERROR is a function and can be embedded in a statement, whereas SIGNAL is a separate statement altogether.

GET DIAGNOSTICS

The GET DIAGNOSTICS statement in DB2 UDB for iSeries has been greatly enhanced. Figure 6.26 shows the syntax diagram for the statement.

```
        .--CURRENT--.
>>-GET--+-----------+--DIAGNOSTICS-+---statement-information--+----->< 
        '--STACKED--'              |--condition-information--|
                                   '--combined-information---'
```

```
statement-information
   .-,-----------------------------------------------------------.
   V                                                             |
|----+--SQL-variable-name----+-=--+---statement-information-item--+--|
     '--SQL-parameter-name---'
condition-information

|-CONDITION---+--+--SQL-variable-name----+---+----------------------->
              |  '--SQL-parameter-name---'   |
              '--integer--------------------'


   .-,-----------------------------------------------------------.
   V                                                             |
>----+--SQL-variable-name----+-=--+--connection-information-item--+--|
     '--SQL-parameter-name---'    '--condition-information-item---'


combined-information

|--+--SQL-variable-name----+-- = ----------------------------------->
   '--SQL-parameter-name---'


>-ALL--+-----------------------------------------------------------------+--|
       |    .-,---------------------------------------------------.      |
       |    V                                                     |      |
       '---'----+--STATEMENT-------------------------------------+--+--'
                '--+--CONDITION---+---+----------------------------+--'
                   '--CONNECTION--'   |--+--SQL-variable-name----+--|
                                      |  '--SQL-parameter-name---'  |
                                      '--integer--------------------
```

Figure 6.26 A simplified *GET DIAGNOSTICS* syntax diagram for iSeries.

The GET DIAGNOSTICS statement can be used to obtain a lot of information about the SQL statement that was just executed. The CURRENT keyword retrieves information about the last SQL statement (not a GET DIAGNOSTIC statement) that executed. The STACKED keyword can only be used from inside a handler, and obtains information on the last SQL statement prior to the handler invocation.

The type of information available is divided into three parts: statement information, connection information, and condition information. It is accessed using the appropriate clause. A clause to obtain the combined information is also provided. The examples in this chapter have shown how to obtain condition-related information. The keyword CONDITION is a synonym for EXCEPTION. Hence, the statement

```
GET DIAGNOSTICS EXCEPTION 1 p_error_message = MESSAGE_TEXT
```

is the same as

```
GET DIAGNOSTICS CONDITION 1 p_error_message = MESSAGE_TEXT
```

Table 6.2 lists all the keywords for information that can be obtained using the GET DIAGNOSTICS statement.

Table 6.2   Information Available from the iSeries *GET DIAGNOSTICS* Statement

Information Type	Information Keyword
STATEMENT	COMMAND_FUNCTION_CODE
	DB2_DIAGNOSTIC_CONVERSION_ERROR
	DB2_LAST_ROW
	DB2_NUMBER_CONNECTIONS
	DB2_NUMBER_PARAMETER_MARKERS
	DB2_NUMBER_RESULT_SETS
	DB2_NUMBER_ROWS
	DB2_NUMBER_SUCCESSFUL_SUBSTMTS
	DB2_RELATIVE_COST_ESTIMATE
	DB2_RETURN_STATUS
	DB2_ROW_COUNT_SECONDARY
	DB2_ROW_LENGTH
	DB2_SQL_ATTR_CONCURRENCY
	DB2_SQL_ATTR_CURSOR_CAPABILITY
	DB2_SQL_ATTR_CURSOR_HOLD
	DB2_SQL_ATTR_CURSOR_ROWSET
	DB2_SQL_ATTR_CURSOR_SCROLLABLE

Information Type	Information Keyword
	DB2_SQL_ATTR_CURSOR_SENSITIVITY
	DB2_SQL_ATTR_CURSOR_TYPE
	DYNAMIC_FUNCTION
	DYNAMIC_FUNCTION_CODE
	MORE
	NUMBER
	ROW_COUNT
	TRANSACTION_ACTIVE
	TRANSACTIONS_COMMITTED
	TRANSACTIONS_ROLLED_BACK
CONNECTION	CONNECTION_NAME
	DB2_AUTHENTICATION_TYPE
	DB2_AUTHID_TRUNCATION
	DB2_AUTHORIZATION_ID
	DB2_CONNECTION_METHOD
	DB2_CONNECTION_NUMBER
	DB2_CONNECTION_STATE
	DB2_CONNECTION_STATUS
	DB2_CONNECTION_TYPE
	DB2_DDM_SERVER_CLASS_NAME
	DB2_DYN_QUERY_MGMT
	DB2_ENCRYPTION_TYPE
	DB2_EXPANSION_FACTOR_FROM
	DB2_EXPANSION_FACTOR_TO
	DB2_PRODUCT_ID
	DB2_SERVER_CLASS_NAME
	DB2_SERVER_NAME
	DB2_USER_ID

Information Type	Information Keyword
CONDITION	CATALOG_NAME
	CLASS_ORIGIN
	COLUMN_NAME
	CONDITION_IDENTIFIER
	CONDITION_NUMBER
	CONSTRAINT_CATALOG
	CONSTRAINT_NAME
	CONSTRAINT_SCHEMA
	CURSOR_NAME
	DB2_ERROR_CODE1
	DB2_ERROR_CODE2
	DB2_ERROR_CODE3
	DB2_ERROR_CODE4
	DB2_INTERNAL_ERROR_POINTER
	DB2_LINE_NUMBER
	DB2_MESSAGE_ID
	DB2_MESSAGE_ID1
	DB2_MESSAGE_ID2
	DB2_MESSAGE_KEY
	DB2_MODULE_DETECTING_ERROR
	DB2_NUMBER_FAILING_STATEMENTS
	DB2_OFFSET
	DB2_ORDINAL_TOKEN_n
	DB2_PARTITION_NUMBER
	DB2_REASON_CODE
	DB2_RETURNED_SQLCODE
	DB2_ROW_NUMBER
	DB2_SQLERRD_SET

Information Type	Information Keyword
	DB2_SQLERRD1
	DB2_SQLERRD2
	DB2_SQLERRD3
	DB2_SQLERRD4
	DB2_SQLERRD5
	DB2_SQLERRD6
	DB2_TOKEN_COUNT
	DB2_TOKEN_STRING
	MESSAGE_LENGTH
	MESSAGE_OCTET_LENGTH
	MESSAGE_TEXT
	PARAMETER_MODE
	PARAMETER_NAME
	PARAMETER_ORDINAL_POSITION
	RETURNED_SQLSTATE
	ROUTINE_CATALOG
	ROUTINE_NAME
	ROUTINE_SCHEMA
	SCHEMA_NAME
	SERVER_NAME
	SPECIFIC_NAME
	SUBCLASS_ORIGIN
	TABLE_NAME
	TRIGGER_CATALOG
	TRIGGER_NAME
	TRIGGER_SCHEMA
	CATALOG_NAME

Figure 6.30 in the next section provides an example of how the GET DIAGNOSTICS statement can be used to obtain several pieces of diagnostic information in one statement. Refer to the DB2 UDB for iSeries SQL Reference manual for a detailed description for each of these options.

DB2 UDB for zSeries Considerations

Most of the material discussed in this chapter thus far applies to DB2 UDB for zSeries. In this section, few considerations that are specific to zSeries are highlighted.

Condition Handlers

Chapter 4, "Using Flow of Control Statements," mentioned that SQL PL does not require the use of a compound statement to execute more than one statement in a branch of a conditional statement. Thus, if you enclose multiple statements within an IF statement, where the condition is always true, you will in fact be able to code several statements inside a condition handler. Figure 6.27 shows an example of this implementation.

```
CREATE PROCEDURE simple_error (IN p_midinit CHAR
                             ,IN p_empno CHAR(6) )
WLM ENVIRONMENT <env>
LANGUAGE SQL
se: BEGIN
   DECLARE SQLSTATE CHAR(5) DEFAULT '00000';
   DECLARE SQLCODE INT DEFAULT 0;
   DECLARE CONTINUE HANDLER FOR SQLEXCEPTION
       IF 1=1 THEN                  -- (1)
           SET ...;
           SET ...;
           SELECT * INTO ...;
           RETURN ...;
       END IF;
   UPDATE employee
      SET midinit = p_midinit
    WHERE empno = p_empno;
END se
```

Figure 6.27   An example of Implementation #1 to code several statements within a condition handler in DB2 for zSeries.

On Line (1), we use the IF condition statement to allow for multiple statements to be coded within the handler. The condition 1=1 always resolves to true, which means all of these statements are always executed.

Another option is to use the handler to set up a flag variable which can be tested with an IF statement after exiting the handler. Figure 6.28 shows an example of this option.

```
CREATE PROCEDURE simple_error (IN p_midinit CHAR
                              ,IN p_empno CHAR(6) )
WLM ENVIRONMENT <env>
LANGUAGE SQL
se: BEGIN
   DECLARE v_flag   SMALLINT DEFAULT 0;
   DECLARE SQLSTATE CHAR(5) DEFAULT '00000';
   DECLARE SQLCODE INT DEFAULT 0;
   DECLARE CONTINUE HANDLER FOR SQLEXCEPTION
          SET v_flag = 1;                      -- (1)
   UPDATE employee
      SET midinit = p_midinit
    WHERE empno = p_empno;
   IF v_flag = 1 THEN                          -- (2)
      . . . ;                                  -- (3)
   END IF;
END se
```

Figure 6.28   An example of Implementation #2 to code several statements within a condition handler in DB2 for zSeries.

On Line (1), we use the condition handler to set the variable v_flag to 1. Later on Line (2), we test if v_flag has a value of 1 and if it does, on Line (3) we perform multiple statements. Later in Figure 6.30, you will see a more complex example which will cover this issue in more detail.

Depending on the type of condition handler and what you are trying to accomplish, you may need to modify the previous example accordingly. Normally you will have to change EXIT handlers to CONTINUE handlers.

Another consideration to keep in mind if you need to set several variables within a condition handler is to use the statements VALUES INTO or SELECT INTO, which allow you to set several variables in one statement.

GET DIAGNOSTICS Statement

The GET DIAGNOSTICS statement has been enhanced considerably in zSeries. Figure 6.29 shows the syntax diagram for the statement.

```
>>-GET-DIAGNOSTICS----+--statement-information--+------------------><
                      |--condition-information--|
                      '--combined-information---'
```

```
statement-information

   .-,-----------------------------------------------------------.
   V                                                             |
|----+---host-variable1-------+-=---+--statement-information-item--+--|
     '----host-variable1--------=---+-DB2_GET_DIAGNOSTICS_DIAGNOSTICS---+'
condition-information

|-CONDITION---+--+--host-variable2-------+---+----------------------->
              '--integer--------------------'


   .-,-----------------------------------------------------------.
   V                                                             |
>----+-----host-variable3----+-=---+--condition-information-item---+-|
                             '--connection-information-item--'


combined-information

|--+--host-variable4------------+-- = ------------------------------------>

>-ALL--+-------------------------------------------------------------+--|
       |   .-,-----------------------------------------------------------. |
       |   V                                                             | |
       '---'----+--STATEMENT---------------------------------------+--+--'
                '--+--CONDITION---+--+----------------------------+--'
                   '--CONNECTION--'  |--+--SQL-variable-name-----+--|
                                     '--integer--------------'
```

Figure 6.29   A simplified *GET DIAGNOSTICS* syntax diagram for zSeries.

The type of information is divided into three parts: statement information, connection information, and condition information. Table 6.3 lists all the keywords for information that can be obtained using the GET DIAGNOSTICS statement.

Table 6.3   Information Available from the zSeries *GET DIAGNOSTICS* Statement

Information Type	Information Keyword
STATEMENT	DB2_LAST_ROW
	DB2_NUMBER_PARAMETER_MARKERS
	DB2_NUMBER_RESULT_SETS

Information Type	Information Keyword
	DB2_RETURN_STATUS
	DB2_SQL_ATTR_CURSOR_HOLD
	DB2_SQL_ATTR_CURSOR_ROWSET
	DB2_SQL_ATTR_CURSOR_SCROLLABLE
	DB2_SQL_ATTR_CURSOR_SENSITIVITY
	DB2_SQL_ATTR_CURSOR_TYPE
	MORE
	NUMBER
	ROW_COUNT
CONNECTION	DB2_AUTHENTICATION_TYPE
	DB2_AUTHORIZATION_ID
	DB2_CONNECTION_STATE
	DB2_CONNECTION_STATUS
	DB2_CONNECTION_TYPE
	DB2_DDM_SERVER_CLASS_NAME
	DB2_PRODUCT_ID
CONDITION	CATALOG_NAME
	CONDITION_NUMBER
	CURSOR_NAME
	DB2_ERROR_CODE1
	DB2_ERROR_CODE2
	DB2_ERROR_CODE3
	DB2_ERROR_CODE4
	DB2_INTERNAL_ERROR_POINTER
	DB2_MESSAGE_ID
	DB2_MODULE_DETECTING_ERROR
	DB2_ORDINAL_TOKEN_n
	DB2_REASON_CODE

Information Type	Information Keyword
	DB2_RETURNED_SQLCODE
	DB2_ROW_NUMBER
	DB2_SQLERRD_SET
	DB2_SQLERRD1
	DB2_SQLERRD2
	DB2_SQLERRD3
	DB2_SQLERRD4
	DB2_SQLERRD5
	DB2_SQLERRD6
	DB2_TOKEN_COUNT
	MESSAGE_TEXT
	RETURNED_SQLSTATE
	SERVER_NAME

Some options discussed earlier for LUW also apply except that MESSAGE_TEXT in zSeries returns only the message text, not the SQLCODE or SQLSTATE. For the example shown earlier where MESSAGE_TEXT returned

```
SQL0727N  An error occurred during implicit system action type "1".  Information
returned for the error includes SQLCODE "-204", SQLSTATE "42704" and message
tokens "DB2ADMIN.EMPLOYEE".  SQLSTATE=56098
```

DB2 for zSeries would only return:

```
DB2ADMIN.EMPLOYEE IS AN UNDEFINED NAME
```

As indicated earlier, the keyword DB2_TOKEN_STRING is not supported in DB2 UDB for zSeries. However, a combination of other different keywords may provide similar information. Figure 6.30 shows an example where an SQL procedure returns the SQLCODE, SQLSTATE, and message text information. This SQL procedure also reflects the way procedure simple_error_token shown in Figure 6.19 would be written in zSeries. Note that this procedure also works for iSeries.

```
CREATE PROCEDURE simple_error_token ( IN  p_midinit       CHAR
                                    , IN  p_empno         CHAR(6)
                                    , OUT p_sqlcode_out   INT
                                    , OUT p_sqlstate_out  CHAR(5)
```

```
                                     ,OUT p_token_string VARCHAR(100) )
    LANGUAGE SQL
 -- SPECIFIC simple_error_token                      -- applies to iSeries
    WLM ENVIRONMENT <env>                            -- applies to zSeries
setk: BEGIN
    -- Declare variables
    DECLARE SQLSTATE CHAR(5) DEFAULT '00000';
    DECLARE SQLCODE  INT     DEFAULT 0;
    -- Declare condition handlers
    DECLARE EXIT HANDLER FOR SQLEXCEPTION
        GET DIAGNOSTICS EXCEPTION 1  p_sqlcode_out   = DB2_RETURNED_SQLCODE,
                                     p_sqlstate_out  = RETURNED_SQLSTATE,
                                     p_token_string  = MESSAGE_TEXT;   -- (1)
    -- Procedure logic
    SET p_token_string = '';
    VALUES (SQLCODE, SQLSTATE)
      INTO p_sqlcode_out
          ,p_sqlstate_out;
    UPDATE employee
      SET midinit = p_midinit
    WHERE empno = p_empno;
END setk
```

Figure 6.30 The *GET DIAGNOSTICS* statement in DB2 for zSeries and iSeries.

On Line (1), you can see that the GET DIAGNOSTICS statement can return several values in one statement. Alternatively, the following options return several groups of values at once:

```
GET DIAGNOSTICS p_error_message = ALL STATEMENT;
GET DIAGNOSTICS p_error_message = ALL CONNECTION;
GET DIAGNOSTICS p_error_message = ALL CONDITION;
```

For example, the ALL CONDITION keyword may return something like the following:

```
CONDITION_NUMBER=1; DB2_RETURNED_SQLCODE=204; RETURNED_SQLSTATE=42704;
DB2_REASON_CODE=0; DB2_ROW_NUMBER=00;DB2_ERROR_CODE1=-
500;DB2_ERROR_CODE2=0;DB2_ERROR_CODE3=0; DB2_ERROR_CODE4=-1; DB2_SQLERRD1=-
500;DB2_SQLERRD2=0;DB2_SQLERRD3=0;DB2_SQLERRD4=-1; DB2_SQLERRD5=0;
DB2_SQLERRD6=0; DB2_INTERNAL_ERROR_POINTER=-
500;DB2_MODULE_DETECTING_ERROR=DSNXOTL ;MESSAGE_ID=DSN00204E ;
SERVER_NAME=MEXICO;DB2_ORDINAL_TOKEN_1
=TS56692.EMPLOYEE;MESSAGE_TEXT=TS56692.EMPLOYEE IS AN UNDEFINED
NAME;CURSOR_NAME= ;
```

For the complete set of keywords that are allowed, refer to the DB2 UDB for z/OS Version 8 SQL Reference Guide.

RETURN Statement

In DB2 UDB for zSeries, a RETURN statement can be coded within a condition handler. Therefore, the stored procedure ret_value shown in Figure 6.21 can be rewritten as shown in Figure 6.31. This also works for iSeries.

```
CREATE PROCEDURE ret_value (   )
    LANGUAGE SQL
 -- SPECIFIC ret_value                          -- applies to iSeries
    WLM ENVIRONMENT <env>                        -- applies to zSeries
rv: BEGIN
    DECLARE EXIT HANDLER FOR SQLEXCEPTION
            RETURN -1;
    <body of procedure>;
END rv
```

Figure 6.31   The *RETURN* statement within a condition handler in DB2 for zSeries and iSeries.

Figure 6.32 shows one way in which the SQL procedure delete_dept (originally shown in Figure 6.23) can be rewritten in DB2 UDB for zSeries.

```
CREATE PROCEDURE delete_dept ( IN p_deptno CHAR(3)
                             ,OUT p_message VARCHAR(100) )
LANGUAGE SQL
WLM ENVIRONMENT <env>
----------------------------------------------------------------------
-- Procedure Description
--
-- Deletes a department, as long as there are no rows with the input
--    department number in any child tables (EMPLOYEE and PROJECT).
--
-- RETURNS:  1 if successful, but now rows existed for deletion
--            0 on successful completion
--            -1 on un-successful complete
--     SETS: Appropriate message in output parameter 'p_message'
----------------------------------------------------------------------
dd: BEGIN
    -- Declare variables
```

```
DECLARE SQLCODE          INT     DEFAULT 0;
DECLARE SQLSTATE         CHAR(5) DEFAULT '00000';
DECLARE v_ret_value      INT     DEFAULT 0;
DECLARE v_num_rows       INT     DEFAULT 0;

-- Declare conditions
DECLARE c_EMP_child_rows_exist  CONDITION FOR SQLSTATE '99001';
DECLARE c_PROJ_child_rows_exist CONDITION FOR SQLSTATE '99002';

-- Declare handlers
DECLARE CONTINUE HANDLER FOR SQLEXCEPTION                         -- (1)
     VALUES ('Unknown error, SQLSTATE: "' ||
             SQLSTATE || '", SQLCODE=' || CHAR(SQLCODE), -1)
        INTO  p_message, v_ret_value;                            -- (2)

-- Declare handlers for custom conditions
DECLARE EXIT HANDLER FOR c_EMP_child_rows_exist, c_PROJ_child_rows_exist
        RETURN -1;                                               -- (3)

-- Child table: EMPLOYEE
SELECT COUNT(1)
  INTO v_num_rows
  FROM employee
 WHERE workdept = p_deptno;
 IF v_ret_value = -1 THEN GOTO BYE; END IF;                      -- (4)

 IF v_num_rows <> 0 THEN
    SET p_message = 'Cannot delete, child EMPLOYEE rows exist.';
    SIGNAL c_EMP_child_rows_exist;
 END IF;

 --Child table: PROJECT
 SELECT COUNT(1)
   INTO v_num_rows
   FROM project
  WHERE deptno = p_deptno;
 IF v_ret_value = -1 THEN GOTO BYE; END IF;                      -- (5)

 IF v_num_rows <> 0 THEN
    SET p_message = 'Cannot delete, child PROJECT rows exist.';
```

```
        SIGNAL c_PROJ_child_rows_exist;
    END IF;


    DELETE FROM department
        WHERE deptno = p_deptno;
    GET DIAGNOSTICS v_num_rows = ROW_COUNT;
    IF v_ret_value = -1 THEN GOTO BYE; END IF;                        -- (6)


    -- Set the appropriate return message
    IF v_num_rows = 0 THEN
        SET v_ret_value = 1;
        SET p_message = 'No rows exist for deletion of department '
        || p_deptno || '.';
    ELSE
        SET p_message = 'Department ' || p_deptno || ' successfully deleted.';
    END IF;


    LEAVE dd;                                                        -- (7)
BYE: RETURN -1;                                                      -- (8)
END dd
```

Figure 6.32   Rewriting *delete_dept* SQL procedure in DB2 UDB for zSeries.

The following notes correspond to the location numbers shown in Figure 6.32:

1. Because nested compound statements are not allowed in DB2 for zSeries, only one statement can be coded within a handler; thus, we were unable to set a variable, and at the same time RETURN -1. The IF statement workaround to code several statements within a condition handler is not used in this implementation. The handler was changed from an EXIT handler in the original implementation to a CONTINUE handler, and test conditions where added in Lines (5), (6), and (7). These test conditions would determine if the CONTINUE handler was invoked and if it was, the rest of the instructions would be skipped and a -1 would be returned as indicated by the BYE label.

2. VALUES INTO and SELECT INTO are handy statements to use within a condition handler because only one statement is allowed inside it, and these statements can set several variables at once.

3. Note that a RETURN statement can be coded within a condition handler in DB2 for zSeries.

4. We tested to see if the CONTINUE handler was invoked. If it was, then we should go to the BYE label and return -1.

5. Same as Line (4).

6. Same as (4)

7. This is required so that the BYE label is only reached when the condition handler was invoked, as tested in Lines (4), (5), and (6).

8. The label BYE should only be reached based on the tests performed in Lines (4), (5), and (6).

Summary

This chapter has shown some techniques for handling exceptions and completion conditions within DB2 SQL procedures. Basic definitions of SQLCODE and SQLSTATE were provided, followed by a description of how to use them in conjunction with condition handlers. Different types of handlers can be declared—namely EXIT, CONTINUE, and UNDO handlers (the UNDO handler is not supported in DB2 UDB for zSeries). The scope of a condition handler is the compound statement in which the handler is declared.

The concept of naming specific conditions was also described. In addition to making the stored procedure code more readable, the ability to name conditions is useful for specifying user-defined conditions. Additionally, the SIGNAL and RESIGNAL statements were discussed to show how you could force a condition in the SQL procedure body by specifying an SQLSTATE or a named condition.

Finally, passing parameters back to calling procedures and retrieving return values from called procedures were considered. The RETURN statement can be used for returning values, and the GET DIAGNOSTICS statement is used to receive the returned value. The GET DIAGNOSTICS statements in DB2 UDB for iSeries and zSeries are more comprehensive, which allows you to obtain information about a statement, a connection, and a condition.

If non-integer or multiple values need to be passed back to a calling application, OUT parameters can always be used.

Working with Dynamic SQL

In this chapter, you will learn

- The two phases of processing an SQL statement
- The difference between dynamic SQL and static SQL
- When and how to use dynamic SQL with the EXECUTE IMMEDIATE statement
- When and how to use dynamic SQL with PREPARE and EXECUTE
- The use of dynamic SQL in cursors
- How to use dynamic CALL statements
- The use of dynamic SQL for DDL
- How to use the escape character in dynamic SQL
- How to use the package cache

Dynamic SQL is a method of SQL programming that allows you to write robust and flexible code. So far, only static SQL has been used in our SQL procedures, and the distinction between dynamic SQL and static SQL has not been made. At this stage, you may not even know that SQL can be classified as static or dynamic, but don't worry—such details will be covered first. Then, this chapter will discuss the different ways of using dynamic SQL in SQL procedures. Then we will highlight restrictions and advanced techniques of using dynamic SQL.

PREPARE and *EXECUTE*: The Two Phases of Any SQL Statement

An SQL statement can be viewed as an operation requested from the application to the database engine, be it to retrieve data, perform an insert, or update existing data. Whenever you submit an SQL statement to DB2, it passes through two general phases called PREPARE and EXECUTE. For the purpose of this discussion, PREPARE and EXECUTE will be discussed in the context of SELECT (that is, retrieving data), but the concepts can be applied to INSERT and UPDATE SQL statements just as easily.

In the PREPARE phase, the DB2 query optimizer examines the SQL statement and determines the most efficient method to retrieve the requested data. Many decisions need to be considered by the optimizer, such as

- Is the query syntax valid and is the query semantically correct?
- How can the query be rewritten so that it can be more easily optimized?
- What is the best index or combination of indexes to use?
- For queries that join tables, in what order should they be joined to minimize disk I/O or optimize memory usage?

The method by which DB2 chooses to retrieve the data is called an **access plan**. Once the optimal access plan has been determined, the query enters the EXECUTE phase. In the EXECUTE phase, the database uses the access plan to fetch the data.

Dynamic SQL Versus Static SQL

In the context of application development, queries can be classified as either dynamic SQL or static SQL. In other words, applications are said to use dynamic SQL, static SQL, or both. Both dynamic and static SQL must go through the PREPARE and EXECUTE phases described in the previous section.

In order to use a static SQL statement, the complete statement must be specified. The names of the tables and columns as well as the data types being reference are known. The only information that can be specified at runtime are values in the WHERE clause of the SQL statement using host variables. Once an access plan for a static SQL is generated, it is stored in the database. The plan is persistent and reusable as long as the same static SQL statement is issued.

Dynamic SQL statements are dynamically processed at run time. Unlike static SQL, the statement structure is not required when the application is precompiled. Dynamic SQL statements are always prepared before execution, whether or not the same statement (and hence the same access plan) is used over and over again. To minimize the preparation cost, DB2 keeps frequently used access plans in the **package cache** (also known as **query cache**). The package cache significantly reduces the cost of repeated SQL requests, but there is still the overhead of issuing and responding to prepare requests.

Writing statements using static SQL, as you can imagine, can yield performance benefits at execution time because DB2 no longer has to "think" about how to resolve the statement.

Dynamic SQL, however, offers flexibility of building an SQL statement at design time that is not possible with static SQL.

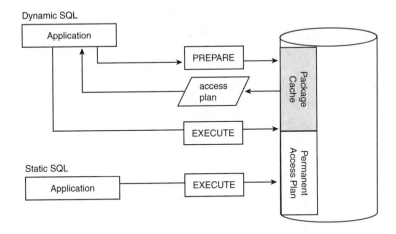

Figure 7.1   Visual comparison of the difference between dynamic and static SQL.

Up to this point in the book, the examples presented have all used static SQL. Programming interfaces such as JDBC, CLI, and ODBC, however, generally use dynamic SQL.

TIP

Dynamic SQL does not necessarily mean that you must take a performance hit relative to static SQL. For applications that use a set of queries very frequently, their access plans are kept and reused in the DB2's package cache (known as **EDM statement cache** in zSeries and **plan cache** in iSeries). The first execution of any given query, however, must incur the full cost of the PREPARE phase.

Static SQL is fast and easy to program in SQL procedures, but there are circumstances where static SQL cannot be used. The most common need for dynamic SQL is when the final form of a query is not known at application design time. In such cases, static SQL is not an option.

Restrictions and Considerations

When you are considering dynamic SQL over static SQL or vice versa, you should also understand that dynamic SQL uses only statements that can be dynamically prepared. Hence, dynamic SQL must be any of the following statements shown in Table 7.1

Table 7.1   Statements That Can Be Dynamically Prepared

Statement	LUW	iSeries	zSeries
ALLOCATE CURSOR	N	NA	Y
ALTER	Y	Y	Y
ASSOCIATE LOCATOR	N	NA	Y
CALL	Y	Y	N
CLOSE	Y	N	N
COMMENT	Y	Y	Y
COMMIT	Y	Y	Y
CONNECT	Y	N	N
CREATE	Y	Y	Y
DECLARE GLOBAL TEMPORARY TABLE	Y	Y	Y
DELETE	Y	Y	Y
DESCRIBE	N	N	N
DISCONNECT	N	N	NA
DROP	Y	Y	Y
EXECUTE	N	N	N
EXECUTE IMMEDIATE	Y	N	N
EXPLAIN	Y	NA	Y
FETCH	N	N	N
FLUSH EVENT MONITOR	Y	NA	NA
FREE LOCATOR	Y	Y	Y
GET DIAGNOSTICS	N	N	N
GRANT	Y	Y	Y
HOLD LOCATOR	N	Y	Y
INSERT	Y	Y	Y
LABEL	N	Y	Y
LOCK TABLE	Y	Y	Y
OPEN	N	N	N

Statement	LUW	iSeries	zSeries
PREPARE	N	N	N
REFRESH TABLE	Y	Y	Y
RELEASE (*Connection*)	N	N	N
RELEASE SAVEPOINT	Y	Y	Y
RENAME INDEX	Y	Y	NA
RENAME TABLE	Y	Y	Y
RENAME TABLESPACE	Y	Y	Y
ROLLBACK	Y	Y	Y
SAVEPOINT	Y	Y	Y
SELECT (statement)	Y	Y	Y
SELECT INTO	Y	N	N
SET CONNECTION	Y	N	N
SET CURRENT APPLICATION ENCODING SCHEME	N	NA	N
SET CURRENT DEFAULT TRANSFORM GROUP	Y	NA	NA
SET CURRENT DEGREE	Y	NA	Y
SET CURRENT EXPLAIN MODE	Y	NA	NA
SET CURRENT EXPLAIN SNAPSHOT	Y	NA	NA
SET CURRENT LOCALE LC_CTYPE	N	NA	Y
SET CURRENT MAINTAINED TABLE TYPES FOR OPTIMIZATION	Y	NA	Y
SET CURRENT OPTIMIZATION HINT	N	NA	Y
SET CURRENT PACKAGE PATH	N	NA	N
SET CURRENT PACKAGESET	N	NA	N
SET CURRENT PRECISION	N	NA	Y
SET CURRENT QUERY OPTIMIZATION	Y	NA	NA
SET CURRENT REFRESH AGE	Y	NA	Y
SET CURRENT RULES	N	NA	Y

Statement	LUW	iSeries	zSeries
SET CURRENT SQLID	N	NA	Y
SET ENCRYPTION PASSWORD	N	Y	Y
SET EVENT MONITOR STATE	Y	NA	NA
SET INTEGRITY	Y	NA	NA
SET PASSTHRU	Y	NA	NA
SET PATH	Y	Y	Y
SET RESULT SETS	NA	N	NA
SET SCHEMA	Y	Y	Y
SET SERVER OPTION	Y	NA	NA
SET TRANSACTION	N	Y	NA
SIGNAL SQLSTATE	N	N	N
UPDATE	Y	Y	Y
VALUES INTO	N	Y	N

Different methods are available for you to work with dynamic SQL in SQL procedures, and the following subsections will discuss each in turn.

NOTE
On zSeries, some statements can be dynamically prepared only if DYNAMICRULES run behavior is implicitly or explicitly specified. Refer to the corresponding SQL Reference manual for details.

Using Dynamic SQL with *EXECUTE IMMEDIATE*

The EXECUTE IMMEDIATE statement is the simplest way to use dynamic SQL. This method tells DB2 to perform the PREPARE and EXECUTE phase for the SQL statement in one step (see Figure 7.2).

```
>>-EXECUTE--IMMEDIATE--sql-statement------->< 
```

Figure 7.2   The syntax diagram for *EXECUTE IMMEDIATE*.

Figure 7.2 shows the syntax diagram for EXECUTE IMMEDIATE. The *sql-statement* parameter is required for the EXECUTE IMMEDIATE statement and is a VARCHAR parameter that contains the dynamic SQL statement you want to execute.

You would use EXECUTE IMMEDIATE if

- You want to execute DML or DDL using dynamic SQL.
- The SQL statement only needs to be executed once or infrequently.
- The SQL statement is not a SELECT statement.

Consider Figure 7.3 that shows the updated employee table and where conditions of the update are generated at runtime.

```
CREATE PROCEDURE CHANGE_BONUS ( IN p_new_bonus DECIMAL
                             , IN p_where_cond VARCHAR(1000)
                             , OUT p_num_changes INT )
    LANGUAGE SQL
    SPECIFIC change_bonus1                      -- applies to LUW and iSeries
 -- WLM ENVIRONMENT <env>                       -- applies to zSeries

cb: BEGIN

    DECLARE v_dynSQL VARCHAR(1000);                         -- (1)

    SET v_dynSQL = 'UPDATE EMPLOYEE SET BONUS = ' ||        -- (2)
                CHAR(p_new_bonus) || ' WHERE ' ||
                p_where_cond;

    EXECUTE IMMEDIATE v_dynSQL;                             -- (3)

    GET DIAGNOSTICS p_num_changes = row_count;
END cb
```

Figure 7.3 *An example of EXECUTE IMMEDIATE to execute dynamic SQL.*

In Figure 7.3, the SQL procedure CHANGE_BONUS takes two input parameters. The IN parameters, p_new_bonus and p_where_cond, specify the new bonus value and the WHERE condition for the change in bonus, respectively. The OUT parameter p_num_changes returns to the SQL procedure caller the number of records that were updated by the SQL procedure.

A variable called v_dynSQL used to store the dynamic SQL statement text is declared on Line (1). The variable is declared with a size that is sufficiently large enough to hold the entire statement. Otherwise, the SQL string is automatically truncated to fit. Next, the base UPDATE statement with two IN parameters is concatenated to produce the final SQL statement shown on Line (2). Finally, the UPDATE statement stored in the variable v_dynSQL on Line (3) is prepared and executed using the EXECUTE IMMEDIATE command.

Here is an example showing how to call the SQL procedure `change_bonus`. Establish a connection from the command line to the sample database. Then, execute the following CALL statement:

```
CALL CHANGE_BONUS (1000, 'year(hiredate) < 1975', ?)
```

The procedure `change_bonus` is invoked to give every employee who was hired before 1975 a bonus of 1000. Notice that a question mark is used as a placeholder for the OUT parameter. Calling the SQL procedure from the command line will result in output that is similar to the following:

```
Value of output parameters
  --------------------------
  Parameter Name   : P_NUM_CHANGES
  Parameter Value : 20

  Return Status = 0
```

From the output, 20 rows were updated by the SQL procedure.

Escaping Single Quotes (')

Let's look at a slightly modified version of the SQL from Figure 7.3. Consider the following UPDATE statement:

```
SET v_dynSQL = 'UPDATE EMPLOYEE SET BONUS=' ||
              CHAR(p_new_bonus) || 'WHERE LASTNAME = ''BROWN'' ';
```

Notice that in this example, the WHERE clause with the search string `''BROWN''` is hard-coded in the statement text. Because LASTNAME is a character column, the search predicate must be a string. It means that the value BROWN must be quoted like `'BROWN'` in the dynamic SQL text. This can be accomplished by prefixing the single quote with an additional single quote, as shown in the previous example. This tells DB2 that the single quotes are escaped and they are part of the SQL statement.

If you were to use the SQL procedure as presented in Figure 7.3, you could simply pass `LASTNAME = 'BROWN'` as `p_where_cond`.

Reusing Dynamic SQL Statements with *PREPARE* and *EXECUTE*

As mentioned in the previous section, EXECUTE IMMEDIATE is ideal if you have a single SQL statement that you need to execute just once. If you have a dynamic SQL statement that needs to be executed many times, however, using EXECUTE IMMEDIATE incurs the unnecessary cost of re-preparing the SQL statement. A better solution is to use PREPARE and EXECUTE separately, but first the concept of parameter markers must be introduced.

Parameter markers are useful if you have a set of very similar queries to execute, but only certain variable values change. Consider the following two UPDATE statements:

```
UPDATE EMPLOYEE SET BONUS=500 WHERE EMPNO='000300';
UPDATE EMPLOYEE SET BONUS=1000 WHERE EMPNO='000340';
```

From DB2's perspective, the access plan used to update the row that contains employee 000300 is the same as the one used to fetch and update the row that has employee 000340. Hence, the value of the bonus and the employee number are irrelevant to the access plan being chosen, and the query can be reduced to the following general form:

```
UPDATE EMPLOYEE SET BONUS=? WHERE EMPNO=?;
```

Here, the question marks are called **parameter markers** and act as placeholders for variables that can be replaced with values at a later time. The ability to use parameter markers is a feature that is specific to dynamic SQL.

In SQL procedures, parameter markers can be used to avoid the overhead of preparing similar SQL statements that result in the same access plan. To do this, instead of using EXECUTE IMMEDIATE, the process is executed in two commands: PREPARE and EXECUTE. The syntax for PREPARE and EXECUTE is presented in Figures 7.4 and 7.5.

```
>>-PREPARE--statement-name--FROM--host-variable--------><
```

Figure 7.4   The syntax diagram for *PREPARE*.

The PREPARE statement has two parameters. The *statement-name* is an identifier for referencing the prepared form of the query. The *host-variable* is a VARCHAR variable that holds the SQL statement text to be prepared.

```
>>-EXECUTE--statement-name-------------------------------------->
>--+-------------------------------------------------+------------->
   |             .-,------------------.              |
   |             V                    |              |
   '-INTO--+---result-host-variable-+-----------+-'
           '-DESCRIPTOR--result-descriptor-name-'

>--+-------------------------------------------------+------------><
   |             .-,------------------.              |
   |             V                    |              |
   '-USING--+---input-host-variable-+-----------+-'
            '-DESCRIPTOR--input-descriptor-name-'
```

Figure 7.5   The syntax diagram for *EXECUTE*.

The EXECUTE statement takes one or more parameters. In the least, *statement-name* must be specified, and it must reference a statement object that has been previously prepared. Optionally, if the SQL statement has one or more parameter markers, a comma-delimited list of *host-variables* can be specified in the USING clause for parameter substitution.

The INTO clause is only used for dynamic CALL statements which are discussed later in this chapter.

Consider the following example in which a company increases bonuses for only department managers. To do this, a cursor is defined for all managers to fetch their current bonuses and then increase them by the amount specified in the p_bonus_increase parameter (see Figure 7.6).

```
CREATE PROCEDURE change_mgr_bonus ( IN p_bonus_increase DECIMAL
                                  , OUT p_num_changes INT )
    LANGUAGE SQL
    SPECIFIC change_mgr_bonus                       -- applies to LUW and iSeries
 -- WLM ENVIRONMENT <env>                           -- applies to zSeries

cmb: BEGIN

    DECLARE v_dynSQL          VARCHAR(200);
    DECLARE v_new_bonus       DECIMAL;
    DECLARE v_no_data         SMALLINT DEFAULT 0;

    DECLARE v_mgrno           CHAR(6);
    DECLARE v_bonus           DECIMAL;

-- cursor of all employees who are also managers
    DECLARE c_managers CURSOR FOR
        SELECT e.empno
             ,e.bonus
          FROM EMPLOYEE e
             ,DEPARTMENT d
         WHERE e.empno=d.mgrno;

    DECLARE CONTINUE HANDLER FOR NOT FOUND
        SET v_no_data=1;

    SET v_dynSQL = 'UPDATE EMPLOYEE SET BONUS=? WHERE EMPNO=?';
    SET p_num_changes=0;
```

```
    PREPARE v_stmt1 FROM v_dynSQL;                  -- (1)


    OPEN c_managers;
    FETCH c_managers INTO v_mgrno, v_bonus;


    WHILE (v_no_data=0) DO
        SET p_num_changes = p_num_changes + 1;
        SET v_new_bonus = v_bonus + p_bonus_increase;


        EXECUTE v_stmt1 USING v_new_bonus, v_mgrno;     -- (2)


        -- fetch the next row to be processed
        FETCH c_managers INTO v_mgrno, v_bonus;
    END WHILE;
    CLOSE c_managers;
END cmb
```

Figure 7.6 A dynamic SQL example using *PREPARE* and *EXECUTE ... USING ...* statements.

In the previous example, there are several concepts to highlight. The SQL procedure starts off with variable declarations. A statement text stored in v_dynSQL is prepared on Line (1) and uses v_stmt1 as the statement name identifier.

Within the WHILE loop, the statement name v_stmt1 is executed repeatedly on Line (2). Because the prepared statement has two parameter markers, the USING clause of EXECUTE is used to substitute the parameter values.

TIP

You can also issue EXECUTE without the USING clause if the dynamic SQL statement has no parameter markers.

Before running the SQL procedure, take a look at the current bonus values for department managers and note their values.

```
SELECT e.empno, e.bonus FROM EMPLOYEE e, DEPARTMENT d WHERE e.empno=d.mgrno

EMPNO   BONUS
------  -----------
000010     1000.00
000020      800.00
000030      800.00
000050      800.00
```

```
000060      500.00
000070      700.00
000090      600.00
000100      500.00
```

Then, call the SQL procedure with the bonus increase value. For example, in LUW you can use
the Command Line Process (CLP):

```
CALL CHANGE_MGR_BONUS (100,?)
```

The output should look something like the following:

```
Value of output parameters
--------------------------

  Parameter Name   : P_NUM_CHANGES
  Parameter Value : 8


  Return Status = 0
```

In this example, eight rows were updated as indicated by P_NUM_CHANGES. To further verify that
the result is correct, query the data once again.

```
SELECT e.empno, e.bonus FROM EMPLOYEE e, DEPARTMENT d WHERE e.empno=d.mgrno

EMPNO  BONUS
------ -----------
000010     1100.00
000020      900.00
000030      900.00
000050      900.00
000060      600.00
000070      800.00
000090      700.00
000100      600.00
```

Figure 7.6 was used to illustrate repeated EXECUTE statements with one PREPARE statement. This
"PREPARE once, EXECUTE many" design will offer much better performance as compared to running a PREPARE and EXECUTE or EXECUTE IMMEDIATE for the same statement over and over again.

Using Dynamic SQL in Cursors

Sometimes it may be necessary to iterate through a set of rows of a result set and determine where
the result set was created using dynamic SQL. In this section, examples of dynamic SQL in cursors will be introduced.

Consider using the same example as shown in the previous section, except that the
c_managers cursor is defined dynamically. Figure 7.7 demonstrates the code.

```
CREATE PROCEDURE change_mgr_bonus2 ( IN p_bonus_increase DECIMAL
                                   , OUT p_num_changes INT)
    LANGUAGE SQL
    SPECIFIC change_mgr_bonus2                 -- applies to LUW and iSeries
 -- WLM ENVIRONMENT <env>                      -- applies to zSeries

cmb2: BEGIN

    DECLARE v_dynMgrSQL       VARCHAR(200);                -- (1)
    DECLARE v_dynSQL          VARCHAR(200);

    DECLARE v_new_bonus       DECIMAL;
    DECLARE v_no_data         SMALLINT DEFAULT 0;

    DECLARE v_mgrno           CHAR(6);
    DECLARE v_bonus           DECIMAL;

    -- cursor of all employees who are also managers
    DECLARE c_managers CURSOR FOR v_cur_stmt;              -- (2)

    DECLARE CONTINUE HANDLER FOR NOT FOUND
        SET v_no_data=1;

    -- SQL for c_managers cursor
    SET v_dynMgrSQL = 'SELECT e.empno,e.bonus FROM EMPLOYEE e, DEPARTMENT d ' ||
                     'WHERE e.empno=d.mgrno';

    SET v_dynSQL = 'UPDATE EMPLOYEE SET BONUS= ? WHERE EMPNO=?';
    SET p_num_changes=0;

    PREPARE v_stmt1 FROM v_dynSQL;

    PREPARE v_cur_stmt FROM v_dynMgrSQL;                   -- (3)
    OPEN c_managers;                                       -- (4)
    FETCH c_managers INTO v_mgrno, v_bonus;
```

```
    WHILE (v_no_data=0) DO
        SET p_num_changes = p_num_changes + 1;
        SET v_new_bonus = v_bonus + p_bonus_increase;
        EXECUTE v_stmt1 USING v_new_bonus, v_mgrno;


        -- fetch the next row to be processed
        FETCH c_managers INTO v_mgrno, v_bonus;
    END WHILE;

    CLOSE c_managers;
END cmb2
```

Figure 7.7   Dynamic SQL cursors

First, a VARCHAR variable large enough to contain the SQL statement must be declared for the cursor as shown on Line (1). In the cursor declaration on Line (2), notice how the cursor has been declared for the v_cur_stmt statement name which will eventually identify the prepared statement held by the v_dynMgrSQL. Finally, before opening the c_managers cursor, the v_cur_stmt statement name must be prepared on Line (3) using the v_dynMgrSQL variable. When the c_managers cursor on Line (4) is opened, DB2 expects that the v_cur_stmt statement name references a prepared SQL statement.

Note that in this example, the parameter markers for p_bonus and p_empno are untyped. Depending on the situation, you may run into a problem where a variable of the wrong type is supplied for the parameter marker. You can protect the application from errors by using CAST to guarantee the proper type. For example, the v_dynSQL variable can be changed to use the following SQL statement instead:

```
SET v_dynSQL = 'UPDATE EMPLOYEE SET BONUS= CAST(? AS DECIMAL) WHERE EMPNO= CAST
(? AS CHAR(6))';
```

Using CAST to guarantee the proper type may not always be necessary. You should only use it if there is the opportunity for type mismatch because CAST adds execution overhead.

Before running the SQL procedure, take a look at the current bonus values for department managers:

```
SELECT e.empno, e.bonus FROM EMPLOYEE e, DEPARTMENT d WHERE e.empno=d.mgrno

EMPNO   BONUS
------  -----------
000010     1100.00
000020      900.00
000030      900.00
```

```
000050        900.00
000060        600.00
000070        800.00
000090        700.00
000100        600.00
```

Then, call the SQL procedure with the value for the bonus increase as the input parameter. Again, you can use the CLP in LUW:

```
CALL CHANGE_MGR_BONUS2 (100,?)
```

The output should look something like the following:

```
Value of output parameters
---------------------------
  Parameter Name   : P_NUM_CHANGES
  Parameter Value : 8


  Return Status = 0
```

In this case, eight rows were updated as indicated by P_NUM_CHANGES. To further verify that the code is correct, query the data once again.

```
SELECT e.empno, e.bonus FROM EMPLOYEE e, DEPARTMENT d WHERE e.empno=d.mgrno

EMPNO   BONUS
------  -----------
000010      1200.00
000020      1000.00
000030      1000.00
000050      1000.00
000060       700.00
000070       900.00
000090       800.00
000100       700.00
```

Dynamic *CALL* Statements

In LUW and iSeries, the CALL statement can be dynamically prepared. You can specify parameter markers through the use of host variables. However, the syntax for LUW and iSeries differ slightly:

- In LUW, the USING clause of the EXECUTE statement is used to provide values for the IN and INOUT parameter. The INTO clause can be used for receiving values from INOUT and OUT parameters of dynamically called procedures. Refer to Figure 7.5 for the complete syntax diagram of the EXECUTE statement.

- In iSeries, the USING clause of the EXECUTE statement is used for all parameter modes: IN, OUT, INOUT.

Figure 7.8 shows an example of how to use the INTO clause.

> **NOTE**
> In zSeries, support for dynamic CALL statements in SQL procedures is only available from some ODBC or CLI drivers such as the ones provided by IBM. Thus, there is no workaround to the sample SQL procedure shown in Figure 7.8.

```
CREATE PROCEDURE dynamicCall( IN procschema VARCHAR(50)
                           , IN procname   VARCHAR(50)
                           , OUT p_total   INTEGER )
    LANGUAGE SQL
    SPECIFIC dynamiccall                          -- applies to LUW and iSeries
dc2: BEGIN

    DECLARE v_dynSQL        VARCHAR(200);
    DECLARE v_p1            INT;
    DECLARE v_p2            INT;
    DECLARE v_p3            INT;


    SET v_p1=100;
    SET v_p2=200;
    -- default to user schema if not supplied
    SET procschema = COALESCE (procschema, USER);      -- (1)

    SET v_dynSQL = 'CALL ' || rtrim(procschema)
                           || '.'
                           || ltrim(procname)
                           || '(?,?,?)';                -- (2)

    PREPARE v_stmt FROM v_dynSQL;
    /* Assumption - SQL procedure being called
     * has 3 parameters :
```

```
    *       v_p1 - IN
    *       v_p2 - INOUT
    *       v_p3 - OUT
    */
    EXECUTE v_stmt INTO v_p2, v_p3 USING v_p1, v_p2;  -- applies to LUW  -- (3)
  --EXECUTE v_stmt USING v_p1, v_p2, v_p3;             -- applies to iSeries
    SET p_total = v_p2 + v_p3;
END dc2
```

Figure 7.8   An example of using *EXECUTE ... USING ... INTO ...* for dynamically prepared *CALL* statements.

In Figure 7.8, the SQL procedure `dynamicCall` takes two parameters: a schema and procedure name. The `procschema` parameter is checked whether it has a NULL value. If NULL is supplied, the current connected user ID will be used as the default schema, shown on Line (1). A CALL statement is then formed by concatenating the SQL procedure schema and name, using the LTRIM and RTRIM functions to strip off blank spaces that may cause problems, as shown on Line (2).

TIP

For best performance, it is always better to use CALL with fully qualified SQL procedure names.

For the purposes of this example, we can assume that whatever SQL procedure is called, the SQL procedure will have exactly three parameters; those parameters are IN, INOUT, and OUT. If an SQL procedure is called that differs in its parameter requirements, the CALL will fail.

After the CALL statement has been prepared, it is executed USING the variables v_p1 and v_p2 as the input values to the IN and INOUT parameters, respectively. The INTO clause is supported by v_p2 and v_p3 to receive values returned from the called SQL procedure.

The dynamically prepared statement was a CALL statement that had v_p2 defined as an INOUT parameter. The statement will run as expected in the rewritten form.

Authorization Consideration

Security for dynamic SQL is evaluated at runtime using the privileges of the user who calls the SQL procedure, rather than the person who builds the SQL procedure. For any dynamic SQL that you use, ensure that the user calling the SQL procedure will have the proper privileges. For more information on how security is resolved, see Appendix E, "Security Considerations in SQL Procedures."

Summary

As you have seen in this chapter, dynamic SQL can be used for executing SQL statements that are not fully known until runtime. Dynamic SQL can be used for single SQL statements, the CALL statement (except in zSeries), and cursors. Such features enhance the flexibility and add more robustness to SQL procedures. You have seen when and how to use the EXECUTE IMMEDIATE, PRE-PARE, and EXECUTE statements.

Additionally, the use of an escape character in dynamic SQL statements was explained. The package cache and how it is used to improve performance of dynamic SQL was discussed indepth. Finally, special registers that can be used to improve performance and further control the environment were examined.

CHAPTER 8

Nested SQL Procedures

In this chapter, you will learn

- What nested SQL procedures are
- How to pass parameters between nested SQL procedures
- How to return values from nested SQL procedures
- How to return and receive result sets from within nested SQL procedures
- How to write recursive SQL procedures
- Various security techniques you should employ in nested SQL procedures

DB2 supports nesting of SQL procedures—that is, invoking an SQL procedure from another SQL procedure.

While all the information described in this book so far is applicable to nested SQL procedures, you need a little more information on how to pass data between SQL procedures so that they work together effectively. For example, some SQL statements are unique to nested SQL procedures. These topics are covered in this chapter.

TIP

In DB2, you can also implement stored procedures in a host programming language such as C or Java.

Basic Nested SQL Procedures

Let's look at Figure 8.1 and Figure 8.2 for examples of two basic nested SQL procedures.

```
CREATE PROCEDURE count_projects ( IN  p_empno CHAR(6)
                                , OUT p_total INT )
   LANGUAGE SQL
   SPECIFIC count_projects                   -- applies to LUW and iSeries
-- WLM ENVIRONMENT <env>                     -- applies to zSeries
cp: BEGIN
   -- Procedure logic
   SELECT COUNT(*)
     INTO p_total
     FROM emp_act
    WHERE empno = p_empno;
END cp
```

Figure 8.1   An example of a called procedure.

```
CREATE PROCEDURE bonus ( IN  p_empno CHAR(6)
                       , OUT p_bonus CHAR(1) )
   LANGUAGE SQL
   SPECIFIC bonus                            -- applies to LUW and iSeries
-- WLM ENVIRONMENT <env>                     -- applies to zSeries
bn: BEGIN
   -- Declare variables
   DECLARE v_min INT DEFAULT 5;
   DECLARE v_total INT DEFAULT 0;

   -- Procedure logic
   CALL count_projects(p_empno, v_total);

   IF ( v_total >= v_min )
   THEN
       SET p_bonus = 'Y';
   ELSE
       SET p_bonus = 'N';
   END IF;
END bn
```

Figure 8.2   An example of a caller procedure.

The procedure `count_projects` in Figure 8.1 returns the number of projects that one employee has completed. Each employee is identified by an employee number. The procedure `bonus` in Figure 8.2 is used to determine whether an employee should be awarded a bonus based on how many projects he or she has completed. It uses the output of the `count_projects` procedure in its calculation.

In procedure `bonus`, which is referred to as the **caller**, a CALL statement is issued to invoke procedure `count_projects`, which is referred to as the **called procedure**.

By using nested SQL procedures, you can encapsulate business logic into smaller separate units. The code becomes more readable, maintainable, and reusable.

Passing Parameters Between Nested SQL Procedures

As with procedures in any programming language, nested SQL procedures are not of much use unless you can pass values between the caller and the called procedures. In the examples shown in Figure 8.1 and Figure 8.2, you can pass values in and out by issuing the CALL statement in the caller procedure. The number of parameters and their data types must match the called procedure signature. After the successful completion of a CALL statement, the OUT parameter values will be available to the caller procedure.

TIP

DB2 SQL PL uses strong data typing. This means that you will have to match the data types of the local variables with those of the parameters in the called procedure's signature, if possible. You will have to use the explicit CAST functions if the specified data type does not support implicit conversion.

The local variables are matched to the called SQL procedure parameters by their positions in the CALL statement.

If you have overloaded the called SQL procedure, DB2 will determine which procedure to invoke by the number of parameters in the CALL statement. Overloading with the same number of parameters is not supported, even if the data types are different. Overloading of procedures is not possible on zSeries. For detailed information on overloaded SQL procedures, refer to Chapter 2, "Basic SQL Procedure Structure."

Returning Values from Nested SQL Procedures

Besides using output parameters to pass values back from the called procedure, you can also return one integer as the return code (also known as the return value).

To return the value, use the SQL control statement RETURN as introduced in Chapter 2, "Basic SQL Procedure Structure." To access the return value, use the SQL control statement GET DIAGNOSTICS. The syntax and a full description of the command can be found in Chapter 6, "Condition Handling."

In Figure 8.3, procedure `get_emp_name` returns the employee first name for an employee number. If the record is found, a value of `99` is returned. Otherwise, the procedure returns a value of `1000`.

```
CREATE PROCEDURE get_emp_name ( IN   p_empno CHAR(6)
                               , OUT p_fname VARCHAR(10) )
   LANGUAGE SQL
   SPECIFIC get_emp_name                         -- applies to LUW and iSeries
-- WLM ENVIRONMENT <env>                         -- applies to zSeries

gen: BEGIN
    -- Declare variables
    DECLARE v_return_code INT DEFAULT 99;

    -- Declare condition handlers
    DECLARE CONTINUE HANDLER FOR NOT FOUND
        SET v_return_code = 1000;

    -- Procedure logic
    SELECT firstnme
      INTO p_fname
      FROM employee
      WHERE empno = p_empno;

    RETURN v_return_code;
END gen
```

Figure 8.3   An example of returning a value from a called procedure.

Using return codes can be arbitrary. However, it is recommended that system-defined SQLCODEs not be used as customized return codes. It may cause unnecessary confusion in interpreting error messages.

The caller procedure find_emp in Figure 8.4 shows how to use the GET DIAGNOSTICS statement to obtain the return code from the called procedure. Notice that the GET DIAGNOSTICS statement on Line (2) immediately follows the CALL statement on Line (1).

```
CREATE PROCEDURE find_emp ( IN   p_empno CHAR(6)
                           , OUT p_output VARCHAR(50) )
   LANGUAGE SQL
   SPECIFIC find_emp                             -- applies to LUW and iSeries
-- WLM ENVIRONMENT <env>                         -- applies to zSeries
```

```
fe: BEGIN
    -- Declare variables
    DECLARE v_rc INT;
    DECLARE v_fname VARCHAR(15);

    -- Procedure logic
    CALL get_emp_name ( p_empno, v_fname );                    --(1)
    GET DIAGNOSTICS v_rc = RETURN_STATUS;                      --(2)

    IF ( v_rc = 99 )
    THEN
        SET p_output = 'The employee is: ' || v_fname || '.';
    ELSEIF ( v_rc = 1000 )
    THEN
        SET p_output = 'The employee does not exist!';
    ELSE
        SET p_output = 'Something else went wrong.';
    END IF;
END fe
```

Figure 8.4 An example of receiving a returned value by a caller procedure.

In Figure 8.4, the caller procedure assesses the execution of the called procedure by checking the return code. This value is then used to formulate more user-friendly messages.

Because an integer can be returned by both the return code and the output parameter, you might wonder which method you should use. A good SQL programming practice is to reserve the use of return codes for status indicators only. For all other situations, use an output parameter even if you only have one integer to return.

TIP
Use a return code for execution status only.

Returning Result Sets from Nested SQL Procedures

In previous chapters, you have learned how to use cursors to return result sets to calling applications. You have an additional consideration, though, with returning result sets when nested SQL procedures are used. You can either

- Return your result set to the (direct) calling procedure.
- Return your result set to the calling application (external client).

The target where you return the result set can be defined by using the WITH RETURN clause of the DECLARE CURSOR statement (see Figure 8.5).

```
>>-DECLARE--cursor-name--CURSOR----+------------+--------------->
                                   '-WITH HOLD--'


>-----+----------------------------+------------------------->
      |                 .-TO CALLER--.  |
      '-WITH RETURN--+------------+--'
                     '-TO CLIENT--'


>----FOR--+-select-statement-+-------------------------------><
          '-statement-name---'
```

Figure 8.5 A partial *DECLARE CURSOR* syntax.

As discussed in Chapter 5, "Understanding and Using Cursors and Result Sets," the DECLARE CURSOR statement defines a cursor. When the WITH RETURN TO CALLER clause is used, the result sets will be returned to the direct caller, which can be either another SQL procedure or an external application. When the WITH RETURN TO CLIENT clause is used, the result sets will be returned to the external application only. The result sets will be invisible to all intermediate SQL procedures.

NOTE

Valid options on zSeries are WITHOUT RETURN (the default) and WITH RETURN TO CALLER. WITH RETURN TO CLIENT is not supported.

Figure 8.6 shows the differences between how cursors will return their result sets depending on the RETURN TO clause. The stored procedures are described in detailed in the next sections.

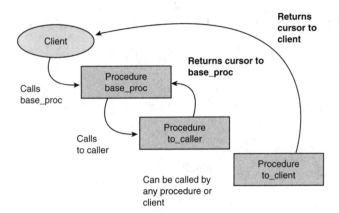

Figure 8.6   Returning cursors in nested stored procedures.

Returning Result Sets to the Client

Figure 8.7 shows an example of an SQL procedure that uses a cursor to return result sets to the client. The procedure returns the first names, the last names, and the salaries of all the employees in one department for a given department number.

```
CREATE PROCEDURE to_client ( IN  p_dept CHAR(3) )
    LANGUAGE SQL
    SPECIFIC to_client                          -- applies to LUW and iSeries
-- WLM ENVIRONMENT <env>                        -- applies to zSeries

    DYNAMIC RESULT SETS 1
tc: BEGIN
    -- Procedure logic
--  DECLARE v_cur CURSOR WITH RETURN TO CALLER   -- use this line for zSeries
    DECLARE v_cur CURSOR WITH RETURN TO CLIENT   -- use this line for LUW and
iSeries
        FOR SELECT firstnme, lastname, salary
            FROM    employee
            WHERE   workdept = p_dept;
    OPEN v_cur;
END tc
```

Figure 8.7   An example of returning result sets to a client.

A simple caller SQL procedure in Figure 8.8 demonstrates how to receive a result set in the caller procedure.

```
CREATE PROCEDURE base_proc (   )
    LANGUAGE SQL
    SPECIFIC base_proc
    DYNAMIC RESULT SETS 1
bp: BEGIN
    -- Declare variables
    DECLARE v_dept CHAR(3) DEFAULT 'A00';

    -- Procedure logic
    CALL to_client(v_dept);
END bp
```

Figure 8.8   An example of receiving result sets from a client for LUW and iSeries.

On zSeries, although the procedure in Figure 8.8 builds and runs, it cannot handle the returned result set. Remember that RETURN TO CLIENT is not an option; therefore, the ASSOCIATE RESULT SET and ALLOCATE CURSOR statements have to be used. These statements are explained later in this chapter; you can also find an example of the base_proc for zSeries in Figure 8.16.

On LUW and iSeries, the procedure simply issues a CALL statement to to_client procedure. If you invoke the SQL procedure base_proc from the command window on LUW, you will see the output depicted in Figure 8.9.

```
FIRSTNME        LASTNAME        SALARY
CHRISTINE       HAAS            52750.00
VINCENZO        LUCCHESSI       46500.00
SEAN            O'CONNELL       29250.00
"BASE_PROC" RETURN_STATUS: "0"
```

Figure 8.9   The output of procedure *base_proc*.

For LUW and iSeries, even though there is no cursor declared in the body of the SQL procedure base_proc and there is no result set specified in its header, the calling application still received the result set. This is because the WITH RETURN TO CLIENT clause in the to_client SQL procedure causes DB2 to bypass any intermediate SQL procedures and return the result sets directly to the application. The output you see is actually from the to_client procedure. You should see the same output if you invoke to_client directly without going through the base_proc caller.

TIP

The cursor with the WITH RETURN TO CLIENT clause and its result sets are invisible to any intermediate SQL procedures.

If you need to use the result sets in both the caller SQL procedure and the client application, you will have to use WITH RETURN TO CALLER clause explained in the next section and re-return the rows in the caller SQL procedure.

The RETURN TO CLIENT option can be very useful when you have stored procedures with many layers of nested logic. You can use complex logic to determine which procedure should be called to generate your result set and then have it returned directly to the calling program. This allows you to have more flexibility in the modularity of your stored procedure design because the original calling procedure(s) do not need to have any idea of the final form of the result set returned to the caller.

Returning Result Sets to the Caller

To understand the difference between the WITH RETURN TO CLIENT and WITH RETURN TO CALLER clauses, let's look at the two nested SQL procedures in Figures 8.11 and 8.12, which are very similar to the two examples presented earlier. The diagram in Figure 8.10 shows how nested stored procedures can return result sets to each other.

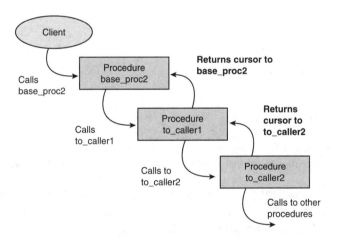

Figure 8.10   Procedures returning cursors to the calling procedure.

Figure 8.11 shows the called SQL procedure using the WITH RETURN TO CALLER clause.

```
CREATE PROCEDURE to_caller1 ( IN  p_dept CHAR(3) )
    LANGUAGE SQL
    SPECIFIC to_caller1                         -- applies to LUW and iSeries
-- WLM ENVIRONMENT <env>                        -- applies to zSeries

    DYNAMIC RESULT SETS 1
tc1: BEGIN
```

```
      -- Procedure logic
      DECLARE v_cur CURSOR WITH RETURN TO CALLER
          FOR SELECT firstnme, lastname, salary
              FROM    employee
              WHERE   workdept = p_dept;
      OPEN v_cur;
END tc1
```

Figure 8.11   An example of returning result sets to the caller.

Figure 8.12 shows the caller SQL procedure that simply invokes the called SQL procedure.

```
CREATE PROCEDURE base_proc2 (  )
    LANGUAGE SQL
    SPECIFIC base_proc2                          -- applies to LUW and iSeries
-- WLM ENVIRONMENT <env>                         -- applies to zSeries

bp2: BEGIN
    -- Declare variables
    DECLARE v_dept CHAR(3) DEFAULT 'A00';

    -- Procedure logic
    CALL to_caller1(v_dept);          -- (1)
END bp2
```

Figure 8.12   An example of invoking a procedure with the *RETURN TO CALLER* clause.

As you can see, the only difference between these two sets of nested SQL procedures is the WITH RETURN clauses in the called SQL procedures. In procedure to_caller1, the result sets are to be passed to its direct caller, be it an SQL procedure or client application.

If another stored procedure invoked the base_proc2 procedure, you may think you would receive a result set because base_proc2 had a result set returned to it within its body. This would not be the case. The result set from the to_proc procedure is returned to base_proc2 on Line (1). However, this result is then not processed at all. It is therefore not passed back to any procedures that called it. If you wanted to pass the result back to the calling procedure, you would have to explicitly receive the result set and return it to the calling procedure. This is covered in the following section.

TIP

If you do not specify TO CLIENT or TO CALLER with the WITH RETURN clause, by default the result sets will be returned to the direct caller.

If you invoke the `to_client` procedure directly, the output will be identical to that of `base_proc2`. Obviously, it makes sense because you are calling two separate procedures directly instead of using nested procedures. The caller and the client application are always the same. There is no difference between the `WITH RETURN TO CALLER` clause and the `WITH RETURN TO CLIENT` clause outside the context of nested SQL procedures.

Receiving Result Sets as a Caller

To make use of the returned result sets from called procedures, you need to know how to access them in the calling procedure.

> **NOTE**
> From the perspective of client applications, there is no difference in handling result sets from nested or non-nested procedures.

On LUW and zSeries, in order to access and make use of the returned result sets, the `ASSOCIATE LOCATORS` statement and the `ALLOCATE CURSOR` statement must be used in the caller SQL procedure. The `ASSOCIATE LOCATORS` syntax is illustrated in Figure 8.13.

```
                .-RESULT SET--.
>>-ASSOCIATE--+-------------+---+-LOCATOR--+-------------------->
                                '-LOCATORS-'


      .-,---------------------.
      V                       |
>----(-----rs-locator-variable---+---)--WITH PROCEDURE--procedure-name-><
```

Figure 8.13   *ASSOCIATE LOCATORS syntax for LUW and zSeries.*

The caller procedure uses `ASSOCIATE LOCATORS` to create pointers to the result sets returned by the nested procedure. The `ALLOCATE CURSOR` statement, shown in Figure 8.14, allocates cursors for the result sets using locator variables obtained by an `ASSOCIATE LOCATORS` statement.

```
>>-ALLOCATE--cursor-name--CURSOR FOR RESULT SET--rs-locator-variable--><
```

Figure 8.14   *ALLOCATE CURSOR syntax for LUW and zSeries.*

> **NOTE**
> On iSeries, `ASSOCIATE LOCATORS` and `ALLOCATE CURSOR` are not supported. In order to have a procedure process result sets, you can create an external stored procedure in C or Java. Appendix H, "Sample Application Code," provides Java alternatives for Figures 8.15 and 8.18.

The example in Figure 8.15 is a caller SQL procedure, which invokes the `to_caller1` called procedure from Figure 8.11. The `to_caller1` procedure returns the first names, the last names, and the salaries of all employees in one department. The caller SQL procedure, `total_salary`, receives the result set and uses it to calculate the total salary of the department.

```
CREATE PROCEDURE total_salary ( IN p_dept CHAR(3)
                            , OUT p_total DECIMAL(9,2) )
   LANGUAGE SQL
   SPECIFIC total_salary                          -- applies to LUW
-- WLM ENVIRONMENT <env>                           -- applies to zSeries

ts: BEGIN
    -- Declare variables
    DECLARE v_fname VARCHAR(12);
    DECLARE v_lname VARCHAR(15);
    DECLARE v_salary DECIMAL(9,2) DEFAULT 0.0;
    DECLARE v_rs RESULT_SET_LOCATOR VARYING;                    --(1)
    -- Declare returncodes
    DECLARE SQLSTATE CHAR(5) DEFAULT '00000';

    -- Procedure logic
    CALL to_caller1(p_dept);                                   --(2)
    ASSOCIATE RESULT SET LOCATOR (v_rs)
        WITH PROCEDURE to_caller1;                             --(3)
    ALLOCATE v_rsCur CURSOR FOR RESULT SET v_rs;               --(4)

    SET p_total = 0;

    WHILE ( SQLSTATE = '00000' ) DO
        SET p_total = p_total + v_salary;
        FETCH FROM v_rsCur INTO v_fname, v_lname, v_salary;
    END WHILE;
END ts
```

Figure 8.15   An example of receiving result sets from the caller procedure for LUW and zSeries.

The result set locator variable is declared on Line (1). After invoking the called SQL procedure on Line (2), the ASSOCIATE LOCATOR statement is used on Line (3) to obtain the result set locator variable. Then the ALLOCATE CURSOR statement is used on Line (4) to open the result set. The cursor name used in the ALLOCATE CURSOR statement must not be declared anywhere prior to the ALLOCATE CURSOR statement in the procedure.

Once declared with ALLOCATE CURSOR, the cursor can be used to fetch rows from the returned result set. In Figure 8.15, a WHILE loop is used to fetch each row in order to calculate the department total salary. The SQLSTATE from the FETCH statement is used as the exit condition for the loop when the end of the result set is encountered.

> **NOTE**
> Recall that on zSeries, you do not have the option of using RETURN TO CLIENT. To simulate RETURN TO CLIENT, use the ASSOCIATE RESULT SET LOCATOR and ALLOCATE CURSOR FOR RESULT SET statements in each intermediate procedure to pass the result set back one level higher. This process should be repeated until the result set is passed to the client.

The example given in Figure 8.16 demonstrates how you could create the base_proc procedure given in Figure 8.8 by using the ALLOCATE CURSOR statement on zSeries.

```
CREATE PROCEDURE base_proc (  )
    LANGUAGE SQL
    WLM ENVIRONMENT <env>
    DYNAMIC RESULT SETS 1
bp: BEGIN
    -- Declare variables
    DECLARE v_dept CHAR(3) DEFAULT 'A00';
    DECLARE v_rs RESULT_SET_LOCATOR VARYING;

    -- Procedure logic
    CALL to_client(v_dept);
    ASSOCIATE RESULT SET LOCATOR (v_rs)
       WITH PROCEDURE to_client;
    ALLOCATE v_rsCur CURSOR FOR RESULT SET v_rs;

    -- <other statements to manipulate the cursor if you want to
    --   send it to the caller>
END bp
```

Figure 8.16   An example of receiving result sets from the client for zSeries.

In Figure 8.16, once the cursor v_rsCur has been allocated, it cannot be directly passed to the caller. If you have this requirement, you can fetch each row of the cursor and insert it into a table, which can be a temporary table (as discussed in Chapter 10, "Leveraging DB2 Application Development Features"), and have another cursor declared WITH RETURN TO CALLER defined on this table.

Receiving Multiple Result Sets as a Caller

A procedure is able to return more than one result set. To process multiple result sets in a caller
procedure, the same statements as described in the previous section can be used. This is best illustrated using the example in Figure 8.17, which shows a called SQL procedure that returns multiple result sets.

```
CREATE PROCEDURE emp_multi ( IN  p_dept CHAR(3) )
    LANGUAGE SQL
    SPECIFIC emp_multi                             -- applies to LUW and iSeries
-- WLM ENVIRONMENT <env>                           -- applies to zSeries

    DYNAMIC RESULT SETS 3
em: BEGIN
    -- Procedure logic
    -- Selects firstname
    DECLARE v_cur1 CURSOR WITH RETURN TO CALLER
        FOR SELECT firstnme
            FROM   employee
            WHERE  workdept = p_dept;
    -- Selects lastname
    DECLARE v_cur2 CURSOR WITH RETURN TO CALLER
        FOR SELECT lastname
            FROM   employee
            WHERE  workdept = p_dept;
    -- Selects salary
    DECLARE v_cur3 CURSOR WITH RETURN TO CALLER
        FOR SELECT salary
            FROM   employee
            WHERE  workdept = p_dept;
    OPEN v_cur1;
    OPEN v_cur2;
    OPEN v_cur3;
END em
```

Figure 8.17   Example of returning multiple result sets to caller procedures.

The called SQL procedure emp_multi, shown in Figure 8.17, is a simple rewrite of the previous
called procedure to_caller1 from Figure 8.11. Instead of returning three columns in one result
set, each column is returned individually in a separate result set. Three cursors are declared and
opened.

   The caller SQL procedure, receive_multi in Figure 8.18, uses ASSOCIATE LOCATORS and
ALLOCATE CURSOR statements multiple times to match the number of result sets returned. Three

result set locator variables are declared and associated with the various result sets. Three cursors
are allocated as well.

```
CREATE PROCEDURE receive_multi ( in  p_dept   CHAR(3)
                               , OUT p_names VARCHAR(100)
                               , OUT p_total DECIMAL(9,2) )

   LANGUAGE SQL
   SPECIFIC receive_multi                     -- applies to LUW and iSeries
-- WLM ENVIRONMENT <env>                      -- applies to zSeries


rm: BEGIN
    -- Declare variables
    DECLARE v_fname VARCHAR(12) DEFAULT '';
    DECLARE v_lname VARCHAR(15) DEFAULT '';
    DECLARE v_salary DECIMAL(9,2) DEFAULT 0.0;
    DECLARE v_rs1, v_rs2, v_rs3 RESULT_SET_LOCATOR VARYING;
    -- Declare returncodes
    DECLARE SQLSTATE CHAR(5) DEFAULT '00000';


    -- Procedure logic
    CALL emp_multi(p_dept);
    ASSOCIATE RESULT SET LOCATOR (v_rs1, v_rs2, v_rs3)
        WITH PROCEDURE emp_multi;
    ALLOCATE v_rsCur1 CURSOR FOR RESULT SET v_rs1;
    ALLOCATE v_rsCur2 CURSOR FOR RESULT SET v_rs2;
    ALLOCATE v_rsCur3 CURSOR FOR RESULT SET v_rs3;


    SET p_names = 'The employees are:';
    WHILE (SQLSTATE = '00000') DO
        SET p_names = p_names || v_fname || ' ' ||  v_lname || ' ';
        FETCH FROM v_rsCur1 INTO v_fname;
        FETCH FROM v_rsCur2 INTO v_lname;
    END WHILE;


    SET p_total = 0;
    WHILE ( SQLSTATE = '00000' ) DO
        SET p_total = p_total + v_salary;
        FETCH FROM v_rsCur3 INTO v_salary;
    END WHILE;
END rm
```

Figure 8.18 An example of receiving multiple result sets from a caller procedure on LUW and
zSeries.

Another point this example demonstrates is that you can use the multiple result sets received both in parallel and sequentially. The first name and last name result sets are used in parallel to generate the string of employee names in the department. The salary result set is used after the first two result sets have been closed. Note that in this example, it is known that the two result sets used in parallel happen to have the same number of rows. In your project, if you choose to use two result sets with different numbers of rows in parallel, you must check the last row condition for each FETCH statement.

Receiving Results from a Procedure in a Trigger

In addition to being able to receive the results of a procedure in another procedure, you can also receive the output in a trigger. This greatly reduces the complexity and maintenance of your triggers by encapsulating code that is repeated in a stored procedure. Triggers are discussed in detail in the next chapter. Figure 8.19 shows a few simple examples are presented to illustrate how a trigger can be rewritten to use a stored procedure.

```
CREATE TRIGGER removeFreeManager
    AFTER DELETE ON department
    REFERENCING OLD AS old_row
    FOR EACH ROW MODE DB2SQL
    BEGIN ATOMIC
        DECLARE staffCount INT DEFAULT 0;
        SET staffCount = (SELECT COUNT(*)             --(1)
                            FROM department
                          WHERE mgrno = old_row.mgrno
                            AND location != 'Head Quarters');
        IF staffCount < 1 THEN                        --(2)
            DELETE FROM employee
            WHERE empno = old_row.mgrno;
        END IF;
    END
```

Figure 8.19   An example of a trigger to remove managers who no longer have any direct reports.

NOTE

On iSeries, for the example in Figure 8.19 to work, you will need to first drop the ROD foreign key on the DEPARTMENT table:

```
ALTER TABLE DEPARTMENT DROP FOREIGN KEY ROD;
```

On zSeries, the trigger in Figure 8.19 cannot be created because the IF statement is not supported in the trigger body (this explained indepth later in the chapter).

The example in Figure 8.19 is a trigger on the department table that removes any manager who no longer has any staff to manage. The logic in section (1) could be much more complex and may be repeated in other triggers. It would be better to move the logic to a stored procedure that could be used by other triggers or procedures. The stored procedure in Figure 8.20 contains the procedure logic.

```
CREATE PROCEDURE count_staff (IN p_mgrNumber char(6),
    OUT p_staffCount INT)
  LANGUAGE SQL
  SPECIFIC count_staff                      -- applies to LUW and iSeries
-- WLM ENVIRONMENT <env>                    -- applies to zSeries


cs: BEGIN
       SELECT COUNT(*) into p_staffCount
         FROM department
        WHERE mgrno = p_mgrNumber
          AND location != 'Head Quarter';

END cs
```

Figure 8.20 An example of a stored procedure to count the number of staff under a particular manager.

```
CREATE TRIGGER removeFreeManager2
    AFTER DELETE ON department
    REFERENCING OLD AS old_row
    FOR EACH ROW MODE DB2SQL
    BEGIN ATOMIC
      DECLARE staffCount INT DEFAULT 0;
   -- DECLARE tmp_mgrno CHAR(6);                --(1) applies to iSeries
   -- SET tmp_mgrno = old_row.mgrno;            --(2) applies to iSeries
   -- CALL count_staff(tmp_mgrno, staffCount);  --(3) use this CALL for iSeries
      CALL count_staff(old_row.mgrno, staffCount);
      IF staffCount < 1 THEN
          DELETE FROM employee
          WHERE empno = old_row.mgrno;
      END IF;
    END
```

Figure 8.21 An example of a trigger that calls a stored procedure.

The CALL statement of the trigger shown in Figure 8.21 uses a transition variable to pass in a parameter. On iSeries, a parameter being passed in a CALL statement cannot be a transition variable, hence one is declared.

A variable tmp_mgrno is declared on Line (1), initialized on Line (2) and then used in the CALL statement on Line (3).

In DB2 for zSeries as in DB2 for LUW, you are allowed to call a stored procedure from a trigger. A DB2 for zSeries trigger, however, has several limitations, such as the fact that the IF statement cannot be coded in the trigger action. These limitations are explained in more detail in Chapter 9, "User-Defined Functions and Triggers."

The sample in Figure 8.21 for the trigger removeFreeManager2 cannot be created as-is in DB2 for zSeries because the trigger contains a DECLARE and an IF statement. Rewriting the trigger so that it calls a stored procedure that includes all the logic including the IF statement should provide a partial workaround. Figure 8.20 can be rewritten as shown in Figure 8.22 and Figure 8.21 can be rewritten as shown in Figure 8.23.

```
CREATE PROCEDURE count_staff (IN  p_mgrNumber char(6))
    LANGUAGE SQL
    WLM ENVIRONMENT <env>
cs: BEGIN
        DECLARE v_staffcount INT DEFAULT 0;
        SELECT COUNT(*)
            INTO v_staffCount
            FROM department
            WHERE mgrno = p_mgrNumber
              AND location != 'Head Quarter';
        IF v_staffCount < 1 THEN                          -- (1)
            DELETE FROM employee
            WHERE empno = p_mgrNumber;
        END IF;
    END cs
```

Figure 8.22   Rewriting the stored procedure *count_staff* for DB2 for zSeries.

On Line (1), you can see how the IF statement logic has been moved from the trigger to the stored procedure.

```
CREATE TRIGGER removeFreeManager2
    AFTER DELETE ON department
    REFERENCING OLD AS old_row
    FOR EACH ROW MODE DB2SQL
    BEGIN ATOMIC
```

```
        CALL COUNT_STAFF(old_row.mgrno);
   END
```

Figure 8.23   Rewriting the trigger *removeFreeManager* for DB2 for zSeries.

Levels of Nesting

If you implement SQL Procedure A which calls SQL Procedure B, which in turn calls Procedure C, you have three levels of nested calls (A->B->C). DB2 LUW and DB2 for zSeries support up to 16 levels of SQL procedure nesting. iSeries has no limit to the number of nesting levels for SQL procedures and user-defined functions.

Recursion

Not only can SQL procedures call other SQL procedures, they can also call themselves. This concept is known as **recursion**. **Recursive SQL procedures** are a special case of nested SQL procedures.

Recursive procedures are sometimes the simplest solution to certain problems, even though they may be rewritten in a non-recursive way with the use of loops. Figure 8.24 shows an example of a recursive procedure.

```
CREATE PROCEDURE managers ( IN  p_deptno CHAR(3)
                          , OUT p_report_chain VARCHAR(100) )
   LANGUAGE SQL
   SPECIFIC managers                            -- applies to LUW and iSeries
-- WLM ENVIRONMENT <env>                        -- applies to zSeries

mn: BEGIN
    -- Declare variables
    DECLARE v_manager_name VARCHAR(15);
    DECLARE v_admrdept CHAR(3);
    DECLARE v_report_chain VARCHAR(100);
    DECLARE v_stmt VARCHAR(100) DEFAULT 'CALL managers(?,?)';      --(1)
applies to LUW or iSeries

    -- Procedure logic
    SELECT admrdept                                               --(2)
      INTO v_admrdept
      FROM department
     WHERE deptno=p_deptno;
```

```
    SELECT lastname                                           --(3)
      INTO v_manager_name
      FROM employee, department
     WHERE empno=mgrno
       AND deptno=p_deptno;


    IF (v_manager_name IS NULL) THEN
         SET v_manager_name = 'VACANT';
    END IF;


    IF ( v_admrdept IS NULL ) THEN
        SET p_report_chain = 'Department ' ||
                        p_deptno || ' not found.';            --(4)
    ELSEIF ( v_admrdept = p_deptno ) THEN                     --(5)
        SET p_report_chain = v_manager_name;
    ELSE
        --applies to LUW or iSeries
        PREPARE v_st from v_stmt;                             --(6)
        --applies to LUW
        EXECUTE v_st INTO v_report_chain USING v_admrdept;    --(7)
        --applies to iSeries
        --EXECUTE v_st USING v_admrdept, v_report_chain;      --(8)
        --applies to zSeries or iSeries
        --CALL managers (v_admrdept, v_report_chain);         --(9)
        SET p_report_chain = v_manager_name || ' -> ' || v_report_chain;
    END IF;
END mn
```

Figure 8.24   An example of a recursive procedure.

The procedure managers find the report chain of a department, which is indicated by a department number. For any department, there is an administrative department. The manager of a
department is not considered a member of this department but rather a member of the administrative department, except at the highest executive level.

   The basic logic is to use a department number to find the administrative department number
on Line (2), then to use the new department number obtained as the input in turn to find the next
level administrative department number on Line (7). The process will continue until the highest
executive level is reached.

   As with all recursive procedures, you need a terminating condition. In this case, the condition is the highest executive level where the department number is the same as the administrative
department number, or if the department number provided to the procedure is incorrect. See
Lines (2), (4), and (5).

The dynamic SQL on Line (1) is required on LUW in order to compile the procedure because the procedure is making a recursive call to call itself, and deferred validation is not supported. If static SQL is used, the procedure name will not be resolved at compile time and will generate a compile error. On zSeries and iSeries, however, deferred object validation is supported, and a static CALL statement can be used as shown on Line (9). In fact, on zSeries you have to use the static CALL statement because it cannot be prepared dynamically. On iSeries, either form of the CALL statement can be used. So the previous example is valid if Lines (6) and (8) are used in conjunction for the dynamic CALL, or just Line (9) for the static CALL.

The limit on the number of recursions is the same as the limit for nesting levels. You need to know how many levels of recursion your recursive SQL procedure will require. You might have to rewrite the code using an iterative solution if the limit is reached, or as a user-defined function.

Security

Detailed information about security issues related to SQL procedures are discussed in Appendix E, "Security Considerations in SQL Procedures."

When you create an SQL procedure, you may specify CONTAINS SQL, READS SQL DATA, or MODIFIES SQL DATA. The NO SQL clause is not valid for SQL procedures. Refer to Chapter 2, "Basic SQL Procedure Structure," for more information.

A nested SQL procedure will not be allowed to call a target procedure with a higher data access level. For example, an SQL procedure created with READS SQL DATA can call SQL procedures created with either CONTAINS SQL or READS SQL DATA, but cannot call SQL procedures created with MODIFIES SQL DATA.

With this restriction, a user without proper privileges will not be able to obtain access to confidential data, even if he knows the name and signature of the SQL procedure that reads or modifies the data. You may have given access to a staff member to a stored procedure that reads the data. If he or she modifies the read-only stored procedure to call a stored procedure that modifies the data, that person would not be allowed. This would prevent unauthorized data manipulation by calling other stored procedures that can modify data.

Summary

This chapter covered nested SQL procedures. Data is passed between the procedures and external applications via parameters or result sets. Output parameters are used to return single values, while result sets are used to return rows of data. The return status, which is of integer type, should be reserved as an execution status indicator only.

You have two options in returning result sets. By using the TO CALLER or TO CLIENT clauses, you can control the destination and the visibility of the result sets. Use TO CLIENT (not supported on zSeries) if the result set is meant for an external application only. Use TO CALLER if the result set is meant for direct callers.

Recursive SQL procedures are special cases of nested SQL procedures. Dynamic SQL is required to implement recursive procedures on LUW.

User-Defined Functions and Triggers

In this chapter, you will learn

- What User-Defined Functions (UDFs) are
- How UDFs can be used to simplify your application development efforts
- What triggers are
- How triggers can be used to transparently and consistently enforce application logic in the database

UDFs and **triggers** are database objects that help reduce the complexity of database application development.

On LUW, although the language syntax for SQL PL is consistent for all types of objects from an application development perspective, the language implementation to support SQL PL for stored procedures is different from that for UDFs and triggers. SQL PL support in UDFs and triggers is a subset of that in stored procedures. It is referred to as the **inline SQL PL**.

NOTE
Although the UDFs and triggers are covered in this chapter, inline SQL PL is not discussed here. Appendix B, "Inline SQL PL for DB2 UDB for Linux, UNIX, and Windows," is fully dedicated to the topic and introduces how to implement stand-alone code as well.

On iSeries and zSeries, SQL UDFs and triggers are implemented just like SQL procedures. They are compiled during the creation process and the corresponding programs are executed when the objects are invoked.

The *CREATE FUNCTION* Statement

There are basically three different types of UDFs. **SQL functions**, as the name implies, are written in SQL PL. The function can be coded to return a scalar value, a single row (LUW only), or a table of data (LUW and iSeries only). **External functions** are defined in the database with references to object code libraries that are written in other languages such as C or Java. **Sourced functions** are registered functions that reference to another built-in or user-defined function. They are useful for supporting existing functions with user-defined types. This book covers only SQL functions.

Like most database objects in DB2, SQL functions are created with a CREATE statement. Complete syntax of the CREATE FUNCTION statement is shown in Figure 9.1.

> **NOTE**
> Differences in the CREATE FUNCTION statement for iSeries and zSeries platforms are discussed at the end of this chapter.

```
>>-CREATE FUNCTION--function-name------------------------------->

>-- (--+-------------------------------+--)--*------------------->
       | .-,-------------------------. |
       | V                           | |
       '---parameter-name--data-type--+-'

>--RETURNS--+-data-type-----------------+--*-------------------->
            '-+-ROW---+--| column-list |-'
              '-TABLE-'

                                  .-LANGUAGE SQL-.
>--+-----------------------+--*--+--------------+--*---------->
   '-SPECIFIC--specific-name-'

   .-NOT DETERMINISTIC-.       .-EXTERNAL ACTION----.
>--+-------------------+--*--+--------------------+--*---------->
   '-DETERMINISTIC-----'       '-NO EXTERNAL ACTION-'

   .-READS SQL DATA---------.       .-STATIC DISPATCH-.
>--+-----------------------+--*--+-----------------+--*-------->
   +-CONTAINS SQL-----------+
   |                        |
   '-MODIFIES SQL DATA------'
```

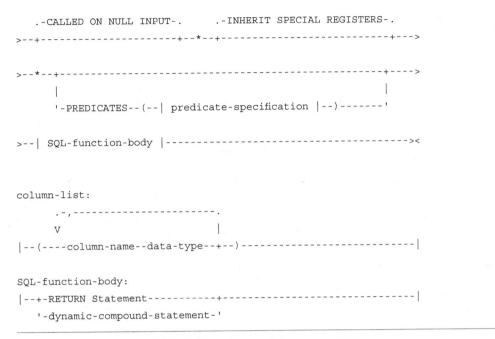

```
        .-CALLED ON NULL INPUT-.      .-INHERIT SPECIAL REGISTERS-.
>--+----------------------+--*--+----------------------------+--->


>--*--+-------------------------------------------------------+---->
      |                                                       |
      '-PREDICATES--(--| predicate-specification |--)-------'

>--| SQL-function-body |---------------------------------------><



column-list:
        .-,----------------------.
        V                        |
|-- (----column-name--data-type--+--)---------------------------|

SQL-function-body:
|--+-RETURN Statement----------+-----------------------------|
   '-dynamic-compound-statement-'
```

Figure 9.1   The *CREATE FUNCTION* statement syntax for LUW.

Function Name and Parameters

The function name specified in the CREATE FUNCTION statement is limited to 18 characters on LUW and 128 characters on iSeries and zSeries. It must begin with a letter, followed by zero or more letters, digits, or underscore characters (_).

A function is said to be **qualified** if it is referenced by a two-part name that is made up of a schema and a function name. The restrictions for schema name on each platform include the following:

- On LUW, the schema of a user-defined function cannot begin with SYS

- On iSeries, the schema name cannot be QSYS2, QSYS, QTEMP, or SYSIBM.

- On zSeries, the schema name can begin with SYS only if the schema is SYSADM or SYSTOOLS, or if the user issuing the statement has SYSADM or SYSCTRL privileges.

Unqualified functions are resolved in the same manner as the unqualified procedures. Refer to Chapter 2, "Basic SQL Procedure Structure," for details.

To uniquely identify a function, DB2 relies on the function signature. A **function signature** is a combination of a schema name, a function name, a list of parameters, and the data types of the parameters. DB2 allows all data types to be used in SQL UDFs, with the exception of LONG VARCHAR and LONG VARGRAPHIC on LUW.

If any parameter is to be used for a UDF, you need to specify the parameter name and its data type inside the parentheses. Use a comma to separate multiple parameters. Figure 9.2 shows an example of functions with zero or more parameters.

```
CREATE FUNCTION functest(). . .
CREATE FUNCTION prod.sum_abc(p_type INTEGER, p_value DECIMAL). . .
CREATE FUNCTION test.getsalary(p_name VARCHAR(10), p_age SMALLINT). . .
```

Figure 9.2   Examples of functions with zero or more parameters.

It is valid to define more than one function with the same name in a database as long as they have unique function signatures. For example, two functions with the same name in the same schema are unique if the number of parameters or the data types of the parameters are different. These functions are known as **overloaded functions**. Figure 9.3 shows some examples of overloaded functions.

```
CREATE FUNCTION db2admin.functest(v_int INT, v_vc VARCHAR(100)) ...
CREATE FUNCTION db2admin.functest(v_double DOUBLE, v_vc VARCHAR(100)) ...
CREATE FUNCTION db2admin.functest(v_vc VARCHAR(100), v_ts TIMESTAMPS) ...
CREATE FUNCTION db2admin.functest(v_vc VARCHAR(100), v_ts TIMESTAMPS, v_si
SMALLINT) ...
```

Figure 9.3   Examples of overloaded functions.

Functions with the same number of parameters and the same data types of the parameters are considered to have the same signature, even if the length or the precision of the parameters are different:

```
CREATE FUNCTION DB2ADMIN.FUNCTEST(V_VC VARCHAR(100))...
CREATE FUNCTION DB2ADMIN.FUNCTEST(V_VC VARCHAR(200))...
```

These functions are considered to have the same signature, even though one uses VARCHAR(100) and the other uses VARCHAR(200). They cannot be overloaded.

As you may have noticed, the functions are overloaded differently from the procedures. While functions with different number of parameters or with the same number of parameters but different parameter data types can both be overloaded, only procedures with different number of parameters can be overloaded. Refer to Chapter 2, "Basic SQL Procedure Structure," for more details on overloaded procedures.

NOTE
Overloaded SQL functions are supported on zSeries, but overloaded SQL procedures are not.

Returns Function Output

The type of data a UDF can return is not restricted only to a single value but also a row (LUW only) or a table of data (LUW and iSeries only). If you want to return a scalar value, simply specify its data type in the RETURNS clause, like this:

```
CREATE FUNCTION functest () RETURNS INTEGER . . .
```

For row and table functions, specify the ROW or TABLE keyword in the RETURNS clause. Following that, you need to provide the name and data type of each column to be returned. Here are some examples:

```
CREATE FUNCTION functest () RETURNS ROW    (name VARCHAR(10), age INTEGER) . . .
CREATE FUNCTION functest () RETURNS TABLE (prod_id SMALLINT, price DECIMAL) . . .
```

> **NOTE**
> On iSeries, the DISALLOW PARALLEL clause must be specified for UDFs that return TABLE.
> Refer to the iSeries section at the end of this chapter for more details.

Specific Name

A **specific name** is used to uniquely identify a UDF, and it is particularly useful when using overloaded functions. The specific name can be used with UDFs in the same manner as with the SQL procedures. Refer to Chapter 2, "Basic SQL Procedure Structure," for more details.

> **NOTE**
> The specific name is supported on zSeries for UDFs, but not for SQL procedures.

Language SQL

On LUW and zSeries, the LANGUAGE SQL clause is optional, and if omitted it is assumed to be an SQL UDF. On iSeries, LANGUAGE SQL must be specified as the first clause following the parameter list and RETURNS clause.

> **TIP**
> For portability, always use LANGUAGE SQL as the first clause after RETURNS.

DETERMINISTIC or *NOT DETERMINISTIC*

This clause allows you to specify if the function is DETERMINISTIC or NOT DETERMINISTIC. A UDF is **deterministic** if it returns the same results for each invocation of identical input parameters. On the other hand, a UDF is **not deterministic** if the results depend on the input values and/or other values that may change, such as the current date or time. Whenever possible, identifying a function as DETERMINISTIC allows DB2 to perform additional optimizations to improve performance.

The default is NOT DETERMINISTIC, which is typically the case for most UDFs.

EXTERNAL ACTION or *NO EXTERNAL ACTION*

This optional clause specifies whether or not the function takes some action that changes the state of an object not managed by the database manager. By specifying NO EXTERNAL ACTION, the system can use certain optimizations that assume functions have no external impacts. The default is EXTERNAL ACTION.

CONTAINS SQL, READS SQL DATA, MODIFIES SQL DATA

This clause restricts the type of SQL statements that can be executed by the function. On top of the standard DB2 security model on database objects, this clause provides extra security control over the function body.

When CONTAINS SQL is specified, only statements that do not read or modify data are allowed in the function. Examples of such statements are DECLARE variables, SET variables, and SQL control statements.

READS SQL DATA is the default option. It can be specified if the function contains only statements that do not modify SQL data. There is one exception case where tables might not be accessible from a function even if READS SQL DATA is specified. Consider this statement:

```
UPDATE EMPLOYEE SET SALARY = SALARY + BONUS(EMPNO)
```

BONUS is a UDF defined with READS SQL DATA. SQL statements that read from the EMPLOYEE table are not allowed in the UDF. This is due to conflict operations on the table where the statement invoking the function is trying to update EMPLOYEE and BONUS only allows READ access.

For nested UDFs (and in fact nested UDFs, triggers, and procedures), data access in the nested object is allowed to be more restrictive, but will fail if the nested object is defined with a less restrictive level.

On LUW, MODIFIES SQL DATA is supported for SQL table functions only. All SQL statements supported in the dynamic compound SQL statement block in the function body are allowed. Refer to the section later in this chapter for an introduction to dynamic compound SQL statements.

On iSeries, MODIFIES SQL DATA is supported for all SQL function types.

On zSeries, MODIFIES SQL DATA is not supported.

STATIC DISPATCH

This optional clause indicates that at function resolution time, DB2 chooses a function based on the static types (declared types) of the parameters of the function. This behavior is the default and the only value that can be specified. This clause is optional.

CALLED ON NULL INPUT

This clause indicates that the function will always be invoked even if its input parameters are null. This behavior is the default and is the only value that can be specified. This clause is optional.

NOTE

On iSeries, a RETURN NULL ON NULL INPUT option is supported, in addition to the CALLED ON NULL INPUT clause. It specifies that if the function is invoked with any NULL parameters, a NULL is returned.

INHERIT SPECIAL REGISTERS (LUW and iSeries Only)

The INHERIT SPECIAL REGISTERS option works the same with UDFs as with the SQL procedures. Refer to Chapter 2, "Basic SQL Procedure Structure," for more details.

PREDICATES (LUW only)

PREDICATES is an optional clause that is valid for scalar functions only. It allows the predicates of an SQL statement that will be using the function to exploit index extensions. An **index extension** is an index object for use with indexes that have structured type or user-defined type columns.

SQL Function Body

The **function body** contains the logic of the SQL function. It is made up of a RETURN statement or a dynamic compound SQL statement. The RETURN statement is used to return the result of a function. The syntax of the statement is shown in Figure 9.4.

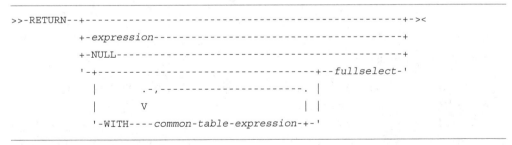

```
>>-RETURN--+-----------------------------------------------+-><
           +-expression------------------------------------+
           +-NULL------------------------------------------+
           '-+-----------------------------------+--fullselect-'
             |          .-,--------------------. |
             |          V                      | |
             '-WITH----common-table-expression-+-'
```

Figure 9.4 *RETURN* statement syntax.

Depending on whether the function output type is a scalar value, a row, or a table of data, different options are supported in the body of the RETURN statement.

An **expression** specifies a value which can be a constant, a special register, CASE expression, or another function invocation. Data type of the expression result must match what is specified in the RETURNS clause of the CREATE FUNCTION statement. An expression is supported for all three UDF types.

Unlike SQL procedures, you can return a NULL value from SQL functions. Because both the expression and NULL clauses return only a single value, they can only be specified in scalar SQL functions.

A **compound statement** combines one or more other SQL statements into one execution block. It is supported on LUW and iSeries only. For more information on compound statement support on LUW, refer to Appendix B, "Inline SQL PL for DB2 UDB for Linux, UNIX, and Windows."

User-Defined Functions by Examples

Examples of scalar UDF, table UDF, and procedure invocation inside UDFs in this section will show you more DB2 UDF features.

A Simple Scalar UDF Example

The example in Figure 9.5 demonstrates a simple UDF, which will trim the blanks off a string from both sides.

> **NOTE**
> A similar built-in function, TRIM, does exist on iSeries. However, the example is provided only as an illustration.

```
CREATE FUNCTION trim_both ( p_var VARCHAR(100) )          --(1)
   RETURNS VARCHAR(100)                                   --(2)
   LANGUAGE SQL
   SPECIFIC trim
   RETURN LTRIM(RTRIM(p_var))                             --(3)
```

Figure 9.5   A simple UDF example.

The UDF uses two DB2 built-in functions: LTRIM and RTRIM, which trims the blanks off the string from the left and the right side, respectively.

This UDF simply takes one VARCHAR input variable on Line (1) and routes the parameter to the LTRIM and RTRIM functions on Line (3). The function is defined with RETURNS VARCHAR(100) on Line (2), which is a single value and, by definition, a scalar function.

To test the UDF in Figure 9.5, you can issue the following SQL statement:

```
SELECT trim_both(' abc ') FROM SYSIBM.SYSDUMMY1


1
------------------------
abc


  1 record(s) selected.
```

The result is that the blanks at both sides are trimmed off.

A Complex Scalar UDF Example

Now that you have a good understanding of UDFs, here is a more complex example. Consider a scenario in which your application frequently retrieves the department name to which an employee belongs. The employee table, however, only contains the department code for employees, and you don't want to write your queries to join the employee table and the department table every time the department name is needed. To simplify this task, a UDF can be created that takes the employee number as a parameter and returns the department name. Figure 9.6 presents code for a function that would satisfy these requirements.

```
CREATE FUNCTION deptname(p_empid VARCHAR(6))                        --(1)
RETURNS VARCHAR(30)                                                 --(2)
LANGUAGE SQL
SPECIFIC deptname                                                   --(3)
d: BEGIN ATOMIC                                                     --(4)
    DECLARE v_department_name VARCHAR(30);
    DECLARE v_err VARCHAR(70);
    SET v_department_name = (
        SELECT d.deptname FROM department d, employee e            --(5)
            WHERE e.workdept=d.deptno AND e.empno= p_empid);
    SET v_err = 'Error: employee ' || p_empid || ' was not found';
    IF v_department_name IS NULL THEN
        SIGNAL SQLSTATE '80000' SET MESSAGE_TEXT=v_err;            --(6)
    END IF;
  RETURN v_department_name;
END d                                                              --(7)
```

Figure 9.6   A scalar UDF that returns a department name, given an employee number (for LUW and iSeries only).

> **NOTE**
>
> The example in Figure 9.6 does not work for zSeries because compound statements (`BEGIN...END`) are not supported.

In Figure 9.6, the SQL UDF `deptname` takes an employee ID as its parameter on Line (1). If you looked at the DDL for the employee table, you would notice that the type for the EMPNO column is actually CHAR(6). The function parameter, however, is defined as VARCHAR(6) because DB2 assumes VARCHAR types to resolve a UDF call. If you defined the input parameter as CHAR(6), every time you called the function you would have to cast the input parameter to CHAR(6) as follows (which is highly inconvenient):

```
SELECT *
  FROM department d
 WHERE d.deptname=deptname(CAST ('000060' AS CHAR(6)))
```

> **TIP**
>
> Use VARCHAR types for character string input in UDF definitions.

On Line (2), the function is defined to return a single value of type VARCHAR(30) which, by definition, makes it a scalar function.

In our first example, the function body was a single line. To use multiple lines of code in the UDF, the body of the function is wrapped with BEGIN ATOMIC on Line (4) and END on Line (7).

> **NOTE**
>
> On LUW, the atomic compound statements must be used in the UDF body.

To get the department name, the `employee` and `department` tables are joined on the department code (`deptno` and `workdept` columns) on Line (5), and further filtered by the employee number (which is unique) to guarantee that at most one row will be returned. Note that the SET statement is used to accomplish this rather than SELECT INTO. On LUW, SELECT INTO is currently not supported in dynamic compound statements, but using the SET statement works just as well. For more information, refer to Appendix B, "Inline SQL PL for DB2 UDB for Linux, UNIX, and Windows." On iSeries, the SELECT INTO is supported.

As a best practice, avoid using variable names that are the same as column names within queries. Within a query, DB2 always resolves column names first before evaluating variable and parameter values. Consider what would happen if the input parameter was called `empno` instead of `p_empid` and replaced on Line (5) in the previous code sample with the SELECT statement:

```
SELECT d.deptname
  FROM department d
       ,employee e
```

```
WHERE e.workdept=d.deptno
  AND e.empno= empno
```

Because of the order in which DB2 evaluates column and variable values, the previous query is equivalent the following query, which is incorrect:

```
SELECT d.deptname
  FROM department d
       ,employee e
 WHERE e.workdept=d.deptno
   AND 1=1
```

If you use the variable naming scheme that has been used throughout the book, (the p_ prefix for parameter names and the v_ prefix for local variable names), you will not run into this problem.

TIP

Do not use the column names as variable names. DB2 always resolves column names first before evaluating variable and parameter values.

Looking at the SELECT statement on Line (5), there is a possibility that an invalid employee number could be passed as a parameter. The SELECT statement will then return no values and v_department_name will be null. To better handle the scenario, SIGNAL SQLSTATE is used on Line (6) to throw an error if the employee ID is not found. The SIGNAL SQLSTATE code is optional because, had it been left out, the function would simply return null which may also be reasonable depending on your needs.

The scalar SQL UDF can be used in a SELECT column list, in a predicate, or as part of an expression, as shown in Figures 9.7, 9.8, and 9.9.

```
SELECT e.empno
      ,e.firstnme
      ,e.lastname
      ,deptname(e.empno) department_name
  FROM employee e
 WHERE e.empno='000060'


EMPNO  FIRSTNME     LASTNAME         DEPARTMENT_NAME
------ ------------ ---------------- ----------------------------------------
000060 IRVING       STERN            MANUFACTURING SYSTEMS

 1 record(s) selected.
```

Figure 9.7 Scalar UDF in a *SELECT* column.

```
SELECT *
  FROM department d
 WHERE d.deptname=deptname('000060')


DEPTNO DEPTNAME                         MGRNO  ADMRDEPT LOCATION
------ ---------------------------- ------ -------- ----------------

D11    MANUFACTURING SYSTEMS            000060 D01        -


  1 record(s) selected.
```

Figure 9.8   Scalar UDF in a predicate.

```
SELECT deptname('000060') || ' department'
  FROM SYSIBM.SYSDUMMY1


1
-----------------------------------
MANUFACTURING SYSTEMS department


  1 record(s) selected.
```

Figure 9.9   Scalar UDF as part of an expression.

NOTE

DB2 on zSeries supports the same UDF usages. However, the examples in Figures 9.7 to 9.9 do not work on zSeries because the particular UDF is not supported.

A Table UDF Example (LUW and iSeries)

Table functions return entire tables and are used in the FROM clause of a SELECT. Suppose you want to have a table function that dynamically returns a result set of all employees in a given department. Use a table UDF that takes a single parameter representing the department ID.

To build the table function, the resulting table structure needs to be determined. In this example, the following should be returned: the employee number, last name, and first name of employees. To ensure that you don't encounter incompatible data type errors, first look at what data types are used for the employee table. From the CLP on LUW, enter the following SQL command:

```
DESCRIBE TABLE employee
```

Column name	Type schema	Type name	Length	Scale	Null
EMPNO	SYSIBM	CHARACTER	6	0	No
FIRSTNME	SYSIBM	VARCHAR	12	0	No
MIDINIT	SYSIBM	CHARACTER	1	0	No
LASTNAME	SYSIBM	VARCHAR	15	0	No
WORKDEPT	SYSIBM	CHARACTER	3	0	Yes
PHONENO	SYSIBM	CHARACTER	4	0	Yes
HIREDATE	SYSIBM	DATE	4	0	Yes
JOB	SYSIBM	CHARACTER	8	0	Yes
EDLEVEL	SYSIBM	SMALLINT	2	0	No
SEX	SYSIBM	CHARACTER	1	0	Yes
BIRTHDATE	SYSIBM	DATE	4	0	Yes
SALARY	SYSIBM	DECIMAL	9	2	Yes
BONUS	SYSIBM	DECIMAL	9	2	Yes
COMM	SYSIBM	DECIMAL	9	2	Yes

```
  14 record(s) selected.
```

From this table description, you can determine that the returned table of our table function will have the following definition:

```
CREATE TABLE  ... (empno CHAR(6), lastname VARCHAR(15), firstnme VARCHAR(20))
```

The table function can now be created with the following code shown in Figure 9.10.

```
CREATE FUNCTION getEmployee(p_dept VARCHAR(3))
RETURNS TABLE                                                           --(1)
    (empno VARCHAR(6), lastname VARCHAR(15), firstnme VARCHAR(12))      --(2)
LANGUAGE SQL
SPECIFIC getEmployee              -- LUW and iSeries
--DISALLOW PARALLEL               -- iSeries
RETURN                                                                  --(3)
SELECT e.empno, e.lastname, e.firstnme
  FROM employee e
 WHERE e.workdept=p_dept
```

Figure 9.10   Example of a user-defined table function.

In Figure 9.10, the UDF is defined to return a table on Line (1), and will have the definition previously composed using the column types found in the employee table on Line (2).

The body of this query is quite simple; the result of a SELECT statement that retrieves all employees for a given department is returned on Line (3).

After the previous table function has been created, it can be used in queries such as the following in Figure 9.11:

```
SELECT * FROM TABLE(getEmployee('E21')) AS emp
ORDER BY lastname


EMPNO   LASTNAME        FIRSTNME
------  --------------- ------------
000340 GOUNOT           JASON
000330 LEE              WING
000320 MEHTA            RAMLAL
000100 SPENSER          THEODORE


  4 record(s) selected.
```

Figure 9.11   Query the simple table UDF example.

Note the following information from Figure 9.11:

- If you have to order the values returned by the table function, you must specify it in the calling SELECT statement as illustrated in the previous figures. ORDER BY cannot be specified inside the table function body.

- The function is called in the FROM clause of a SELECT statement, and the table function must be cast to a table type by using the TABLE() function. Furthermore, you must alias the table returned by the table function (such as emp as shown previously).

The example in Figure 9.10 shows the simplest case of a table function. It is only useful if all the data you need already exists in the table. What if you want to build some of your business logic into the table function? Assume now you received a new request to insert a default record to the employee table if the input department number does not exist. Figure 9.12 shows how you can build this business logic in an SQL table function.

```
CREATE FUNCTION getEmployee2(p_dept VARCHAR(3))
RETURNS TABLE
    (empno VARCHAR(6),
     lastname VARCHAR(15),
     firstnme VARCHAR(12))
LANGUAGE SQL
```

```
SPECIFIC getEnumEmployee2                    -- LUW and iSeries
MODIFIES SQL DATA                                            -- (1)
--DISALLOW PARALLEL                    -- iSeries
ge2: BEGIN ATOMIC
  DECLARE v_cnt int DEFAULT 0;                               -- (2)

  SET v_cnt = (SELECT COUNT(*) FROM employee WHERE workdept = p_dept);  -- (3)

  IF (v_cnt = 0) THEN
    INSERT INTO employee                                     -- (4)
      (empno, firstnme, midinit, lastname, workdept, edlevel)
    VALUES ('000000', 'No Record', 'N', 'New Department', p_dept, 0);
  END IF;

  RETURN                                                     --(5)
    SELECT e.empno, e.lastname, e.firstnme
    FROM employee e
    WHERE e.workdept=p_dept;
END ge2
```

Figure 9.12   Example of a complex table UDF.

Figure 9.12 is a modified table UDF based on the function in Figure 9.10. To be able to modify the employee table as the business logic required, the MODIFIES SQL DATA clause has to be included in the function header on Line (1). Otherwise, you will receive an SQL error.

```
On LUW:
SQL0374N  The "MODIFIES SQL DATA" clause has not been specified in the CREATE
FUNCTION statement for LANGUAGE SQL function "DB2ADMIN.GETENUMEMPLOYEE2" but an
examination of the function body reveals that it should be specified.  LINE
NUMBER=26.  SQLSTATE=428C2

On iSeries (shortened):
SQL State: 2F002
Vendor Code: -577

Message: [SQL0577] Modifying SQL data not permitted.
```

A local variable v_cnt is declared on Line (2) and used on Line (3) to check for any record in the
employee table for the department whose number is passed in as the input parameter. If there is
no record found, a default record with dummy names will be inserted into the employee table on
Line (4) before the content of the table is returned on Line (5). Note that because the SELECT
statement after the RETURN statement on Line (5) is now part of the compound statement, a semicolon is required at the end of the statement as the delimiter. If you compare this code snippet
with Figure 9.10, you will notice that the SELECT statement is not followed by a semicolon.

Test the table function using a similar query as shown in Figure 9.11; you should get the
same result set. However, if you query with a new department number, you will see a dummy row
being returned. These two sample queries are shown in Figure 9.13.

```
SELECT * FROM TABLE(getEmployee2('E21')) AS emp


EMPNO   LASTNAME           FIRSTNME
------  ----------------   ------------

000100 SPENSER             THEODORE
000320 MEHTA               RAMLAL
000330 LEE                 WING
000340 GOUNOT              JASON


  4 record(s) selected.


SELECT * FROM TABLE(getEmployee2('111')) AS emp


EMPNO   LASTNAME           FIRSTNME
------  ----------------   ------------
000000 New Department      No Record


  1 record(s) selected.
```

Figure 9.13   Query the complex table UDF example.

NOTE
If the iSeries sample database is being used, you will need to drop the red foreign key constraint on the employee table for the example in Figure 9.13 to work.

Invoking SQL Procedures in UDFs (LUW and iSeries Only)

On LUW and iSeries, it is possible to invoke SQL procedures from UDFs. This is particularly
useful on LUW, because it provides a way to overcome limitations of inline SQL PL. The ability
to invoke SQL procedures allows you to use any DB2 SQL PL features in your UDFs directly or
indirectly.

> **TIP**
>
> On LUW, use SQL procedures to work around inline SQL PL limitations in SQL UDFs.

The example in Figure 9.6 only supports simple error handling. Any SQL error will force the function to stop and the standard DB2 SQL error codes return to the application. The application has to be able to analyze and handle DB2-specific SQL error codes. This could be inconvenient if your application works with multiple DBMSs.

To make this transparent to the application, a simple UDF can be used as a wrapper, as shown in Figure 9.14. It calls an SQL procedure where all business logic is implemented (demonstrated in Figure 9.15), captures errors returned from the stored procedure, and returns a user-defined error code.

```
CREATE FUNCTION deptname2 (p_empid VARCHAR(6))
RETURNS VARCHAR(30)
LANGUAGE SQL
SPECIFIC deptname2
READS SQL DATA                                               -- (1)
d2: BEGIN ATOMIC
    DECLARE v_department_name VARCHAR(30);
    DECLARE v_error INT;

    CALL deptname_sp (p_empid, v_department_name, v_error);  -- (2)

    IF (v_error = 1) THEN                                    -- (3)
        SIGNAL SQLSTATE '80001' SET MESSAGE_TEXT='The employee is not found';
    ELSEIF (v_error= 2) THEN
        SIGNAL SQLSTATE '80002' SET MESSAGE_TEXT='The department is not found';
    ELSEIF (v_error= 3) THEN
        SIGNAL SQLSTATE '80003' SET MESSAGE_TEXT='Duplicate department numbers';
    ELSEIF (v_error= 4) THEN
        SIGNAL SQLSTATE '80004' SET MESSAGE_TEXT='Other fatal errors';
    END IF;

    RETURN v_department_name;                                -- (4)
END d2
```

Figure 9.14   Example of an SQL UDF invoking an SQL procedure.

Because the business logic is moved to the supporting SQL stored procedure, the UDF shown in Figure 9.14 is only a wrapper. The UDF serves three purposes:

- It invokes the SQL procedure on Line (2).

- It generates customized error code and user-friendly error message at the IF...ELSE block on Line (3).

- It returns the department name to the application on Line (4).

The READS SQL DATA option on Line (1) is the default value. It is spelled out here to make it clear that the data access restrictions in the UDF and the procedure are at the same level. More details on the data access are discussed in the later section of this chapter.

```
CREATE PROCEDURE deptname_sp
  ( IN  p_empid VARCHAR(6),
    OUT p_department_name VARCHAR(30),
    OUT p_error INT)
LANGUAGE SQL
SPECIFIC deptname_sp
READS SQL DATA                                        -- (1)
ds: BEGIN
    -- Declare variables
    DECLARE SQLSTATE CHAR(5) DEFAULT '00000';
    DECLARE v_cnt INT;

    -- Declare condition handlers
    DECLARE EXIT HANDLER FOR SQLEXCEPTION             -- (2)
        SET p_error = 4;
    DECLARE EXIT HANDLER FOR SQLSTATE '21000'         -- (3)
        SET p_error = 3;
    DECLARE EXIT HANDLER FOR NOT FOUND                -- (4)
        SET p_error = 2;
    DECLARE EXIT HANDLER FOR SQLSTATE '99999'         -- (5)
        SET p_error = 1;

    -- Procedure logic
    SET p_error = 0;
    SET p_department_name = '';

    SELECT COUNT(*)                                   -- (6)
    INTO v_cnt
    FROM employee
```

```
   WHERE empno = p_empid;

   IF (v_cnt = 0) THEN
     SIGNAL SQLSTATE '99999';                           -- (7)
   END IF;

   SELECT d.deptname                                    -- (8)
   INTO p_department_name
   FROM department d, employee e
   WHERE e.workdept=d.deptno
AND e.empno= p_empid;


END ds
```

Figure 9.15   Use an SQL procedure to support an SQL UDF.

Because a UDF with the READS SQL DATA option cannot call a procedure with the MODIFIES SQL DATA option, the READS SQL DATA option on Line (1) of Figure 9.15 is required. More details on the data access are discussed in the later section of this chapter.

The business logic is moved from the SQL UDF to the supporting SQL procedure on Line (8). Because the SQL procedures support the complete set of SQL PL, more sophisticated error handlings are implemented. Four error handlers are declared on Lines (2) to (5) to provide more details on exactly what goes wrong if an error happens.

The extra SELECT statement on Line (6) and the SIGNAL statement on Line (7) are used to check if the employee exists. If the employee does not exist, the SELECT statement on Line (6) sets the v_cnt to 0, which will raise SQLSTATE '99999' on Line (7). The raised SQLSTATE is captured by EXIT HANDLER on Line (5), which returns customized error code 1 to the calling UDF for further process.

Only if the employee exists does the SELECT statement on Line (8) execute. If the statement returns no rows, you know it is caused by the department table. The EXIT HANDLER on Line (4) for the NOT FOUND condition captures the error and returns error code 2 to the calling UDF for further process. Please note that due to the validation of the employee table on Lines (6) and (7), the NOT FOUND condition can only be caused by the department table.

DB2 does not allow more than one row returned in a SELECT ... INTO ... statement such as the statement on Line (8). If more than one department name is returned for one department number, DB2 will not simply pick the first one. DB2 will raise an SQL error instead.

```
SQL0811N  The result of a scalar fullselect, SELECT INTO statement, or   VALUES
INTO statement is more than one row.  SQLSTATE=21000
```

This error is captured by an exit handler on Line (3). The EXIT HANDLER on Line (2) simply captures all other SQL errors. If the error handler on Line (2) is not declared, unhandled SQL errors will cause the SQL procedure to stop and error code to be returned to the UDF. Because the UDF in Figure 9.14 cannot handle the error code either, the UDF is stopped in turn. The DB2 error code is further passed to your application by the UDF.

Invoke the deptname2 UDF with a valid employee ID, and the result is a valid department number in the sample database.

```
SELECT deptname2('000010') FROM SYSIBM.SYSDUMMY1


1
------------------------------
SPIFFY COMPUTER SERVICE DIV.


  1 record(s) selected.
```

If a nonexisting employee ID is used, a more meaningful customized error message tells you exactly what happened.

```
SELECT deptname2('123456') FROM SYSIBM.SYSDUMMY1


1
------------------------------
SQL0438N  Application raised error with diagnostic text: "The employee is not
found".  SQLSTATE=80001
```

Some extra invalid data are needed to see other newly implemented error messages. Invoking the UDF with the employee number of a newly inserted employee who has an invalid department number produces the following:

```
INSERT INTO employee
(empno, firstnme, midinit, lastname, workdept, edlevel) VALUES ('010010', 'No
Record', 'N', 'New Record', 'FAK', 0)
DB20000I  The SQL command completed successfully.


SELECT deptname2('010010') FROM SYSIBM.SYSDUMMY1


1
------------------------------
SQL0438N  Application raised error with diagnostic text: "The department is
not found".  SQLSTATE=80002
```

Some data setup is required if you are interested in seeing how the new implementation works with duplicate department numbers:

```
INSERT INTO employee
(empno, firstnme, midinit, lastname, workdept, edlevel) VALUES ('010020', 'No
Record', 'N', 'New Record', 'AAA', 0)
DB20000I  The SQL command completed successfully.


INSERT INTO department (deptno, deptname, admrdept) VALUES ('AAA', 'Duplicate
Name', 'A00')
DB20000I  The SQL command completed successfully.


INSERT INTO department (deptno, deptname, admrdept) VALUES ('AAA', 'Duplicate
Name', 'A00')
DB20000I  The SQL command completed successfully.


SELECT deptname2('010020') FROM SYSIBM.SYSDUMMY1


1
-------------------------------
SQL0438N  Application raised error with diagnostic text: "Duplicate department
numbers".  SQLSTATE=80003
```

For other considerations of invoking SQL procedures in UDFs and triggers, refer to the later section of this chapter.

NOTE

If the iSeries sample database is being used, in order for the series of examples above to work you will need to drop the red foreign key on the employee table, drop the q_<schema>_department_deptno_00001 primary key constraint on the department table, and drop the xdept1 unique index on the department table.

The *CREATE TRIGGER* Statement

Triggers are database objects associated with a table or a view to define operations that should occur automatically upon an INSERT, UPDATE, or DELETE operation (hereafter called the **triggering SQL statement**) on that table or view. Operations performed by triggers occur within the database engine and are therefore transparent to the application.

There is often application logic (or rules) that should always be enforced across all applications. These rules may exist because data in one table may be related to data in others. If you have many applications that share a set of tables, it can be cumbersome to ensure that all applications follow and enforce these logic rules consistently and properly. To compound the problem, if the logic or rules change, application code changes are required for all affected applications.

Triggers can solve this problem by moving logic from the application level to the database level so that all applications share the same code which enforces these rules. If there is ever a change in the rules, you only need to change the trigger definitions in the database, and all applications will follow the new rules without requiring any additional changes.

Here are some examples of how triggers might be used:

- When inserting, triggers can be used to supply, validate, or manipulate data before allowing an insert operation to occur.

- When updating, triggers can be used to compare the new value (supplied by the UPDATE statement) with the existing value in the table to ensure that the transition from old value to new value follows proper state transitions. For example, a trigger could be created to allow a column value to change from NO to YES only and not vice versa.

- Upon deletion, triggers can be used to automatically insert logging information into another table for audit trail purposes.

On LUW, the INSTEAD OF triggers can be used to insert, update, or delete from views where these operations are otherwise not allowed. The views are not insertable, updatable, or deletable because the columns of the views cannot be automatically mapped to underling table columns. However, if you know your business logic and you know how the changes in views can be mapped to changes in underlying tables, you can put the logic into the body of INSTEAD OF triggers and use INSTEAD OF triggers to work around SQL limits.

TIP

On LUW, use INSTEAD OF triggers to support insert, update, or delete statements through the views, which are otherwise not insertable, updatable, or deletable.

The complete syntax of the CREATE TRIGGER statement is shown in Figure 9.16.

```
>>-CREATE TRIGGER--trigger-name--+-NO CASCADE BEFORE-+---------->
                                 +-AFTER-------------+
                                 '-INSTEAD OF--------'


>--+-INSERT-------------------------+--ON--+-table-name-+------->
   +-DELETE-------------------------+      '-view-name--'
   '-UPDATE--+--------------------+-'
             |     .-,----------. |
             |     V            | |
             '-OF---column-name-+-'
```

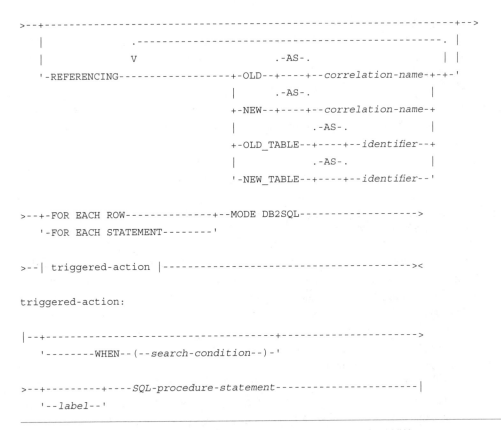

```
>--+----------------------------------------------------------------+-->
   |              .---------------------------------------------. |
   |          V                          .-AS-.                 | |
   '-REFERENCING----------------+-OLD--+----+--correlation-name-+-+-'
                                |        .-AS-.                 |
                                +-NEW--+----+--correlation-name-+
                                |            .-AS-.             |
                                +-OLD_TABLE--+----+---identifier--+
                                |                 .-AS-.         |
                                '-NEW_TABLE--+----+---identifier--'

>---+-FOR EACH ROW--------------+---MODE DB2SQL------------------>
    '-FOR EACH STATEMENT--------'

>--| triggered-action |-----------------------------------------><

triggered-action:

|--+--------------------------------------+-------------------->
   '--------WHEN--(--search-condition--)-'

>--+----------+----SQL-procedure-statement----------------------|
   '--label--'
```

Figure 9.16   The complete *CREATE TRIGGER* statement syntax for LUW.

Trigger Name

The unqualified trigger name specified in the CREATE TRIGGER statement is limited to 18 characters for LUW and 128 characters for iSeries and zSeries. It must begin with a letter, followed by zero or more letters, digits, or underscore characters (_).

A trigger is said to be **qualified** if it is referenced by a two-part name that is made up of a schema and a trigger name. The schema name limitation of triggers is the same as that of SQL procedures. The qualified trigger name, including the implicit or explicit schema name, must be unique.

BEFORE, AFTER, or INSTEAD OF

DB2 supports triggers defined on tables on all platforms, and triggers defined on views for LUW only. The view trigger is also known as the INSTEAD OF trigger. There are two types of table triggers: BEFORE and AFTER triggers. When a trigger begins its execution because of a triggering SQL statement, the trigger is said to be **activated**.

A BEFORE trigger will be activated before any table data is affected by the triggering SQL statement. You would use BEFORE triggers to intercept data provided by the application to validate or supply missing values, for example. If the triggering SQL statement affects more than one row, the BEFORE trigger will be activated for every row that is affected.

A BEFORE trigger is always defined with the NO CASCADE clause. This means that operations performed within this trigger do not activate other triggers in the database. This has the implicit restriction that no INSERT, UPDATE, or DELETE statements are allowed in the body of BEFORE triggers. If you want to perform INSERT, UPDATE, or DELETE statements in a trigger body, you must define them as AFTER triggers.

TIP

NO CASCADE is optional and is the default behavior on iSeries. Always specify NO CASCADE for BEFORE triggers for portability.

AFTER triggers are activated after the triggering SQL statement has executed to completion successfully. In general, you would use AFTER triggers to post-process data. You would also use AFTER triggers if your logic required you to perform any INSERT, UPDATE, or DELETE operations because these statements are not supported in BEFORE triggers. AFTER triggers also offer additional options in how they can behave. With AFTER triggers, you can optionally define them to activate on a per-statement basis rather than on a per-row basis. This topic is discussed further in the upcoming sections in this chapter.

On LUW, an INSTEAD OF trigger is activated after the triggering SQL statement has been issued to the base view. A fundamental difference exists between a table trigger and a view trigger. For a table trigger, regardless of a BEFORE or an AFTER trigger, both the trigger actions and the triggering statements are executed eventually. For a view trigger, also known as an INSTEAD OF trigger, the trigger action is used to replace the triggering statement. In other words, the trigger action is executed instead of the triggering statement. The triggering statement is only attempted on the base view and is only used to fire the INSTEAD OF trigger. The triggering statement will never be executed.

INSERT, DELETE, or UPDATE

Triggers can be defined for INSERT, DELETE, or UPDATE triggering statements. On LUW and zSeries, there is no limit to how many triggers you can define on a table. On iSeries, the limit is 300. However, it is not a good idea to define too many triggers. When more than one trigger is defined for one type of triggering statement—for example, for an INSERT statement—they are fired in the order of their creation.

TIP

Consolidate your triggers into one if the result depends on the trigger firing sequence. You can explicitly control the sequences of the trigger actions within one trigger. The firing sequence can be changed when some triggers involved are rebuilt in a different order.

On iSeries, a DELETE trigger cannot be created on a table that has a referential constraint of ON DELETE SET NULL. Similarly, an UPDATE trigger cannot be created on a table that has a referential constraint of ON UPDATE SET NULL or ON UPDATE SET DEFAULT.

On LUW, you can only define one INSTEAD OF trigger for each type of triggering statements on each view. In other words, you can only define one INSTEAD OF delete trigger, one INSTEAD OF insert trigger, and one INSTEAD OF update trigger for a view.

TIP

If you need to create more than one INSTEAD OF trigger for one type of triggering statement (INSERT, UPDATE, or DELETE), you can create two identical views with different names.

You should always try to specify the column name list for UPDATE triggers. If the optional column name list is not specified in an UPDATE trigger, every column of the table is implied. Omission of the column-name list implies that the trigger will be activated by the update of any column of the table. The column-name list is not supported in INSTEAD OF triggers.

TIP

Define an optional column-name list for your UPDATE triggers to prevent your triggers being activated unnecessarily.

REFERENCING Clauses

REFERENCING NEW is used to define a qualifier to reference transition values supplied by INSERT and UPDATE statements. REFERENCING OLD is used to define a qualifier to reference transition data that will be discarded by UPDATE and DELETE statements. REFERENCING OLD_TABLE specifies a transition table name that identifies the set of affected rows prior to the triggering SQL operation. REFERENCING NEW_TABLE specifies a transition table name that identifies the affected rows as modified by the triggering SQL operation and by any SET statement in a BEFORE trigger that has already executed. This option can be referred to in AFTER triggers only.

FOR EACH ROW or FOR EACH STATEMENT

Triggers defined with FOR EACH ROW will fire once for each row. Both BEFORE and AFTER triggers support activation FOR EACH ROW.

Triggers defined with FOR EACH STATEMENT will fire once for each statement only, no matter how many rows are affected in that statement. Only AFTER triggers can be defined to activate FOR EACH STATEMENT. For update and delete triggers defined with FOR EACH STATEMENT, they will be activated even if no rows are affected by the triggering UPDATE or DELETE statement. For example, if a single delete statement results in 1,000 rows deleted, an AFTER/FOR EACH STATEMENT trigger defined on that table will activate just once at the end of the entire delete operation. On the other hand, if the trigger was defined as AFTER/FOR EACH ROW, it will activate 1,000 times, once for each row affected by the triggering SQL statement.

MODE DB2SQL

MODE DB2SQL is simply a clause that must be included as part of the CREATE TRIGGER syntax. DB2SQL is the only mode currently supported on LUW and zSeries. For iSeries, mode DB2ROW is also supported. Triggers on iSeries defined with mode DB2ROW are activated on each row operation whereas triggers defined with mode DB2SQL are activated after all of the row operations have been activated.

Triggered Action

On LUW, the SQL procedure statements in the body of the triggered action are implemented by inline SQL PL. The previous sections in this chapter on user-defined SQL functions have already explained the inline SQL PL and its limitations. For more information, refer to Appendix B, "Inline SQL PL for DB2 UDB for Linux, UNIX, and Windows."

On iSeries, you can specify processing options to be used to create the trigger by using the SET OPTION clause. This clause can be specified as part of the **triggered action**, just before the WHEN clause.

The optional WHEN clause defines the conditions for trigger activation. You could, for example, define the trigger to activate only if certain data existed in another table. For better performance, it is recommended that you specify trigger activation conditions with the WHEN clause if it is reasonable to do so. The WHEN clause is not supported in INSTEAD OF triggers.

TIP

Use the WHEN clause to define the trigger activation condition to prevent your triggers being activated the unnecessarily.

NOTE

On zSeries, labels are not allowed in triggers.

Triggers by Examples

Now after you know the basics of the DB2 triggers, it is the time to look at a few examples which will show you how to use DB2 triggers to enforce your business logic.

A *BEFORE* Trigger Example

BEFORE triggers are activated before the triggering SQL statement executes. By using a BEFORE trigger, you have the opportunity to supply values, validate data, and even reject the triggering SQL statement according to user-defined rules. In this section, a trigger will be created to activate before an INSERT into a table. Using similar code, you can create triggers to activate before UPDATE and DELETE operations.

In the SAMPLE database, a table called cl_sched is used to store data for class schedules. Two columns in cl_sched—starting and ending—define when the class starts and ends, respectively.

A simple rule might be to assume that a class ends one hour after it begins if the ending time is not provided upon INSERT into this table. The trigger in Figure 9.17 will enforce this.

```
CREATE TRIGGER default_class_end
NO CASCADE BEFORE INSERT ON cl_sched                -- (1)
REFERENCING NEW AS n                                -- (2)
FOR EACH ROW                                        -- (3)
MODE DB2SQL
WHEN (n.ending IS NULL)                             -- (4)
    SET n.ending = n.starting + 1 HOUR             -- (5)
```

Figure 9.17   Example of a basic *BEFORE INSERT* trigger

Figure 9.17 shows how to create a trigger called default_class_end which activates before an insert on table cl_sched on Line (1). To intercept and supply a default-ending time, the trigger needs to make reference to values provided by the triggering INSERT statement. The REFERENCING NEW AS *n* clause on Line (2) associates the transition values provided by the INSERT statement with the qualifier *n*. The ending time of the INSERT statement can then be checked and/or supplied by referring to *n.ending* on Lines (4) and (5).

On Line (3), FOR EACH ROW means that this trigger will activate for every row that is inserted. Therefore, if you had executed the following INSERT statement:

```
INSERT INTO cl_sched (class_code, day, starting)
VALUES ('DB20002', 1, '12:00'), ('DB20003', 3, '9:00')
```

NOTE

DB2 on zSeries does not support multiple-row INSERT with the previous syntax. You need to modify the previous INSERT statement to two INSERT statements, one for each row.

The trigger would be activated twice, once for each row inserted, even though only a single INSERT statement was issued.

The trigger is defined to activate only when the ending time is null using the optional WHEN clause on Line (4), which ensures that the trigger only activates if a value has not been supplied.

Finally, if the trigger is activated, the ending time is supplied automatically and is set to one hour after the starting time on Line (5).

To test this trigger, execute the following SQL statement:

```
INSERT INTO cl_sched (class_code, day, starting)
VALUES ('DB20001', 1, '10:00')
```

Now, if you select all rows from `cl_sched`, you'll see that the class has been automatically set to have an ending time of 11:00.

```
SELECT * FROM cl_sched

CLASS_CODE DAY    STARTING ENDING
---------- ------ -------- --------
DB20001         1 10:00:00 11:00:00
  1 record(s) selected.
```

Similarly, the trigger does not execute if an ending time is supplied:

```
INSERT INTO cl_sched (class_code, day, starting, ending)
VALUES ('DB20002', 2, '12:00', '15:00')
```

Now, selecting from the `cl_sched` will show that the ending time remains at 15:00.

```
SELECT * FROM cl_sched

CLASS_CODE DAY    STARTING ENDING
---------- ------ -------- --------
DB20001         1 10:00:00 11:00:00
DB20002         2 12:00:00 15:00:00
  2 record(s) selected.
```

An *AFTER* Trigger Example

As stated earlier, unlike BEFORE triggers, AFTER triggers allow you to use INSERT, UPDATE, or DELETE statements inside the trigger body. This would be useful if you wanted to transparently keep an audit trail of when certain events occurred.

To support the following example, connect to the sample database and execute the following DDL to create a table called `audit`:

```
CREATE TABLE AUDIT (event_time TIMESTAMP, desc VARCHAR(100))
```

Figure 9.18 includes a trigger that can be used to keep an audit trail of salary changes with related information such as date and time of the change, as well as the person who made the change.

```
CREATE TRIGGER audit_emp_sal
AFTER UPDATE OF salary ON employee
REFERENCING OLD AS o NEW AS n                                    --(1)
FOR EACH ROW
MODE DB2SQL
```

```
INSERT INTO audit VALUES                                    --(2)
(CURRENT TIMESTAMP, ' Employee ' || o.empno ||
' salary changed from ' || CHAR(o.salary) || ' to ' ||
CHAR(n.salary) || ' by ' || USER)
```

Figure 9.18   An example of a basic *AFTER UPDATE* trigger.

NOTE
If the iSeries `sample` database is being used, you will need to drop the foreign key named `red` from the `employee` table for the example in Figure 9.18 to work.

In Figure 9.18, the trigger is able to reference to both `old` and `new` values because it is defined to activate upon table updates on Line (1). Upon any change in salary for any employee, the trigger will insert into the `audit` table a record of when the update occurred, what the old and new values are, and who executed the UPDATE statement on Line (2). USER is a DB2 special register that holds the connection ID of the application. Refer to Chapter 2, "Basic SQL Procedure Structure," for more information. Also, the WHEN clause in this example has been left out so that this trigger will activate unconditionally.

To test this trigger, update Theodore Spenser's salary because he seems to be underpaid relative to other managers. To see the salaries of current managers, issue the following query:

```
SELECT empno, firstnme, lastname, salary FROM employee
WHERE job='MANAGER'


EMPNO   FIRSTNME      LASTNAME          SALARY
------  ------------  ----------------  -----------
000020  MICHAEL       THOMPSON            41250.00
000030  SALLY         KWAN                38250.00
000050  JOHN          GEYER               40175.00
000060  IRVING        STERN               32250.00
000070  EVA           PULASKI             36170.00
000090  EILEEN        HENDERSON           29750.00
000100  THEODORE      SPENSER             26150.00

  7 record(s) selected.
```

To give Theodore a 15 percent raise, issue the following UPDATE statement:

```
UPDATE employee e SET salary=salary*1.15 WHERE e.empno= '000100';
```

Now you can check the status of the employee table to see Theodore's new salary.

```
SELECT empno, firstnme, lastname, salary FROM employee e
WHERE e.empno='000100'

EMPNO  FIRSTNME     LASTNAME         SALARY
------ ------------ ---------------- -----------
000100 THEODORE     SPENSER             30072.50

  1 record(s) selected.
```

Finally, verify that the salary update has been logged in the AUDIT table:

```
SELECT * FROM AUDIT

EVENT_TIME               DESC
------------------------ -----------------------------------------------------------
2002-04-21-21.26.07.665000 employee 000100 salary changed from 0026150.00  to
0030072.50  by DB2ADMIN

  1 record(s) selected.
```

A Complex *AFTER* Trigger Example

In the examples presented thus far, the trigger code bodies have only contained single SQL statements. In this section, previous examples will be extended to show you how to incorporate more complex logic using the SQL PL elements you've already seen in previous chapters.

Returning to the example in Figure 9.17, with the default class time suppose that some restrictions have been added with respect to when a class can be scheduled:

- A class cannot end beyond 9 PM.
- A class cannot be scheduled on weekends.

A trigger could be defined to disallow the INSERT, UPDATE, or DELETE on table cl_sched that violates the aforementioned rules and returns a descriptive error to the application.

If you created the trigger from the previous example, drop it before continuing with this example. Note that an ALTER TRIGGER statement does not exist. Therefore, to modify a trigger you must drop and re-create it:

```
DROP TRIGGER default_class_end
```

Figure 9.19 contains the trigger code to enforce the new rules.

```
CREATE TRIGGER validate_sched
NO CASCADE BEFORE INSERT ON cl_sched
REFERENCING NEW AS n
FOR EACH ROW
MODE DB2SQL
vs: BEGIN ATOMIC                                                    --(1)
   -- supply default value for ending time if null
   IF (n.ending IS NULL) THEN                                       --(2)
      SET n.ending = n.starting + 1 HOUR;
   END IF;


   -- ensure that class does not end beyond 9PM
   IF (n.ending > '21:00') THEN                                     --(3)
      SIGNAL SQLSTATE '80000'
         SET MESSAGE_TEXT='class ending time is beyond 9pm';        --(4)
   ELSEIF (n.DAY=1 or n.DAY=7) THEN                                 --(5)
      SIGNAL SQLSTATE '80001' SET MESSAGE_TEXT='class cannot
      be scheduled on a weekend';                                   --(6)
   END IF;
END vs                                                              --(7)
```

Figure 9.19   An advanced *BEFORE INSERT* trigger using SQL PL (for LUW and iSeries only).

NOTE
The example in Figure 9.19 does not work on zSeries due to a limitation of the statements that can be used in the trigger body. The list of supported SQL statements as well as an alternative example (shown in Figure 9.33) is provided in the zSeries considerations section.

The trigger works by first supplying a default ending time, if it has not already been provided on Line (2). Then, it ensures that the ending time does not exceed 9PM on Line (3) and has not been scheduled for a weekend on Line (5).

Here are the highlights of the example in Figure 9.19:

- In order to use multiple statements in the trigger body, the SQL PL statements must be wrapped within an atomic compound statement using BEGIN ATOMIC (1) and END (7).
- Within the atomic compound statement, SQL PL flow control elements like IF at (2), (3), and (5) and SIGNAL at (4) and (6) can be used.
- Note that the maximum length of the error message used with SIGNAL SQLSTATE is 70 characters. If you exceed this limit, the message will be truncated without warning at run time.

To test the trigger, execute the following SQL statements:

1. First, attempt to insert a class where the starting time is 9 PM. Because the ending time is not supplied, 10p.m. will be assumed.

```
INSERT INTO CL_SCHED (class_code, day, starting)
    VALUES ('DB20005', 5, '21:00')
```

This insert statement results in the following custom error, as desired:

```
DB21034E  The command was processed as an SQL statement because it was not a
valid Command Line Processor command.  During SQL processing it returned:
SQL0438N  Application raised error with diagnostic text: "class ending time is
beyond 9pm".  SQLSTATE=80000
```

2. Next, attempt to insert a class where the day of the week is Sunday (the value of DAY starts from Sunday with a value of 1).

```
INSERT INTO CL_SCHED (class_code, day, starting, ending)
    VALUES ('DB20005', 1, '13:00', '15:00')
```

Again, the insert statement results in the following custom error, as expected:

```
DB21034E  The command was processed as an SQL statement because it was not a
valid Command Line Processor command.  During SQL processing it returned:
SQL0438N  Application raised error with diagnostic text: "class cannot be
scheduled on a weekend".  SQLSTATE=80001
```

3. Finally, insert a valid value into the class schedule table (Thursday, 1 to 3 PM).

```
INSERT INTO CL_SCHED (class_code, day, starting, ending)
    VALUES ('DB20005', 5, '13:00', '15:00')
```

By selecting from the `cl_sched` table, you will see the row that was just inserted. (You may see another row, as shown next, if you attempted the previous example.)

```
SELECT * FROM cl_sched

CLASS_CODE DAY    STARTING ENDING
---------- ------ -------- --------
DB20001        1 10:00:00 11:00:00
DB20002        2 12:00:00 15:00:00
DB20005        5 13:00:00 15:00:00
  3 record(s) selected.
```

An *INSTEAD OF* Trigger Example (for LUW Only)

Figure 9.20 displays a view based on table `org` in the `sample` database. It gives you the department count by divisions.

```
CREATE VIEW org_by_division
  (division, number_of_dept)
AS
  SELECT division, count(*)
  FROM org
  GROUP BY division
```

Figure 9.20　An example of an un-updatable view.

A simple `SELECT` query

```
SELECT * FROM org_by_division
```

shows the content of the view as following:

```
DIVISION   NUMBER_OF_DEPT
---------- --------------
Corporate              1
Eastern                3
Midwest                2
Western                2

  4 record(s) selected.
```

In DB2, if a view contains the GROUP BY clause, the view is not updatable, which means you can not issue an UPDATE statement against the view. Try the following UPDATE statement, which attempts to change the Midwest division name to Southern division:

```
UPDATE org_by_division SET division='Southern' WHERE division='Midwest'
```

You will receive the following SQL error indicating that the operation is not supported:

```
DB21034E  The command was processed as an SQL statement because it was not a
valid Command Line Processor command.  During SQL processing it returned:
SQL0150N The target fullselect, view, typed table, materialized query table,
or staging table in the INSERT, DELETE, UPDATE, or MERGE statement is a target
for which the requested operation is not permitted.  SQLSTATE=42807
```

As discussed earlier, an INSTEAD OF trigger can be used to implement the UPDATE operation you want to perform on the view which is not updatable. Figure 9.21 is such an example.

```
CREATE TRIGGER upd_org
INSTEAD OF UPDATE
ON org_by_division
REFERENCING OLD AS o NEW AS n
FOR EACH ROW
MODE DB2SQL
BEGIN ATOMIC
  IF (o.number_of_dept != n.number_of_dept) THEN         -- (1)
    SIGNAL SQLSTATE '80001' SET MESSAGE_TEXT =
        'The number of department is not updatable.';
  END IF;

  UPDATE org                                             -- (2)
  SET division = n.division
  WHERE division = o.division;
END
```

Figure 9.21   An example of an *INSTEAD OF* trigger.

After the trigger is created, when an UPDATE statement is issued against the view the trigger body will be executed instead. If the query is to update the number of department, it will be rejected on Line (1). It is reasonable as you cannot update the counts without adding rows into the base table. If the query is to update the division name, the UPDATE statement on Line (2) will be executed to update all corresponding rows in the org table from the old division name to the new division name.

A simple SELECT query shows the content of the base table:

```
SELECT * FROM org


DEPTNUMB DEPTNAME        MANAGER DIVISION    LOCATION
-------- --------------- ------- ---------- -------------
      10 Head Office     160     Corporate  New York
      15 New England     50      Eastern    Boston
      20 Mid Atlantic    10      Eastern    Washington
      38 South Atlantic  30      Eastern    Atlanta
      42 Great Lakes     100     Midwest    Chicago
      51 Plains          140     Midwest    Dallas
      66 Pacific         270     Western    San Francisco
      84 Mountain        290     Western    Denver


  8 record(s) selected.
```

To see the effect of the trigger, issue an UPDATE query that attempts to update the number of department. The customized error message defined in the trigger body is returned:

```
UPDATE org_by_division SET number_of_dept=2 WHERE division='Corporate'


DB21034E  The command was processed as an SQL statement because it was not a
valid Command Line Processor command.  During SQL processing it returned:
SQL0438N  Application raised error with diagnostic text: "The number of
department is not updatable.".  SQLSTATE=80001
```

Issue the previously failed UPDATE query again to update the division name:

```
UPDATE org_by_division SET division='Southern' WHERE division='Midwest'


DB20000I  The SQL command completed successfully.
```

The query was successful because of the INSTEAD OF trigger. All the query did was to activate the trigger. It was the body of the trigger that really went through. Issue the SELECT query again to exam the content of the org table:

```
SELECT * FROM org


DEPTNUMB DEPTNAME        MANAGER DIVISION    LOCATION
-------- --------------- ------- ---------- -------------
      10 Head Office     160     Corporate  New York
      15 New England     50      Eastern    Boston
      20 Mid Atlantic    10      Eastern    Washington
```

```
38 South Atlantic 30       Eastern    Atlanta
42 Great Lakes    100      Southern   Chicago
51 Plains         140      Southern   Dallas
66 Pacific        270      Western    San Francisco
84 Mountain       290      Western    Denver
```

```
8 record(s) selected.
```

Comparing with the previous content, you may notice that all Midwest division rows are renamed into the Southern division.

The IF...ELSE...block in the trigger body in Figure 9.18 cannot be replaced by the UPDATE OF or the WHEN clause because they are not supported in INSTEAD OF triggers.

A Comparison of View Triggers and Table Triggers (LUW only)

The **view trigger** is a relatively new concept for DBMSs. A fundamental difference exists between the table triggers and the view triggers. Figure 9.22 is used to further illustrate the difference. It consists of a simple base table, a trivial view (which is defined the exactly the same as the base table), a simple table insert trigger, and a view insert trigger.

```
CREATE TABLE t_airport
( airport_code char(3) not null,
  airport_name char(50) );

CREATE VIEW v_airport
AS
  SELECT * FROM t_airport;

CREATE TRIGGER insert_t_airport
AFTER INSERT
ON t_airport
FOR EACH ROW
MODE DB2SQL
BEGIN ATOMIC
END;

CREATE TRIGGER insert_v_airport
INSTEAD OF INSERT
ON v_airport
FOR EACH ROW
MODE DB2SQL
BEGIN ATOMIC
END;
```

Figure 9.22   A comparison of a view trigger and a table trigger.

Both triggers are very similar. They both have an empty trigger body. There is no triggered action defined. Without the triggers, the following INSERT statements through the view or to the table generates the same results:

```
INSERT INTO t_airport VALUES ('YYZ', 'TORONTO');
INSERT INTO v_airport VALUES ('YYZ', 'TORONTO');
```

After the triggers are defined, however, the results of the INSERT statements become different. Execute the INSERT statement on the empty table:

```
INSERT INTO t_airport VALUES ('YYZ', 'TORONTO');
```

You will see the content of the table t_airport as the following:

```
AIRPORT_CODE AIRPORT_NAME
------------ -------------------------------------------------
YYZ          TORONTO

  1 record(s) selected.
```

This result is expected. The values in the INSERT statement are all valid. The INSERT statement completed without a problem. Then the AFTER trigger is activated. Because the trigger has no action defined, it did nothing as expected.

What if you execute the INSERT statement through a view now?

```
INSERT INTO v_airport VALUES ('SFO', 'SAN FRANCISCO');
```

You can probably expect the same behavior. After all, the two triggers look very similar. Query the table t_airport again, and you should see the following:

```
AIRPORT_CODE AIRPORT_NAME
------------ -------------------------------------------------
YYZ          TORONTO

  1 record(s) selected.
```

Nothing changed. There is no new row. Where does the record go? Is there anything wrong? Not really. Everything worked as designed. Remember if an INSTEAD OF trigger is defined, the triggering statement will only serve the pupose of activating the trigger. It will not be executed at all. Instead, the trigger body, the triggered actions, will be executed. In this example, the triggered action is not defined, to the trigger did nothing, as designed.

A slight modification of the INSTEAD OF trigger in Figure 9.21 is needed to make it work the same away as the table trigger. The result is shown in Figure 9.23.

```
CREATE TRIGGER insert_v_airport
INSTEAD OF INSERT
ON v_airport
REFERENCING NEW AS n                              -- (1)
FOR EACH ROW
MODE DB2SQL
BEGIN ATOMIC
    INSERT INTO t_airport                         -- (2)
    VALUES (n.airport_code, n.airport_name);
END
```

Figue 9.23   The modified *INSTEAD OF* trigger.

In order to behave the same as the table trigger in Figure 9.22, the INSERT statement to the base table has to be explicitly implemented on Line (2), and the REFERENCING clause on Line (1) has to be included in the header.

Invoking UDFs and SQL Procedures from Triggers

Both UDFs and SQL procedures can be invoked from triggers. The ability to invoke SQL procedures is particularly useful on LUW if you need to use DB2 SQL PL features that are not yet supported in the inline SQL PL subset.

TIP
On LUW, use SQL procedures to work around inline SQL PL limitations in triggers.

An example of how triggers invoke functions and procedures is illustrated in Figures 9.24, 9.25, and 9.26.

NOTE
The examples in Figures 9.24, 9.25, and 9.26 do not work on zSeries due to some restrictions in UDFs and triggers. Refer to the zSeries considerations section for details.

```
CREATE TRIGGER insert_employee
NO CASCADE BEFORE INSERT
ON employee
REFERENCING NEW AS n
FOR EACH ROW
MODE DB2SQL
ie: BEGIN ATOMIC
  DECLARE v_valid CHAR(1) DEFAULT 'N';
```

```
IF (n.empno = '') THEN
  SET n.empno = new_empno();                              -- (1)
END IF;


CALL validate_dept(n.workdept, v_valid);                 -- (2)


IF (v_valid = 'N') THEN
  SIGNAL SQLSTATE '80001'
      SET MESSAGE_TEXT= 'Incorrect department number';   -- (3)
END IF;
END ie
```

Figure 9.24   An example of a trigger invoking a function and a procedure (for LUW and iSeries).

Figure 9.24 shows a BEFORE INSERT trigger that performs data validation on the input data. It creates a new employee number if the input employee number is an empty string. It validates the department number, raises an SQL error, and stops the INSERT statement if the department number is not validated. A business decision has been made to implement the logic to produce a new employee number by a function so that the function can be used by other triggers, procedures, and functions if needed. The trigger only invokes the UDF on Line (1).

Another business decision is also made to use a cursor to implement the logic of department number validation. The example only illustrates how to invoke procedures in triggers as a method to use cursors indirectly. The cursor is used in a simple example. In real life, you should only use cursors when necessary; for example, you may consider using cursors because the department table is very large and because the business logic is too complex for a query to handle. For more information, refer to Chapter 5, "Understanding and Using Cursors and Result Sets." The trigger only invokes the SQL procedure on Line (2).

The only logic implemented in the trigger is to raise an SQL error if the department number is not valid on Line (3).

```
CREATE FUNCTION new_empno ( )
RETURNS CHAR(6)
LANGUAGE SQL
SPECIFIC new_empno
ne: BEGIN ATOMIC
  DECLARE v_max_empno INT;
  DECLARE v_next_empno VARCHAR(12);

  SET v_max_empno =                                       -- (1)
    (SELECT INT(MAX(empno)) FROM employee);
```

```
  SET v_next_empno =                                        -- (2)
    ( '000000' || RTRIM(CHAR(v_max_empno + 10)) );

  RETURN SUBSTR(v_next_empno, LENGTH(v_next_empno)-5, 6);    -- (3)
END ne
```

Figure 9.25   The supporting UDF for the trigger in Figure 9.24.

The UDF in Figure 9.25 generates a new employee number by adding 10 to the largest employee number that currently exists. The employee number is defined as CHAR(6) in the employee table. However, the contents are numeric strings. Because DB2 SQL PL is a strong typed language, explicit casting is needed. The maximum employee number on Line (1) needs to be cast into an integer for the next employee number calculation. The result is cast back to characters on Line (2). The RTRIM function is used on Line (2) to remove the trailing blanks after the conversion from an integer to a character string. Concatenating leading zeros on Line (2) and taking the rightmost six characters on Line (3) formats the employee number in the proper style.

The body of the UDF can be implemented in one line of the RETURN statement. It is implemented as shown in Figure 9.25 for better readability. In your own project, it is recommended that a numeric column is used as the IDs and that a DB2 SEQUENCE object or a DB2 IDENTITY column is used for auto-incremental IDs. The implementation in Figure 9.25 illustrates using UDFs with triggers. Using maximum value to calculate the next ID may cause concurrent problems in a real-life application. For more information on the SEQUENCE object or the IDENTITY column, refer to Chapter 3, "Overview of SQL PL Language Elements."

```
CREATE PROCEDURE validate_dept
  ( IN p_deptno VARCHAR(3),
    OUT p_valid CHAR(1) )
    LANGUAGE SQL
    SPECIFIC validate_dept                    -- Applies to LUW and iSeries
-- WLM ENVIRONMENT <env>                       -- Applies to zSeries
    READS SQL DATA
vd: BEGIN
  -- Declare variables
  DECLARE v_deptno CHAR(3);
  DECLARE SQLSTATE CHAR(5) DEFAULT '00000';

  -- Procedure logic
  DECLARE c_dept CURSOR FOR
    SELECT deptno FROM department;

  OPEN c_dept;
```

```
  SET p_valid = 'N';

  FETCH FROM c_dept INTO v_deptno;

  w1: WHILE ( SQLSTATE = '00000' ) DO
    IF (v_deptno = p_deptno) THEN
      SET p_valid = 'Y';
      LEAVE w1;
    END IF;

    FETCH FROM c_dept INTO v_deptno;
  END WHILE w1;

  CLOSE c_dept;
END vd
```

Figure 9.26   The supporting SQL procedure for the trigger in Figure 9.24.

The `validate_dept` procedure checks to see whether the input department number is correct. A `'Y'` is returned for a department number found in the department table; otherwise, an `'N'` is returned. A cursor is used in this simple example to illustrate how to use SQL procedures that implement SQL PL features that are not currently supported in triggers.

If an `'N'` is returned to the trigger in Figure 9.24, the IF...ELSE block on Line (3) will raise an SQL error and pass a customized error message to the application.

The use of a UDF in this example allows the trigger to reuse the new employee number-generating code, which might be shared by many database objects. Implementing SQL procedures allows the trigger to use the cursor indirectly.

To test the trigger, use a new employee record with a valid employee number but an invalid department number as shown in the following code. The shown customized error message indicates that the procedure is invoked properly, because the business logic of department number checking is only implemented in the SQL procedure.

```
INSERT INTO employee (empno, firstnme, midinit, lastname, workdept, edlevel)
VALUES('000400', 'Firstname', 'T', 'Lastname', 'ABC', 1)

DB21034E  The command was processed as an SQL statement because it was not a
valid Command Line Processor command.  During SQL processing it returned:
SQL0438N  Application raised error with diagnostic text: "Incorrect department
number".  SQLSTATE=80001
```

Now test again with a valid department number but without an employee number. A new record is successfully created. The employee number is created from the maximum existing employee number as implemented in the UDF.

```
INSERT INTO employee (empno, firstnme, midinit, lastname, workdept, edlevel)
VALUES('', 'Firstname', 'T', 'Lastname', 'A00', 1)
DB20000I  The SQL command completed successfully.


SELECT empno, firstnme, midinit, lastname, workdept, edlevel FROM employee


EMPNO   FIRSTNME        MIDINIT LASTNAME          WORKDEPT EDLEVEL
------  ------------    ------- ----------------  -------- -------
000010 CHRISTINE        I       HAAS              A00           18
...
000340 JASON            R       GOUNOT            E21           16
000350 Firstname        T       Lastname          A00            1


  33 record(s) selected.
```

For other considerations of invoking SQL procedures in UDFs and triggers, refer to the next section of this chapter.

Considerations for Invoking SQL Procedures from UDFs and Triggers

To preserve the data integrity in the database, certain rules are implemented for SQL procedures that are to be invoked by UDFs and triggers. The same rules apply when the SQL procedures are invoked in DB2 stand-alone code for LUW, which is discussed in Appendix B, "Inline SQL PL for DB2 UDB for Linux, UNIX, and Windows."

Data Access Restrictions

Both UDFs and SQL procedures have three data access options: CONTAINS SQL, READ SQL DATA, and MODIFIES SQL DATA, as discussed in Chapter 2, "Basic SQL Procedure Structure," and in earlier sections within this chapter. AFTER and INSTEAD OF triggers can always modify data. BEFORE triggers cannot UPDATE, INSERT, or DELETE. For practical purposes, you can think of these two types of triggers as having a MODIFIES SQL DATA access level and BEFORE triggers as having a READ SQL DATA access level.

DB2 does not allow UDFs or SQL procedures with lower data access levels to invoke UDFs or SQL procedures with higher data access levels.

- UDFs or SQL procedures with the MODIFIES SQL DATA option can invoke any other valid UDFs and SQL procedures.
- UDFs and SQL procedures with the READS SQL DATA option can only invoke UDFs and SQL procedures with either the READS SQL DATA or CONTAINS SQL option.
- UDFs and SQL procedures with the CONTAINS SQL option can only invoke UDFs and SQL procedures with the CONTAINS SQL option.

Because READS SQL DATA is the default option for UDFs but MODIFIES SQL DATA is the default option for SQL procedures, you need to use the explicit data access options if you need to invoke SQL procedures in your UDFs. This was demonstrated in Figures 9.14 and 9.15.

The MODIFIES SQL DATA option is not supported in row functions. An SQL procedure that modifies tables cannot be invoked in row functions. It, however, can be invoked in table functions and triggers.

> **TIP**
>
> Use an explicit data access option in both UDFs and SQL procedures for readability. It is easier to find UDFs and procedures with incompatible data access levels.

Transaction Control in SQL Procedures

If a procedure is invoked by either a UDF or a trigger, the ROLLBACK and COMMIT statements are not allowed in the body of the procedure, unless it is rolled back to a save point that is defined in the same procedure.

> **NOTE**
>
> On iSeries, in addition to ROLLBACK and COMMIT, a procedure invoked by a UDF or trigger cannot contain the CONNECT, SET CONNECTION, RELEASE, DISCONNECT, or SET TRANSACTION statements, either.
>
> On zSeries, the examples in Figures 9.27, 9.28, and 9.29 only work for the stored procedures and triggers, but not for the table UDFs. Table UDFs are not supported on zSeries. For an illustration of transaction control on zSeries, replace the table UDFs with scalar UDFs.

In Figure 9.27, the show_trans_sp procedure has a COMMIT statement at the end. A table UDF and a trigger are created to invoke the procedure.

```
CREATE PROCEDURE show_trans_sp()
   LANGUAGE SQL
   SPECIFIC show_trans_sp                     -- applies to LUW and iSeries
-- WLM ENVIRONMENT <env>                      -- applies to zSeries
   MODIFIES SQL DATA
sts: BEGIN
  INSERT INTO cl_sched (class_code) VALUES ('AAA');
  INSERT INTO cl_sched (class_code) VALUES ('BBB');
  INSERT INTO cl_sched (class_code) VALUES ('CCC');

  COMMIT;                                     -- (1)
END sts
```

```
CREATE FUNCTION show_trans_func()
RETURNS TABLE (subject CHAR(64))
LANGUAGE SQL
SPECIFIC show_trans_func
MODIFIES SQL DATA
-- DISALLOW PARALLEL                            -- applies to iSeries
stf: BEGIN ATOMIC
  CALL show_trans_sp();
  RETURN
    SELECT subject FROM in_tray;
END stf

CREATE TRIGGER show_trans_trig
AFTER INSERT ON in_tray
FOR EACH ROW MODE DB2SQL
BEGIN ATOMIC
  CALL show_trans_sp();
END
```

Figure 9.27   Examples of transaction control in procedures invoked by UDFs and triggers.

When executed, the function and trigger produce the following error messages because of the COMMIT statement on Line (1).

```
SELECT * FROM TABLE(show_trans_func()) AS t

SQL0751N  Routine "DB2ADMIN.SHOW_TRANS_SP" (specific name "SQL040222031129103")
attempted to execute a statement that is not allowed.

INSERT INTO in_tray (subject) VALUES ('ABCD')

DB21034E  The command was processed as an SQL statement because it was not a
valid Command Line Processor command.  During SQL processing it returned:
SQL0723N  An error occurred in a triggered SQL statement in trigger
"DB2ADMIN.SHOW_TRANS_TRI".  Information returned for the error includes SQLCODE
"-751", SQLSTATE "    " and message tokens
"DB2ADMIN.SHOW_TRANS_SP|SQL040222031129103".  SQLSTATE=09000
```

Both the UDF and the trigger work if the COMMIT statement is removed. Replacing the COMMIT statement on Line (1) with a ROLLBACK statement produces the same error message.

As you might already notice, the errors produced are runtime errors. As long as the COMMIT or ROLLBACK statement is not executed, both the UDF and the trigger will work. Figure 9.28 shows the modified version of Figure 9.27, where the COMMIT statement will never be executed.

```
CREATE PROCEDURE show_trans_sp2()
   LANGUAGE SQL
   SPECIFIC show_trans_sp2                    -- applies to LUW and iSeries
-- WLM ENVIRONMENT <env>                      -- applies to zSeries
   MODIFIES SQL DATA
sts2: BEGIN
  INSERT INTO cl_sched (class_code) VALUES ('AAA');
  INSERT INTO cl_sched (class_code) VALUES ('BBB');
  INSERT INTO cl_sched (class_code) VALUES ('CCC');

  IF (1=0) THEN
    COMMIT;
  END IF;
END sts2


CREATE FUNCTION show_trans_func2()
RETURNS TABLE (subject CHAR(64))
LANGUAGE SQL
SPECIFIC show_trans_func2
-- DISALLOW PARALLEL                          -- applies to iSeries
MODIFIES SQL DATA
stf2: BEGIN ATOMIC
  CALL show_trans_sp2();
  RETURN
    SELECT subject FROM in_tray;
END stf2


CREATE TRIGGER show_trans_trig2
AFTER INSERT ON in_tray
FOR EACH ROW MODE DB2SQL
BEGIN ATOMIC
  CALL show_trans_sp2();
END
```

Figure 9.28   A modified version of Figure 9.27.

Both the UDF and the trigger work in this example. The following INSERT statement invokes the trigger, which in turn invokes the modified procedure

```
INSERT INTO in_tray (subject) VALUES ('ABCD')
```

produces the following results:

```
SELECT class_code FROM cl_sched

CLASS_CODE
----------
AAA
BBB
CCC

  3 record(s) selected.

SELECT subject FROM in_tray

SUBJECT
-----------------------------------------------------------------
ABCD

  1 record(s) selected.
```

The execution of the function in Figure 9.28 will produce the same result in table cl_sched.

The examples in Figures 9.27 and 9.28 can be modified further to demonstrate how save points are supported in such SQL procedures. The modified code is shown in Figure 9.29.

```
CREATE PROCEDURE show_svpt_sp()
   LANGUAGE SQL
   SPECIFIC show_svpt_sp                 -- Applies to LUW and iSeries
-- WLM ENVIRONMENT <env>                 -- Applies to zSeries
   MODIFIES SQL DATA
sss: BEGIN
   SAVEPOINT svpt1 ON ROLLBACK RETAIN CURSORS;
      INSERT INTO cl_sched (class_code) VALUES ('AAA');
      INSERT INTO cl_sched (class_code) VALUES ('BBB');

   ROLLBACK TO SAVEPOINT svpt1;
      INSERT INTO cl_sched (class_code) VALUES ('CCC');
   END sss
```

```
CREATE FUNCTION show_svpt_func()
RETURNS TABLE (subject CHAR(64))
LANGUAGE SQL
SPECIFIC show_svpt_func
MODIFIES SQL DATA
-- DISALLOW PARALLEL                        -- applies to iSeries
ssf: BEGIN ATOMIC
  CALL show_svpt_sp();
  RETURN
    SELECT subject FROM in_tray;
END ssf



CREATE TRIGGER show_svpt_trig
AFTER INSERT ON in_tray
FOR EACH ROW MODE DB2SQL
BEGIN ATOMIC
  CALL show_svpt_sp();
END
```

Figure 9.29   Examples of save point support.

Compare the result of the execution of the trigger in the following code snippet with the result of the execution of the trigger in Figure 9.28.

```
INSERT INTO in_tray (subject) VALUES ('ABCD');
DB20000I  The SQL command completed successfully.

SELECT class_code FROM cl_sched

CLASS_CODE
----------
CCC

  1 record(s) selected.


SELECT subject from in_tray

SUBJECT
----------------------------------------------------------------
ABCD

  1 record(s) selected.
```

There is now only one row left in table `cl_sched` as the first two rows are rolled back.

Table Read or Write Conflict in SQL Procedures on LUW

DB2 enforces a set of rules to avoid data integrity violation when an SQL procedure is invoked by a UDF or trigger. For simplicity, triggers are used in this section as examples. Please note that all discussions in this section apply to both UDFs and triggers as well as stand-alone code unless otherwise specified.

When an SQL procedure is invoked by a trigger, if both the trigger and the SQL procedure are working with the same table at the same time, the result could be unpredictable. Because the statements in a trigger and the statements in an SQL procedure invoked by that trigger can access a table at the same time, the status of the table is unknown from the perspective of the SQL procedure. Some rows of the table might have been updated by the trigger action; some might have not. Actions taken based on the partially modified rows can be incorrect. To avoid the potential read or write conflict in this type of situation, DB2 does not allow statements that conflict on any table.

The restrictions are implemented in DB2 using the concept of table access contexts. A **table access context** is created when the trigger invokes an SQL procedure. A separate table access context is created when the same trigger issues other SQL statements.

The following rules are enforced by DB2:

- Within the same table access context, different statements can both read from and write to the same table without causing a conflict.
- When a table is being read within a given table access context, contexts can also read the table. If any other context attempts to write to the table, however, a conflict occurs.
- When a table is being written within a table access context, then no other context can read or write to the table without causing a conflict.

If a conflict occurs, an error (`SQLCODE -746`, `SQLSTATE 57053`) is returned to the statement that caused the conflict at the runtime.

Please do not mistake the read and write conflict restrictions by the regular row and table level data access control. DB2 controls the data access and guarantees the data integrity by isolation levels and database locking mechanism, which is beyond the scope of this book. For this section, all you need to remember is that statements that cause a conflict are not allowed. Statements that do not cause a conflict will still need to wait to receive the proper locks before they can actually read from or write to a table.

The concept of read and write conflict is illustrated by the examples in Figure 9.30.

```
CREATE PROCEDURE show_conflict_sp()
LANGUAGE SQL
SPECIFIC show_conflict_sp
MODIFIES SQL DATA
scs: BEGIN
```

```
    INSERT INTO cl_sched (class_code) VALUES ('AAA'); -- (1)
    INSERT INTO cl_sched (class_code) VALUES ('BBB');
    INSERT INTO cl_sched (class_code) VALUES ('CCC'); -- (2)
END scs


CREATE TRIGGER show_conflict_trig
AFTER INSERT ON in_tray
FOR EACH ROW MODE DB2SQL
sct: BEGIN ATOMIC
    INSERT INTO cl_sched (class_code) VALUES ('DDD'); -- (3)
    CALL show_conflict_sp();                          -- (4)
END sct
```

Figure 9.30 Examples illustrating read and write conflict (LUW only).

In Figure 9.30, the procedure show_conflict_sp is to be called from the trigger show_conflict_trig. Both the procedure and the trigger contain SQL statements that write to the cl_sched table. When the SQL procedure is invoked on Line (4), a table access context—calling it context1 for easy referral—is created. The three INSERT statements inside the procedure body are to be executed within context1. Another table access context—context2—is created when the trigger issues the INSERT statement on Line (3). The INSERT statement on Line (3) is to be executed within context2.

Recall the three rules enforced by DB2; the third rule is violated in this example. Both context1 and context2 are trying to write to the same table cl_sched. This is not allowed.

When the trigger is executed, you will see the following error message:

```
INSERT INTO in_tray (subject) VALUES ('ABCD')

DB21034E  The command was processed as an SQL statement because it was not a
valid Command Line Processor command.  During SQL processing it returned:
SQL0723N  An error occurred in a triggered SQL statement in trigger
"DB2ADMIN.SHOW_CONFL".  Information returned for the error includes SQLCODE
"-746", SQLSTATE "57053" and message tokens
"DB2ADMIN.SHOW_CONFLICT_SP|SQL040222032202703|".  SQLSTATE=09000
```

Because the conflicts are only reported at the runtime, it is important that you test all your conditions to catch this type of error.

DB2 for iSeries Considerations

For completeness, the syntax diagram for the iSeries CREATE FUNCTION statement is shown in Figure 9.31, followed by an explanation of differences from DB2 on LUW.

```
>>-CREATE FUNCTION---function-name ---------------------------->

>--(--+-------------------------------+--)--*------------------->
      | .-,------------------------. |
      | V                          | |
      '---parameter-name--data-type1-+-'

>--RETURNS--+-data-type--------------------------+---*--------->
            |          .-,-----------------------. |
            |          V                          | |
            '-TABLE----column-name--data-type2---+-'

>--LANGUAGE SQL------------------------------------------------+->

   .-NOT DETERMINISTIC--  .    .-MODIFIES SQL DATA--.
>--+-------------------+-----+--------------------+------------->
   '-DETERMINISTIC------'       +-CONTAINS SQL-------+
                               '-READS SQL DATA-----'

   .-CALLED ON NULL INPUT-------.
>--+--------------------------+--+------------------------+-->
   '-RETURNS NULL ON NULL INPUT-'  '-SPECIFIC--specific-name--'

   .-EXTERNAL ACTION-----.      .-FENCED-----.
>--+--------------------+-----+-----------+------------------->
   '-NO EXTERNAL ACTION--'      '-NOT FENCED-'

   .-STATIC DISPATCH------.
>--+--------------------+-----+-------------------+--------->
                               '-ALLOW PARALLEL------'
                               '-DISALLOW PARALLEL---'

                               .-INHERIT SPECIAL REGISTERS-.
>--+------------------------+-+-------------------------+-->
   '-CARDINALTITY integer------'

>--+---------------------+---SQL-routine-body-----------------><
   '-SET OPTION-statement-'
```

Figure 9.31   *CREATE FUNCTION* statement syntax for iSeries.

A ROW is not a valid RETURN type option. It is considered a special case of a TABLE.

A UDF specified with the UNFENCED option executes in a thread within the same environment as the database manager, in contrast to the FENCED option which executes in a thread outside the environment. The UNFENCED option has the potential to perform better.

The ALLOW PARALLEL option permits multiple instances of the UDF to execute at the same time, and the DISALLOW PARALLEL option gives you the option of serializing the execution of the UDF. For table functions, only the DISALLOW PARALLEL option is valid and is mandatory.

The CARDINALITY clause is only used for table functions and provides an estimate on the number of rows returned. This information, if available, is used by the optimizer.

The SET OPTION option statement is used to specify processing options that will be used to create the function. For a complete list of options, refer to the SET OPTION statement information found in the "Statements" chapter of the DB2 UDB for iSeries SQL Reference. If the SET OPTION clause is specified, it must be the last clause before the SQL routine body.

DB2 for zSeries Considerations

The differences in the support of UDFs and triggers on zSeries are highlighted in this section.

The *CREATE FUNCTION* Statement

For completeness, the syntax diagram for the zSeries CREATE FUNCTION statement is shown in Figure 9.32, followed by an explanation of differences from DB2 on LUW.

```
>>-CREATE FUNCTION--function-name------------------------------->


>--(--+-------------------------------+--)--*------------------->
      |  .-,-------------------------. |
      |  V                           | |
      '---parameter-name--data-type--+-'


>--RETURNS--+-data-type-----------------+--*------------------->


                                   .-LANGUAGE SQL-.
>--+-------------------------+--*--+---------------+--*--------->
   '-SPECIFIC--specific-name-'


>--+-----------------------------+----------------+----------->
   +-PARAMETER CCSID -+---ASCII----+
                      |- EBCDIC  -|
                      '- UNICODE -'
```

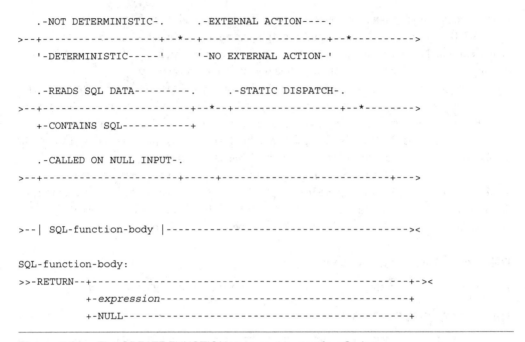

```
    .-NOT DETERMINISTIC-.        .-EXTERNAL ACTION----.
>--+-------------------+--*--+--------------------+--*---------->
    '-DETERMINISTIC-----'        '-NO EXTERNAL ACTION-'


    .-READS SQL DATA---------.        .-STATIC DISPATCH-.
>--+---------------------+--*--+-----------------+--*-------->
    +-CONTAINS SQL-----------+


    .-CALLED ON NULL INPUT-.
>--+---------------------+-----+--------------------------+--->



>--| SQL-function-body |------------------------------------><


SQL-function-body:
>>-RETURN--+--------------------------------------------------+-><
           +-expression-----------------------------------+
           +-NULL-----------------------------------------+
```

Figure 9.32   The *CREATE FUNCTION* statement syntax for zSeries.

Only SQL scalar UDFs are supported.

The PARAMETER CCSID clause indicates the encoding scheme for string parameters as ASCII, EBCDIC, or UNICODE.

Compound statements (identified by BEGIN ... END blocks) are not supported in the SQL function body. Only the RETURN clause followed by an expression or NULL is supported. This implies that a stored procedure cannot be called from a function on zSeries because the CALL statement cannot be specified anywhere in the function body.

Trigger Considerations

Table 9.1 shows the subset of SQL statements supported in the trigger body on zSeries.

Table 9.1   SQL Statements Supported in the Trigger Body on zSeries

SQL Statement	Before Trigger	After Trigger
fullselect	X	X
CALL	X	X
SIGNAL	X	X
VALUES	X	X
SET transition variable	X	

SQL Statement	Before Trigger	After Trigger
INSERT		X
DELETE (searched)		X
UPDATE (searched)		X
REFRESH TABLE		X

Because the IF statement is not supported in the trigger body, the example in Figure 9.19 does not work on zSeries. One possible workaround is to split the trigger into three separate triggers as shown in Figure 9.33.

```
CREATE TRIGGER validate_sched_1
NO CASCADE BEFORE INSERT ON cl_sched
REFERENCING NEW AS n
FOR EACH ROW
MODE DB2SQL
-- supply default value for ending time if null
WHEN (n.ending IS NULL)
BEGIN ATOMIC
    SET n.ending = n.starting + 1 HOUR;
END


CREATE TRIGGER validate_sched_2
NO CASCADE BEFORE INSERT ON cl_sched
REFERENCING NEW AS n
FOR EACH ROW
MODE DB2SQL
-- ensure that class does not end beyond 9pm
WHEN (n.ending > '21:00')
BEGIN ATOMIC
    SIGNAL SQLSTATE '80000' SET MESSAGE_TEXT='class ending time is beyond 9pm';
END


CREATE TRIGGER validate_sched_3
NO CASCADE BEFORE INSERT ON cl_sched
REFERENCING NEW AS n
FOR EACH ROW
MODE DB2SQL
-- supply default value for ending time if null
WHEN (n.DAY=1 or n.DAY=7)
```

```
BEGIN ATOMIC
SIGNAL SQLSTATE '80001' SET MESSAGE_TEXT='class cannot be scheduled on a
weekend';
END
```

Figure 9.33   An advanced *BEFORE INSERT* trigger using SQL PL in DB2 for zSeries.

The triggers in Figure 9.33 need to be created in the order shown so that they are fired in the proper sequence to maintain the original logic.

Invoking UDFs and SQL Procedures from Triggers

To invoke UDFs from a trigger, use SELECT or VALUE statements. The SET statement can also be used to assign the value returned by a function to a variable.

To invoke SQL procedures from a trigger, use CALL statements. The parameters of this stored procedure call must be literals, transition variables, table locators, or expressions.

The trigger example in Figure 9.24 does not work on zSeries because it contains unsupported statements, such as the IF and DECLARE statements. A possible workaround is to move all the logic other than the function call into the procedure.

The function example in Figure 9.25 needs to be implemented as an external UDF because the BEGIN...END compound statements are not supported on zSeries.

Nesting SQL Statements

An SQL statement can explicitly invoke UDFs or stored procedures, or can implicitly activate triggers that invoke UDFs or stored procedures. This is known as **nesting SQL statements**. DB2 for zSeries supports up to 16 levels of nesting.

Restrictions on nested SQL statements include the following:

- When you execute a SELECT statement on a table, you cannot execute INSERT, UPDATE, or DELETE statements on the same table at a lower level of nesting.

- When you execute an INSERT, DELETE, or UPDATE statement on a table, you cannot access that table from a UDF or stored procedure that is at a lower level of nesting.

Although trigger activations count in the levels of SQL statement nesting, the previous restrictions on SQL statements do not apply to SQL statements that are executed in the trigger body.

Summary

In this chapter, UDFs and triggers were discussed. DB2's support for advanced SQL PL logic in UDFs and triggers allows you to encapsulate both simple and complex logic at the database server to simplify application development.

Both scalar UDFs and table UDFs are illustrated by examples. UDFs can be directly used in the SQL statements. Invoking SQL procedures in UDFs enables you to use all DB2 SQL PL features directly or indirectly.

Triggers are an ideal mechanism to facilitate global enforcement of business logic for all applications and users. Examples of BEFORE, AFTER, and INSTEAD OF triggers were illustrated, and the purpose and limitations of using each type were discussed. Both UDFs and SQL procedures can be invoked in the triggers. Similarly, invoking SQL procedures in triggers enables you to use all DB2 SQL PL features directly or indirectly.

You should give extra attention when invoking SQL procedures from UDFs and triggers. The considerations for data access control, transaction control, and read and write conflicts should be carefully reviewed.

CHAPTER **10**

Leveraging DB2 Application Development Features

In this chapter, you will learn how to

- Take advantage of enhanced SQL features for better performance
- Use declared global temporary tables
- Share temporary table data across multiple procedure calls
- Use save points for finer transaction control
- Wrap sequence objects in stored procedures to improve application portability

At this point, you should know almost everything about writing DB2 SQL procedures. You have learned about SQL PL structure, flow control, cursor usage, condition handling, dynamic SQL, and using nested procedure calls. The focus of this chapter is on DB2 application development features that are not part of SQL PL per se but are commonly employed in SQL procedures, functions, and triggers, because they offer significant benefits in the areas of functionality, performance, and manageability.

Using more efficient SQL is arguably the best way to improve performance of stored procedures. If SQL is inefficient, database tuning can only get you so far. Increasing memory or adding more disks to the system may be a way to make DB2 run larger, but rewriting SQL for more efficient execution allows DB2 to run smarter.

Declared global temporary tables can be used when you need to have a table exist only for a particular user and only for the duration of his or her session. They are also used for staging data for manipulation using SQL, and have the option of disabling transaction logging to improve performance of data-intensive operations.

Using save points and nested save points can give you greater control over transactions. **Save points** allow you to start a transaction and keep portions of a transaction while rolling back other portions, without committing the overall unit of work.

Sometimes it may be useful to use stored procedures as wrappers for sequence objects for increased portability. This will appeal mostly to application developers who wish to create applications to run on multiple database platforms.

Leveraging Advanced SQL

Some lesser-known SQL features exist that can dramatically improve performance. Namely, SELECT from INSERT, UPDATE, and DELETE, and the MERGE SQL statement. These SQL enhancements can greatly improve performance by unifying one or more SQL statements.

The SQL features discussed in this section (NEW TABLE, OLD TABLE, FINAL TABLE, and MERGE SQL statements) are currently supported on LUW and partially on zSeries. On zSeries, FINAL TABLE is supported with INSERT statements (you can learn more details in upcoming sections).

Combining *SELECT* with *INSERT*, *UPDATE*, and *DELETE*

Consider the procedure in Figure 10.1, which deletes an employee using an employee number and returns the name of the deleted employee as output. This procedure works on all platforms.

```
CREATE PROCEDURE delete_employee1 ( IN p_empno VARCHAR(6)
                                  , OUT p_fullname VARCHAR(100))
    LANGUAGE SQL
    SPECIFIC delete_employee1                    -- applies to LUW and iSeries
  --WLM ENVIRONMENT <env>                        -- applies to zSeries
de: BEGIN
    DECLARE EXIT HANDLER FOR NOT FOUND
        SET p_fullname = 'employee not found';

    SELECT firstnme || ' ' || lastname INTO p_fullname
      FROM EMPLOYEE
      WHERE EMPNO = p_empno;

    DELETE FROM EMPLOYEE
      WHERE EMPNO = p_empno;
END de
```

Figure 10.1   Fetching and deleting a row using two SQL statements.

To execute this procedure, you can use

```
CALL delete_employee1 ('000210',?)
```

The key observation here is that the procedure must execute the same query twice: first to retrieve the employee name, and then again to delete the employee row (you can think of UPDATES and DELETES as SELECT statements with side effects). This procedure looks straight forward, and at first glance you would think it cannot be improved. However, as demonstrated in Figure 10.2, the procedure can be optimized to use just one SQL statement.

```
CREATE PROCEDURE delete_employee2 ( IN p_empno VARCHAR(6)
                                    , OUT p_fullname VARCHAR(100) )

    LANGUAGE SQL
    SPECIFIC delete_employee2
de: BEGIN
    -- OLD TABLE clause currently valid on LUW only

    DECLARE EXIT HANDLER FOR NOT FOUND
        SET p_fullname = 'employee not found';

    SELECT firstnme || ' ' || lastname INTO p_fullname
        FROM OLD TABLE (DELETE FROM EMPLOYEE WHERE EMPNO = p_empno);   --1
END de
```

Figure 10.2   Fetching and deleting a row using a single SQL statement on LUW.

NEW TABLE and OLD TABLE

Whenever a table is inserted into, updated, or deleted from, DB2 maintains something internally called **transition tables**. These transition tables are referred to as the NEW TABLE and OLD TABLE. In the case of INSERT or UPDATE, the NEW TABLE contains the new row to be inserted or the new value to use for update. In the case of UPDATE or DELETE, the OLD TABLE contains the old value before an update or the value that is to be deleted.

By using NEW TABLE or OLD TABLE with a SELECT statement, you can effectively combine SELECTs with INSERT, UPDATE, and DELETE for situations such the one described in the previous example. For clarity, this concept can be illustrated in the context of INSERT, UPDATE, and DELETE independently.

SELECT from DELETE is most useful when you need to be able to delete from a table and return information about the row that was deleted. You have already seen an example of this. Another good example is where a table is being used as a queue, and you must consume from the queue (delete the row) and then do something else with the de-queued data.

```
CREATE TABLE queue (data int)
INSERT INTO queue VALUES (1),(2),(3)
SELECT *
FROM OLD TABLE (DELETE FROM (SELECT * FROM queue
FETCH FIRST ROW ONLY))
```

SELECT from UPDATE is useful when you need to know something about either the new or old values of the row being updated. A good example of this is where you give an employee a 10 percent raise but you also want to know his or her original salary.

```
SELECT salary
FROM OLD TABLE
(UPDATE EMPLOYEE SET salary = salary * 1.1 WHERE EMPNO= '000340')
```

Similarly, if you wanted to retrieve the new salary, you can use NEW TABLE instead:

```
SELECT salary
FROM NEW TABLE
(UPDATE EMPLOYEE SET salary = salary * 1.1 WHERE EMPNO= '000340')
```

What if you wanted to retrieve both the old salary and new salary in a single statement? This topic is discussed in the next subsection on INCLUDE columns.

SELECT from INSERT is useful if you want to know about the value being inserted and that value is not immediately available. A good example of this is where you are inserting into a table with an identity column. Normally, you would call the function IDENTITY_VAL_LOCAL to retrieve the value used for the most recently inserted identity value.

When more than one row is inserted using a single SQL statement, IDENTITY_VAL_LOCAL cannot return all generated identity values. In other words, if the table identity_tab was defined as follows:

```
CREATE TABLE identity_tab
(id INT NOT NULL GENERATED ALWAYS AS IDENTITY, data VARCHAR(100))
```

the function IDENTITY_VAL_LOCAL cannot be used after statements, such as

```
INSERT INTO identity_tab (data) VALUES ('A'), ('B'), ('C');
```

or (t2 has multiple rows)

```
INSERT INTO identity_tab (data) SELECT data FROM t2
```

The procedure in Figure 10.3 demonstrates how you can use NEW TABLE to retrieve all generated identity values after a multi-row insert.

```
CREATE PROCEDURE insert_identities()
    LANGUAGE SQL
    SPECIFIC insert_identities
ii: BEGIN
-- This procedure requires a table defined as follows:
-- CREATE TABLE identity_tab (id INT NOT NULL GENERATED ALWAYS AS IDENTITY,
data VARCHAR(100));

    DECLARE c1 CURSOR WITH RETURN TO CALLER FOR
        SELECT id FROM NEW TABLE (INSERT INTO identity_tab (data) SELECT
deptname FROM department);
    OPEN c1;
END ii
```

Figure 10.3   Using *NEW TABLE* to retrieve identity values for a multi-row insert on LUW.

When you call this procedure, the department names are inserted into the identity_tab table, and identity values are generated for each row. The cursor returns to the client all the identity column values used for the multi-row insert.

NOTE
The INSERT operation is not executed until the cursor is opened.

INCLUDE

The previous section discussed how an UPDATE statement has access to both NEW TABLE and OLD TABLE values. The example demonstrated how you can retrieve the old or new salary of an employee after a salary increase of 10 percent. The SQL statements are repeated here for the purpose of introducing INCLUDE columns.

```
SELECT salary FROM OLD TABLE (UPDATE EMPLOYEE SET salary = salary * 1.1 WHERE
EMPNO= '000340')
SELECT salary FROM NEW TABLE (UPDATE EMPLOYEE SET salary = salary * 1.1 WHERE
EMPNO= '000340')
```

By using NEW TABLE and OLD TABLE alone, however, it is not possible to retrieve both the old and new salary value. An INCLUDE column can be used to fill this gap.

```
SELECT salary as new_salary, old_salary
  FROM NEW TABLE ( UPDATE employee INCLUDE (old_salary DECIMAL(9,2))
                   SET salary      = salary * 1.10,
                       old_salary = salary
                 WHERE empno='000340')
```

The INCLUDE clause in the nested UPDATE statement creates a new column that can be selected from the outer SELECT statement. You can see that the old_salary retrieves the old salary value while the table column salary is increased by 10 percent. If p_empno is 000340, the output would be

```
NEW_SALARY  OLD_SALARY
----------- -----------
  26224.00    23840.00
```

FINAL TABLE

In addition to OLD TABLE and NEW TABLE, there is also something called FINAL TABLE. When executing INSERT, UPDATE, or DELETE, there may still be AFTER triggers or referential constraints that result in further modification of data. FINAL TABLE can be used to ensure that such changes cannot occur.

> **NOTE**
> On zSeries, FINAL TABLE is supported for INSERT statements only.

Consider the following example where, using the same identity_tab table defined earlier in this section, an AFTER trigger is created that sets all data values to NULL. That is, any data value provided on INSERT to table identity_tab *always* is wiped out. While this is not particularly useful, it clearly demonstrates the difference between NEW TABLE and FINAL TABLE.

```
CREATE TRIGGER trig1
    AFTER INSERT ON identity_tab REFERENCING NEW AS n
    FOR EACH ROW MODE DB2SQL
    UPDATE identity_tab SET data=null
```

If you used NEW TABLE after performing the INSERT, the SELECT would retrieve the inserted data value even though the AFTER trigger ultimately sets it to NULL.

```
SELECT data FROM NEW TABLE (INSERT INTO identity_tab VALUES (default,'x'))
DATA
--------------------------------
x

  1 record(s) selected.
```

However, when using FINAL table, the SQL statement is not allowed to succeed because DB2 sees the AFTER trigger. This protects you from any unforeseen side effects not visible to the application.

```
SELECT data FROM FINAL TABLE (INSERT INTO identity_tab VALUES (default,'x'))
SQL0989N  AFTER trigger "TRIG1" attempted to modify a row in table
"IDENTITY_TAB" that was modified by an SQL data change statement within a FROM
clause.  SQLSTATE=560C3
```

Deleting a Few Rows at a Time

When you want to delete a large amount of data, one major concern can be transaction log space consumption. There are not many situations more painful than starting a DELETE operation that runs for hours, only to be forced to roll back due to a log full condition.

> **TIP**
>
> On LUW, if you want to purge all data from a table rather than using DELETE, you can use ALTER TABLE *table-name* ACTIVATE NOT LOGGED INITIALLY WITH EMPTY TABLE to purge the table data without any transaction logging.

And even if you do have sufficient log space, you generally do not want to have a single transaction consume the majority of active online log files. The solution is to delete from the table in groups of rows with intermittent COMMITs. Figure 10.4 provides an example of how to perform deletes in this manner.

The emp_act table can grow quickly because employees log their project activity hours. As time passes, older data can be purged. In Figure 10.4, data that is older than the current year is being purged.

```
CREATE PROCEDURE chunk_delete (OUT p_batches INT)
    LANGUAGE SQL
    SPECIFIC chunk_delete
cd: BEGIN
    -- This example is currently supported on LUW only
    DECLARE SQLSTATE CHAR(5) DEFAULT '00000';
    DECLARE v_cnt INT DEFAULT 0;
    DECLARE rows_deleted INT DEFAULT 1;

    REPEAT
        SET v_cnt = v_cnt + 1;
        DELETE FROM (SELECT 1 FROM EMP_ACT
                        WHERE YEAR(EMENDATE) < YEAR(current date)
                        FETCH FIRST 10 ROWS ONLY);
        GET DIAGNOSTICS rows_deleted = ROW_COUNT;
        COMMIT;
        UNTIL rows_deleted = 0
    END REPEAT;

    SET p_batches = v_cnt;
END cd
```

Figure 10.4   Deleting from a table in groups on LUW.

The key feature of this procedure is the DELETE from SELECT statement that limits its result set to a fixed number of rows using FETCH FIRST ... ROWS ONLY. In this example, the rows are deleted in groups of 10 and committed (however, in your own situations, you should find that significantly higher values in the hundreds or thousands will yield significantly better performance). This is repeated until no rows are left to delete as determined by GET DIAGNOSTICS.

MERGE Statement

The MERGE SQL statement is used to unify INSERT, UPDATE, and DELETE statements into one, with which may result in better performance.

TIP

MERGE is currently available on LUW. However, the procedure that implements merging of data without the MERGE statement (see Figure 10.6) works for all platforms.

To demonstrate, consider an example where you have a staging table that contains both updates to existing data and new data to be inserted into a primary table. The following tables and data are used to support the following examples.

```
CREATE TABLE master_table (id INT NOT NULL, data VARCHAR(100));
CREATE UNIQUE INDEX ix1 ON master_table (id);
ALTER TABLE master_table ADD CONSTRAINT master_pk PRIMARY KEY (id);
CREATE TABLE stage_table LIKE master_table;

INSERT INTO master_table VALUES (1,'a');
INSERT INTO master_table VALUES (2,'b');
INSERT INTO master_table VALUES (3,'c');
INSERT INTO master_table VALUES (4,'d');

INSERT INTO stage_table VALUES (1,'A');
INSERT INTO stage_table VALUES (3,'C');
INSERT INTO stage_table VALUES (10,'j');
INSERT INTO stage_Table VALUES (11,'k');
```

Figure 10.5   Scenario setup for merging data from two tables.

The table `master_table` in this case is the primary table, whereas `stage_table` is the staging table. If a row in `stage_table` also exists in `master_table`, the existing row in `master_table` should be updated. If a row in `stage_table` does not exist in `master_table`, it should be inserted into `master_table`. Figure 10.6 demonstrates how one might do this.

```
CREATE PROCEDURE old_merge ()
    LANGUAGE SQL
    SPECIFIC old_merge                              -- applies to LUW and iSeries
  --WLM ENVIRONMENT <env>                           -- applies to zSeries
om: BEGIN
    DECLARE v_id INT;
    DECLARE v_data VARCHAR(100);

    DECLARE SQLSTATE CHAR(5) DEFAULT '00000';

    DECLARE cur CURSOR FOR
        SELECT id, data FROM stage_table;                        -- (1)

    DECLARE CONTINUE HANDLER FOR SQLSTATE '23505'
        -- Primary key violation. Perform update instead.
        UPDATE master_table SET data = v_data WHERE id = v_id; -- (2)

    OPEN cur;
    FETCH cur INTO v_id, v_data;

    WHILE (SQLSTATE = '00000') DO
        INSERT INTO master_table VALUES (v_id, v_data);          -- (3)
        FETCH cur INTO v_id, v_data;
    END WHILE;

END om
```

Figure 10.6   Merging data from two tables using *INSERT* and *UPDATE* statements.

The procedure works by creating a cursor on Line (1) for table `stage_table` and attempts insert each row into `master_table` on Line (3). Should the insert fail due to a primary key violation, the row must already exist in `master_table`. The CONTINUE handler on Line (2) then performs an UPDATE instead using the primary key value of the row to be merged.

The procedure can be dramatically simplified and execute with greater efficiency using a MERGE statement. Compare Figure 10.6 with Figure 10.7.

```
CREATE PROCEDURE new_merge()
    LANGUAGE SQL
    SPECIFIC new_merge
nm: BEGIN

    -- the MERGE statement is currently support on LUW only
    MERGE INTO master_table as M
    USING (SELECT id, data FROM stage_table) AS S
       ON M.id=S.id
    WHEN NOT MATCHED THEN
        INSERT VALUES (S.id, S.data)
    WHEN MATCHED THEN
        UPDATE SET M.data=S.data;
END nm
```

Figure 10.7   Merging data from two tables using the *MERGE* statement on LUW.

Now that you have seen a basic example, additional detail about the MERGE statement can be introduced. The MERGE statement can be broken down as follows:

```
MERGE INTO <target> USING <source> ON <match-condition>
{WHEN [NOT] MATCHED [AND <predicate>]
 THEN [UPDATE SET ...|DELETE|INSERT VALUES ....|SIGNAL ...]}
[ELSE IGNORE]
```

The <target> is the primary table and the <source> is a SELECT statement defining the source of rows to be merged into the primary table. In Figure 10.7, the source was simply the set of all rows from table stage_table. The source, however, can be any valid SELECT statement and might even join multiple tables.

The <match condition> is a unique column value that defines the relationship between the source and target tables. In the previous example, this was the primary key column shared by both master_table and stage_table.

Once the source and target and their relationship has been defined, you can decide what to do when there is or is not a match. You can even have multiple matched and not matched conditions.

MERGE has a number of intricate details that are best served by the DB2 SQL Reference. Refer to the SQL Reference for more examples or if you need additional information.

Declared Global Temporary Tables

Declared global temporary tables are like regular database tables but offer performance benefits:

- They can store data with minimal infrastructure and resource requirements.
- They can be tuned to be memory bound for better performance.
- Because they are accessible only from the connection that creates it, there is no need for locking mechanisms
- They can be manipulated without transaction logging on some platforms.

In the following sections, you will learn how to employ temporary tables in your applications.

Introduction to Temporary Tables

Declared global temporary tables are often referred to as **DGTTs** or simply, **temporary tables**. As the name implies, temporary tables are not persistent database objects. Temporary tables are much like normal tables except that they persist only for the duration of a connection and can only be accessed by the connection that declares it. If two connections each create a temporary table with the same name, each instance of the temporary table is unique. When a database connection is closed, all temporary tables declared through that connection are dropped automatically.

Temporary tables are not owned by a particular user; they belong to the session in which they are created. All temporary tables belong to schema SESSION. You have to fully qualify the temporary tables with SESSION for all temporary table references; otherwise, DB2 will look for a persistent table in the current schema instead (for example, SESSION.temptable1).

Creating the Environment for Temporary Tables

On DB2 LUW and zSeries, some setup is required before temporary tables can be used. On iSeries, no setup is required (temporary tables will be created in the library QTEMP).

On DB2 LUW, a user temporary table space must exist (which is different from, and often confused with, a SYSTEM temporary table space). Like all other table space types, the user temporary table space requires that a buffer pool be assigned to it. When a temporary table is declared and populated, the data will use the buffer pool assigned to the table space to keep the data in memory. If the memory requirements for the temporary table exceed the size of the buffer pool assigned to the table space, DB2 will automatically page some of the data to disk.

Here is a simple example of creating a simple user temporary table space on LUW:

```
CREATE USER TEMPORARY TABLESPACE usertempspace
    MANAGED BY SYSTEM USING ('usertempspace')
    BUFFERPOOL ibmdefaultbp
```

Temporary tables that use `usertempspace` table space will be held in the `IBMDEFAULTBP` buffer pool. If you are concerned that your temporary tables may consume too much of your primary buffer pool, you may want to create a dedicated buffer pool for the user temporary table space.

On zSeries you need to

- Create a database and use the `AS TEMP` clause to ensure this database is only used for temporary tables.
- Create a user temporary table space in the TEMP database.

For example, this statement will create the database `tempdb` that will only be used by temporary tables:

```
CREATE DATABASE tempdb AS TEMP
```

Only one TEMP database can be created for each DB2 subsystem or data sharing member. A TEMP database cannot be shared between DB2 subsystems or data sharing members.

Once a TEMP database has been created, you must create a table space in this database. For example, the following statement will create table space `temptbl` in database tempdb using 8K page buffer pool BP8K0:

```
CREATE TABLESPACE temptbl in tempdb bufferpool BP8K0
```

Declaring Global Temporary Tables

Let's now look at the many ways in which you can declare and use a temporary table. The syntax for declaring a temporary table looks a lot like creating standard tables. The syntax and options available for declared global temporary tables varies slightly by platform. Therefore, a basic syntax diagram is provided for each platform in Figures 10.8, 10.9, and 10.10. For a full description of the DECLARE GLOBAL TEMPORARY TABLE, consult the SQL Reference for your platform. The following examples will also call out some of the slight differences in options and syntax you should be aware of.

```
>>-DECLARE GLOBAL TEMPORARY TABLE--table-name------------------->


        .-,--------------------.
        V                      |
>--+-(----| column-definition|-+--)----------------------------+-->
   +-LIKE--+-table-name1-+---+-----------------+-----------------+
   |       '-view-name---' '-| copy-options |-'                 |
   '-AS--(--fullselect--)-+-DEFINITION ONLY-+---+-----------------+-
                                             '-| copy-options |-'
```

```
      .-ON COMMIT DELETE ROWS---.
>--*--+-----------------------+--*---------------------------->
      '-ON COMMIT PRESERVE ROWS-'


>--+----------------------------------------+---------------->
   |                  .-ON ROLLBACK DELETE ROWS---. |
   '-NOT LOGGED--+---------------------------+-'
                 '-ON ROLLBACK PRESERVE ROWS-'


>--*--+--------------+--*--+--------------------+-------------->
      '-WITH REPLACE-'     '-IN--tablespace-name-'
```

Figure 10.8 *DECLARE GLOBAL TEMPORARY TABLE* syntax for DB2 LUW.

```
>>-DECLARE GLOBAL TEMPORARY TABLE--table-name------------------>


       .-,-------------------------------------------.
       V                                             |
>--+-(----+-column-definition---------------------+-+--)-+----->
   |       '-LIKE--+-table-name-+--+-------------+-'     |
   |               '-view-name--' '-copy-options-'       |
   +-LIKE--+-table-name-+--+-------------+--------------+
   |       '-view-name--' '-copy-options-'              |
   '-as-subquery-clause--------------------------------'


   .------------------------------------------------.
   V                                                |
>----+-WITH REPLACE--------------------------------+-+---------><
     | .-ON COMMIT DELETE ROWS---.                 |
     +-+-----------------------+--------------+
     | '-ON COMMIT PRESERVE ROWS-'             |
     |                  .-ON ROLLBACK DELETE ROWS---. |
     '-NOT LOGGED--+---------------------------+-'
                   '-ON ROLLBACK PRESERVE ROWS-'
```

Figure 10.9 *DECLARE GLOBAL TEMPORARY TABLE* syntax for iSeries.

```
>>-DECLARE GLOBAL TEMPORARY TABLE--table-name------------------->


       .-,--------------------.
       V                      |
>--+-(----+-column-definition---+-----------------------------------------+---->
   |                                                --COLUMN ATTRIBUTES--  |
   |                          --EXCLUDING IDENTITY--|-------------------|  |
   |--LIKE-- --table-name-- ----|-----------------------------------|  |
   |       |--view-name----|                        |--COLUMN ATTRIBUTES--|  |
   |                       |--INCLUDING IDENTITY-|-------------------|  |  |
   |--AS--(fullselect)--WITH NO DATA---------------------------------|
                                   |--copy-options--|


     .-----------------------------------------------.
     V                                               |
>----+-----------------------------------------------+-+----------->< 
      | .-ON COMMIT DELETE ROWS---.                  |
      +-+------------------------+--------------'
      | |-ON COMMIT PRESERVE ROWS-|
      | '-ON COMMIT DROP TABLE----|
      '-----CCSID--+-ASCII---+----'
                   |-EBCIDIC-|
                   '-UNICODE-'
```

Figure 10.10 *DECLARE GLOBAL TEMPORARY TABLE* syntax for zSeries.

An example of declaring a temporary table is shown in Figure 10.11.

```
DECLARE GLOBAL TEMPORARY TABLE session.tempnewproj ( projno CHAR(6)
                                                    , projname VARCHAR(24)
                                                    , projsdate DATE
                                                    , projedate DATE
                                                    , category VARCHAR(10)
                                                    , desc VARCHAR(100) )
        ON COMMIT PRESERVE ROWS
        NOT LOGGED                  -- applies to LUW and iSeries
        ON ROLLBACK PRESERVE ROWS   -- applies to LUW and iSeries
        WITH REPLACE                -- applies to LUW and iSeries
        IN usertempspace            -- applies to LUW
;
```

Figure 10.11 An example of declaring a temporary table.

The example demonstrates creating a temporary table called `tempnewproj`. The columns and data types are defined explicitly the same way you would for standard tables.

On LUW, BLOB, CLOB, DBCLOB, LONG VARCHAR, LONG VARGRAPHIC, DATALINK, reference, and structured types are not supported in temporary tables. On zSeries, all built-in data types are supported in temporary tables except for BLOB, CLOB, DBCLOB, and ROWID data types. On iSeries, BLOB, CLOB, DBCLOB, VARCHAR, VARGRAPHIC, and DATALINK are supported, but with minor restrictions. Refer to the iSeries SQL Reference for these restrictions.

The IN clause is used to specify a temporary table space for the temporary table and applies to DB2 LUW only. If you do not specify it, DB2 will automatically select one by default. DB2 UDB for iSeries does not have the concept of table space, and on zSeries temporary tables are created in a table space with the appropriate page size that belongs to the TEMP database. For portability, leave this option out of the temporary table definition.

Before you can declare another temporary table with the same name in the same session, the existing temporary table has to be dropped. You can do this by explicitly using the DROP TABLE statement.

```
DROP TABLE session.tempnewproj
```

On DB2 LUW and iSeries, a WITH REPLACE option is available, as shown in Figure 10.8. When using this option, should you declare a table with the same name (within the same session), DB2 will automatically drop the existing temporary table and re-create it with the new definition. The WITH REPLACE option is particularly useful in connection pooled environments (where connections are returned to a pool rather than released by applications). With connection pooling, it is possible that previously used temporary tables have not been dropped when the connection is returned to the pool. Using the WITH REPLACE option ensures that next application using a pooled connection will not pick up data left over from its previous use.

The ON COMMIT option allows you to specify whether you want to preserve or delete data in the temporary table on commit. The default behavior is to flush the temporary table's contents on commit.

The NOT LOGGED clause is used to indicate that data changes in this table are not logged (for better performance). On zSeries, minimal logging is required and the NOT LOGGED clause is currently not available.

There are other methods for declaring temporary tables as well.

```
DECLARE GLOBAL TEMPORARY TABLE TEMP_EMPLOYEE LIKE EMPLOYEE
```

Often, temporary tables take the same form of a real table because the temporary table will be used to stage a subset of data from another table for processing. Figure 10.11 demonstrates the use of the LIKE clause to easily accomplish this. The main benefit of this is simplicity because there is no need to provide the column definitions for the temporary table. The source table definition can be a real table, another temporary table, a view, or a nickname (for a remote table). Only column names, their types, and nullable attribute are copied. Indexes and constraints are not copied.

Figure 10.12 illustrates yet another way to declare temporary tables. The column names and types of the full select determine the structure of the temporary table. The temporary table does not get populated by the SELECT statement.

```
DECLARE GLOBAL TEMPORARY TABLE TEMP_EMPDEPT AS
    ( SELECT E.FIRSTNME, E.LASTNAME, D.DEPTNAME
         FROM EMPLOYEE E, DEPARTMENT D WHERE E.WORKDEPT=D.DEPTNO)
    DEFINITION ONLY
    -- on zSeries and iSeries, this is a synonym for WITH NO DATA
```

Figure 10.12   Declaring a temporary table using a full-select.

Using Temporary Tables in SQL Procedures

You can declare, manipulate, and drop temporary tables in an SQL procedure. Figure 10.13 demonstrates the basic elements of declaring and using temporary tables in the context of a stored procedure. It also highlights a potential problem that is not immediately evident.

```
CREATE PROCEDURE temp_table_demo()
    LANGUAGE SQL
    SPECIFIC temp_table_demo                    -- applies to LUW and iSeries
  --WLM ENVIRONMENT <env>                       -- applies to zSeries
DYNAMIC RESULT SETS 1
BEGIN
    DECLARE v_sql VARCHAR(100) DEFAULT 'SELECT * FROM session.temp_table';
    DECLARE c_cur CURSOR WITH RETURN TO CALLER FOR stmt;            -- (1)

    DECLARE GLOBAL TEMPORARY TABLE
        session.temp_table ( id INT, value VARCHAR(10))
        ON COMMIT PRESERVE ROWS;

    INSERT INTO session.temp_table VALUES (1,'a');
    INSERT INTO session.temp_table VALUES (2,'b');
    INSERT INTO session.temp_table VALUES (3,'c');

    PREPARE stmt FROM v_sql;
    OPEN c_cur;
END
```

Figure 10.13   A simple example of using a temporary table.

Looking carefully at the sample code, you will notice that the cursor c_cur on Line (1) is declared to return the contents of the temporary table to the calling application. However, rather than declaring the cursor to directly select from the temporary table, dynamic SQL is used to do this. Use of dynamic SQL (discussed in Chapter 7, "Working with Dynamic SQL") is required on LUW because object dependencies are resolved at procedure build time.

Use of dynamic SQL to open a cursor on a temporary table is not required on zSeries and iSeries. On zSeries, procedures are created with the VALIDATE (RUN) bind option by default. The example is applicable, however, if the procedure is created with the VALIDATE (BIND) option. On iSeries, object dependencies are always deferred until execution time. Using dynamic SQL for cursors is recommended for compatibility on all DB2 platforms.

Sharing Temporary Tables Between Multiple Procedures

This section demonstrates how to share temporary tables between procedures. The examples are designed such that they work on all platforms.

Before you can reference a temporary table, it must first be declared so that DB2 knows its structure. Complications can arise when the location where a temporary table is declared differs from the location(s) where it may be referenced. Consider the following scenarios:

- An application wants to declare temporary table T, populate it, and then call procedure P to process the data. How can both the application and procedure P make reference to T without procedure P re-declaring T?

- A stored procedure P1 may declare a temporary table T, populate it, and wish to call procedures P2 and P3 to process the data. How can P2 and P3 reference a temporary table declared in P1 without re-declaring it themselves?

In both cases, attempts to re-declare a temporary table within the same session will result in either SQLSTATE 42710 (the object already exists) or the first table being replaced by subsequent declarations if WITH REPLACE is specified.

The solution to this problem is to recognize that the declaration and reference(s) do not have to be contained in the same procedure body. The only requirement is that the temporary table must be declared in the current session at procedure build time. In the following example, two procedures that share a temporary table called SESSION.temp will be demonstrated.

Figure 10.14 shows a procedure called init_temp that simply encapsulates the declaration of the temporary table SESSION.temp.

```
CREATE PROCEDURE init_temp()
    LANGUAGE SQL
    SPECIFIC init_temp                      -- applies to LUW and iSeries
  --WLM ENVIRONMENT <env>                   -- applies to zSeries
it: BEGIN
    DECLARE GLOBAL TEMPORARY TABLE
```

```
        session.temp (id INT, data VARCHAR(10))
        WITH REPLACE                        -- applies to LUW and iSeries
        ON COMMIT PRESERVE ROWS;
END it
```

Figure 10.14   A procedure for encapsulating the declaration of a temporary table.

Using a procedure to initialize the temporary table yields three key benefits:

- It allows temporary tables to be easily declared for the database connection used by the DB2 Development Center.
- The procedure developer does not have to hunt through application code (that may be maintained by another person) to find the DDL of the temporary table.
- If the same temporary table may be instantiated from multiple locations in application code, the definition of the table is centralized at one place.

With the procedure `init_temp`, it is relatively easy to manage an environment for building procedures which share temporary tables. You can build a procedure which references the temporary table as long as `init_temp` is executed first in the current database connection.

To complement `init_temp`, define a procedure to drop the temporary table as illustrated in Figure 10.15. This is necessary for zSeries because the `WITH REPLACE` option is not currently available on that platform. On LUW or iSeries, if the temporary table `SESSION.temp` exists in the current session, calling `init_temp` automatically drops any existing table.

```
CREATE PROCEDURE close_temp()
    LANGUAGE SQL
    SPECIFIC CLOSE_TEMP        -- applies to LUW and iSeries
    -- WLM ENVIRONMENT <env>   -- applies to zSeries
BEGIN
    DROP TABLE SESSION.TEMP;
END
```

Figure 10.15   A procedure to encapsulate the dropping of a temporary table.

Using a procedure to drop the temporary table has these two benefits:

- It allows one to drop temporary tables for the session when working in DB2 Development Center.
- It completes the encapsulation of the temporary table declaration through stored procedures.

To build the procedure `insert_to_temp` in Figure 10.16, execute the procedure `init_temp`. Notice that `insert_to_temp` statically refers to `SESSION.temp` but does not contain `DECLARE TEMPORARY TABLE` in its body.

```
CREATE PROCEDURE insert_to_temp()
    LANGUAGE SQL
    SPECIFIC insert_to_temp                -- applies to LUW and iSeries
  --WLM ENVIRONMENT <env>                  -- applies to zSeries
BEGIN
    INSERT INTO SESSION.TEMP VALUES (1, 'one');
    INSERT INTO SESSION.TEMP VALUES (2, 'two');
    INSERT INTO SESSION.TEMP VALUES (3, 'three');
END
```

Figure 10.16   A procedure that references a temporary table without a declaration.

Another procedure, `show_rows` in Figure 10.17, shares the temporary table data. It returns the contents of the temporary table to the application.

```
CREATE PROCEDURE show_rows()
    LANGUAGE SQL
    SPECIFIC show_rows                     -- applies to LUW and iSeries
  --WLM ENVIRONMENT <env>                  -- applies to zSeries
DYNAMIC RESULT SETS 1
BEGIN
    DECLARE cur CURSOR WITH HOLD WITH RETURN TO CALLER FOR
        SELECT * FROM session.temp;

    OPEN cur;
END
```

Figure 10.17   A procedure that returns the contents of a temporary table.

To wrap up this example, Table 10.1 lists the calling sequence:

Table 10.1   Calling Sequence for Sharing Temporary Tables

Step 1:	CALL init_temp	This will re-initialize the SESSION.temp table.
Step 2:	CALL insert_to_temp	This will insert three rows into SESSION.temp.
Step 3:	CALL show_rows	The result set returned will be the three rows contained in the temporary table populated by insert_to_temp.
Step 4:	CALL close_temp	Drops the temporary table.

Considerations

On iSeries temporary tables are supported in both user-defined functions and triggers. On zSeries, temporary tables are supported in user-defined functions but not in triggers. On LUW, temporary tables are not supported in user-defined functions or triggers. However, functions and triggers can call stored procedures that use temporary tables.

Created Global Temporary Tables

On zSeries, there are two types of temporary tables:

- Temporary tables created with the `DECLARE GLOBAL TEMPORARY TABLE` statement (declared).
- Temporary tables created with the `CREATE GLOBAL TEMPORARY TABLE` statement (created).

This chapter has discussed the first type of temporary tables. For portability with the other platforms, this is the type of temporary tables that should be used. If you are developing applications exclusively on zSeries, however, you may want to consider using the second type of temporary tables.

Created temporary tables put a description of the table in the catalog. This description is persistent and can therefore be shared across application processes. Though the description is shared, an instance of this table is distinct for each application process, and it will not persist beyond the life of the application process.

The name for this table follows the rules of any standard table, and the schema name does not need to be `SESSION`.

Indexes, `UPDATE` operations, and `DELETE` (positioned only) operations are not supported with the created temporary tables. Locking, logging, recovery, table space, and database operations do not apply to this type of table as well.

The created global temporary table is stored in table spaces in the work file database. It is not stored in a database created as TEMP as with declared global temporary tables.

For more detail about created global temporary tables, refer to the DB2 for zSeries SQL Reference.

Working with Save Points

A **save point** is a server side mechanism that can give you greater control over transactions. Save points enable you to start a transaction and keep portions of a transaction while rolling back other portions, without committing the overall unit of work. In the following sections, you will see how to employ them in your stored procedures.

Introduction to Application Save Points

An **application save point** is a mechanism to control transactions within an application program such as an SQL procedure. There are three kinds of save points:

- Statement save point
- Compound SQL save point
- External save point

By default, a save point is internally created before the execution of each SQL statement. If an SQL statement fails with an error, DB2 will roll back to the internal save point. Statement save points are used internally by DB2.

If you use an atomic compound statement, DB2 performs a block of SQL statements as one statement. If any substatement fails, all actions within the compound SQL block are rolled back. Atomic compound SQL actually uses an internal compound SQL save point. See Chapter 4, "Using Flow of Control Statements," for a discussion of atomic compound SQL. The third kind of save point, an external save point, is the focus of this section. From this point on, any reference to the term "save point" implies external save point.

An **external save point** is similar to an atomic compound block but with more granular transaction control. After establishing a save point within a transaction, you have the option to roll back substatements of a transaction to a save point without affecting other operations in the transaction.

Syntax diagrams for creating, releasing, and rolling back to a save point are shown in Figures 10.18, 10.19, and 10.20, respectively.

```
>>-SAVEPOINT--savepoint-name----+---------+-------------------->
                                '-UNIQUE--'
                                  .-ON ROLLBACK RETAIN LOCKS--.
>----ON ROLLBACK RETAIN CURSORS--+---------------------------+--><
```

Figure 10.18   Syntax diagram of creating a save point.

The keyword UNIQUE indicates that this save point name will not be reused in the transaction. If you want to establish another save point with the same name within the same transaction, you need to explicitly release the save point or end the whole transaction with COMMIT or ROLLBACK statements.

ON ROLLBACK RETAIN CURSORS is a mandatory clause that describes cursor behavior within the save point. If a cursor is opened or referenced in a save point, rolling back to the save point will keep the cursor open and positioned at the next logical row of the result set. At the completion of a transaction, DB2 by default releases all database locks acquired in it. This is also the default behavior when you roll back to a save point. With the ON ROLLBACK RETAIN LOCKS option, DB2 will not release locks obtained within the save point.

```
        .-TO-.
>>-RELEASE--+----+--SAVEPOINT--savepoint-name------------------><
```

Figure 10.19   Syntax diagram of releasing a save point.

```
           .-WORK-.
>>-ROLLBACK--+------+--+----------------------------------+----><
                        '-TO SAVEPOINT--+---------------+-'
                                        '-savepoint-name-'
```

Figure 10.20   Syntax diagram of rolling back to a save point.

After the last substatement of the block, you may choose to roll back to the save point or release the save point. Once the save point is released, rolling back to the save point is no longer possible. A save point is implicitly released when the transaction is completed. Rolling back to a save point is not considered to be the end of a transaction so the save point is not released.

Using Save Points in SQL Procedures

In Figure 10.21, an SQL procedure bonus_incr is illustrated. It is used to automate bonus increases for employees in a company. Company ABC is doing so well that every employee is receiving a 10 percent bonus increase. Given that the total amount of bonuses for some departments is already quite high, management has decided that if the total bonus of a department is greater than $3,000, its employees will not receive the increase immediately and will be evaluated individually.

```
CREATE PROCEDURE bonus_incr ()
    LANGUAGE SQL
    SPECIFIC bonus_incr      -- applies to LUW and iSeries
    -- WLM ENVIRONMENT <env> -- applies to zSeries
bi: BEGIN
    -- DECLARE VARIABLES
    DECLARE v_dept, v_actdept CHAR(3);
    DECLARE v_bonus, v_deptbonus, v_newbonus DECIMAL(9,2);
    DECLARE v_empno CHAR(6);
    DECLARE v_atend SMALLINT DEFAULT 0;

     -- DECLARE CURSORS
    DECLARE c_sales CURSOR WITH HOLD FOR                          -- (1)
```

```
    SELECT workdept, bonus, empno FROM employee
    ORDER BY workdept;

-- DECLARE HANDLERS
DECLARE CONTINUE HANDLER FOR NOT FOUND
    SET v_atend=1;
DECLARE EXIT HANDLER FOR SQLEXCEPTION                          -- (2)
    SET v_atend=1;

-- Procedure body
OPEN c_sales;
FETCH c_sales INTO v_dept, v_bonus, v_empno;

    WHILE (v_atend = 0) DO
        SAVEPOINT svpt_bonus_incr ON ROLLBACK RETAIN CURSORS;     -- (3)
        SET v_actdept = v_dept;
        SET v_deptbonus = 0;
        WHILE ( v_actdept = v_dept ) AND ( v_atend = 0 ) DO
            SET v_newbonus = v_bonus * 1.1;
            UPDATE employee
                SET bonus = v_newbonus
                WHERE empno = v_empno;
            SET v_deptbonus = v_deptbonus + v_newbonus;
            FETCH c_sales INTO v_dept, v_bonus, v_empno;
        END WHILE;

        IF v_deptbonus <= 3000.00 THEN
            COMMIT;                                               -- (4)
        ELSE
            ROLLBACK TO SAVEPOINT svpt_bonus_incr;                -- (5)
            RELEASE SAVEPOINT svpt_bonus_incr;                    -- (6)
        END IF;
    END WHILE;

END bi
```

Figure 10.21   SQL procedure *BONUS_INCR*.

The statement on Line (1) displays a cursor that is declared to retrieve a result set of every employee sorted by department number. The statement on Line (3) defines a save point svpt_bonus_incr. This is the point to which the application can roll back. The WHILE loop iterates through the employee table for a given department and performs the bonus increase. If the total amount of bonus for a department is 3000 or less, changes made since the save point are committed on Line (4). In order to keep the cursor open so that other departments can be processed, the cursor is declared on Line (1) with the WITH HOLD option. On the other hand, if the total bonus for a department is greater than 3000, updates to the database since the last save point will be rolled back on Line (5). The save point is also released on Line (6) so that it can be created again on Line (4) before processing the next department.

What happens if a statement used in the save point fails? Does DB2 roll back only the statement, the save point block, or the whole SQL procedure? The answer depends on whether a HANDLER is defined to catch the error. Without a HANDLER declared for the error, any statement failure raised in a save point will cause all changes made in the SQL procedure to be rolled back regardless of whether they are defined inside or outside of the save point. Conversely, if a HANDLER is defined for the error, only the failed statement is rolled back. This is the expected behavior when a save point is used. To make the example in Figure 10.21 more complete, an EXIT HANDLER is defined on Line (2). This makes sure that only the statement in error is rolled back and exits the stored procedure call.

Nested save points are also supported for more granular transaction control. Figure 10.22 illustrates usage of nested save points.

```
CREATE PROCEDURE nested_savepoint ( )
    LANGUAGE SQL
    SPECIFIC nested_savepoint    -- applies to LUW and iSeries
    -- WLM ENVIRONMENT <env>     -- applies to zSeries
nsp: BEGIN

CREATE TABLE SP_TABLE (c1 INT);
COMMIT;

SAVEPOINT sp1 ON ROLLBACK RETAIN CURSORS;
INSERT INTO sp_table VALUES (1);

SAVEPOINT sp2 ON ROLLBACK RETAIN CURSORS;
INSERT INTO sp_table VALUES (2);

savepoint sp3 on rollback retain cursors;
INSERT INTO sp_table VALUES (3);
```

```
ROLLBACK TO SAVEPOINT sp2;
COMMIT;

DROP TABLE SP_TABLE;
COMMIT;
END nsp
```

Figure 10.22   Nested save point example.

The procedure shown in Figure 10.22 demonstrates the use of nested save points. The procedure contains three transactions: one to create the table SP_TABLE, another to perform some inserts, and a third transaction to drop the table. The procedure does nothing useful except to demonstrate the use of nested save points.

As you can see, three save points are set in the second transaction. Before the end of transaction, a ROLLBACK TO SAVEPOINT is used to roll back changes up to the save point sp2. That is, the following statements are rolled back:

```
INSERT INTO sp_table VALUES (2);
INSERT INTO sp_table VALUES (3);
```

The resulting table at the end of the second transaction is a single row with a value of 1. Another observation is that you can roll back to any save point within a transaction.

Sequence Objects

In Chapter 3, "Overview of SQL PL Language Elements," you learned how to use sequence objects and identity columns to generate incremental numeric values. These methods are commonly used to generate ID values for primary keys. Other relational database products on the market each have their own way of generating incremental values. For vendors who need to create applications to support multiple database products, stored procedures are sometimes used to encapsulate database-specific syntax so that the application layer remains database-agnostic.

Here, the previous discussion of sequence objects is extended to demonstrate how a stored procedure can be used to provide a consistent syntax (across multiple database vendors) for obtaining the next value of a given sequence object. The stored procedures can be maintained along with other database objects. An example is shown in Figure 10.23.

Whereas code manageability is improved by wrapping NEXTVAL in stored procedures, keep in mind the overhead needed to load and run stored procedures.

```
CREATE PROCEDURE seqnextval ( IN   p_seqname VARCHAR(50)
                            , OUT p_nextval INT )
    LANGUAGE SQL
    SPECIFIC seqnextval        -- applies to LUW and iSeries
```

```
    -- WLM ENVIRONMENT <env> -- applies to zSeries
snv: BEGIN
    -- DECLARE VARIABLES
    DECLARE v_dynstmt VARCHAR(100);

    -- DECLARE CONDITIONS                                        -- (1)
    -- SQLSTATE 42704, object not found
    DECLARE seq_notfound CONDITION FOR SQLSTATE '42704';
    -- SQLSTATE 42501, object privilege error
    DECLARE obj_access_error CONDITION FOR SQLSTATE '42501';

    -- DECLARE CURSORS
    DECLARE c_nextval CURSOR FOR v_prepstmt;

    -- DECLARE HANDLERS                                          -- (2)
    DECLARE EXIT HANDLER FOR seq_notfound
        RESIGNAL SQLSTATE '70000'
          SET MESSAGE_TEXT = 'Sequence Object NOT FOUND';
    DECLARE EXIT HANDLER FOR obj_access_error
        RESIGNAL SQLSTATE '70001'
          SET MESSAGE_TEXT = 'User encounters privilege problems';

    -- Procedure body
    SET v_dynstmt = 'SELECT NEXTVAL for ' || p_seqname || ' FROM
SYSIBM.SYSDUMMY1' ; -- (3)
    PREPARE v_prepstmt FROM v_dynstmt;                          -- (4)
    OPEN c_nextval;
    FETCH c_nextval INTO p_nextval;                             -- (5)
    CLOSE c_nextval;

END snv
```

Figure 10.23   Sequence value generation wrapped in an SQL procedure.

This stored procedure takes a sequence object name as input and returns the next sequence value. The statement on Line (3) is used to generate the value and must be prepared dynamically on Line (4) because the sequence object name is not known until the time of execution. The generated value is then fetched on Line (5) and stored in the OUT parameter.

Conditions and error handlers are defined on Lines (1) and (2) to catch object-not-found and privilege errors. If the given sequence is not defined or the sequence schema name is not correctly provided, the stored procedure will result in an OBJECT NOT FOUND error. A privilege error may result if the user does not have USAGE on the sequence or the user does not have EXECUTE on the stored procedure package itself. For more information about privileges required for creating or executing a stored procedure, refer to Appendix E, "Security Considerations in SQL Procedures."

The behavior of a sequence object can be changed with the ALTER SEQUENCE. Another stored procedure can be defined to alter a sequence object with specific options (see Figure 10.24).

```
CREATE PROCEDURE alterseq   ( IN p_seqname VARCHAR(50)
                            , IN p_options VARCHAR(100) )
    LANGUAGE SQL
    SPECIFIC alterseq          -- applies to LUW and iSeries
    -- WLM ENVIRONMENT <env> -- applies to zSeries
aseq: BEGIN
    -- DECLARE VARIABLES
    DECLARE v_dynstmt VARCHAR(100);
    DECLARE v_retcode INTEGER DEFAULT 0;

    -- DECLARE CONDITIONS
    -- SQLSTATE 42704, object not found
    DECLARE seq_notfound CONDITION FOR SQLSTATE '42704';
    -- SQLSTATE 42501, object privilege error
    DECLARE obj_access_error CONDITION FOR SQLSTATE '42501';

    -- DECLARE HANDLERS
    DECLARE EXIT HANDLER FOR seq_notfound
        RESIGNAL SQLSTATE '70000'
          SET MESSAGE_TEXT = 'Sequence Object NOT FOUND';
    DECLARE EXIT HANDLER FOR obj_access_error
        RESIGNAL SQLSTATE '70001'
          SET MESSAGE_TEXT = 'User encounters privilege problems';
    DECLARE EXIT HANDLER FOR SQLEXCEPTION
        RESIGNAL SQLSTATE '70002'
          SET MESSAGE_TEXT = 'SQL Exception raised';

    -- Procedure body
    SET v_dynstmt = 'ALTER SEQUENCE ' || p_seqname || ' ' || p_options;
    PREPARE v_prepstmt FROM v_dynstmt;
    EXECUTE v_prepstmt;

END aseq
```

Figure 10.24   Sequence object alteration wrapped in an SQL procedure.

To test the `ALTERSEQ` stored procedure, you can issue

```
CALL alterseq('staff_seq', 'restart with 500')
```

This will `RESTART` the sequence number at `500`.

Summary

The focus of this chapter was to highlight important DB2 application development features that are not part of the SQL PL language, but are frequently employed in DB2 application objects to improve performance and simplify SQL PL application development.

You saw how advanced SQL can be used to access internal transition tables by combining `SELECT`s with `INSERT`, `UPDATE`, and `DELETE`, and how `MERGE` can simplify the task of merging data from two tables. The concept of declared global temporary tables was introduced, as well as a lesser known technique for sharing temporary tables between the application and other procedures. Save points can be employed to partially rollback transactions. Finally, an example of how to encapsulate sequence objects was presented for applications that want to maintain a high degree of database independence.

Deploying SQL Procedures, Functions, and Triggers

In this chapter, you will learn

- Several methods for deploying SQL procedures
- How to deploy functions and triggers
- The pros and cons associated with each of the various deployment methods
- Considerations for deploying and working with SQL procedures

Deployment of SQL procedures is the task of moving SQL procedures from one environment to another—for example, moving SQL procedures from a development environment to a test or production environment. This chapter discusses several ways in which this can be done. The method chosen to deploy your procedures will depend on your requirements.

The DB2 Development Center can be used to deploy SQL procedures on the following platforms: LUW, iSeries, and zSeries. The deployment process on LUW and zSeries is very similar, and hence there will be material that is relevant for both platforms. There are additional methods and considerations for each platform, and these (in addition to the iSeries deployment methods) are covered later in the chapter.

Deploying on Linux, UNIX, and Windows

This section covers deployment issues for DB2 on Linux, UNIX, and Windows.

Deploying SQL Procedures Using DDL

The most straightforward way to deploy SQL procedures is to export them in DDL form from the source environment and apply them against the target environment. The Export command in the

DB2 Development Center can be used to generate the DDL file. To do this, after launching the
DB2 Development Center, right-click on the Stored Procedures folder within a project and select
Export (see Figure 11.1) to launch the Export Wizard.

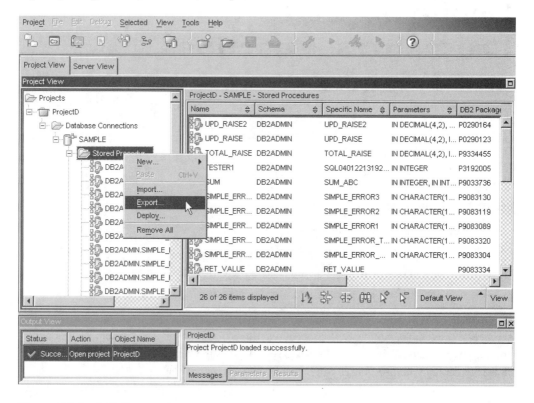

Figure 11.1   Initiating export.

The first screen of the wizard gives you the option of choosing which SQL stored procedures you
would like to export (see Figure 11.2).

TIP

Select the procedures you want to export in the order that you want to create them. For
example, if there are any interdependencies between the stored procedures, you must
ensure that the called procedures are selected before the calling procedure. If stored procedures are created first that are dependent on other procedures which do not exist, then
the compilation of the stored procedures with the dependencies will fail.

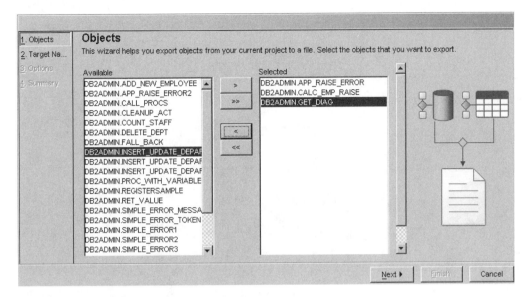

Figure 11.2   Selecting stored procedures for export.

Clicking Next will take you to thescreen in the wizard, in which you can specify the location and name of an output file. In Figure 11.3, the target filename is `sample_proc`. The generated file will be a .DB2 file, contained in a zipped file with the same name.

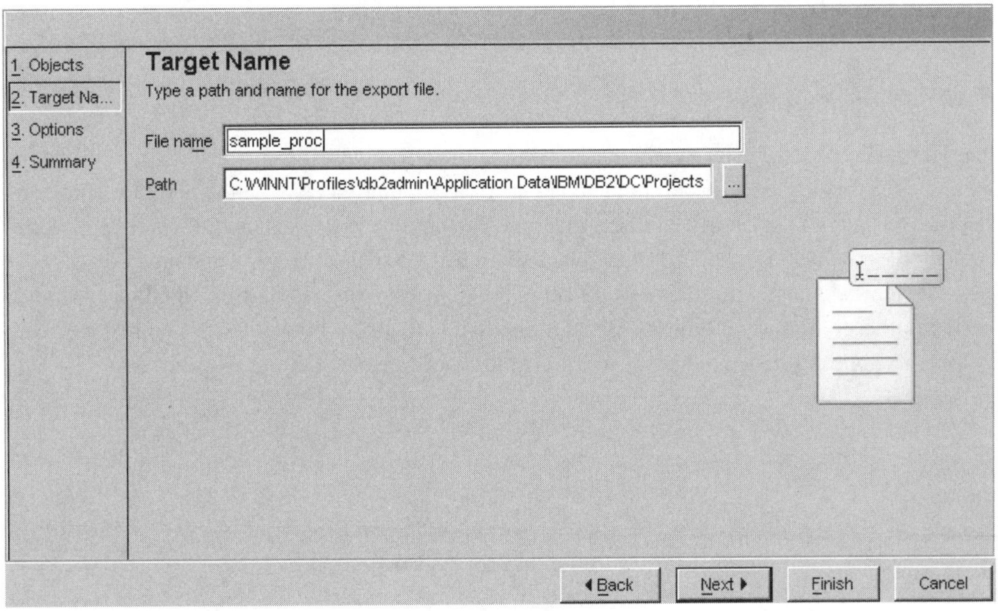

Figure 11.3   Saving the export file.

The next screen (shown in Figure 11.4) offers up some alternatives for the output file. To export in DDL form, you need to select the *Create an export script* radio button. The *Export as project* radio button will bundle all of the procedures into a single zip file. The *Include source files* checkbox can be checked or unchecked. It makes no difference when exporting SQL procedures; it is only used when exporting Java stored procedures.

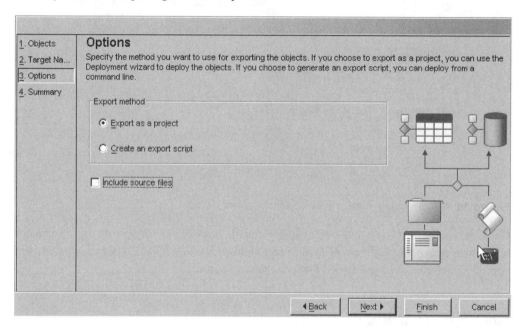

Figure 11.4   Export options.

The next screen in the wizard summarizes the options that were selected; clicking Finish will generate the file. Figure 11.5 shows the contents of the output file. Notice the first line of the output file is a database CONNECT statement that has been commented out. The file can be modified to remove the comments and specify the values for a different database, user, and password. Notice also that the statement termination character is the @ symbol instead of the semicolon (;). This is done in order to remove ambiguity, because the SQL procedure body contains embedded semicolons. The line delimiters are also needed for the procedures to compile properly.

```
-- connect to SAMPLE user DB2ADMIN using Password
-- DROP PROCEDURE smp_export_proc1 (CHARACTER, CHARACTER(6), CHARACTER(7))
-- @
CREATE PROCEDURE smp_export_proc1 ( IN p_midinit CHAR
                              ,IN p_empno CHAR(6)
                              ,OUT p_empno_mid CHAR(7))
      LANGUAGE SQL
```

```
    SPECIFIC export_proc1
sep: BEGIN
   -- Declare return codes
   DECLARE SQLSTATE CHAR(5) DEFAULT '00000';
   DECLARE SQLCODE INT DEFAULT 0;

   SET p_empno_mid = p_empno || p_midinit;
END sep
@
-- DROP PROCEDURE simple_export_proc2 (CHARACTER, CHARACTER(6), INTEGER)
-- @
CREATE PROCEDURE simple_export_proc2 ( IN p_midinit CHAR
                                      ,IN p_empno CHAR(6)
                                      ,OUT p_mid_empno INT)
    LANGUAGE SQL
    SPECIFIC simple_export_proc2
sep2: BEGIN
    -- Declare variables
    DECLARE SQLSTATE CHAR(5) DEFAULT '00000';
    DECLARE SQLCODE INT DEFAULT 0;

    SET p_mid_empno = length(rtrim(p_midinit || p_empno));
END sep2
@
-- DROP PROCEDURE empty_proc ()
-- @
CREATE PROCEDURE empty_proc ()
    LANGUAGE SQL
    SPECIFIC empty_proc
ep: BEGIN
END ep
@

--CONNECT RESET
-- @
```

Figure 11.5   Contents of the export file.

> **TIP**
>
> In order to be able to use the script repeatedly against the same database, you can edit the file and modify it to uncomment out the DROP statements that have been included before the CREATE statements in the script. The SPECIFIC name of the procedure can be used in the DROP statements to avoid ambiguity for any overloaded procedures. The example in Figures 11.6 and 11.7 show how this can be done.

```
-- DROP PROCEDURE sum (INTEGER, INTEGER, INTEGER)
-- @
CREATE PROCEDURE sum(IN p_a INTEGER,IN p_b INTEGER,OUT p_s INTEGER)
SPECIFIC sum_ab
LANGUAGE SQL
    BEGIN
        SET p_s = p_a + p_b;
    END
@
```

Figure 11.6   Procedure text created by the Export command.

The modified script in Figure 11.7 will return an error the first time it is run because there will be no procedure sum to drop. If the script is run multiple times, then it will run properly because it will first drop the old version of the script and then re-create it. The script in Figure 11.6 would never re-create the sum procedure if executed multiple times because the DROP statement is commented out, and would instead return an error on the Create Procedure command.

```
DROP PROCEDURE sum (INTEGER, INTEGER, INTEGER)
@f
CREATE PROCEDURE sum(IN p_a INTEGER,IN p_b INTEGER,OUT p_s INTEGER)
SPECIFIC sum_ab
LANGUAGE SQL
    BEGIN
        SET p_s = p_a + p_b;
    END
@
```

Figure 11.7   Script modifications for multiple script executions.

TIP

It's a good idea to remove the comment on the CONNECT statement. When uncommenting the CONNECT statement, specify a database and user but remove *using <Password>* altogether. This way, every time the script is invoked, it will prompt you for a password. This will help catch situations in which the script is invoked inadvertently, because it gives you the option of canceling out at the password prompt.

Other options exist for exporting SQL procedures. For example, you can SELECT the procedure body text directly from the system catalog tables and pipe the output directly to a file. If you want to have a more robust solution, then you can write a little SQL procedure to extract the procedure body, format the output, and generate the corresponding DROP statements. However, because the utility exists in the DB2 Development Center, why not use it?

Now that you have the SQL procedure in a DDL file, you can apply the script to a target environment. This can be done through the command line. Of course, you will have to make sure that any database objects which are accessed by any of the SQL procedures have been created prior to running the script on the target server. To import (and create the SQL procedures), you can enter the following from the command line:

```
db2 -td@ -f SAMPLE_PROC.db2
```

The -td@ option specifies that the @ symbol is to be used for the statement termination character and the -f option specifies that the input comes from a file. Refer to Appendix C, "Building from the Command Line," for more information

You may also have noticed while using the DB2 Development Center, you have an option to import. You can use this option to import an SQL procedure (instead of the command line option described earlier); however, this option has limited use when importing from a file. Only one procedure can be imported at a time, and the input file can only contain CREATE PROCEDURE statements. The file that is generated by the export utility is also zipped. You will have to unzip it before you can import any stored procedures from it.

Deploying Functions

There are multiple methods to deploy functions with DB2. The Development Center's GUI is an ideal method to learn how to deploy functions. The script-based method covered later in the chapter is recommended for more experienced users who have already stabilized their functions and want to deploy them across one or more test or production environments.

Deploying Functions Using the Development Center

In addition to deploying procedures, you can use the Development Center to develop and deploy your functions. The main Project View menu provides a listing of the functions that are part of your project. The menu is shown in the upper-left corner of Figure 11.8.

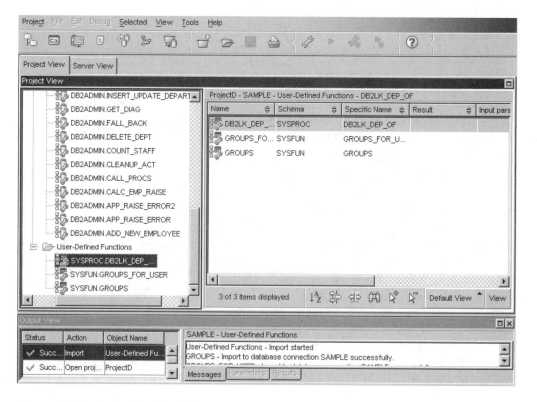

Figure 11.8   Project function list.

To deploy a function, right-click over the function and select the Deploy option. This will open the Deployment Wizard for functions. The deployment option is shown in Figure 11.9.

Figure 11.10 demonstrates the the Target Database screen in the wizard, which will allow you to specify the connection details for the database to which you will be deploying. The Options screen will allow you to control how the function is deployed to the target database. You can control if the source code is deployed and available on the target by selecting the Deploy Source to Database option. The Error Handling option specifies how an error should be handled during the compilation of a function.

One of the more important options is how duplicates should be handled. Often when you deploy functions to a target server, functions might already exist with identical names and inputs. If you want to overwrite the existing functions, then select Drop Duplicates. If , you do not want to compile any functions that already exist, then select Ignore Duplicates.

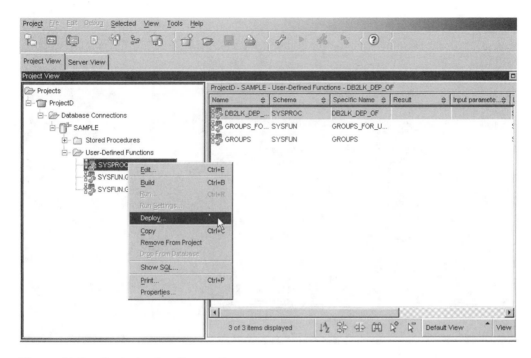

Figure 11.9 Deploying functions option.

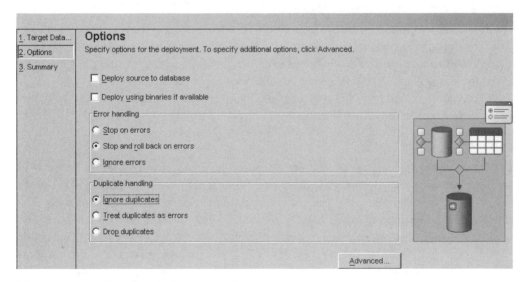

Figure 11.10 Function deployment options.

The final Summary screen, shown in Figure 11.11, will summarize all the options that you have selected. This process will have to be repeated for each of the functions that you are working with.

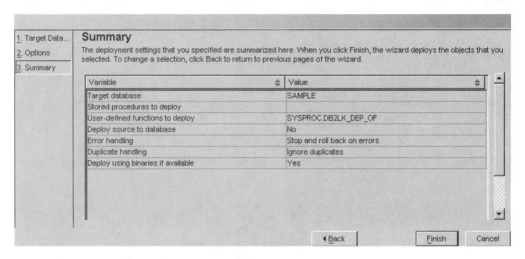

Figure 11.11   Function deployment summary screen.

Deploying Functions Using Scripts

The most common method for deploying functions is still to use scripts. Having the functions in a script allows you to group all of the functions into one unit. You can also control that the functions are all compiled in the proper order. As stated earlier, this is important because functions often have dependencies, and if they are created out of order then the creation may fail.

Appendix C, "Building from the Command Line," contains a detailed overview of how to deploy scripts from the command line.

Deploying Triggers

The Development Center does not currently support the deployment of triggers. In order to deploy triggers on your systems, you will have to write scripts. These scripts can also contain functions and stored procedures so you can combine your deployment into one large script. The best practice, however, is to break your scripts into separate files for functions, triggers, and stored procedures. This makes debugging easier because you can isolate any script failures to a particular group of functions. The overview of how to deploy your scripts can be found in Appendix C, "Building from the Command Line."

Deploying Using *GET ROUTINE* and *PUT ROUTINE*

In previous releases of DB2 UDB, a C compiler was required to create stored procedures. The GET ROUTINE and PUT ROUTINE commands were used to overcome the compiler requirement when deploying stored procedures. The commands can still be useful for deploying procedures if you do not want to have the procedure logic exposed in scripts. You need to have database administrator (DBADM) or higher authority to execute either of the commands.

GET ROUTINE retrieves necessary information about an SQL procedure from the source environment and places that information in an SQL archive (SAR) file. PUT ROUTINE deploys the SQL procedure to the target environment, taking the SAR file generated from the GET ROUTINE command as input.

Figure 11.12 shows the syntax diagram for the GET ROUTINE command.

```
>>-GET ROUTINE--INTO--file_name--FROM--+----------+-------------->
                                       '-SPECIFIC-'


>--PROCEDURE--routine_name--+----------+--------------------->< 
                            '-HIDE BODY-'
```

Figure 11.12   Syntax diagram for *GET ROUTINE*.

As you can see, the command is self-explanatory. If the SPECIFIC keyword is used, then you must use the specific name of the procedure in place of routine_name; otherwise, the procedure name must be used.

The HIDE BODY keyword is used in cases where you do not want to expose the content of the procedure when it is deployed. The text of the SQL procedure will not be inserted into the system catalog tables; only the compiled code for the SQL procedure will be transferred. This helps protect your code, because it can be used to hide the business logic contained in it.

Figure 11.13 shows two examples of the command.

```
GET ROUTINE INTO procs/prod_ddl.sar FROM SPECIFIC PROCEDURE db2admin.proc_ddl
HIDE BODY@

GET ROUTINE INTO procs/simple_result_set.sar FROM SPECIFIC PROCEDURE
db2admin.simple_result_set@
```

Figure 11.13   Example of *GET ROUTINE*.

This command will have to be executed once for each procedure that you want to deploy. This task can get cumbersome, Figure 11.14 demonstrates a SQL query to generate a command file for all SQL procedures in a given database. The path to where the SAR files will reside will need to be updated. You also have the option of changing the WHERE clause if you want to be more selective.

```
SELECT 'GET ROUTINE INTO procs\'
       || SPECIFICNAME || '.sar FROM SPECIFIC PROCEDURE '
       || RTRIM(PROCSCHEMA) || '.' || SPECIFICNAME
       || ' HIDE BODY' || '@'
  FROM SYSCAT.PROCEDURES
 WHERE LANGUAGE = 'SQL';
```

Figure 11.14   Generate *GET ROUTINE* SQL script.

Assuming that the script is saved in a file called `get_routine_script.db2`, you can use the following command to direct the output to another file called `get_routine_all.db2`:

```
db2 -txf get_routine_script.db2 -z get_routine_all.db2
```

The `-x` option suppresses column headings and the row count, and the `-z` option directs output to a file. Following is a sample of the contents of the `get_routine_all.db2` file:

```
GET ROUTINE INTO procs\PROC_DDL.sar FROM SPECIFIC PROCEDURE DB2ADMIN.PROC_DDL
HIDE BODY@
GET ROUTINE INTO procs\SIMPLE_RESULT_SET.sar FROM SPECIFIC PROCEDURE
DB2ADMIN.SIMPLE_RESULT_SET HIDE BODY@
```

You can then run the `get_routine_all.db2` file against the source database. This will extract all the information on SQL procedures into SAR files.

TIP

Create the directory in which you want to store the SAR files prior to running the script. You may want to give it a descriptive name that indicates the date and time of when the SAR files were generated. Often, you will generate the SAR files but at a later date not remember when they were generated.

The SAR files can then be used by the PUT ROUTINE command to deploy the SQL procedures to the target environment. Figure 11.15 shows the syntax diagram for the PUT ROUTINE command.

```
>>-PUT ROUTINE----FROM----file-name---------------------------->

>------+------------------------------------------+----------------><
       '-OWNER--new-owner--+----------------+--'
                           '-USE REGISTERS--'
```

Figure 11.15   Syntax diagram for *PUT ROUTINE*.

The options for the PUT ROUTINE command may not be as intuitive as GET ROUTINE. Typically, the owner of the SQL procedure in a development environment is not the same as the owner of the procedure in the production environment. Hence, the PUT ROUTINE command gives you the option of overriding the owner by using the OWNER keyword when deploying. Additionally, the default schema names and the path for function resolution will also likely be different between environments. The register values for CURRENT SCHEMA and CURRENT PATH can be set on the target server, and can be used by the PUT ROUTINE command using the USE REGISTERS keyword.

Figure 11.16 shows two examples of the PUT ROUTINE command. In both of the examples, the OWNER of the SQL procedure on the target system will be the user db2admin. To issue this command, the user db2admin must have sufficient authority to create the procedure (the user must have SYSADM or DBADM authority, or must have IMPLICIT SCHEMA authority on the database, or CREATEIN privilege on the default schema of the procedure). The second routine the CURRENT SCHEMA and CURRENT PATH values will be used for the procedure's schema and path values instead of the default values.

```
PUT ROUTINE FROM procs/proc_ddl.sar OWNER db2admin@
PUT ROUTINE FROM procs/simple_result_set.sar OWNER db2admin USE REGISTERS@
```

Figure 11.16 Example of a *PUT ROUTINE*.

You can use the sample script shown in Figure 11.17 (against the source database) to generate a script for each of your PUT ROUTINE statements.

```
SELECT 'PUT ROUTINE FROM procs\'
       || SPECIFICNAME || '.sar OWNER db2admin@'
  FROM SYSCAT.PROCEDURES
 WHERE LANGUAGE = 'SQL';
```

Figure 11.17 Generate *PUT ROUTINE* SQL script.

The following is a sample of the output generated from this command:

```
PUT ROUTINE FROM procs\PROC_DDL.sar OWNER db2admin@
PUT ROUTINE FROM procs\SIMPLE_RESULT_SET.sar OWNER db2admin@
```

The GET ROUTINE and PUT ROUTINE commands use the pre-installed procedures GET_ROUTINE_SAR() and PUT_ROUTINE_SAR() in schema SYSFUN. These procedures have been externalized, and can be used by you to write your own interface or application to perform the GET ROUTINE and PUT ROUTINE.

> **NOTE**
>
> On UNIX systems, special consideration should be given to the users and the owners of files. The instance owner must belong to the primary group of the fenced user. If these conditions are not met, the commands will not work.

Using GET ROUTINE and PUT ROUTINE is the primary method for SQL procedure distribution in packaged applications. For example, you could be a vendor developing an application that requires stored procedures. GET ROUTINE would be used to create the SAR files. PUT ROUTINE would be then used by the application's install process to deploy the procedures.

Using the GET ROUTINE and PUT ROUTINE commands can also save time during installation because the code does not have to be recompiled.

> **TIP**
>
> The DB2 Development Center can be used for quickly deploying stored procedures. Similar to the Import and Export options, a Deploy option is also available. In cases where you might have separate databases for development and testing, the Deploy option allows you to quickly deploy procedures directly from the source database to the target database.

Deploying Using Older Releases of DB2

When deploying procedures, it is very important to consider which release of DB2 you will be using as the source and which will be the target. Releases of DB2 before V8.2 required the use of a C compiler to create SQL stored procedures. The introduction of the use of Native PSM in V8.2 has eliminated the need for a C compiler. It is, however, important to remember that previous releases of DB2 still require it, and you must plan accordingly.

Deploying from Pre-V8.2 to Post-V8.2

All releases of DB2 before V8.2 required the use of a C compiler. The GET ROUTINE and PUT ROUTINE commands can be used to overcome the need for a C compiler on the target system. There is one limitation of this method of deployment that may not be obvious. When you compile a procedure using a C compile on the earlier versions of DB2, the compiled code is platform-specific. You can therefore only deploy the procedures onto a system with the same operating system.

The GET ROUTINE and PUT ROUTINE commands can still be used for deploying your procedures, but you will have to issue the GET ROUTINE command on each particular operating system to which you need to deploy. Make sure you keep track of which files are for which operating system. A simple method would be to change the name of the output file to *filename_OS*.DB2. You can then deploy the procedures to the appropriate operating system.

Deploying from Pre-V8.2 to V8.2

Despite V8.2 using Native PSM for its procedures, it still also supports procedures that were previously compiled using C. If you are going to be using V8.2 as a database for your application, it is recommended that you compile all your procedures on V8.2 to ensure they are all in Native PSM. If, however, there is a business need for you to develop on an earlier release of DB2, then it is still possible to deploy your procedures onto V8.2 databases.

When you compile your procedures on pre-V8.2 databases, you will have to have a C compiler installed on the system. When you deploy the procedures to a V8.2 system, the code will still be compiled C code. You will therefore have the same restrictions as with pre-V8.2 procedures concerning only being able to deploy to the same operating system on which you compiled.

Deploying from V8.2 to Pre-V8.2

All procedures that are compiled on V8.2 are compiled in Native PSM. This code is platform-independent, but it does require the new features built into the V8.2 database engine to read it. You will therefore not be able to deploy procedures that are created on V8.2 databases to any previous releases of DB2. To deploy these procedures to databases on an earlier release, you will have to upgrade the target database to at least V8.2 which is the same as V8.1 FixPak 7.

Code Page Considerations

When building applications in mixed code-page environments, you need to give some thought to deployment. For example, if the database server is created with a UNICODE code page, a client with any code page can connect to it.

As client applications connect to the database to invoke stored procedures, input character string parameters are converted from the client application's code page to the database server's code page. Because the stored procedure is on the database server, it uses the same code page as the database server, thus no more code page conversion will occur until the stored procedure completes. At this point, all output character string parameters are converted to the client application's code page and sent back to the caller.

This implies that when building the stored procedure (which will later be deployed using GET ROUTINE or PUT ROUTINE) on a development or test server, the build steps (PREP, COMPILE, and BIND) must be executed against a database with the same code page as the code page of the database on the target server.

Backup and Recovery Considerations

Although not directly related to deployment, you need to give special consideration to the recovery of a database and its SQL procedures.

Specifically, for databases containing SQL procedures the RESTORE DATABASE command or the first connection after the RESTORE command may fail. This will occur if the KEEPFENCED DB2 configuration parameter is set to YES, and the DLL associated with the stored procedures is still resident in memory. To get around this, you need to restart the instance prior to issuing the `RESTORE` command. Stopping the instance will unload any DLLs associated with the stored procedures from memory.

TIP

Always restart the instance prior to issuing a `RESTORE` if your database contains SQL procedures.

Deployment Considerations for DB2 for zSeries

Many of the deployment considerations and techniques for DB2 on LUW also apply to DB2 on zSeries. The skills and tools you have learned for DB2 LUW can be leveraged for zSeries.

Deploying SQL Procedures

In order to build an SQL stored procedure on zSeries, you can use JCL or the DB2 Development Center. Issuing the `CREATE PROCEDURE` statement only registers the procedure to the DB2 catalog; however, it does perform the compilation and bind steps required for the procedure to be ready to be executed. If you store your `CREATE PROCEDURE` statements in a script file and execute this script from the CLP at the DB2 client machine while connected to a DB2 for zSeries subsystem, you will receive an error and the procedures will not build. Therefore, in order to deploy SQL procedures on zSeries, we recommend you use the DB2 Development Center. The methodology for using the Development Center to deploy a stored procedure is similar to LUW:

- Use the Export function to generate a file containing the `CREATE PROCEDURE` statements. Though the resulting script cannot be used to build the stored procedure from the command line, you can use it as a base for a JCL job that can include bind and compilation steps.

- Use the Import function from a file that was exported from another zSeries system. By using this function, all the bind and compilation steps will be handled by the Development Center. As explained earlier, Import can only be used one stored procedure at a time.

- Use the Deploy function to deploy directly one or more stored procedures from a source DB2 subsystem to a target DB2 subsystem. This is the recommended method for zSeries, and is explained in more detail later in this chapter.

Deploying Functions and Triggers

In order to build functions on zSeries, you can use `CREATE FUNCTION`. Unlike stored procedures, this statement is enough to register and build the function. Therefore, in order to deploy functions on zSeries, you can include in a script file all the `CREATE FUNCTION` statements and execute them from the command line, either using SPUFI or from a DB2 LUW client connected to the DB2 for series zSeries subsystem. Moreover, there is no support in the Development Center to work with functions on zSeries.

Similar to functions, a CREATE TRIGGER statement is enough to register and build a trigger on zSeries. Triggers can only be deployed from the command line; the Development Center cannot be used because there is no support to develop triggers from this tool.

TIP

As with LUW, we recommend you create separate scripts for functions and triggers. SQL stored procedures cannot be deployed with scripts.

Deployment Considerations Based on Your C Compiler Requirements

A DB2 for zSeries SQL stored procedure is converted into a C language program as part of the build process. To deploy a procedure from a source DB2 for zSeries subsystem to a target DB2 for zSeries subsystem, you need to consider if the target system has a C/C++ compiler enabled or not. If the target system does not have a C/C++ compiler enabled, a methodology similar to deploying other programs on the mainframe can be followed:

1. Copy the load module (executable) from the source to the target.
2. Copy the DBRMs from the source to the target.
3. Bind the DBRMs to create a package in the target database.
4. Issue the CREATE PROCEDURE statements from the mainframe to register the procedure in the DB2 catalog of the target database. You may need to change the WLM environment, schema, and collection ID for the target subsystem.
5. Grant execute authorization on the stored procedure.

If you were developing your procedures using the Development Center, the Export option can be used to extract the CREATE PROCEDURE statements. If the Development Center was not used, these statements are stored in the source DB2 subsystem catalog table SYSIBM.SYSROUTINES_SRC.

This method will not work for zSeries UDFs and triggers where CREATE FUNCTION and CREATE TRIGGER not only register these objects but also create the corresponding packages using a C compiler; therefore, they cannot be deployed if the target system does not have this compiler.

If the target system does have a C/C++ compiler enabled, in addition to the method already mentioned, the methods described in earlier sections of this chapter can be followed.

Common Deployment Considerations for LUW and zSeries

DB2 LUW and DB2 on zSeries have a number of common options for deploying DB2 objects. This section covers the common deployment methods and traits.

Deploying from One Database to Another

Often procedures need to be moved from a test environment to a production environment, and having a complicated system of recording files and redeploying may not be practical. To simplify the movement from one system to another, you can instead use the Deploy option in the Development Center. This allows you to move the procedures directly from one cataloged system to another.

To use the Deploy option, you can either right-click on the Stored Procedure folder or right-click on an individual stored procedure and choose Deploy. The individual option is shown in Figure 11.18. You may also start the deployment option directly from the Development Center start-up menu. The Deploy option is recommended when you are supporting multiple environments, because it will work with both LUW and with zSeries. It also allows you to deploy several stored procedures at a time, unlike the Import option.

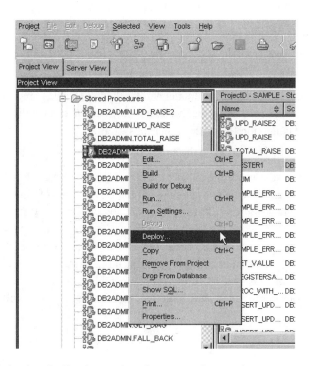

Figure 11.18   Selecting the Deploy options for a stored procedure.

Once you have selected which procedure you are going to deploy, you can select the target server. The wizard will offer you a list of all the databases that you have cataloged on the system you are using. The tool will not check if the required tables and objects for the stored procedure on the source server exist on the target server. It is therefore important that you have your target database properly set up. The database selection of TEST2 as the target database is shown in Figure 11.19.

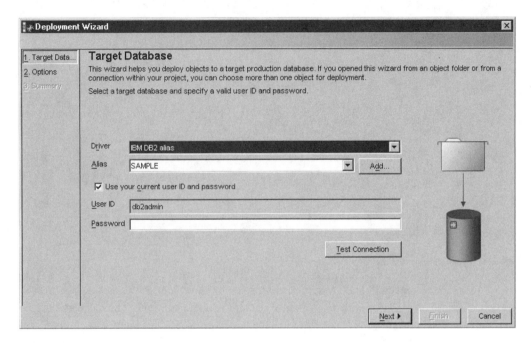

Figure 11.19   Selecting the target database.

> **NOTE**
> Figure 11.19 shows three steps on the left side of the window: Target database, Options, and Summary. If you had right-clicked on the Stored Procedure folder instead of right-clicking on an individual stored procedure, another step would have given you the option to choose the stored procedures to deploy.

A number of options control how the stored procedures are deployed on the target database. In Figure 11.20, if you select the Deploy Source to Database option, the procedure source will be placed in the catalog tables. The Deploy Using Binaries If Available option is used when a C compiler is required on the target server. If the option was chosen, the binaries—which are the .SAR files—would be exported to the target server. This option is no longer needed for DB2 for LUW with the addition of Native PSM. It should also not be applicable to zSeries. The Error

Handling options allow you to control how the deploy process is handled. By not having the entire script roll back on a single failure, you can then correct your error and rerun just a small section of the script. Creating smaller scripts will also result in easier error detection and correction.

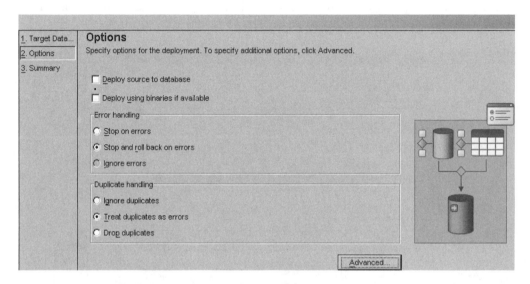

Figure 11.20   Deploy options.

The deployment options will make it a lot easier for you to move your procedures across the systems. Often your test and production systems are almost identical, and your changes may be fairly minor. By choosing DROP DUPLICATES, all the duplicate procedures on the target server will be dropped and replaced by those coming from the source server. This would be the best method for moving your tested changes into production. If you only want to deploy new procedures, and are concerned about overwriting duplicaate procedures on you production system, then make sure to select Treat Duplicates as Errors.

If you are performing a large-scale deployment of several stored procedures, then using scripts would probably be the most effective method. If, however, you would like to deploy the scripts on zSeries, you will also need to write the JCL to execute them and add the bind and compile steps. However, if you are only moving a few procedures from test to production, then the Deploy tool will make your life a lot easier.

Deploying in DB2 UDB for iSeries

Many methods exist for deploying stored procedures, triggers, and functions in DB2 UDB for iSeries. You can use the DB2 UDB for Linux, UNIX, and Windows client; the IBM iSeries Navigator for Windows; or commands natively on the iSeries server.

Using the Development Center

If you are connected remotely and have the DB2 UDB for Linux, UNIX, and Windows client, then you can use the Development Center for deploying stored procedures. Triggers and functions for iSeries are not supported in the Development Center. Within this environment, you can only deploy from one iSeries server to another.

There are two methods that you can use within this environment. The first method is to use the Export Wizard from the pop-up menu which appears after right-clicking on the Stored Procedure folder. The wizard will step you through, allowing you to pick and choose the procedures to export. The Export Wizard gives you the option of saving the procedures to a script, or exporting the procedures as a project. In both cases, a .zip file is created.

Saving them to a script will enable you to import the procedures one at time; however, you will have to unzip the file before you can import. You can import using the Import Wizard provided from inside the Development Center. Alternatively for DB2 LUW, the DB2 Command Line Processor can be used to issue the CREATE PROCEDURE statements directly.

Exporting as a project allows you to use the **Deployment Tool**, available from the Tools menu in the Development Center. This tool provides an interface where you can pick and choose which procedures you want to deploy to the target server.

> **TIP**
>
> Saving to a file allows you to deploy across platforms, as long as the procedure is portable.

Using iSeries Navigator and CL Commands in iSeries

The IBM iSeries Navigator for Windows can be used as well to help with deployment. You can drill down to the schema you are working on, multi-select the objects you want to deploy, and use the context menu (via right-clicking on the mouse) to select the Generate SQL option, as shown in Figure 11.21. The output of Generate SQL is a series of CREATE statements for the objects selected.

The Generate SQL option launches a wizard, shown in Figure 11.22, which allows you to add or remove objects to the list. The wizard also prompts you to select where you want the output; to a file or in the Run and SQL Script window. Saving it to a file saves the output on the iSeries server. Opening in a SQL script window allows you to modify, run, and/or save to a file on the remote client.

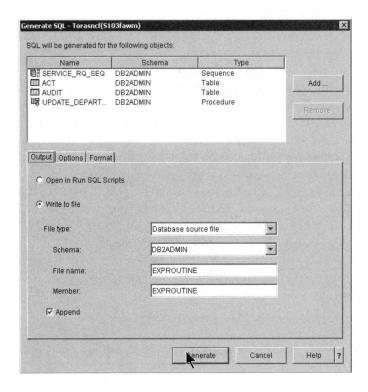

Figure 11.21   Using the IBM iSeries Navigator to generate SQL.

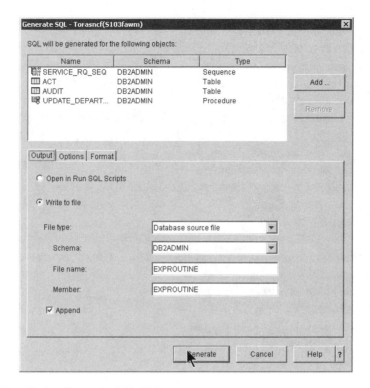

Figure 11.22 iSeries Generate SQL GUI.

The Generate SQL option can be used to generate DDL for tables, indexes, aliases, views, user-defined types, or SQL functions. If a table has triggers associated with it, then selecting the table will also generate the DDL for the corresponding triggers. Once the file is saved, you can launch a Run an SQL script window for a database on the target server. You can then load the file from the remote client's file system and execute the script through this interface. Figure 11.23 shows an example of a generated script.

```
--   Generate SQL
--   Version:               V5R3M0 040528
--   Generated on:          06/16/04 19:55:43
--   Relational Database:   S103FAWM
--   Standards Option:      DB2 UDB iSeries
CREATE SEQUENCE DB2ADMIN.SERVICE_RQ_SEQ
     AS SMALLINT
     START WITH 1
     INCREMENT BY 1
     MINVALUE 1
     MAXVALUE 5000
```

```
      NO CYCLE CACHE 50 NO ORDER ;
CREATE TABLE DB2ADMIN.ACT (
      ACTNO SMALLINT NOT NULL ,
      ACTKWD CHAR(6) CCSID 37 NOT NULL ,
      ACTDESC VARCHAR(20) CCSID 37 NOT NULL ,
      CONSTRAINT DB2ADMIN.Q_DB2ADMIN_ACT_ACTNO_00001 PRIMARY KEY( ACTNO ) ) ;

CREATE TABLE DB2ADMIN.AUDIT (
      EVENT_TIME TIMESTAMP DEFAULT NULL ,
      DESC VARCHAR(100) CCSID 37 DEFAULT NULL ) ;

SET PATH "DB2ADMIN","SYSIBM" ;

CREATE PROCEDURE DB2ADMIN.UPDATE_DEPARTMENT ( )
      LANGUAGE SQL
      SPECIFIC DB2ADMIN.UPD_DEPT
      NOT DETERMINISTIC
      MODIFIES SQL DATA
      CALLED ON NULL INPUT
      UD : BEGIN
      -- Declare variable
      DECLARE V_DEPTNO CHAR ( 3 ) ;
      -- Declare returncode
      DECLARE SQLSTATE CHAR ( 5 ) ;

      DECLARE C_DEPT CURSOR WITH HOLD FOR
      SELECT DEPTNO
      FROM DEPARTMENT
      FOR UPDATE OF LOCATION ;

      -- Declare condition handler
      DECLARE CONTINUE HANDLER FOR SQLSTATE '24504' , SQLSTATE '24501'
      L1 : LOOP                                              -- (1)
      LEAVE L1 ;
      END LOOP ;

      -- Procedure logic
      OPEN C_DEPT ;

      SAVEPOINT A ON ROLLBACK RETAIN CURSORS ;
```

```
FETCH FROM C_DEPT INTO V_DEPTNO ;                                    -- (2)
UPDATE DEPARTMENT SET LOCATION = 'FLOOR1' WHERE CURRENT OF C_DEPT ; -- (3)
COMMIT ;                                                             -- (4)

FETCH FROM C_DEPT INTO V_DEPTNO ;                                    -- (5)
COMMIT ;   -- (6)
UPDATE DEPARTMENT SET LOCATION = 'FLOOR2' WHERE CURRENT OF C_DEPT ; -- (7)

FETCH FROM C_DEPT INTO V_DEPTNO ;                                    -- (8)
UPDATE DEPARTMENT SET LOCATION = 'FLOOR3' WHERE CURRENT OF C_DEPT ; -- (9)
COMMIT ;                                                             -- (10)

FETCH FROM C_DEPT INTO V_DEPTNO ;                                    -- (11)
UPDATE DEPARTMENT SET LOCATION = 'FLOOR4' WHERE CURRENT OF C_DEPT ; -- (12)
ROLLBACK ;   -- (13)

FETCH FROM C_DEPT INTO V_DEPTNO ;   -- (14)
UPDATE DEPARTMENT SET LOCATION = 'FLOOR5' WHERE CURRENT OF C_DEPT ; -- (15)

CLOSE C_DEPT ;

RETURN 0 ;
END UD  ;
```

Figure 11.23   Sample iSeries script.

If the file output was saved on the iSeries server, the file can be transferred to a target server and the RUNSQLSTM CL command can be used to execute the script. For example, if the file is named EXPROUTINE, contains a member EXPROUTINE, and is saved in library TARGET, you would issue the following command:

```
RUNSQLSTM SRCFILE(TARGET/EXPROUTINE) SRCMBR(EXPROUTINE) NAMING(*SQL)
```

If you do not want to use the GUI tools, then you can use CL commands on the server to save and restore objects. Basically, you would need to save the objects on the source server and restore them on the target server. For example, if you wanted to save to a file (rather than to tape or some other device), you would need to create a SAVEFILE, save the objects to that file, transfer the file to the target server, and restore the objects from that file.

Figure 11.24 lists a the series of commands that you would execute in order to copy all program (stored procedures and triggers) and service program (functions) objects, from the SOURCE library and save them to a file called `SAVEIT`, and the corresponding restore command to restore to the TARGET library.

```
On source server:
CRTSAVF FILE(SOURCE/SAVEIT)
SAVOBJ OBJ(*ALL) LIB(SOURCE) DEV(*SAVF) OBJTYPE(*PGM *SRVPGM)
SAVF(SOURCE/SAVIT)
On target server:
RSTOBJ OBJ(*ALL) SAVLIB(SOURCE) DEV(*SAVF) OBJTYPE(*PGM *SRVPGM)
SAVF(SOURCE/SAVIT) RSTLIB(TARGET)
```

Figure 11.24 Save and restore on iSeries.

There are likely more methods and combination of methods that you can use to deploy stored procedures. Which method you choose will depend on your level for comfort and familiarity with the tools shown to you.

Summary

This chapter has described several methods for deploying SQL procedures. The deployment of SQL procedures for DB2 LUW and zSeries was grouped into one section because the DB2 Development Center can be used for both. One simple method described was exporting the procedure DDL via the DB2 Development Center, and then using the DB2 Command Line Processor to import it into the target database. The different issues that you can face when deploying procedures across multiple releases of DB2 were covered. DB2 for LUW specific issues, such as code pages and backup and recovery, were presented. The CLP commands GET ROUTINE and PUT ROUTINE were also shown as an alternative for deployment, in environments where the code needs to be hidden, or when working with earlier releases of DB2 for LUW that required a C compiler.

The deployment of SQL procedures for DB2 for iSeries was covered separately because they can be deployed differently. SQL procedures for iSeries can be deployed using the DB2 Development Center, which is used for DB2 LUW and for zSeries, and also the IBM iSeries Navigator tool. Finally, the differences in deployment methods specific to iSeries were discussed.

Performance Tuning

In this chapter, you will learn

- How to tune your database
- How to analyze and improve SQL access plans
- Performance tuning tips for each of the platforms (LUW, iSeries, zSeries)
- How to use the Design Advisor on LUW to create efficient indexes

This chapter is divided into three sections, one for each of the platforms.

Performance Considerations for LUW

This section discusses how to obtain the best performance of your database system with relative ease. When available, the focus is placed on the GUI tools of the various platforms; otherwise, commands will be discussed.

The Configuration Advisor

After you have created stored procedures, triggers, and UDFs, it is a good idea to perform an overall tuning of the database system to ensure that they have a properly configured environment in which to run. The easiest and quickest way to tune your database is through the **Configuration Advisor GUI**, which is launched from the Control Center. Using this utility allows you to tune in a matter of minutes what used to take days, and provides for a great initial starting point from which additional tuning, if desired, can be applied.

The Configuration Advisor will ask you a series of questions about your environment that you answer during the course of several screens. At the end, it will generate a script of recommendations that can be instantly applied, or it can be saved and applied at a later time. The script can even be scheduled through the Task Scheduler.

To launch the Configuration Advisor, from the Control Center right-click on the database that you want to configure and select Configuration Advisor. Figure 12.1 displays one of the "interview" screens.

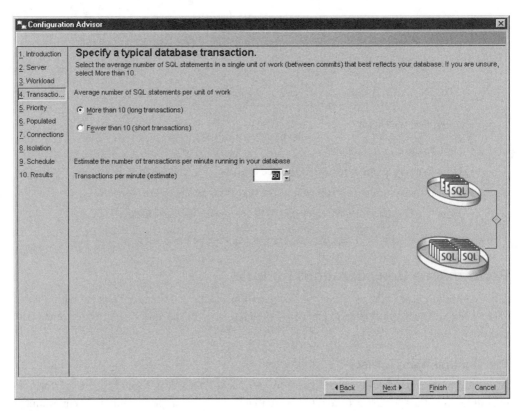

Figure 12.1   The Configuration Advisor.

When you complete the interview, you will see a list of recommendations similar to what appears in Figure 12.2.

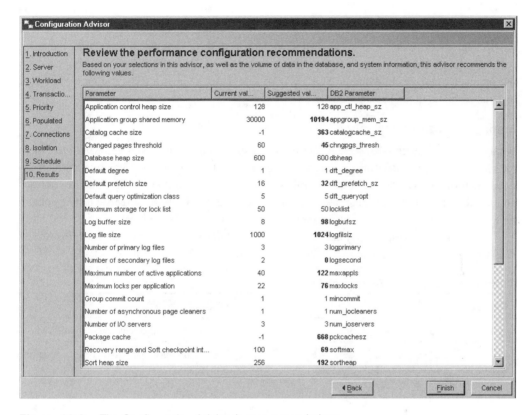

Figure 12.2   The Configuration Advisor's recommendations.

The **package cache** is a repository for statement information of both dynamic and static SQL. It increases the performance of statements by reducing lock contention in the system catalog tables, keeping frequently used access plans in memory, and increasing the sharing of dynamic SQL statements between applications.

A **package** is made up of sections and information about the compilation environment, such as optimization level, isolation level, and so on. A **section** is a compiled executable object that contains logic to satisfy the SQL. Every SQL request is associated with a specific section. These sections and their related packages can be found in the SYSCAT.PACKAGES system catalog view.

The package cache is created when the database is activated (either from the ACTIVATE DB command or first user connection) and will remain in memory until the database is deactivated (either through the DEACTIVATE DB command or when all users have disconnected). It is a performance consideration to ACTIVATE a database and to not rely on the first connection to load DB2's memory structures. The package cache is shared amongst all connections to the database.

When a DB2 agent servicing a connection is about to execute a dynamic SQL, it will check the package cache for the existence of an identical text of the statement. If it is found, the agent will copy the package into its own memory and execute the section. This is why it is important to use parameter markers in dynamic SQL, as it will increase the chances that the same statement text can be found in the Package Cache.

Monitoring SQL Performance

Sometimes you may find that certain queries are not executing as quickly as you would like them to. This is typically caused by a number of factors, the most common of which is a table scan being performed instead of an index. A **table scan** may be chosen if the current database statistics are out of date, and indicates the table consists of very few rows when in reality it may contain thousands. It can also be caused by an appropriate index simply not existing.

The best way to find slowly executing SQL is by using a **Statement Event Monitor**, which will capture both dynamic and static SQL. The basic steps are described in Table 12.1.

Table 12.1   Creating a Statement Event Monitor

Command	Description
`connect to <db_name>`	Obtain a connection to the database to monitor
`create event monitor stmtmon for STATEMENTS write to file 'D:\temp\ eventmonitoring' buffersize 64 nonblocked`	Create an event monitor that will record statement events as they occur
`set event monitor stmtmon state 1`	Enable the statement event monitor to begin recording statement activity
`*run the application*`	Run the application to generate statements to be recorded
`set event monitor stmtmon state 0`	Turn off the statement event monitor.
`db2evmon -db <db_name> -evm stmtmon > D:\temp\eventmonitoring\mon.txt`	Output the recorded information to a text file for analysis purposes.
`drop event monitor stmtmon`	Drop the statement event monitor object once it is no longer needed.

Figure 12.3 shows a sample of output generated by the statement monitor.

```
12) Statement Event ...
  Appl Handle: 8
  Appl Id: *LOCAL.DB2.014B04013609
  Appl Seq number: 0001

  Record is the result of a flush: FALSE
  -----------------------------------------
  Type     : Static
  Operation: Open
  Section  : 2
  Creator  : DB2ADMIN
  Package  : P6280365
  Consistency Token  : MBDcQXBU
  Package Version ID  :
  Cursor    : CURS2
  Cursor was blocking: TRUE
  -----------------------------------------
  Start Time: 02-23-2004 20:36:09.070311
  Stop Time:  02-23-2004 20:36:09.098640
  Exec Time:  0.028329 seconds
  Number of Agents created: 1
  User CPU: 0.000000 seconds
  System CPU: 0.010014 seconds
  Fetch Count: 0
  Sorts: 0
  Total sort time: 0
  Sort overflows: 0
  Rows read: 8
  Rows written: 0
  Internal rows deleted: 0
  Internal rows updated: 0
  Internal rows inserted: 0
  Bufferpool data logical reads: 0
  Bufferpool data physical reads: 0
  Bufferpool temporary data logical reads: 0
  Bufferpool temporary data physical reads: 0
  Bufferpool index logical reads: 0
  Bufferpool index physical reads: 0
```

```
Bufferpool temporary index logical reads: 0
Bufferpool temporary index physical reads: 0
SQLCA:
 sqlcode: 0
 sqlstate: 00000


13) Statement Event ...
 Appl Handle: 8
 Appl Id: *LOCAL.DB2.014B04013609
 Appl Seq number: 0001


 Record is the result of a flush: FALSE
 -----------------------------------------
 Type      : Dynamic
 Operation: Execute
 Section  : 4
 Creator  : NULLID
 Package  : SYSSH200
 Consistency Token  : SYSLVL01
 Package Version ID  :
 Cursor   : SQL_CURSH200C4
 Cursor was blocking: FALSE
 Text     : SELECT * FROM DB2ADMIN.EMPLOYEE
            WHERE EMPNO = ?
 -----------------------------------------
 Start Time: 02-23-2004 20:36:09.065773
 Stop Time:  02-23-2004 20:36:09.099012
 Exec Time:  0.033239 seconds
 Number of Agents created: 1
 User CPU: 0.000000 seconds
 System CPU: 0.000000 seconds
 Fetch Count: 39
 Sorts: 0
 Total sort time: 0
 Sort overflows: 0
 Rows read: 39
 Rows written: 0
 Internal rows deleted: 0
 Internal rows updated: 0
 Internal rows inserted: 0
```

```
Bufferpool data logical reads: 39
Bufferpool data physical reads: 0
Bufferpool temporary data logical reads: 0
Bufferpool temporary data physical reads: 0
Bufferpool index logical reads: 0
Bufferpool index physical reads: 0
Bufferpool temporary index logical reads: 0
Bufferpool temporary index physical reads: 0
SQLCA:
 sqlcode: 100
 sqlstate: 02000
```

Figure 12.3   Sample statement event monitor output.

As you can see, the text of dynamic SQL statements is displayed, but for static statements you only see a package and a section. You need to perform one more step to view the static SQL. But before you do that, there are some things that you should look for in the output. Expensive SQL usually has one or more of the following characteristics:

- `Rows Read`. Identifies the number of rows read by a statement and does not count index rows or direct table reads. A very high number could mean that an index is needed or that statistics are out of date.
- `Exec Time`. The actual execution time for the statement. High execution times should be investigated further.
- `Sort Overflows`. Identifies where costly sort overflows are occurring. This could indicate the need for an index, execution of the RUNSTATS command, or a larger sort heap.

Once you have found some statements to investigate, make note of the following:

- For dynamic SQL: `Text`
- For static SQL: `Section` and `Package`

Using *Explain* to Analyze Access Plans

As mentioned, for static SQL you only see the Section and Package number. In order to determine the SQL, you will need to use the db2expln utility:

```
db2expln -database <dbname> -schema <schema> -package <package> -section <sec-
tion> -output <outfile.txt>
```

The output you see is actually an Explain diagram. The reference does not cover interpreting the text-based explain. Instead, it will simply be used to determine the text of the SQL statement. Once you have the statement, we can use Visual Explain (see Figure 12.4) to see what is happening in terms of the access plan.

From the Control Center, right-click on the database for which you want to explain an SQL statement and select Explain SQL. In the SQL text box, you can input your SQL statement. In this case, we will explain SELECT * FROM DB2ADMIN.EMPLOYEE WHERE EMPNO = ?. Then click on OK to generate the query graph.

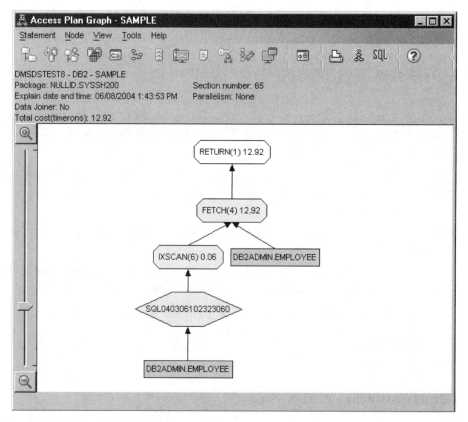

Figure 12.4   Visual Explain graph.

When analyzing the Explain output, try to identify the following:

- Expensive operations such as large sorts, sort overflows, and heavy table usage that could benefit from more sort space, better indexes, updated statistics, or different SQL.
- Table scans that could benefit from an index.
- Poor predicate selectivity that could be caused by outdated statistics.

If you see table scans and you believe that a proper index exists and is simply not being chosen by the optimizer, you will want to perform a REORG followed by a RUNSTATS on the table(s) in question (explained later in the chapter). If you find the table scan is still occurring, it's time to use the Design Advisor.

The Design Advisor

The **Design Advisor** is used to recommend indexes, Materialized Query Tables (MQTs), and Multidimensional Clustering tables (MDCs) for a selected set of SQL statements. You can input SQL manually, import SQL from packages, or import the SQL of explained statements. Having the DB2 Wizard generate your MQTs, MDCs, and indexes based on your specified workload greatly reduces what could be a complicated analysis.

To launch the Design Advisor, right-click on the target database within the Control Center and select Design Advisor. The Design Advisor is straightforward to use. Figure 12.5 shows you how to define a workload.

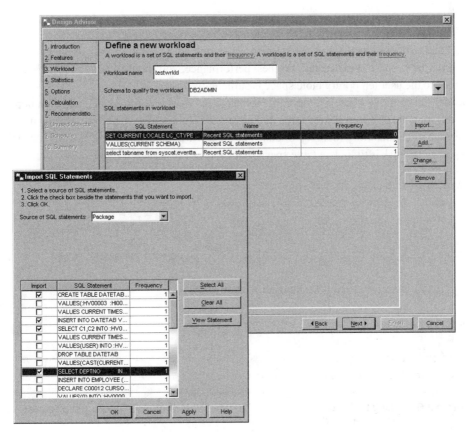

Figure 12.5 Importing statements into the Design Advisor.

Large Object (LOB) Considerations

With regular data types, DB2 uses buffer pool(s) to cache data and index pages for faster in-memory reads and writes. However, LOBs can be as large as 2GB and the system may not have that much memory. Even if there is that much memory, it does not make sense to page all existing data out of the buffer pool just to serve one LOB data object. Therefore, LOBs are accessed directly from disk without going through the buffer pool. This is called a **direct I/O operation**. As you may imagine, such access is slower than in-memory buffer pool access. In such a case, the system cache may be useful, because the O/S can cache the LOBs instead of DB2. This is advantageous if the LOBs are reused.

> **NOTE**
> For storage and performance reasons, do not use LOBs for small data values. Use VARCHAR or VARCHAR FOR BIT DATA if possible, which can hold a maximum of 32,672 bytes of data.

Temporary Tables Considerations

Recall that temporary tables can remain memory bound until the buffer pool assigned to the user temporary table space is exhausted. For best performance, you should ensure that the buffer pool assigned to the user temporary table space is sufficiently large.

Consider the scenario where a temporary table session.employee is created and then populated with the contents of the employee table in the SAMPLE database. We want to determine if the temporary table remains fully memory-bound. The easiest way to determine if a temporary table is being paged to disk is to look at table space snapshots as illustrated in Figure 12.6.

```
CREATE USER TEMPORARY TABLESPACE usertempspace
    MANAGED BY SYSTEM USING ('usertempspace')
    BUFFERPOOL ibmdefaultbp


DECLARE TABLE SESSION.EMPLOYEE LIKE EMPLOYEE ON COMMIT PRESERVE ROWS


INSERT INTO SESSION.EMPLOYEE SELECT * FROM EMPLOYEE


UPDATE MONITOR SWITCHES USING BUFFERPOOL ON          -- (1)


RESET MONITOR ALL                                    -- (2)

GET SNAPSHOT FOR TABLESPACES ON SAMPLE               -- (3)
```

Figure 12.6   Using table space snapshots to determine whether temporary tables are memory-bound.

After declaring and populating the temporary table, we turn on the buffer pool monitor switch on Line (1) and reset DB2's monitors on Line (2). We then populate the temporary table by copying the contents of the employee table into `session.employee`. `GET SNAPSHOT FOR TABLESPACES` on Line (3) reveals on whether any parts of the temporary table was flushed to disk.

The snapshot output will be grouped into logical sections by table space. The section of interest, of course, will be the data collected for the user temporary table space we created (`usertempspace`). Figure 12.7 provides parts of this output. Because the full output is very large, only the statistics that are of primary interest in this example are listed.

```
Tablespace name                             = USERTEMPSPACE
  Tablespace ID                             = 3
  Tablespace Content Type                   = User Temporary data
  Buffer pool ID currently in use           = 1
  Number of used pages                      = 1
...
  Buffer pool temporary data logical reads  = 37
  Buffer pool temporary data physical reads = 0
...
  Buffer pool temporary index logical reads = 0
  Buffer pool temporary index physical reads = 0
```

Figure 12.7   Snapshot output is grouped into logical sections by table space.

You can see from the output in Figure 12.7 that there have been no temporary data physical reads and no temporary index physical reads. The temporary table, therefore, has been memory-bound. Had any portion of the temporary table been paged to disk, the physical read counters would not be zero. If physical reads are occurring, one solution may be to increase size of the buffer pool assigned to the user temporary table space. If your temporary tables are quite large, simply adding more memory may not yield sufficient performance gains, and other alternatives should be investigated, which are discussed in the following subsections.

Improving Performance

Temporary tables perform well because

- Data manipulation is not logged.
- There is no need for locking.
- Temporary tables can be memory-bound.

The only characteristic that is tunable is in the way memory is used by the temporary table. In the following sections, we will discuss the methods of tuning the performance of temporary tables.

Creating Indexes

In some cases, you may want to store a large amount of data in temporary tables. Large table scans on temporary tables will consume precious CPU cycles. DB2 allows you to create indexes on temporary tables; the syntax is the same as for persistent tables. Like temporary tables, indexes on temporary tables must also be created in the SESSION schema. Figure 12.8 illustrates.

```
DECLARE GLOBAL TEMPORARY TABLE session.temp1 (id INT, c2 INT)
CREATE INDEX session.temp1idx ON session.temp1(id)
```

Figure 12.8   An example of creating an index on a temporary table.

Ongoing Maintenance to Keep Performance at Its Peak

You should perform two very important maintenance activities on a regular basis to keep your database performing consistently well—namely, REORG and RUNSTATS. REORG is used to eliminate fragmented data and reclaim space from deleted rows of tables and indexes. It should be run whenever there have been a considerable number of INSERT, UPDATE, or DELETE operations. RUNSTATS is used to collect statistics for tables and indexes that are used by the DB2 cost-based optimizer to make educated decisions when it comes to generating access plans for SQL. It is always a good idea to perform a RUNSTATS after a large number of INSERT, UPDATE, or DELETE operations; after adding an index; and after performing a REORG. All tables (including System Catalog tables) typically benefit from running RUNSTATS. RUNSTATS can now be throttled so that it can run while the database is being used with little (if any) impact on the users.

You can use the Control Center to configure these activities. In the Control Center, right-click on your database and select Configure Automatic Maintenance. Inside, you can specify online and offline maintenance windows and define the exact behavior of the maintenance commands. You can also optionally supply a list of contacts who should be notified of operational outcomes. Figure 12.9 shows the Summary page.

In order for your static SQL to take advantage of the new statistics, packages containing SQL will need to be rebound to the database. This is most easily accomplished through the db2rbind command, which will rebind all the packages in the database. When the package is rebound, a new access plan will be generated for the static SQL, and this plan will be optimized using the current statistics.

The specific command is: db2rbind <dbname> -l <logfile.out> ALL. REBIND can also be used to rebind individual packages.

To avoid having to manually run this command, open the DB2 Task Center and define a DB2 command task that is the previous db2rbind command. You can also enable notification in the Task Center similar the notification described previously.

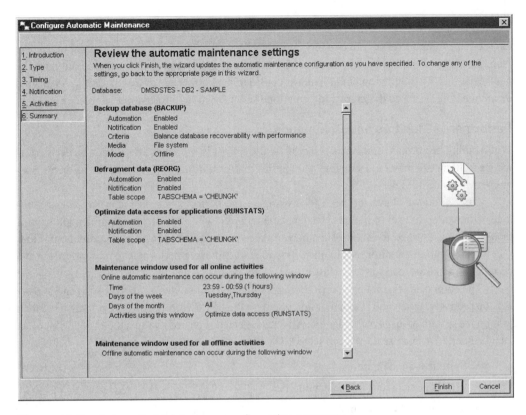

Figure 12.9   Automatic Maintenance configuration summary.

DB2 for iSeries Considerations

i5/OS for iSeries automates many of the configuration tasks for you, such as physical data place-
ment or memory management. In addition to these tasks, DB2 UDB for iSeries handles query
optimization as well. You may encounter situations where you would want to change or influence
the default behaviors of these optimizations, and hence this section is focused on improving and
monitoring query performance.

NOTE

DB2 UDB for iSeries is tightly integrated with the operating system; thus, tuning the performance at the operating system level may also impact the database. For a detailed look at
improving performance at the operating system level, refer to the Performance section
under System Administration in the IBM eServer iSeries Information Center.

Monitoring Memory Usage

On iSeries, tuning memory usage of any application is managed by the operating system. Hence, memory usage of the database is managed by the operating system, and you should not have the need to do this. To monitor and tune requires considerable knowledge of the operating system and its architecture. Refer to the iSeries Information Center for more information on this.

Performance Monitors and Commands

When tuning performance, it is necessary to analyze what is running to determine where performance bottlenecks may be occurring. The iSeries platform offers several avenues for investigating performance of SQL.

Often, you will have the need to investigate the performance characteristics of a workload—for example, a set of queries. This may be required while you are developing applications, or while you are tasked to investigate a performance problem. The iSeries environment provides you with a database monitor tool to allow you to start capturing performance measurements at a certain point in time, and to stop measuring at a later point.

The commands that allow you to start and stop database monitors are STRDBMON and ENDDBMON, respectively. When you start a monitor, you have the option of collecting query statistics for all jobs on the system or just a particular job. All data collected is placed in a specified table, which can later be queried to analyze the data collected. The type of information collected is

- System and job name
- SQL statement and sub-select number
- Start and end timestamp
- Estimated processing time
- Total rows in table queried
- Number of rows selected
- Estimated number of rows selected
- Estimated number of joined rows
- Key columns for advised index
- Total optimization time
- Join type and method
- ODP implementation

This information can be used to target queries that require performance tuning. For example, you can look for long-running queries, or queries that have a high number of rows selected or joined.

The query optimizer (see the next section) is invoked for each statement that is captured. One of the tasks of the query optimizer is to evaluate if additional indexes can improve performance, and if so, provide advice on what indexes to create. This information is captured by the monitor and can be very useful in improving performance.

The table in which the data is captured is specified in the STRDBMON command. The definition for the table can be found in the IBM eServer iSeries Information Center in the Performance and Optimization section under Database. Commonly used queries against database monitor captured data can be found at www.iseries.ibm.com/db2/dbmonqrys.htm.

NOTE

Due to the high volume of information captured, when running the database performance monitor, system resources can become constrained. The iSeries server does provide a memory-resident database monitor tool, which can be accessed through APIs. This tool greatly reduces the overhead on system resources. Details can be found in the Information Center.

The iSeries Navigator is a very user-friendly tool in helping with performance monitoring. It basically provides a GUI interface to the STRDBMON and ENDDBMON commands. In addition, it provides a standard set of reports, which can be modified if you want, that can be run against the data collected from the monitor. Figure 12.10 shows how a monitor can be started from the iSeries Navigator.

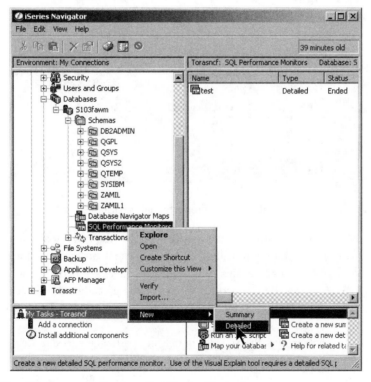

Figure 12.10   Starting a monitor from the iSeries Navigator.

To stop the monitor, you can select the monitor, right-click, and select End. Once you have ended the monitor, you can analyze the results, again by right-clicking on the monitor and selecting Analyze Results. This will present you with a window that allows you to select the information you are interested in. Figure 12.11 shows the some of choices you have available to you.

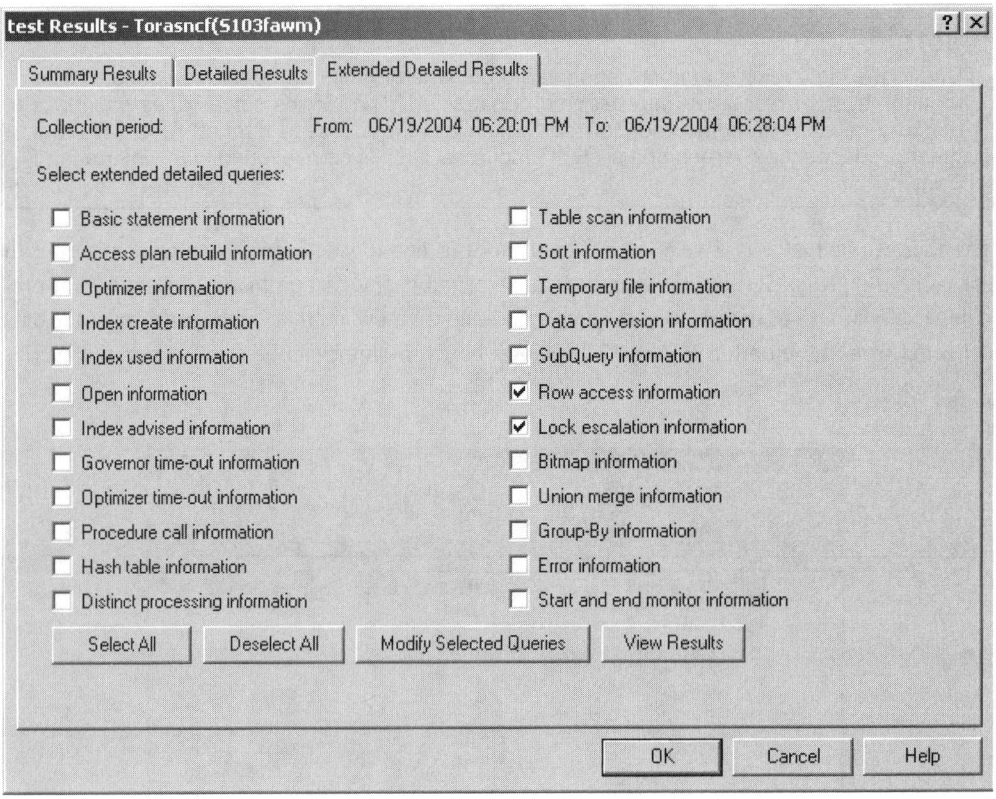

Figure 12.11   Sample of available monitor reports through iSeries Navigator.

In contrast to the database monitor that captures data on real time workloads, the PRTSQLINF command is provided to capture information about SQL statements embedded in a program, an SQL package, or a service program. This command is the iSeries version of the db2expln command on the LUW platforms. Remember that when a stored procedure or trigger is created, it is compiled and a program is created. Similarly, when a function is created, the resulting object is a service program.

So if you wanted to analyze the SQL statements in a particular stored procedure, you would need to obtain the corresponding program that was created and specify it in the PRTSQLINF command. The information is analyzed and printed (sent to spooled output). The type of information captured is the same as in the database monitor.

Figure 12.12 shows an example of how to query the system catalogs to determine the system name for an SQL procedure, and then uses it as input for the PRTSQLINF command.

```
Query the system catalog:
SELECT external_name
  FROM qsys2.sysroutine
 WHERE specific_schema = 'DB2ADMIN'
   AND specific_name = 'BONUS_INCR';


Issue the PRTSQLINF command:
PRTSQLINF OBJ(DB2ADMIN/BONUS_INCR) OBJTYPE(*PGM)


Output found under WRKSPLF:
                                      Display Spooled File
 File  . . . . . :    BONUS_INCR
Page/Line   1/1
 Control . . . . .
Columns     1 - 130
 Find  . . . . . .


*...+....1....+....2....+....3....+....4....+....5....+....6....+....7....+....
8....+....9....+....0
 5722SS1 V5R3M0 040528  Print SQL information  Program DB2ADMIN/BONUS_INCR
06/11/04 08:52:57 Page   1
 Object name..............DB2ADMIN/BONUS_INCR
 Object type..............*PGM
   CRTSQLCI
        OBJ(DB2ADMIN/BONUS_INCR)
        SRCFILE(QTEMP/QSQLSRC)
        SRCMBR(BONUS_INCR)
        COMMIT(*NONE)
        OPTION(*SQL *PERIOD *NOCNULRQD)
        TGTRLS(V5R3M0)
        ALWCPYDTA(*OPTIMIZE)
        CLOSQLCSR(*ENDACTGRP)
        RDB(*LOCAL)
        DATFMT(*ISO)
        TIMFMT(*ISO)
        DFTRDBCOL(DB2ADMIN)
        DYNDFTCOL(*NO)
        SQLPKG(DB2ADMIN/BONUS_INCR)
```

```
          ALWBLK(*ALLREAD)

          DLYPRP(*YES)

          DYNUSRPRF(*USER)

          SRTSEQ(*HEX)

          LANGID(ENU)

          RDBCNNMTH(*DUW)

          TEXT('SQL PROCEDURE BONUS_INC                        ')

          STATEMENT TEXT CCSID(37)

          SQLPATH("DB2ADMIN" "SYSIBM")

          DECRESULT(31 31 0)
DECLARE C_SALES CURSOR WITH HOLD FOR SELECT WORKDEPT , BONUS , EMPNO FROM
     EMPLOYEE ORDER BY WORKDEPT
   SQL4021   Access plan last saved on 06/10/04 at 23:42:56.
   SQL4020   Estimated query run time is 0 seconds.
   SQL4027   Access plan was saved with DB2 UDB Symmetric Multiprocessing
installed on the system.
   SQL4002   Reusable ODP sort used.
   SQL4010   Table scan access for table 1.
   SQL4006   All indexes considered for table 1.
OPEN C_SALES
FETCH C_SALES INTO : H : H , : H : H , : H : H
SAVEPOINT SVPT_BONUS_INCR ON ROLLBACK RETAIN CURSORS
SET : H : H = : H : H * 1.1
   SQL4021   Access plan last saved on 06/10/04 at 23:42:56.
   SQL4020   Estimated query run time is 0 seconds.
   SQL4027   Access plan was saved with DB2 UDB Symmetric Multiprocessing
installed on the system.
   SQL4010   Table scan access for table 1.
UPDATE EMPLOYEE SET BONUS = : H : H WHERE EMPNO = : H : H
5722SS1 V5R3M0 040528     Print SQL information          Program
DB2ADMIN/BONUS_INCR                    06/11/04 08:52:57    Page   2
   SQL4021   Access plan last saved on 06/10/04 at 23:42:56.
   SQL4020   Estimated query run time is 0 seconds.
   SQL4027   Access plan was saved with DB2 UDB Symmetric Multiprocessing
installed on the system.
   SQL4008   Index EMPLOYEE  used for table 1.
   SQL4026   Index only access used on table number 1.
   SQL4011   Index scan-key row positioning used on table 1.
   SQL4006   All indexes considered for table 1.
 SET : H : H = : H : H + : H : H
   SQL4021   Access plan last saved on 06/10/04 at 23:42:56.
```

```
   SQL4020   Estimated query run time is 0 seconds.
   SQL4027   Access plan was saved with DB2 UDB Symmetric Multiprocessing
installed on the system.
   SQL4010   Table scan access for table 1.
 FETCH C_SALES INTO : H : H , : H : H , : H : H
 COMMIT
 ROLLBACK TO SAVEPOINT SVPT_BONUS_INCR
 RELEASE SAVEPOINT SVPT_BONUS_INCR
 CLOSE C_SALES
 SELECT 1 INTO : H FROM QSYS2 . QSQPTABL WHERE ( : H : H = : H : H ) AND ( : H :
    H = 0 )
   SQL4021   Access plan last saved on 06/10/04 at 23:42:56.
   SQL4020   Estimated query run time is 0 seconds.
   SQL4027   Access plan was saved with DB2 UDB Symmetric Multiprocessing
installed on the system.
   SQL4010   Table scan access for table 1.
 CLOSE C_SALES
```

Figure 12.12   An example of *PRTSQLINF* output.

Query Optimizer and Access Plans

The previous section alluded to the concept of a query optimizer. Each time a query is processed (or prepared), an access plan is created. An **access plan** directs the database manager on how to execute the query. In particular, it defines which indexes would be used, what type of scan operations will occur, if any intermediate sorts are required, the order of the operations, if any operations can execute in parallel, and more.

In order to compile the access plan, a key input to the query optimizer are the statistics on various database objects gathered by the Statistics Manager (see the next section). This information, along with other environment settings—such as the number of processors, the commitment level (isolation level) under which the query will execute, and the row blocking options—is used to generate the plan.

To help assess whether the optimizer will choose an efficient access plan, you can use the **Visual Explain tool**. This tool is available from the Run SQL Scripts window of the IBM iSeries Navigator. It takes as input a query and produces a visual representation of the access plan. In addition to the access plan, for each operation in the access plan very detailed information about the query and the particular operation is provided.

The best way to show the value of the tool is to show an example. Assume that there are no indexes in the database, and you want to see the access plan for the query shown in Figure 12.13.

```
SELECT e.firstnme
      ,e.midinit
      ,e.lastnme
      ,e.deptname
  FROM employee e
      ,department d
 WHERE e.workdept = d.deptno
```

Figure 12.13   Simple query to be explained.

The access plan generated by the Visual Explain is shown in Figure 12.14.

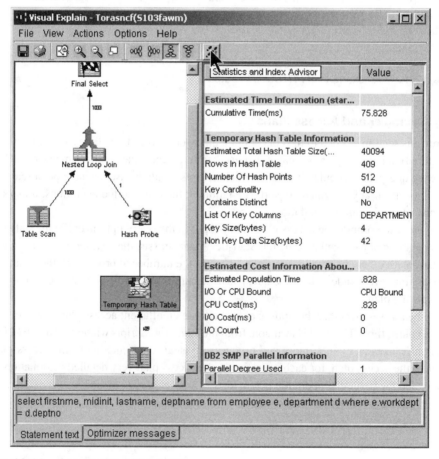

Figure 12.14   Access plan without index.

Looking at the access plan graph, you see that a temporary hash table will be created to obtain the result set. The information on the right displays information about the temporary hash table. If this query was to be used many times, then it may be wise to add a permanent index on the DEPTNO column in DEPARTMENT. To help with determining which indexes to create, the tool also provides an Index Advisor. It can be accessed by clicking the footprints icon in the Visual Explain tool as shown in Figure 12.14. Figure 12.15 shows the recommended indexes based on the Index Advisor.

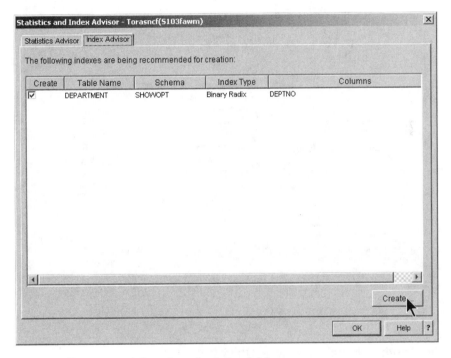

Figure 12.15   Recommendations from the Index Advisor.

Not surprisingly, the DEPTNO column on the DEPARTMENT table is recommended. This interface can also be used to create the index. Once created, you can re-run your Visual Explain and see the resulting access plan with the unique index, shown in Figure 12.16.

The revised access plan no longer creates a temporary has table, but uses the permanent index that was created.

The example, though simple, demonstrates the value of such a tool. It would be a good development practice to generate an access plan for every statement that is developed, and validate that an efficient plan is generated. In general, the goal would be to minimize the number of full table scans.

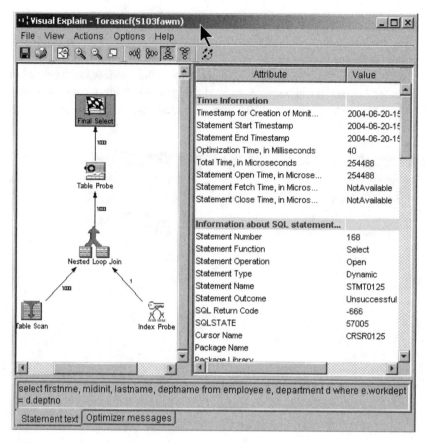

Figure 12.16   Access plan with index.

Variable Length Columns and Large Objects

On iSeries, a row has two sections: a fixed length portion and a variable length portion. The variable length columns (VARCHAR, VARGRAPHIC, VARBINARY) and large objects (CLOB, BLOB, DBCLOB) are stored in the variable length portion of the row. Access to these columns typically requires a secondary I/O operation; however, unlike on LUW, this I/O operation is buffered.

TIP

Use the ALLOCATE clause of the column definition in the CREATE TABLE statement to reserve a portion of the variable length columns in the fixed-length portion of the row to avoid a secondary I/O operation.

Database Statistics

Database table, column, and index statistics are vital to generating the most efficient query access plans. The **Statistics Manager** is tasked with collecting and keeping the statistics up to date. It keeps track of the following information:

- Cardinality of column values
- Selectivity (distribution of values in a column)
- Frequent values (top values in a column and associated frequency)
- Metadata information on a table (number of rows and indexes)
- Estimate of I/O operation (for access to table or index)

The information is collected automatically, but updates to statistical information are not immediate, with the exception of indexes. Statistics on indexes are updated as changes occur. For other objects such as tables or columns, collection occurs in the background as system resources become available.

Because index statistics are immediately updated, they act as the primary source of statistical information for the DB2 UDB iSeries optimizer. One of the biggest causes of poor performance on iSeries is the absence of the correct indexes.

When the Statistics Manager receives requests from the query optimizer, estimates for column statistics are returned, regardless of whether the statistics have been collected. If a request for a column with no statistical data is received, a default value is returned and the column is marked for collection. The next time collection starts, statistics for that column will be collected.

To determine when to re-calculate statistics after they have been collected, the Statistics Manager relies on the Plan Cache. Recall from Chapter 7, "Working with Dynamic SQL," that the plan cache is an area in memory where generated access plans are stored. Each time a new access plan is created or an existing plan is re-used, the Statistics Manager will validate to see if more than 15 percent of the data in the underlying table(s) has changed. If it has, then the corresponding columns will be marked for collection. Additionally, the access plan will also be marked so the next time it is accessed, a new plan is generated.

The automation of the collection works well; however, there are cases when you may want to force the collection of statistics—for example, if you've completed some mass updates or added large volumes of data. You have two options available to you for forcing the collection of statistics. You can use the IBM iSeries Navigator to select tables and columns for which to collect statistics, or you can do it programmatically through the use of APIs.

> **NOTE**
> If your system resources are busy for long periods of time, statistics collection will not occur because the Statistics Manager waits for system resources to become available.

DB2 for zSeries Considerations

This section provides an overview of performance, monitoring, and tuning considerations in a DB2 for zSeries environment. For detailed explanation of the topics described in this section, refer to the DB2 UDB for z/OS V8 Administration Guide.

Before you analyze DB2 for performance problems, you should look at the overall system. In general, try to see why application processes are running slowly or why a given resource is being heavily used. The resource measurement facility (RMF) of z/OS is the best tool to use for such tasks.

If your analysis suggests that the performance problem is within DB2, follow these steps to further pinpoint where the problem is:

1. Turn on Classes 1, 2, and 3 of the accounting trace with the -START TRACE command to determine which resources DB2 is waiting on. In particular, stored procedure processing is included in Class 1 and cCass 2 times.

2. Narrow your range by specifying application processes or a time interval. Once you determine which application is not performing well, you can look at detailed traces for these slow tasks.

3. Use the DB2 performance trace to distinguish slow responsiveness, lack of real storage, contention, high use of resources, and so on.

4. For information about packages or DBRMs, run accounting trace Classes 7 and 8. To determine which packages are consuming excessive resources, compare accounting trace Classes 7 and 8 to the elapsed time for the whole plan on accounting Classes 1 and 2.

The EDM Statement Cache

In DB2 for zSeries, the **EDM Statement cache** contains the skeletons of dynamic SQL. This cache is part of the EDM Pool and is equivalent to the package cache in DB2 for LUW. To turn on the EDM Statement cache, make sure to specify YES for the field CACHE DYNAMIC SQL of installation panel DSNTIP8 (Performance and Optimization Panel) or, if you need to update its value, use panel DSNTIPB, option 19.

For information about packages, plans, and DBRMs, you can review the following catalog tables:

- SYSIBM.SYSPACKAGE contains a row for every package.
- SYSIBM.SYSPLAN contains a row for every application plan.
- SYSIBM.SYSDBRM contains a row for each DBRM of each application plan.

If a plan or package is bound with the REOPT(ALWAYS) bind option, the statement will not be saved in the cache. This option ensures that a statement is optimized with the latest statistics; therefore, DB2 for zSeries will not used the cached information.

In addition to the EDM Statement cache, the **Routine Authorization cache** can be used to save authorization information for SQL procedures and user-defined functions. The field ROUTINE AUTH CACHE in panel DSNTIPP can be used to indicate how much storage to allocate for this cache. If you would like to update this value, use option 22 on panel DSNTIPB.

The Performance Expert Tool

The output of your traces can be analyzed through reports generated by tools such as the DB2 Performance Expert. The **DB2 Performance Expert** is a licensed program that integrates the function of two other tools, the **DB2 Buffer Pool Analyzer** and the **DB2 Performance Monitor (DB2 PM)**. This tool provides performance monitoring, reporting, buffer pool analysis, and a performance-warehouse all-in-one tool.

The data collected from the traces can be presented in the following ways:

- **The Batch report sets** present the data in comprehensive reports or graphs containing system-wide and application-related information for both single DB2 subsystems and DB2 members of a data-sharing group. They can be used to examine performance problems and trends over a period of time.

- The **Online Monitor** gives a current "snapshot" view of a running DB2 subsystem, including applications that are running. It is equivalent to DB2 LUW snapshots. The Online Monitor comes in two flavors: host-based and Workstation. The Workstation version is simpler to use and offers significant advantages. For example, from the Workstation Online Monitor, you can launch Visual Explain so you can examine the access paths and processing methods chosen by DB2 for the currently executing SQL statement. Note that the Visual Explain for DB2 for zSeries does not use the same code base as the Visual Explain provided in DB2 LUW; however, they both serve the same purpose. Figure 12.17 shows an example of Visual Explain for DB2 for zSeries. The graph shows the access plan for the query SELECT salary into:H FROM employees where name='Gene' where there are no indexes defined on table employees.

- The accounting report tells you if your problem is related to an application or data, a concurrency problem, or a global problem.

When you need to obtain more information about these problems, use the following Performance Expert reports:

- **For application and data problems:** Use Explain, SQL Activity, and Record trace reports.

- **For concurrency problems:** Use Deadlock trace, Timeout trace, Locking, and Record trace reports.

- **For global problems:** Use Statistics, I/O activity, CICS or IMS monitor, RMF, or the Console log.

For stored procedures in particular, the accounting report provides the following information:

- The part of the total CPU time spent on stored procedure requests.

- The amount of time spent waiting for a stored procedure to be scheduled and the time needed to return control to DB2 after the stored procedure has completed.

- The number of calls to stored procedures.

- The number of times a stored procedure timed out waiting to be scheduled.

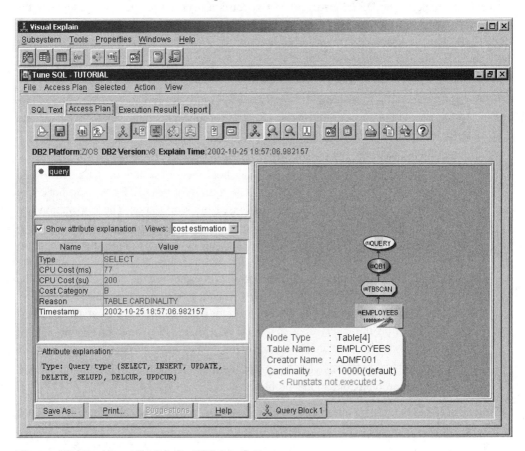

Figure 12.17   Visual Explain for DB2 for zSeries.

Improving Response Time and Throughput

To improve response time and throughput, you should take into account the following items discussed in the following subsections.

Buffer Pool Size

Make buffer pools as large as you can afford for your workload because they will minimize I/O. You also need to monitor the different buffer pool thresholds for best performance. The Buffer Pool Analyzer and the Statistics Report (both part of the Performance Expert tool) can help you with this.

RID Pool Size

The **RID pool** is used to store all record identifiers (RIDs), and is used for unique key enforcing, RID sorting during list prefetches, and so on. The DB2 for zSeries optimizer takes into account the RID pool size and may choose a table space scan if this pool is too small.

RUNSTATS

Similar to DB2 for LUW, the RUNSTATS utility in DB2 for zSeries should be run frequently to update the catalog statistics that are used by the DB2 for zSeries optimizer to calculate the best access plan. REORG and REBIND work similarly as in DB2 LUW.

PCTFREE and *FREEPAGE*

You can use the PCTFREE and FREEPAGE clauses of the CREATE and ALTER TABLESPACE statements and CREATE and ALTER INDEX statements to improve the performance of INSERT and UPDATE operations because free space on pages is reserved.

Distribute Your Datasets Efficiently

To avoid I/O contention, place your frequently used datasets in fast devices and across your available disk volumes to distribute the I/O load.

Create Additional Work File Table Spaces

Work file table spaces are used as temporary spaces when sort operations, joins, temporary tables, and so on are used. By creating more work files, you reduce contention among these table spaces.

Space Formatting

When inserting records, DB2 pre-formats space within a page set as needed. The allocation amount, which is either CYLINDER or TRACK, determines the amount of space that is preformatted at any one time. Choose CYLINDER particularly if you are performing mass inserts.

Avoid Excessive Extents

Try to minimize the number of extents, as the extent size is more important to performance than the number of extents for a data set.

Maximum Number of Open Datasets

Use parameter DSMAX to control the limit of open datasets, and also the number of datasets that are closed when that limit is reached.

Resolving Excessive Wait Time or Timeouts for UDFs and Stored Procedures

Possible causes include:

- The goal of the service class that is assigned to the WLM stored procedure's address space, as it was initially started, is not high enough. The address space uses this goal to honor requests to start processing stored procedures.
- The priority of the service class that is running the stored procedure is not high enough.
- Make sure that the application environment is available by using the z/OS command DISPLAY WLM, APPLENV=*applenv*. If the application environment is quiesced, WLM does not start any address spaces for that environment; CALL statements are queued or rejected.

Tuning Your Queries

Use Visual Explain or the BIND option EXPLAIN to obtain more information about the access path chosen by the optimizer for a given query. If you are performing a table scan, for example, make sure you have appropriate indexes or increase your RID pool size. Reviewing the Visual Explain output should provide you with useful information to determine which actions to perform to improve performance.

Giving Optimization Hints to DB2

This feature is very helpful in a production environment where you have critical queries performing well. If you want to upgrade your DB2 for zSeries code to a higher version or maintenance level, you may want to ensure that such change will not affect the access plan for your critical queries. By executing the EXPLAIN statement on these critical queries, you store their access plans in the PLAN_TABLE. After upgrading your code, if the access plan changes you can give DB2 optimization hints so that it looks in the PLAN_TABLE for the old access plan and uses it instead. There are some restrictions to optimization hints, so make sure to review the DB2 for zSeries Administration Guide, because the optimizer may not necessarily choose to use the hint.

Limit Resources for a Stored Procedure

DB2 for zSeries allows you to establish limits for stored procedures. This can be accomplished by either of these methods:

- Update the ASUTIME column of the SYSIBM.SYSROUTINES catalog table for a given procedure with the processor limit. This limit allows DB2 to cancel procedures that loop.

- Set a limit for the maximum number of times that a procedure can terminate abnormally, by specifying a value in the MAX ABEND COUNT field on installation panel DSNTIPX. This limit is a system limit that applies to all stored procedures, and prevents a problem procedure from overwhelming the system with abend dump processing.

- Set a limit for the maximum number of times that a specific procedure can terminate abnormally, by specifying the STOP AFTER FAILURES option on the ALTER or CREATE PROCEDURE statement. This limit allows you to override the system limit specified in MAX ABEND COUNT and specify different limits for different procedures.

Considerations for Stored Procedures in a Distributed Environment

Consider using the COMMIT ON RETURN YES clause of the CREATE PROCEDURE statement to indicate that DB2 should issue an implicit COMMIT on behalf of the stored procedure upon return from the CALL statement. Using the clause can reduce the length of time locks are held, and can reduce network traffic. With COMMIT ON RETURN YES, any updates made by the client before calling the stored procedure are committed with the stored procedure changes.

Summary

As you can see, you can use many different techniques to get the optimal performance out of your stored procedures. Information was grouped by platform, because performance tuning is very platform-specific. Both monitoring and basic tuning were covered.

To ensure top-notch performance, have a properly configured environment, proper indexes, and current statistics available.

Best Practices

In this chapter, you will learn how to

- Create optimal tables and indexes
- Create easily maintainable code
- Code with performance in mind
- Work more efficiently with result sets

To start off, it is important to recognize that there are different types of best practices. A **best practice** can be a programming guideline that enables easier maintenance through standardized coding techniques, code readability, and code documentation through the use of comments. Alternatively or additionally, a best practice can be a guideline to ensure that you receive the maximum performance from your system resources.

Sometimes these practices compete with each other, and you have to choose one over the other. For example, often performance-related practices are specific to an operating system and are very focused on one platform. If you have a requirement to develop applications that are portable across platforms, it may not be easy to implement a performance-related best practice having IF conditions in your code, or creating multiple code bases targeted at different platforms.

With that said, the implementation of the best practice is left to you, depending on your specific requirement and circumstance.

In this chapter, a variety of best practices will be discussed. First, some features of tables and indexes are examined to help improve performance. Next, we mention things you can do while coding to make sure that your SQL procedure is easy to read and maintain, keeping performance in mind. Finally, we touch upon the topic of result sets.

Table and Index Best Practices

Several SQL options can be applied to both tables and indexes to make them more efficient for your specific SQL workload. Deciding on what features to take advantage of should be based on how your application behaves. If you are unaware of the behavior, you can use statement event monitoring to capture all SQL that is sent to the database engine (discussed in Chapter 12, "Performance Tuning").

Table Considerations

For LUW and zSeries, you can take advantage of the following features when either creating or altering tables:

- APPEND ON (LUW only). Used for tables that have heavy INSERTs to avoid searching the table for free space. With this option, you simply append the row to the end of the table.

- LOCKSIZE TABLE. Change a table's behavior from row-level locking to table-level locking. Use this option for read-only or exclusive access tables, which reduces the amount of time to lock rows and reduces the amount of memory used for locks. On zSeries, DB2 normally chooses page-level locking as the default, and the LOCKSIZE is set at the table space level.

- PCTFREE. Used to maintain free space on each data page of the table, which helps speed up INSERTS, LOADS, and REORGS (don't use with APPEND ON). In zSeries, PCTFREE and FREEPAGE clauses are part of both the CREATE and ALTER TABLESPACE statements and CREATE and ALTER INDEX statements.

- VOLATILE. Used to encourage an index scan on tables whose cardinality changes frequently. This will only work in the cases where the index contains all the columns referenced or when the index is able to apply a predicate in the index scan.

- ACTIVATE VALUE COMPRESSION (LUW only). Can save disk space when a table uses many null and system default values. This can help improve query time when the volume is significant.

On iSeries, you can use the ALLOCATE clause of the column definition in the CREATE TABLE statement to reserve a portion of the variable length columns in the fixed-length portion of the row to avoid a secondary I/O operation.

Temporary Table Considerations

Temporary tables are ideally suited for SQL procedures that generate large amounts of temporary data which need to be stored for no longer than an application connection session. If the table is only needed for the duration of the SQL procedure execution (including the returning of a result set from it), you can declare the temporary table within the SQL procedure. If the temporary table will be shared among SQL procedures of the same session, the table should be declared outside the SQL procedures to increase manageability.

You may find that defined global temporary tables are a nice fit to your application. Especially, if you need a table that

- Does not require locking.
- Does not cause inserts into the system catalog tables.
- Can have minimal logging or no logging.
- Is only visible to the application that created it.

Now with DB2, you can define indexes on these tables so that they can efficiently handle very large data volumes. Additionally, on LUW and zSeries they also support the collection of statistics. This makes temporary tables increasingly important to SQL procedure developers.

NOTE

On zSeries, there are two types of temporary tables: the first one uses the CREATE GLOBAL TEMPORARY TABLE statement, and the second one uses the DECLARE GLOBAL TEMPORARY TABLE statement. For portability with the other platforms, use the second type of temporary tables. Refer to Chapter 10, "Leveraging DB2 Application Development Features," for a comparison between these two statements. In this chapter, temporary tables on zSeries refer to the DECLARE TEMPORARY TABLEs.

Index Considerations

On LUW and zSeries, the following list includes some of the features that can optionally be applied to indexes (the Design Advisor will make full use of these in LUW) to enhance performance:

- PCTFREE (LUW and zSeries only). Used to keep free space on pages of the index. If the index is on a read-only table, there is no need for free space, so a PCTFREE of 0 will use pages more efficiently. However, if the table is not read-only, a PCTFREE of 10 can help speed up inserts by having approximately 10 percent of the page size available as free space. This should be higher for tables with clustered indexes to ensure that the clustered indexes do not become too fragmented. In such a case where there is a high volume of inserts, a value of 15–40 may be more appropriate.

- ALLOW REVERSE SCANS (LUW only). Allows for an index to be scanned bi-directionally, which means quicker retrieval of ascending and descending result sets. This has no negative performance impact because it is done by default at the DB2 code level.

- INCLUDE (LUW only). Can be used to include additional non-indexed columns in the index to promote faster index-only access and avoid fetches.

- UNIQUE. Used to efficiently enforce the uniqueness of a column or set of columns.

- CLUSTER (LUW and zSeries only). Allows the contents of the table physically ordered by the index, which can help greatly improve the efficiency of ORDER BY statements using the same ordering as the columns of the clustered index.

On zSeries, backward-index scans will occur automatically under the following conditions:

- The index is defined on the same columns as the columns in the ORDER BY clause, or the index is defined on the same columns as the columns in the ORDER BY clause followed by other columns.
- For each column that is in the ORDER BY clause, the ordering that is specified in the index is the opposite of the ordering that is specified in the ORDER BY clause.

On iSeries, consider using ENCODED VECTOR indexes for decision support and reporting environments.

Best Practices for Easier Code Maintenance

The following suggestions will help ensure that your code is easy to understand and follow.

Code Readability

The following tips will help you maintain optimal code readability:

- Use indentation! For example, when creating the body of a FOR loop, indent all nested lines by three spaces.
- Use meaningful labels in the body of the SQL procedure.
- Avoid declaring variables with the same name in different compound statements of a same program. Though supported, this can often lead to confusion.
- Avoid using the GOTO statement, because it can lead to spaghetti code which is both difficult to read and maintain. If you have to use the GOTO statement, try to skip to the end of the SQL procedure or the loop.
- Use SQL procedure nesting to break up a complex task into smaller and more manageable components.

Code Size

If a trigger or function body becomes too large, try converting it to a SQL procedure. Triggers can call SQL procedures in DB2, as long as certain rules are not violated. Functions in LUW and iSeries can also call SQL procedures.

If an SQL procedure is very small, consider converting it to a function.

Grouping SQL Procedures by Schema

Use schemas to group application objects by functional component. For example, if you have a group of triggers, functions, and SQL procedures that are responsible for day-to-day maintenance of a payroll invoice system, you may want to group them under the schema PAYROLL. You would then have objects like PAYROLL.ADD_EMPLOYEE and PAYROLL.REMOVE_EMPLOYEE.

Naming Conventions

Always use naming conventions that suggest what the trigger, function, or SQL procedure is responsible for. For example, if creating a trigger, its name should suggest its type (DELETE, UPDATE, or INSERT) and its firing sequence (before or after). For example, a trigger by the name of tab1_bupt could represent a trigger that performs a before update of tab1.

On LUW and iSeries, when creating a SQL procedure or function, always specify a specific name in the CREATE procedure or function header. This makes SQL procedure management much easier, especially when it comes to dropping the SQL procedure. On iSeries, the specific name has the added benefit of specifying the name of the C program that is created by the system (as long as it is a valid system name).

Avoid using the same name for both a variable and a table column. Such naming is allowed but typically causes confusion. If the variable and column names are the same, DB2 will resolve the name to the table column.

On iSeries, further consideration needs to be given when naming triggers, functions, and SQL procedures. For object names that are greater than 10 characters, a system name is generated. When any SQL statement accesses an object with a long name, it is converted internally to the system name. The conversion process may have a small performance impact. This is only an issue when using *SYS naming and when the SQL object names are unqualified.

Return Values Versus Out Parameters

Only use the RETURN statement to return integers as status indicators; anything else convolutes its use. Typically, a status of 0 means successful execution, while a negative value means an error and a positive value means a warning. Out parameters should be used for everything other than status indicators.

Exception Handling

To make code more portable, use SQLSTATE for exception handling instead of SQLCODE. In addition to SQLSTATE being standard across the DB2 family of products, a large proportion of the SQLSTATES are also standard across the different database vendors.

To make the code more readable, declare condition names for specific SQLSTATES and then declare handlers for the named condition. Figure 13.1 demonstrates this.

```
DECLARE FOREIGN_KEY_VIOLATION CONDITION FOR SQLSTATE '23503';
DECLARE EXIT HANDLER FOR FOREIGN_KEY_VIOLATION ... ;
```

Figure 13.1   Declaring condition names.

Some SQLSTATE ranges are reserved for customized SQLSTATES for your application. This prevents the unintentional use of an SQLSTATE value that might be defined by DB2. The customizable SQLSTATES begin with the characters 7 through 9 or I through Z—for example:

```
SIGNAL SQLSTATE '70001' SET MESSAGE_TEXT = 'custom error'
```

Commit and Rollback

Be explicit with transaction control, because DB2 SQL procedures neither COMMIT nor ROLLBACK for you by default at the end of execution. When running SQL procedures through the DB2 Development Center, it may appear as though SQL procedures COMMIT on completion. In reality, it is the Development Center issuing the commit. (See the RUN settings in Appendix D, "Using the DB2 Development Center.") On zSeries, you can use the CREATE PROCEDURE clause 'COMMIT ON RETURN' to tell the database manager to commit the transaction when returning from the SQL procedure call.

Best Practices for Performance

The following recommendations provide alternate ways to perform common tasks to achieve better performance. These suggestions cover both SQL and SQL PL.

Exceptions

On LUW and iSeries, use nested compound statements to localize exception handling and cursors. If the cursors and handlers for specific exceptions are scoped to a compound statement, processing for these exceptions and cursors does not occur outside the compound statements.

Repetitive SQL

Repeated statements should use parameter markers instead of literals to avoid the cost of recompilation.

Table Truncation

On LUW, mass DELETES can be accomplished with the command ALTER TABLE ... ACTIVATE NOT LOGGED INITIALLY EMPTY TABLE. Because these operations are not logged, they will avoid using log space.

Reducing Locking

Avoid using an isolation level higher than what you need. DB2 supports No Commit (NC, iSeries only), Uncommitted Read (UR), Cursor Stability (CS), Read Stability (RS), and Repeatable Read (RR), where RR requires the most locks (it locks every row it reads) and UR or NC requires no locks and can read uncommitted data. The more locks held, the less concurrency exists between applications that are trying to acquire locks on the same objects. By default, on LUW and zSeries, SQL procedures use CS; on iSeries, the commit level at the time of the create is used.

On LUW

Two new procedures have the ability to set and unset PREP options: SET_ROUTINE_OPTS() and GET_ROUTINE_OPTS(). These are the recommended ways of changing options rather than using DB2_SQLROUTINE_PREPOPTS, because you can control the options on a per-procedure level rather than instance-wide. Additionally, you do not have to stop and start the instance for the change to take effect.

For example, to set the isolation level to Uncommitted Read:

```
CALL SET_ROUTINE_OPTS('ISOLATION UR')
```

You can also specify the isolation level to use at a statement level using the option WITH <isolation level> at the end of your statement.

On iSeries

The SET OPTION clause's COMMIT option of the CREATE PROCEDURE statement can be used to specify the isolation level. See the section on iSeries precompile options later in this chapter for more details.

On zSeries

In DB2 for zSeries, use the BIND option ISOLATION to specify the isolation level. The isolation levels supported are the same as DB2 LUW. In addition, DB2 for zSeries uses the ACQUIRE and RELEASE bind parameters to determine when to acquire the locks and when to release them, respectively. ACQUIRE(USE) and RELEASE(COMMIT) will provide for most concurrency.

> **NOTE**
> Use the parameter EVALUATE UNCOMMITTED found in the panel DSNTIP8 to reduce locking. This parameter is equivalent to the registry variable DB2_EVALUNCOMMITTED in DB2 LUW.

In addition, DB2 for zSeries has mechanisms to avoid locking on rows and pages with committed data; this is known as **lock avoidance**. Review the DB2 for zSeries considerations section in Chapter 5, "Understanding and Using Cursors and Result Sets," for details about lock avoidance.

Dynamic SQL for DDL

Dynamic SQL is often used for DDL statements to get around dependency problems on LUW. To illustrate usages of dynamic DDL statements, implement the following SQL procedure (shown in Figure 13.2) that uses a static SQL to create a table called audit, if the table does not already exist.

```
CREATE PROCEDURE flush_audit()

    LANGUAGE SQL
    SPECIFIC flush_audit            -- applies to LUW and iSeries
 -- WLM ENVIRONMENT <env>           -- applies to zSeries
fa: BEGIN

    DECLARE tabcount INT DEFAULT 1;
    DECLARE table_not_found CONDITION FOR SQLSTATE '42704';

    DECLARE CONTINUE HANDLER FOR table_not_found
        SET tabcount=0;

    DROP TABLE AUDIT;
 -- COMMIT;                         -- (1) applies to zSeries

    CREATE TABLE AUDIT (AUD_ID INT, OP_TIME TIMESTAMP, OPERATION VARCHAR(500));

    RETURN tabcount;
END fa
```

Figure 13.2   DDL in SQL procedures using static SQL. This sample can lead to errors on LUW.

At first glance, the code in Figure 13.2 appears fine because it will build and run without errors. Upon trying to rebuild after running the SQL procedure on LUW, however, you will get the following error:

```
[IBM][CLI Driver][DB2/NT] SQL0601N  The name of the object to be created is iden-
tical to the existing name "DB2ADMIN.AUDIT" of type "TABLE".  LINE NUMBER=12.
SQLSTATE=42710
```

The error occurs because on LUW, DB2 checks for object dependency when the SQL procedure is created. In the case of the static CREATE TABLE statement, DB2 found that the AUDIT table already existed and therefore the SQL procedure creation fails. The simple workaround is to drop the existing table and then attempt to rebuild the SQL procedure again. However, this may be a hassle or not feasible if you need to preserve the information in the existing table. The recommendation for DDL, then, is to use dynamic SQL for any DDL Statements to defer dependency checking until execution time.

On iSeries and zSeries, this would not be a problem. On iSeries, the dependency checking is deferred until runtime (if it cannot resolve an object at build time), and hence the form shown in Figure 13.3 can be built without any errors.

On zSeries, dependency checking is also deferred until runtime when the BIND parameter VALIDATE is set to a value of RUN which is the default. Notice that on Line (1), an explicit COMMIT is coded. If this had been omitted and the table audit existed, DB2 on zSeries would have raised an SQLCODE -679 (the object cannot be created because a drop is pending on the object).

Figure 13.3 illustrates how the previous example can be rewritten using dynamic SQL to avoid object dependency errors on LUW.

```
CREATE PROCEDURE flush_audit2 ()
    LANGUAGE SQL
    SPECIFIC flush_audit2                           -- applies to LUW and iSeries
  --WLM ENVIRONMENT <env>                           -- applies to zSeries
fa2: BEGIN

    DECLARE vide VARCHAR (100);
    DECLARE tabcount INT DEFAULT 0;

    SELECT count (*) INTO tabcount
        FROM SYSCAT.TABLES WHERE TABNAME='AUDIT' AND TABSCHEMA=USER;
      -- applies to iSeries
      -- FROM SYSTABLES WHERE TABLE_NAME='AUDIT' AND TABLE_SCHEMA=USER;
      -- applies to zSeries
      -- FROM SYSIBM.SYSTABLES WHERE NAME='AUDIT' AND CREATOR=USER;

    IF tabcount=1 THEN
        SET vide='DROP TABLE ' || USER || '.AUDIT';
        EXECUTE IMMEDIATE vide;
      -- COMMIT;                                     -- (1) applies to zSeries
    END IF;

    SET vide='CREATE TABLE ' || USER || '.AUDIT ' ||
            '(AUD_ID INTEGER, OP_TIME TIMESTAMP, ' ||
            'OPERATION VARCHAR (500))';
```

```
    EXECUTE IMMEDIATE vide;

    RETURN tabcount;
END fa2
```

Figure 13.3   Executing DDL using dynamic SQL.

Now with Figure 13.3, the same duplicate object error will not be encountered because the CREATE TABLE statement is dynamic, and therefore dependency checking for the tables is deferred until runtime. On Line (1), a COMMIT is needed on zSeries for the same reasons that were explained earlier for Figure 13.2.

Using a Single Insert to Replace Multiple Insert Statements

On LUW and iSeries, you can use a single INSERT statement to insert multiple rows at the same time. This pays best performance dividends when used inside some kind of repetitious code, such as a loop. Simply group each row's values in a set of parenthesis and separate the rows by a comma, as shown in the following example:

```
INSERT INTO employee (empono, firstnme, lastname, midinit, edlevel)
  VALUES (empnum1, empfname1, emplname1, empinit1, empedulvl1),
         (empnum2, empfname2, emplname1, empinit1, empedulvl1),
         (empnum3, empfname3, emplname1, empinit1, empedulvl1)
```

Value Assignment

On LUW, SET statements allow for variables to be assigned in parallel (the database manager will take care of this). Using a SELECT ... INTO or VALUES ... INTO statement will actually cause the values to be assigned in a serial fashion, which is not as efficient as SET.

```
VALUES value1, value2, value3 INTO v_1, v_2, v_3;
```

should be rewritten as

```
SET v_1, v_2, v_3 = value1, value2, value3;
```

Deterministic Versus Not Deterministic

Like UDFs, SQL procedures can be defined as DETERMINISTIC or NOT DETERMINISTIC. A DETERMINISTIC SQL procedure helps avoid the cost of repeated execution by giving the database manager the option of caching the result from the first execution.

An SQL procedure should be declared as DETERMINISTIC if for the same input parameter values and same database state (for example, tables referenced by the SQL procedure have not changed), the same result set and/or output parameters values will be returned. That is, if you call ProcA with a single input parameter of "100" and a result of "50" is returned in an output parameter, then if you call the same procedure again with the same input parameter of "100", a DETERMINISTIC procedure would return "50" as long as no database tables have been modified between procedure calls.

Case Statement

Procedural code is generally more expensive to execute than SQL. Sometimes you can use a CASE expression instead of ELSE or IF statements. This leads to more compact and more efficient code. For example, the following procedural logic shown in Figure 13.4 could be replaced with a single CASE expression.

```
IF (NumEmployees < MaxEmployees) THEN
    INSERT INTO smb VALUES (CompanyID, ContactID, NumEmployees);
ELSE
    INSERT INTO smb VALUES (CompanyID, ContactID, MaxEmployees);
END IF;
```

Figure 13.4   *IF* statement logic.

This could be better written as the code that appears in Figure 13.5.

```
INSERT INTO smb VALUES (CompanyID,
                        ContactID,
CASE
    WHEN (NumEmployees < MaxEmployees)
        THEN NumEmployees
    ELSE MaxEmployees
END);
```

Figure 13.5   *CASE* statement logic.

Functions

To improve performance, always declare functions as DETERMINISTIC, if possible. This will specify that the function always returns the same results for a given argument. The database manager may be able to avoid execution of the entire function if this is performed.

On LUW, whenever you are simply reading information from the database and returning some kind of value, consider using a function instead because they are more efficient than SQL procedures (the function is executed as part of the SQL, instead of as a separate package). However, if you are performing any data changes, you must use an SQL procedure.

Working with Result Sets

The following suggestions can help you work with result sets more efficiently.

Cursor Considerations

When you create a cursor, you can specify what kind of operations the cursor may be performing. If you do not provide such a specification, the cursor is referred to as **ambiguous**, and DB2 will only be able to provide minor optimization. You specify the type of cursor by providing the FOR READ ONLY or FOR UPDATE clause in the cursor's SELECT statement. DB2 will perform specific optimizations for the type of cursor defined.

Row blocking is very useful when SQL procedures are returning large result sets. Instead of sending a row at a time to the client, sets of rows are sent together.

On LUW, when FOR READ ONLY is specified, DB2 is able to perform row blocking (unless the BLOCKING NO bind option has been used). You can also specify to use blocking for ambiguous cursors by providing the BLOCKING ALL bind option.

The BLOCKING bind option can be set using a command similar to the following:

```
db2set DB2_SQLROUTINE_PREOPTS="BLOCKING ALL"
```

To set blocking options on iSeries, see the section on Precompile Options on iSeries later in this chapter.

Limiting Result Sets

You can limit query result set size using the FETCH FIRST n ROWS clause, which is useful when you do not need the entire result set. For example, SELECT * FROM table1 FETCH FIRST 10 ROWS ONLY would fetch only the first 10 rows of the result set.

Optimizing Result Set Returns

When you only need a subset of the query at one time (for example, displaying results to a user's screen), you may want to obtain that subset as quickly as possible. You can optimize query return time with the OPTIMIZE FOR n ROWS clause. This will cause DB2 to optimize the return of the specified number of rows, instead of preparing to return all satisfying rows. In addition, the READ ONLY clause will influence the number of rows that will be returned in each block (there will not be more than n rows in a block). This does not limit the number of rows that can be fetched, but may degrade performance if more than *n* rows are fetched.

> **NOTE**
>
> On LUW, in order for this clause to have an impact on data buffers, the value of `n * row size` cannot exceed the size of the communication buffer (defined by DBM CFG RQRIOBLK or ASLHEAPSZ).
>
> An example of the statement would be
>
> ```
> SELECT * FROM table1 OPTIMIZE FOR 10 ROWS
> ```

The `OPTIMIZE FOR n ROWS` clause also applies to DB2 for zSeries, though it is not used for blocking. It does influence the optimizer to choose a different access path. For example, if you add `OPTIMIZE FOR 1 ROWS` in your query, the optimizer will likely not use sorting.

Minimize Result Set Columns

It is often easy to code quick statements with `SELECT * FROM` ...; however, selecting columns that are not required by the calling application can have performance impacts. The obvious benefit to reducing the number of columns is that less data would need to be passed back and forth between the calling application and the database manager. Additionally, a reduced column list may increases the likelihood of an access plan to use an existing index, if one exists.

Precompile Options on iSeries

The `SET OPTION` clause of the `CREATE PROCEDURE` statement on iSeries is used to specify precompile options for the SQL procedure. These can also be specified on the `RUNSQLSTM` command, allowing the options to be propagated to the SQL procedure creation. The precompile options used can have an impact on performance. A few of these options are described here.

The `COMMIT` option specifies the isolation level to use. Using a higher isolation level than required increases the amount of locking, thus reducing concurrency. For a description of isolation levels, refer to Chapter 5, "Understanding and Using Cursors and Result Sets." The valid values for this option ordered from lowest isolation level to highest isolation level are

- *NONE. Isolation level no commit, implies no ROLLBACK/COMMIT operations possible and any logging/journaling is not required.
- *CHG. Isolation level uncommitted read.
- *CS. Isolation level cursor stability.
- *ALL. Isolation level read stability.
- *RR. Isolation level repeatable read.

Specify the lowest isolation level that is possible for your application.

The `ALWBLK` option specifies the degree to which blocking will be used when processing cursors in the SQL procedure. **Row blocking** means the database manager will send data to the client in sets of rows, rather than one row at a time. **Enabling blocking** will increase performance. It is good practice to explicitly define the type of operation when opening a cursor through the use of the FOR READ ONLY or FOR UPDATE clauses. The valid values for the ALWBLK option are

- *ALLREAD. Blocking for read-only cursors when COMMIT is *NONE or *CHG.
- *NONE. No blocking.
- *READ. Blocking of cursors declared as READ ONLY, or when COMMIT is *NONE.

Where possible, use the ALLREAD option.

The ALWCPYDATA option is used to specify whether a copy of the data can be used when processing a SELECT statement. This option is especially important when you have a query that has multiple choices for index usage. The valid options for this clause are

- *OPTIMIZE. A copy of the data is used only when necessary, and the access plan is optimized to yield the fastest way to process the query.
- *YES. A copy of the data is used only when necessary.
- *NO. Data copying is not allowed. If the query processing requires a copy of the data, an error is returned.

Use the OPTIMIZE option. This option will use a combination of existing indexes and copies of data to process the query in the fastest time possible.

The DBGVIEW options specify the type of debug information to be provided by the compiler:

- *NONE. No debug information will be generated.
- *SOURCE. Allows debugging at the SQL statement level.
- *STMT. Allows debugging at the program statement number level.
- *LIST. Generates a listing view for debugging.

Using the SOURCE option makes debugging a lot easier, because you can debug at the actual SQL statement level as opposed to the generated C program statement level.

The DLYPRP option specifies whether to delay the dynamic statement validation in a PREPARE statement until an OPEN, EXECUTE, or DESCRIBE statement is encountered. Validation will always occur with OPEN, EXECUTE, or DESCRIBE, so the validation on PREPARE is redundant. The values are

- *NO. Do not delay validation.
- *YES. Delay validation.

Use the YES option to avoid redundancy and duplicate processing.

Summary

By following these aforementioned best practices, you should be able to write well-organized and logical code that performs well. Specifically, index and table creation were examined, where some options were discussed to squeeze additional performance out of them. Next, code maintenance was covered, where taking a little more time up front in the coding phase can save time and make your SQL procedures more manageable later. Finally, some performance best practices for SQL and SQL PL were shown.

Getting Started with DB2

If you have not used DB2 before, this appendix is the perfect place to start. It covers DB2 fundamentals and commands that will prepare you to work with the SQL procedure examples demonstrated in this book.

The first part of this appendix is focused on DB2 LUW. DB2 commands are illustrated to show how to create and manipulate DB2 instances, databases, buffer pools, table spaces, and tables. A set of DB2 graphical tools is also available to accomplish the same tasks, and more information can be found in the Online Help for the DB2 Administration Tools manual. Focus is on the executing from the command line using a DB2 Command window on Windows or a UNIX shell.

The second part of this appendix covers the iSeries and zSeries platforms—more specifically, tips to get you started quickly on these platforms. Commonly used access methods for developing on these platforms is covered here.

Getting Started with DB2 UDB for LUW

The following section covers the fundamentals of interacting with DB2 for LUW. After reviewing this section, you should have a good understanding of basic DB2 architecture, how to perform several important administrative duties, and how to work with DB2 for everyday activities.

Launching the DB2 Command Window

The first thing you must learn is how to launch the DB2 Command window. From the Windows Start menu, click Programs > IBM DB2 > Command Line Tools and select Command Window (see Figure A.1).

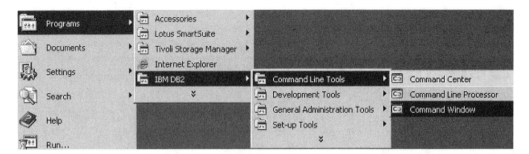

Figure A.1   Launching the DB2 Command window using the Windows Start menu.

Another way to launch the Command window is by running db2cmd from the Windows Run window (see Figure A.2).

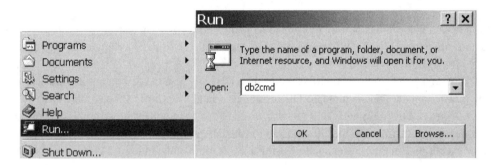

Figure A.2   Launching the DB2 Command window using *db2cmd*.

The DB2 Command Window is the command-line interface to DB2. At first glance, it appears exactly the same as the standard Windows DOS prompt, except that the title bar says "DB2 CLP." DB2 commands cannot be executed within the normal Windows DOS prompt because the DB2 command-line environment has not been initialized. If you have problems executing the commands presented in this appendix, make sure that you are in the DB2 command-line environment by verifying that the title bar reads "DB2 CLP," as shown in Figure A.3.

Launching the DB2 Command Line Processor

Besides the DB2 Command window, you can also issue DB2 commands in DB2's interactive mode by launching the DB2 Command Line Processor. From the Windows Start menu, click Programs > IBM DB2 > Command Line Tools and select Command Line Processor (see Figure A.4).

Figure A.3 The DB2 Command window with "DB2 CLP" in the title bar.

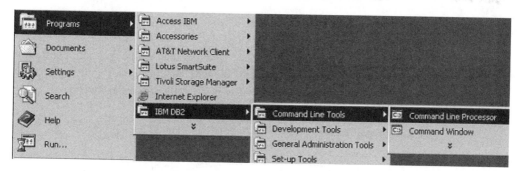

Figure A.4 Launching the DB2 Command Line Processor using the Windows Start menu.

You should see a window similar to Figure A.5.

Notice that the DB2 Command Line Processor window is loaded with a db2 => prompt as compared to a DOS prompt in DB2 Command Line window. The db2 => prompt indicates that you are in the DB2 interactive mode. You can issue any DB2 commands in this mode without a db2 prefix. To exit from the interactive mode, simply issue quit. This will bring you back to the DB2 Command window described in Figure A.3.

```
DB2 CLP - db2setcp.bat DB2SETCP.BAT DB2.EXE                          _ □ ×
(c) Copyright IBM Corporation 1993,2002
Command Line Processor for DB2 SDK 8.1.4

You can issue database manager commands and SQL statements from the command
prompt. For example:
     db2 => connect to sample
     db2 => bind sample.bnd

For general help, type: ?.
For command help, type: ? command, where command can be
the first few keywords of a database manager command. For example:
 ? CATALOG DATABASE for help on the CATALOG DATABASE command
 ? CATALOG          for help on all of the CATALOG commands.

To exit db2 interactive mode, type QUIT at the command prompt. Outside
interactive mode, all commands must be prefixed with 'db2'.
To list the current command option settings, type LIST COMMAND OPTIONS.

For more detailed help, refer to the Online Reference Manual.

db2 =>
```

Figure A.5   The DB2 Command Line Processor.

Overview of DB2 Architecture

There is no better place to start describing the DB2 architecture than with a diagram. Figure A.6 shows the basic components of a DB2 environment. We will start from the top at the instance level, and drill down into the details of databases, buffer pools, table spaces, and so on.

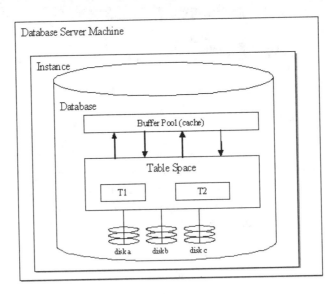

Figure A.6   Overview of the DB2 architecture.

DB2 Instances

A **DB2 instance** is a logical context in which DB2 commands and functions are executed. You can think of an instance as a service or a daemon process that manages access to database files. More than one instance can be defined on a server machine. Each instance is independent of the others, meaning that they are managed, manipulated, and tuned separately.

With the default installation of DB2 v8 (including v8.1 and v8.2), one instance is automatically created called **DB2** on Windows and **db2inst1** on UNIX. The default instance is sufficient for creating a database to run the examples contained in this book.

If you want to list the instances defined on your machine, you can issue the following command in a DB2 Command window or a DOS window:

```
db2ilist
```

Because this command is an executable, it is not recognized in the DB2 interactive mode.

Creating Databases

Each DB2 database is made up of buffer pools, table spaces, tables, metadata information, database log files, and many other components. Once an instance has been created and started, databases can be created within it.

A SAMPLE database comes with every DB2 server installation, but you must manually initiate its creation. The database is used by all the examples illustrated in this book. The command `db2sampl -k` will create the SAMPLE database, create tables and primary keys in the database, and populate the tables with data. Notice that the command is `db2sampl` without the letter e. Table structures and content for all examples used in this book can be found in Appendix F, "DDL."

If you want to create your own database, use the CREATE DATABASE command. Many options are supported by this command, which allows for customization such as the location of the database, database code page settings, default table space characteristics, and so on. However, the command for creating a database can be as simple as the following:

```
db2 CREATE DATABASE <dbname>
```

A complete syntax diagram of the CREATE DATABASE command is available in the DB2 Command Reference.

Before you can work with database objects such as tables, you must first connect to the database. The command to make a database connection is very simple:

```
db2 CONNECT TO <dbname>
```

This command will connect to the database with the user ID currently logged on to the operating system. If you want to connect to the database as a different user ID, specify the USER option:

```
db2 CONNECT TO <dbname> USER <username>
```

DB2 will then ask for the password and send it to the operating system for authentication. Figure A.7 illustrates the creation of the SAMPLE database and establishment of a connection from the command line.

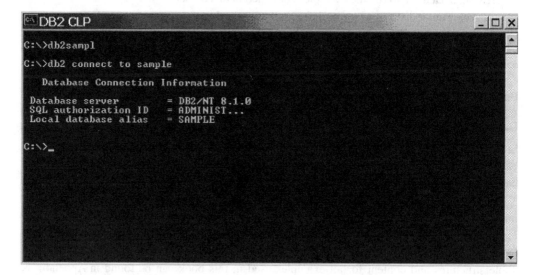

Figure A.7   Creating the SAMPLE database and establishing a connection from the command line.

To disconnect from a database, use

```
db2 CONNECT RESET
```

Note that DB2 does not manage and authenticate user IDs and passwords. They are validated by the operating system or other supported external security facilities. Therefore, there is no need to create database users in order to connect to the database.

Executing SQL in the DB2 Command Window

At this point, you are all set to perform some data manipulation. Just like other database management systems, data is manipulated by means of SQL statements. To execute a single SQL statement from the DB2 Command window, pass the SQL statement as a parameter to the db2 command:

```
db2 "SELECT * FROM EMPLOYEE"
```

It is often useful to group SQL statements together in a script and execute them using one command. To do this, save the set of SQL statements to a file and use the `db2` command with the `-tf` option. For example, assume you have a file called sqlstmt.db2 that contains a number of SQL statements as shown in Figure A.8.

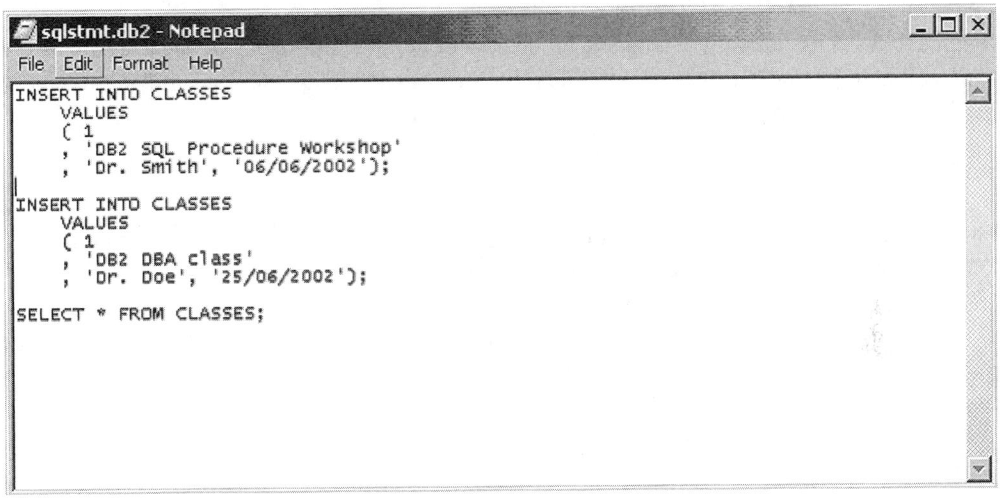


```
INSERT INTO CLASSES
    VALUES
    ( 1
    , 'DB2 SQL Procedure Workshop'
    , 'Dr. Smith', '06/06/2002');

INSERT INTO CLASSES
    VALUES
    ( 1
    , 'DB2 DBA Class'
    , 'Dr. Doe', '25/06/2002');

SELECT * FROM CLASSES;
```

Figure A.8 Example of a text file with multiple SQL statements.

In Figure A.8, each statement is separated by the default statement terminator, the semicolon (;). Use the following command to execute the statements contained in the input file:

```
db2 -tf sqlstmt.db2
```

In some cases, the semicolon cannot be used as the statement terminator. For example, scripts containing the `CREATE PROCEDURE` statement cannot use the default terminator because SQL procedure bodies themselves already use semicolons for statement terminators. An additional option, `-td`, is available to change the termination character. If sqlstmt.db2 had instead used @ as the statement terminator, you would use this command to execute the script:

```
db2 -td@ -f sqlstmt.db2
```

Note that there is no space between the `-td` option and the delimiter character.

All the examples presented in this book are executed using the DB2 Command window. However, you should also learn about the DB2 interactive mode because it supports some unique features.

NOTE
Remember to first connect to the target database before the script can be executed successfully.

Executing SQL in DB2 Interactive Mode

If you choose to use the DB2 interactive mode, you must enter the statement one at a time. Execution of multiple statements in an input file is not supported. A single SQL statement is executed
in DB2 interactive mode like this:

```
db2 => select * from employee
```

The DB2 interactive mode has a memory of all the commands and statements issued in the current session. You can use the `History` or `H` (case is not sensitive) command to obtain a list of
commands executed thus far (see Figure A.9).

```
db2 => History
1     connect to sample
2     select * from employee
3     h
4     update employee set salary=10000 where empno='000010'
5     insert into class values (a, b, c)
6     History
```

Figure A.9   Example of using the *History* command in DB2 interactive mode.

You can also pick a particular command from the list and edit it in your default word processor.
The `Edit` or `E` (case is not sensitive) command is used to accomplish that. For example, using the
history list from Figure A.9, the following command will bring up the Notepad as shown in Figure A.10.

```
db2 => Edit 2
```

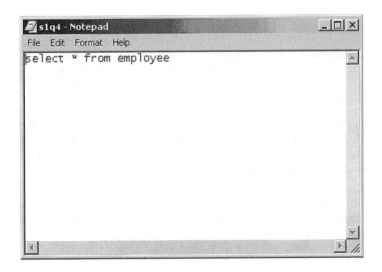

Figure A.10   Edit a previously executed DB2 statement in Notepad.

Configuring the DB2 Environment

Now we'll discuss how to configure the DB2 environment. Proper setup of the DB2 environment is very important because it controls how DB2 operates and functions. It can also be used to customize creation, development, and deployment of SQL procedures. The DB2 configuration parameters, operating system environment variables, and DB2 profile registry variables make up the DB2 environment.

You can change instance and database level configuration parameters that affect the behavior of DB2. With the following commands, you can obtain the instance (also called **database manager**) and database configuration parameters:

```
db2 GET DATABASE MANAGER CONFIGURATION
db2 GET DATABASE CONFIGURATION FOR <dbname>
```

To modify database manager or database configuration parameters, use

```
db2 UPDATE DATABASE MANAGER CONFIGURATION USING <parameter> <new value>
db2 UPDATE DATABASE CONFIGURATION FOR <dbname> USING <parameter> <new value>
```

More than 150 configuration parameters are online–configurable, which means that changes to these parameters can be in effect immediately if the requested resource is available. Changes to the other parameters become effective only after the instance is re-started or the database is re-activated.

This behavior can be explicitly specified with the IMMEDIATE option in the UPDATE DATABASE MANGER CONFIGURATION command, like this:

```
db2 UPDATE DATABASE MANAGER CONFIGURATION
USING <parameter> <new value> IMMEDIATE
db2 UPDATE DATABASE CONFIGURATION FOR <dbname>
USING <parameter> <new value> IMMEDIATE
```

You can also choose to defer the changes until the instance is re-started or the database is re-activated. Simply use the same command described previously, but specify the DEFERRED option:

```
db2 UPDATE DATABASE MANAGER CONFIGURATION
USING <parameter> <new value> DEFERRED
db2 UPDATE DATABASE CONFIGURATION FOR <dbname>
USING <parameter> <new value> DEFERRED
```

The majority of the parameters are related to performance, and they are not covered in detail here in this book. The DB2 Administration Guide provides detailed descriptions of each configuration parameter at both instance and database levels.

Operating system environment variables, as the name implies, are set at the operating system level. The syntax for setting an operating system environment variable depends on the platform and the type of shell you are using. For example, to set the current instance environment to PRODINST on a Windows platform, you use

```
set DB2INSTANCE=PRODINST
```

On AIX with the korn shell, you use

```
export DB2INSTANCE=PRODINST
```

DB2 Profile Registries

DB2 profile registries are DB2-specific variables that affect the management, configuration, and performance of the DB2 system. DB2 profile registries have no relation to the Windows registries. The db2set command is used to view and update the variables. To view all available options, you can use

```
db2set -?
```

To list out the values of the DB2 profile registry variables currently set on the server, use the -all option as illustrated in Figure A.11.

```
db2set -all

[e] DB2PATH=C:\SQLLIB
[i] DB2INSTPROF=C:\SQLLIB
[i] DB2COMM=TCPIP,NPIPE                -- (1)
[g] DB2SYSTEM=DB2NTSERV
[g] DB2PATH=C:\SQLLIB
[g] DB2INSTDEF=DB2
[g] DB2COMM=TCPIP,NPIPE                -- (2)
[g] DB2ADMINSERVER=DB2DAS00
```

Figure A.11   Usage and sample output of *db2set –all*.

The db2set -all command displays the settings of the environment. Indicators such as [e], [i], and [g] represent the scope of the setting:

```
[e] represents the setting of the environment
[u] represents the user level registry
[n] represents node level registry
[i] represents instance level registry
[g] represents global level registry
```

In Figure A.11, you may notice that some registry variables appear twice: one at the instance level on Line (1) and one at the global level on Line (2). Which one does DB2 use if values are set differently? The instance level profile registry variables take precedence over the same named global level registry variables. Some operating system environment variables that DB2 recognizes may also have the same identifier as the profile registry variables. In this case, the operating system environment variable is used.

Figure A.12 illustrates some options on how to set DB2 profile registry variables.

```
db2set VARIABLE=VALUE                    -- (1)
db2set VARIABLE=VALUE -i <instname>      -- (2)
db2set VARIABLE=VALUE -g                 -- (3)
```

Figure A.12   Example of the *db2set* command.

Line (1) of Figure A.12 sets the variable for your current instance as defined by the DB2INSTANCE environment variable. Line (2) uses the -i option to set the variable for the <instname> instance. Line (3) uses the -g option to set the variable globally for all instances defined on the server.

Changes made to DB2 profile registry variables are not dynamic, meaning that new values do not immediately take effect. To implement the new changes, you need to stop and start the instance.

Before you can use an instance, you must start the instance using the db2start command. If you select the default install options, the default instance is configured to start up automatically. To stop an instance, use db2stop.

If there are connections already made to the database and you try to stop the instance, you will receive this error:

```
SQL1025N The database manager was not stopped because databases are still active.
```

All connections made to databases that are defined in an instance must be terminated before that instance can be stopped. To list the applications currently connected to the databases managed by the current instance, you can use the LIST APPLICATIONS command (see Figure A.13).

```
db2 LIST APPLICATIONS

Auth Id    Application    Appl.      Application Id                 DB       # of
           Name           Handle                                    Name     Agents
--------   -------------  ---------- ----------------------------   -------  -----
SQLSPUSER  db2bp.exe      5          *LOCAL.DB2.020606173650        EFORMDB  1
DB2ADMIIN  db2cc.exe      4          *LOCAL.DB2.020606173635        SAMPLE   1
SQLSPUSER  java.exe       6          7F000001.5505.020606173800     SAMPLE   1
SQLSPUSER  db2bp.exe      7          *LOCAL.DB2.020606173811        SAMPLE   1
```

Figure A.13   Sample output of the *LIST APPLICATIONS* command.

Figure A.13 shows a sample output of LIST APPLICATIONS. The Auth Id column of the output represents the authentication ID used to connect. The second column is the application name for the connection. Each connection has a unique application handle (Appl. Handle) and Application Id. The DB Name column tells you which database each connection is connected to.

The last column is the number of database agent processes working for the connection.

With this information, you can identify and ask the users to log out from the database. Sometimes, expecting users to do this is not feasible. In these circumstances, you can use the FORCE APPLICATION command to terminate their connections. The following command will disconnect every connection from all the databases defined in an instance:

```
db2 FORCE APPLICATION ALL
```

To selectively terminate a single or a number of connections, you specify the application handles obtained from the output of the LIST APPLICATIONS command in the FORCE APPLICATION command.

For example, you might want to terminate every connection made to the SAMPLE database. Using the sample output in Figure A.13, application handles 4, 6, and 7 can be terminated by executing

```
db2 "FORCE APPLICATION (4, 6, 7)"
```

NOTE
Double quotes ("") are used here because different operating systems may treat parentheses differently. Enclosing the command with double quotes ensures that the whole command is sent to DB2 for processing.

Internally, this command will terminate the appropriate database processes and roll back any uncommitted changes for the terminated connections asynchronously. Thus, you may not see the effect of the command immediately.

Understanding Buffer Pools

Instances and databases have been discussed at a high level, and we can now dig deeper into the details of databases, starting with buffer pools. To reduce the number of I/O operations to the physical disk where data is stored, DB2 uses **buffer pools** to cache data and index pages in memory. Every database must have at least one buffer pool defined. The default buffer pool created in each database is called IBMDEFAULTBP. The default buffer pool is sufficiently large enough for you to work with the examples presented in this book. If you are creating a database for real workloads, however, the default size of IBMDEFAULTBP is typically not sufficient. You should refer to the DB2 Administration Guide for a more in-depth discussion on buffer pools.

You can find out what buffer pools are currently defined by connecting to the database and executing the following SQL statement:

```
db2 "SELECT * FROM SYSCAT.BUFFERPOOLS"
```

> **NOTE**
>
> Similar to the example shown above asterisk (*) are treated as special characters in most operating systems, enclose the SQL statement with double quotes ("") so that it can be executed successfully on any Linux, UNIX, and Windows platforms.

Creating a buffer pool is also quite easy. To create a buffer pool called BP16K that uses a 16K page size and is 1,000 pages large (page size and pages will be discussed shortly), use the CREATE BUFFERPOOL statement:

```
db2 CREATE BUFFERPOOL BP16K size 1000 pagesize 16K
```

You can also change the size of a buffer pool using the ALTER BUFFERPOOL statement. For example, to reduce the size of the previously listed buffer pool to just 500 pages, execute this code:

```
db2 ALTER BUFFERPOOL BP16K size 500
```

Working with Table Spaces

A **table space** can be viewed as a container for tables, and its responsibility is to manage how table data is physically stored on disk. In other words, tables are logical objects that are created within table spaces.

One of the main characteristics of table spaces is page size. When table data is stored on disk, data is stored on data pages that can range in size. DB2 supports 4K, 8K, 16K, and 32K page sizes. If you create a table space TS16K that uses a 16K page size and create a table T1 in TS16K, then all data inserted into T1 is stored physically on disk using 16K data pages.

Each table space is mapped to a buffer pool, and the buffer pool must use the same page size as the table space. So naturally, buffer pool page sizes of 4K, 8K, 16K, and 32K are also supported. For example, if you want to create a table space of 16K page size, a 16K page size buffer pool must exist before the table space can be created. The IBMDEFAULTBP buffer pool uses a 4K page size.

Three default table spaces are created at database creation time:

- SYSCATSPACE (catalog)
- TEMPSPACE1 (temporary)
- USERSPACE1 (user)

All use a 4K page size and use IBMDEFAULTBP as their buffer pool.

The catalog table space, SYSCATSPACE, stores tables that contain metadata about the database. These metadata tables are commonly referred to as the **system catalog tables**. SYSCATSPACE is created during database creation. No user objects can be defined in it.

The temporary table space, TEMPSPACE1, is used to store temporary data. Temporary table spaces are used by DB2 implicitly for tasks such as sorting, and can be used explicitly for tasks such as table reorganization. Therefore, you must have at least one temporary table space defined in each database.

USERSPACE1 is a REGULAR table space that stores user-defined objects like tables and indexes. You can create more than one user table space with different characteristics in a database.

When creating a table space, in addition to page size you also need to specify one or more table space containers that map to actual physical storage such as an operating system directory, file, or raw device. You will also need to specify whether the table space will be managed by the database (known as **Database Managed Space**, or DMS), or by the operating system (known as **System Managed Space**, or SMS). Containers for SMS table spaces are operating system directories; whereas containers for DMS table spaces can be pre-allocated files or raw devices. If you create a database without any options to the CREATE DATABASE command, the three default table spaces are created as SMS table spaces.

Figure A.14 shows some simple examples of how REGULAR, LARGE, and TEMPORARY table spaces can be created.

```
CREATE REGULAR TABLESPACE userdata_ts              -- (1)
    MANAGED BY SYSTEM
    USING ( 'c:\userdata1'
          , 'e:\userdata2' );


CREATE LARGE TABLESPACE largedata_ts               -- (2)
    MANAGED BY DATABASE
    USING ( file 'c:\largedata\largefile.f1' 3M
          , file 'd:\largedata\largefile.f2' 3M );


CREATE TEMPORARY TABLESPACE temp_ts                -- (3)
    MANAGED BY SYSTEM
    USING ( 'c:\tempdata1' );
```

Figure A.14 Examples of creating REGULAR, LARGE, and SYSTEM TEMPORARY table spaces.

On Line (1), userdata_ts is a REGULAR table space. The keyword REGULAR is optional. It is MANAGED BY SYSTEM that means it is an SMS table space. User-defined database objects can be stored in it. Data will be striped across two containers, and they are operating system directories.

The second table space on Line (2), largedata_ts, is a LARGE table space. LARGE table spaces are used to store only large objects such as Binary Large Objects (BLOB) or Character

Large Objects (CLOB). LARGE table spaces must be defined as DMS with the MANAGED BY DATABASE clause. Notice that two files are defined as the containers for this table space, and each of them is 3MB in size.

The last example on Line (3) creates an SMS system temporary table space with only one container.

Detailed characteristics and differences between SMS and DMS table spaces are not discussed here. More information can be obtained from the DB2 Administration Guide or references listed in Appendix G, "Additional Resources," of this book. By using some DB2 commands, you can easily obtain the list of table spaces defined in a database, their status, and location of the containers for each table space.

To list all the table spaces of a database, connect to the database and issue

```
db2 LIST TABLESPACES
```

You will receive output similar to Figure A.15.

```
            Tablespaces for Current Database

Tablespace ID                    = 0
Name                             = SYSCATSPACE
Type                             = System managed space
Contents                         = Any data
State                            = 0x0000
   Detailed explanation:
     Normal


Tablespace ID                    = 1
Name                             = TEMPSPACE1
Type                             = System managed space
Contents                         = System Temporary data
State                            = 0x0000
   Detailed explanation:
     Normal


Tablespace ID                    = 2
Name                             = USERSPACE1
Type                             = System managed space
Contents                         = Any data
State                            = 0x0000
   Detailed explanation:
     Normal
```

```
Tablespace ID                          = 3
Name                                   = LARGEDATATS
Type                                   = Database managed space
Contents                               = Any data
State                                  = 0x0000
  Detailed explanation:
    Normal
```

Figure A.15   Sample output of the *LIST TABLESPACES* command.

The output provides the unique table space ID, table space name, type of the table space (for example, SMS or DMS), and status of the table space.

To obtain information about the containers used for a specific table space, execute

```
db2 LIST TABLESPACE CONTAINERS FOR <table-space-id>
```

You need to provide the table space ID in this command and this information is available from the output of the LIST TABLESPACES command. An example of using this command and the result is shown in Figure A.16.

```
db2 LIST TABLESPACE CONTAINERS FOR 3

            Tablespace Containers for Tablespace 3

Container ID                           = 0
Name                                   = c:\largedata\largefile.f1
Type                                   = File

Container ID                           = 1
Name                                   = d:\largedata\largefile.f2
Type                                   = File
```

Figure A.16   Example of the *LIST TABLESPACE CONTAINERS* command.

Working with Tables

Now it's time to learn how to create some tables. Again, tables are created within table spaces. A default table space called USERSPACE1 is created for you upon database creation so that you can begin creating tables right away.

```
CREATE TABLE classes
    ( classid      INTEGER NOT NULL
    , classname    VARCHAR(50) NOT NULL
    , instructor   VARCHAR(50)
    , classdate    DATE
    , PRIMARY KEY ( classid ) )          -- (1)
    IN userdata_ts                       -- (2)
```

Figure A.17 Example of table creation.

Figure A.17 shows an example of creating a table with a primary key defined on the `classid` column on Line (1).

To explicitly specify which table space you want a table to be created in, use the `IN <table-space-name>` clause as illustrated on Line (2). If the `IN` clause is not specified, the table will be created in a table space that has a sufficiently large page size, given the row size of the table, and where the user has privileges to do so. Every user object in DB2 must belong to a schema. A **schema** is a logical grouping of database objects such as tables and stored procedures. It is possible to have tables with the same name but in different schemas. You can explicitly reference a database object by its schema and object name using `<schema-name>.<db-object>`. Notice that schema is not specified as part of the statement in Figure A.17. In such cases, the authorization ID used to connect and execute the `CREATE TABLE` statement will be used for the schema.

In some situations, you may want to create tables in a schema other than your authorization ID but don't want to fully qualify all the object names. There is a DB2 special register called CURRENT SCHEMA that can be used to obtain or set the current schema. To obtain the current schema, simply do this:

```
db2 VALUES CURRENT SCHEMA
```

The default value of the CURRENT SCHEMA is the authorization ID used to connect to the database.

To change the current schema, use this command:

```
db2 SET CURRENT SCHEMA = NEWSCHEMA
```

Once the new schema is set, any references to database objects that are not explicitly qualified with a schema will implicitly use this new schema for the duration of the session.

To list the tables defined in a database, you can use the LIST TABLES command. This command has several options.

```
db2 LIST TABLES
```

This command lists tables that belong to the schema assigned to the CURRENT SCHEMA register mentioned above.

If you want to list all the tables under a specific schema, you can extend the previous command to:

```
db2 LIST TABLES FOR SCHEMA <schema-name>
```

The FOR ALL option shown below will then list all the tables under every schema defined in the database.

```
db2 LIST TABLES FOR ALL
```

One other useful thing to know is how to easily find out the structure of a table. For example, you may want to insert a row in a table for which you do not know the data type for a specific column. This command will definitely save you time in searching for the answer:

```
db2 DESCRIBE TABLE <table-name>
```

To *describe* the STAFF table of the SAMPLE database, you can issue

```
db2 DESCRIBE TABLE staff
```

You should receive output similar to Figure A.18.

Column name	Type schema	Type name	Length	Scale	Nulls
ID	SYSIBM	SMALLINT	2	0	No
NAME	SYSIBM	VARCHAR	9	0	Yes
DEPT	SYSIBM	SMALLINT	2	0	Yes
JOB	SYSIBM	CHARACTER	5	0	Yes
YEARS	SYSIBM	SMALLINT	2	0	Yes
SALARY	SYSIBM	DECIMAL	7	2	Yes
COMM	SYSIBM	DECIMAL	7	2	Yes

```
  7 record(s) selected.
```

Figure A.18   Example output of the *DESCRIBE TABLE* command.

Introducing the System Catalog Tables

Most commands demonstrated in this appendix so far obtain information about the database. For example, the LIST TABLESPACES and LIST TABLES commands list the table spaces and tables defined in a database, respectively. Where is the information actually stored? The information about data (also known as **metadata**) is contained in the system catalog tables. These tables are defined under the SYSIBM schema. Because the amount of information stored in the SYSIBM tables is usually more than what database administrators or users want to know, filtered information is extracted through the use of views. These views are defined under the SYSCAT schema.

Table A.1 shows some common SYSCAT views that may be useful when developing your SQL procedures. For a complete list, refer to the DB2 SQL Reference Guide.

Table A.1   Common System Catalog Views

CatalogViews	Descriptions
SYSCAT.BUFFERPOOLS	Buffer Pool configuration
SYSCAT.COLUMNS	Columns
SYSCAT.FUNCTIONS	Functions
SYSCAT.PACKAGES	Packages
SYSCAT.PROCEDURES	Stored procedures
SYSCAT.TABLES	Tables
SYSCAT.TABLESPACES	Table spaces
SYSCAT.TRIGGERS	Triggers

Getting Started with DB2 UDB for iSeries

This section describes how you would get started in a DB2 UDB for iSeries environment. The appendix first describes the DB2 UDB for iSeries architecture, followed by some typical activities and associated interfaces you would use to get started. Where appropriate, comparisons to DB2 LUW will be called out, and equivalent concepts will be highlighted.

There are several interfaces for working with iSeries platforms and databases on that platform. Possible options are

- Using the interactive SQL interface from the i5/OS native system.
- Using the IBM iSeries Navigator shipped as part of IBM iSeries Access for Windows.
- Using the DB2 UDB Client for Windows to work with an iSeries database. The client includes tools such as the Command Center, Control Center, Development Center, and Command Line Processor. DB2 Connect would be required to use this interface.

This section focuses on the first two interfaces. However, in some cases, some other interfaces may be discussed as well.

Launching the Interface

In order to start working with an iSeries environment, you will need access to an iSeries server. You can use the native interface to work with iSeries, in which case you would log on directly on the server, or use an emulator from a Windows environment to log on as shown in Figure A.19.

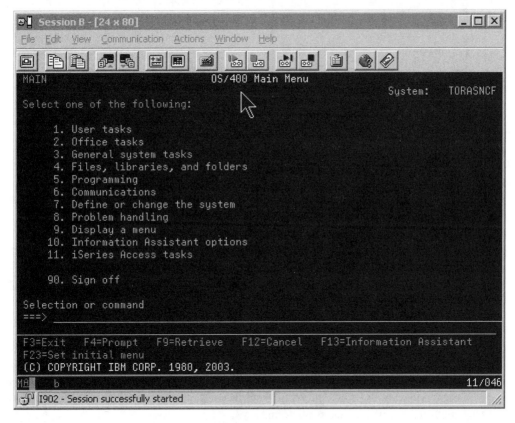

Figure A.19   Logged in to a native environment.

Alternatively, you can install the IBM iSeries Access for Windows software and use the iSeries Navigator for Windows. To launch this environment, from the Windows Start menu click Programs > IBM iSeries Access for Windows > iSeries Navigator (see Figure A.20).

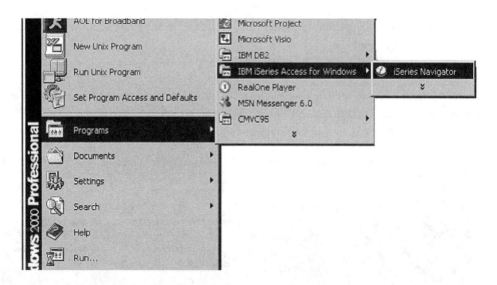

Figure A.20   Launching the iSeries Navigator.

Once the environment is launched, you will need to create a connection to your server. By using the connection, you can then explore and navigate through your iSeries environment (see Figure A.21).

Overview of the DB2 UDB for iSeries Architecture

DB2 UDB for iSeries is part of the i5/OS operating system. It has always been a part of the operating system and was branded as DB2 UDB in February 1999. As new functions are added, DB2 UDB on iSeries remains fully integrated with the operating system.

Any database operations on a DB2 UDB for iSeries database can be performed using one of two methods:

- **Traditional system file access**. The i5/OS native interface to a relational database. It was originally introduced and used before SQL became popular. Traditional iSeries users prior to V3R7 would prefer this interface if they are not familiar with SQL and are comfortable with the iSeries platform.

- **SQL, or Structured Query Language**. The interface fully compliant with the SQL-92 Entry Level Standard. This interface is ideal for users who are used to working with relational databases on other platforms, because the SQL follows a standard and is similar except for minor differences across platforms. It is also the strategic direction for all platforms that DB2 supports.

Either one of the methods can be used to access DB2 UDB of iSeries data. Table A.2, taken from the iSeries V5R3 Information Center, shows some of the differences in terminology and concepts between the two methods.

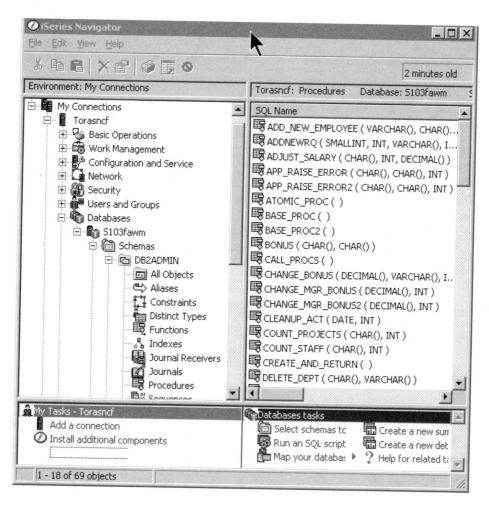

Figure A.21   iSeries Navigator interface.

Table A.2   DSS Versus SQL Comparison and Concepts

SQL Term	Traditional File Access Term
Collection. Consists of a library, a journal, a journal receiver, an SQL catalog, and an optional data dictionary. A collection groups related objects and allows you to find the objects by name.	**Library.** Groups related objects and allows you to find the objects by name.

SQL Term	Traditional File Access Term
Table. A set of columns and rows.	**Physical file.** A set of records.
Row. The horizontal part of a table containing a serial set of columns.	**Record.** A set of fields.
Column. The vertical part of a table of on data type.	**Field.** One of more bytes of related information of one data type.
View. A subset of columns and rows of one or more tables.	**Logical file.** A subset of fields and/or records of up to 32 physical files.
Index. A collection of data in the columns of a table, logically arranged in ascending or descending order.	A type of logical file.
Package. An object that contains control structures for SQL statements to be used by an application server.	**SQL Package.** Has the same meaning as the SQL term.
Catalog. A set of tables and views that contain information about tables, packages, views, indexes, and constraints.	**No similar object.** However, the Display File Description (DSPFD) and Display File Field Description (DSPFFD) commands provide some of the same information that querying an SQL catalog provides.

Now that you've been introduced at a high level to the iSeries platform, we can delve a little deeper into the architecture of the database within the platform. Refer to Figure A.22.

As you can see from Figure A.22, an iSeries server (in general) has only one system-wide database. All database objects are available to the entire system, as long as the user has authority to access them.

The concept of an instance does not exist. Another way of looking at it is that only a single instance is supported on an iSeries server. Because the database is part of the operating system, there is no explicit CREATE DATABASE command. The database already exists and is available.

Typically, additional databases are not created. Different database environments are handled using different schemas. Objects from different schemas can be accessed using a single query. It is possible, however, to create additional independent databases by creating independent disk pools. When an independent disk pool is created, it appears to the system as another database. These independent databases can be made available (varied on) and not-available (varied off) to the system. Typical uses for them are for infrequently used data or as a high availability solution for clustered environments.

The CREATE SCHEMA statement can be used to create schemas explicitly. Explicit creation of a schema will automatically create catalog views (discussed later) to database objects created under that schema.

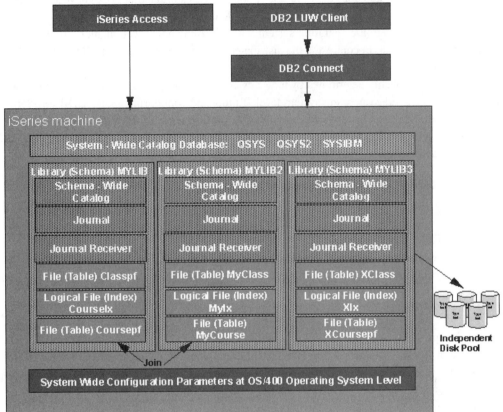

Figure A.22   DB2 UDB for iSeries architecture.

Additionally, a Journal and a Journal Receiver is also created. The **Journal** is used to log database activity, and records this activity to a **Journal Receiver**. A key benefit in employing Journal Management is faster recovery time after an outage. If you are familiar with DB2 on distributed platforms, Journal Management is comparable archive logging. Journaling can be turned on and off at the table level. In this case, changes made to the table are not logged. This is equivalent to using the NOT LOGGED INITIALLY table option on the distributed platforms.

Disk management is performed automatically by the underlying operating system. When a table is created, its association to the physical disk is managed by the operating system. The table is automatically striped across physical disks, and data is balanced across them as required. iSeries administrators can have some influence over how physical disk is utilized through the management and control of disk pools; however, this topic is beyond the scope of this book. In contrast to the distributed platforms, the concept of a table space does not exist on iSeries.

Memory management is also performed automatically by the underlying operating system. Through management and control of memory pools, iSeries administrators can have some influence over how memory is utilized; however, this topic is beyond the scope of this book. When an SQL statement is issued, the operating system will determine how much memory to allocate to the executing statement. In contrast to the distributed platforms, the concept of a buffer pool does not exist on iSeries.

As you've probably determined by now, any configuration on a DB2 UDB for iSeries database is performed at the operating system level. Tuning and configuring a DB2 UDB for iSeries database requires a more indepth understanding of the iSeries platform and operating system. However, many administrative tasks, including the collecting of statistics on tables and indexes, are handled automatically on the iSeries platform.

Executing SQL in DB2 UDB for iSeries

You can use several methods to issue SQL commands; however, as specified earlier, we will focus on two methods: the interactive SQL interface from the i5/OS native system, and the iSeries Navigator for Windows.

To start the interactive SQL interface form the i5/OS native system, issue the following command, which invokes the utility with the option of using SQL naming conventions:

```
STRSQL NAMING(*SQL)
```

You will be presented with a screen similar to the one shown in Figure A.23.

Alternatively, you can use the Run SQL Scripts window of the iSeries Navigator. Drill down to the left-hand side in the Database folder and click on one of the databases. In the bottom-right hand pane entitled Database Tasks, you should see a link for Run an SQL Script. Click on that, and it will open a window as shown in Figure A.24.

SQL statements can be entered in either one of these interfaces. iSeries system commands can be entered through the Run SQL Scripts interface by prefixing the command with CL:, for example:

```
CL: CHGQRYA QRYOPTLIB(DB2ADMIN)
```

The default isolation level for the Run SQL Scripts window is NO COMMIT. This means that if this environment is used to create SQL procedures or functions, The SQL procedures or functions will be created with the NO COMMIT isolation level. This isolation level is often not desired for managing transactions, because COMMIT and ROLLBACK statements are not allowed.

Change the default isolation level of the Run SQL Scripts window using the Connection -> JDBC Setup menu option, or explicitly set it prior to issuing your statement using the SET statement:

Figure A.23 iSeries Interactive SQL screen.

```
SET TRANSACTION ISOLATION LEVEL CS
```

Other interfaces, such as Query for iSeries, can be used in addition to the two methods shown here.

If you are using a DB2 UDB for Windows Client and want to use the CLP, then refer to the previous section on how to use that environment.

So far, you've seen that a database already exists on an iSeries system. Once a user logs on, he or she will be able to execute SQL statements. The first step in starting to work with a database is to create your own work area or schema. Typically, you would name the schema after your user ID to indicate the owner. For production databases, the schema could be something more relevant to the database and its application.

```
CREATE SCHEMA <schemaname>;
```

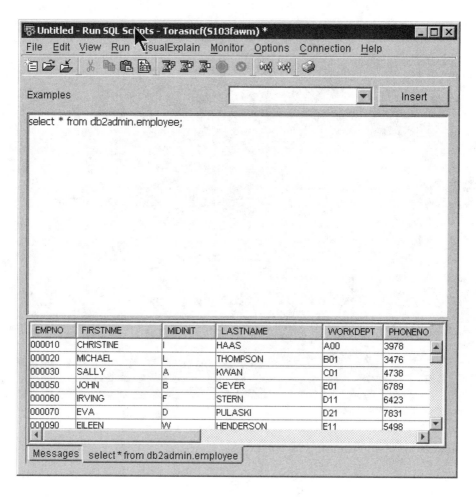

Figure A.24   iSeries Navigator Run SQL Scripts window.

The CREATE SCHEMA command will create a schema-level set of catalog views and set up Journal Management for all tables created under that schema as well.

Working with Tables

Once you've created a schema, you can then create database objects such as tables. Because there is no concept of table spaces, you do not need to specify a table space in which to create the table. Recall that you can use special registers to define the default schema and path. So if you wanted to create a schema and objects within that schema, without qualifying the objects, you can use a script similar to the one shown in Figure A.25.

```
CREATE SCHEMA appendixA;

SET SCHEMA appendixA;

SET PATH appendixA, SYSTEM;


CREATE TABLE classes
    ( classid      INTEGER NOT NULL
    , classname    VARCHAR(50) NOT NULL
    , instructor   VARCHAR(50)
    , classdate    DATE
    , PRIMARY KEY ( classid ) )        -- (1)
```

Figure A.25   Example of table creation on iSeries.

The table will also create an associated primary key on the column classid. Notice that there is no high-level qualifier for the table name. In this case, the value of the CURRENT SCHEMA special register will be used as the high-level qualifier. The CURRENT SCHEMA special register defaults to the current user ID, if it is not explicitly set. Alternatively, a high-level qualifier could have been specified in the table definition itself.

The command LIST TABLES, which is available on the DB2 UDB distributed platforms, is not supported on DB2 UDB for iSeries. Similarly, the DESCRIBE TABLE statement is not supported interactively on iSeries. It is supported through a programming interface using the DESCRIBE TABLE ... INTO clause. The commands, however, can be mimicked interactely by querying the catalog tables.

Catalog

The terms **schema-wide catalog** and **system-wide catalog** have been mentioned earlier in the iSeries section. The **catalog** is a series of system tables and views that holds the metadata for any database object which is created.

The system-wide catalog tables and views are stored under the QSYS and QSYS2 schema, and contain information about every database object that is created on the system.

ODBC and JDBC catalog tables and views reside under the SYSIBM schema. This catalog supports ODBC and JDBC catalog API requests.

The schema-wide catalog is created when the CREATE SCHEMA statement is issued. It consists of a set of views against the system-wide catalog tables, but restricted to objects in that schema. Table A.3 lists the views that are created when the CREATE SCHEMA statement is issued and their associated description.

Table A.3   Catalog View in an iSeries Schema

Catalog View	Description
SYSCHKCST	Information about check constraints.
SYSCOLUMNS	Information about column attributes.
SYSCST	Information about all constraints.
SYSCSTCOL	Information about columns referenced in a constraint.
SYSCSTDEP	Information about constraint dependencies on tables.
SYSINDEXES	Information about indexes.
SYSKEYCST	Information about unique, primary, and foreign keys.
SYSKEYS	Information about index keys.
SYSPACKAGE	Information about packages.
SYSREFCST	Information about referential constraints.
SYSTABLEDEP	Information about materialized query table dependencies.
SYSTABLES	Information about tables and views.
SYSTRIGCOL	Information about columns used in a trigger.
SYSTRIGDEP	Information about objects used in a trigger.
SYSTRIGGERS	Information about triggers.
SYSTRIGUPD	Information about columns in the WHEN clause of a trigger.
SYSVIEWDEP	Information about view dependencies on tables.
SYSVIEWS	Information about the definition of a view.

If you wanted to use the catalog views to list the tables in the current schema, you could issue the statement as shown in Figure A.26. The associated output is also shown.

In addition to using the schema-wide catalog views to query catalog information, the IBM-supplied objects for iSeries under the SYSIBM schema can also be used. This schema contains a richer set of views on the system-wide catalog, as compared to the schema-wide views. Refer to the SQL Reference for a listing of the views under the SYSIBM schema.

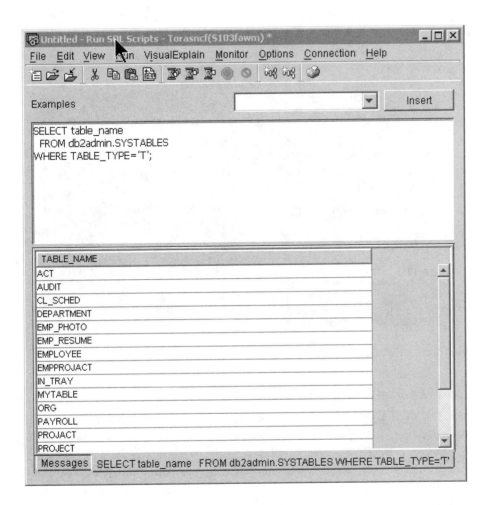

Figure A.26   An example of querying a catalog view.

Getting Started with DB2 UDB for zSeries

This section describes how you would get started in a DB2 UDB for zSeries environment. The DB2 UDB for zSeries architecture is first described, followed by some typical activities and associated interfaces you would use to get started. Where appropriate, comparisons to DB2 LUW will be mentioned, and equivalent concepts will be highlighted.

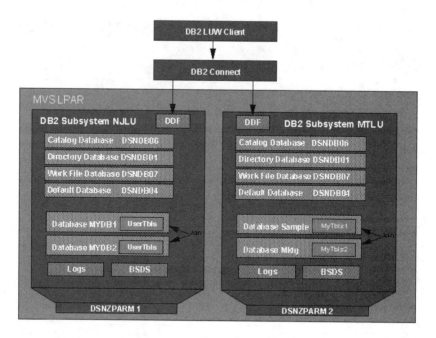

Figure A.27   DB2 UDB for zSeries architecture.

Overview of the DB2 UDB for zSeries Architecture

Figure A.27 shows a simplified view of the DB2 for zSeries system structure.

In DB2 for zSeries, a DB2 subsystem provides a separate DB2 environment similar to a DB2 LUW instance. Several DB2 for zSeries subsystems can be installed in the same machine logical partition (LPAR), and they can only communicate with each other through the Distributed Data Facility (DDF). (Data sharing provides another way that DB2 subsystems work together, but we don't discuss this here.)

A DB2 for zSeries subsystem can contain several databases. Databases in this subsystem interact with each other. In fact, as you can see from Figure A.27, the catalog itself (DSNDB06) is a database. The work file database (DSNDB07) would correspond to the temporary space used in DB2 LUW. The default database (DSNDB04) is used to store objects that users create without explicitly indicating the database to which they belong. DSNDB04 would correspond to USER-SPACE1 in DB2 LUW. Another database—the directory (DSNDB01)—keeps track of internal system information and is kept in sync with the catalog.

The catalog, directory, and other system structures are created once at DB2 subsystem installation time, not like in DB2 LUW where a catalog and other system structures are created for every CREATE DATABASE that is executed.

Within the DB2 for zSeries structure, you can perform SQL operations using tables from different databases. For example, say you have table TS56692.testtbl in database MYDB1 and table DSN8810.emp in the default database DSNDB04. Then, you can execute the following query:

```
SELECT  B.name, B.salary
FROM    TS56692.testtbl A, DSN8810.emp B
WHERE   A.id = B.edlevel
```

Table spaces are physical objects containing logical tables. The page size of the table space is determined by the buffer pool chosen to work with the given table space. There are four types of table spaces:

- Simple
- Segmented
- Partitioned
- Large objects (LOB)

Refer to the DB2 for z/OS SQL Reference for more detail about them.

DB2 for zSeries uses predefined buffer pools with different page sizes (4K, 8K, 16K, and 32K). Most of these buffer pools start with a size of zero which means they are not active. In order to make a buffer pool active or "create" it, use the ALTER BUFFERPOOL command and change the size to a value greater than zero.

Storage groups are used to group different volumes of DASD (Direct Access Storage Devices) that hold datasets in which tables and indexes are actually stored. The default storage group SYSDEFLT is created after installing DB2. All volumes of a given storage group must have the same device type, but parts of a single database can be stored in different storage groups.

Transaction logging in DB2 for zSeries is similar to LUW. Active and archive logs are used. A data set called the **bootstrap data set (BSDS)** keeps track of its logs.

With respect to configuration parameters, in zSeries they are often called **zparms** (for the default name of the parameter module, which is DSNZPARM). Only one set of parameters would affect the entire DB2 subsystem and its databases. The job DSNTIJUZ is used to specify the desired values for these parameters. When run, this job will assemble and link-edit the DSNZPARM module as well as the application program's default module DSNHDECP. The assembled zparm module can be specified when starting DB2. If it is not specified, the module with name DSNZPARM will be used. In versions prior to V7, changes to zparms required DB2 for zSeries to be recycled (stopped and started) to load the new parameter module into memory. With V7 and beyond, this is still the case for some parameters, but not for all. The new SET SYSPARM command allows you to load a new parameter module without recycling DB2.

Catalog

The **catalog** is a series of system tables that hold the metadata for any database object that is created. Catalog tables have a schema of SYSIBM. Some of the DB2 for zSeries catalog tables are updatable, including some of columns that hold statistics information about the data.

Table A.4 shows some common catalog tables that may be useful when developing your SQL procedures. For a complete list, refer to the DB2 UDB for z/OS SQL Reference Guide.

Table A.4   Common System Catalog Views

Catalog Table	Description
SYSIBM.SYSCOLUMNS	Column information for each table or view.
SYSIBM.SYSROUTINES	Information about stored procedures and user-defined functions.
SYSIBM.SYSPLAN	Information about plans.
SYSIBM.SYSPACKAGE	Information about packages.
SYSIBM.SYSTABLES	Information about tables, views, or aliases.
SYSIBM.SYSTABLESPACE	Information about table spaces.
SYSIBM.SYSTRIGGERS	Information about triggers.

Interacting with DB2 for zSeries

There are several interfaces for working with DB2 for zSeries platforms and databases on that platform. Possible options include the following:

- Using DB2 Interactive (DB2I) interface from a Time Sharing Option (TSO) subsystem.
- Using the DB2 LUW Client to work with a DB2 for zSeries database. The client includes tools such as the Command Center, Control Center, Development Center, and Command Line Processor. The DB2 Connect software would be required to use this interface.

Using DB2I

In order to start working with zSeries natively, you will need access to a zSeries server. Use an emulator from a Windows environment to log on to a TSO subsystem on the mainframe, and invoke DB2I which should be available from an Interactive System Productivity Facility (ISPF) menu. Depending on the way your environment was set up in your company, DB2I may be in a different ISPF menu. Contact your system administrator if you cannot find a way to invoke DB2I from ISPF. Figure A.28 shows the DB2I primary option menu.

The DB2I Primary Option Menu has several options, and each of them is briefly explained in Figure A.28. The most common option used to execute SQL queries is option 1 (SPUFI). Figure A.29 shows an example.

In Figure A.29, two datasets are specified: one to be used as input containing the SQL statement to be executed, and the other one to be used as the output of the statement execution. For the example, in the figure TS56692.CNTL.SQL(SELECT) is a dataset that contains this statement (not shown in the figure):

```
SELECT * FROM DSN8810.EMP;
```

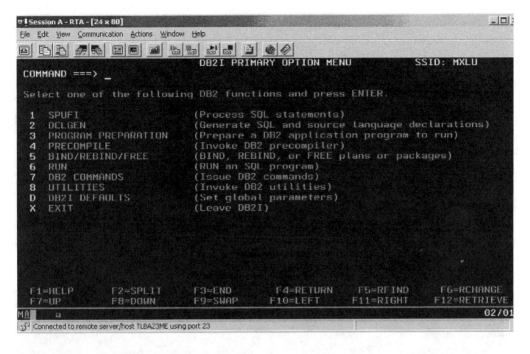

Figure A.28   The DB2I primary option menu.

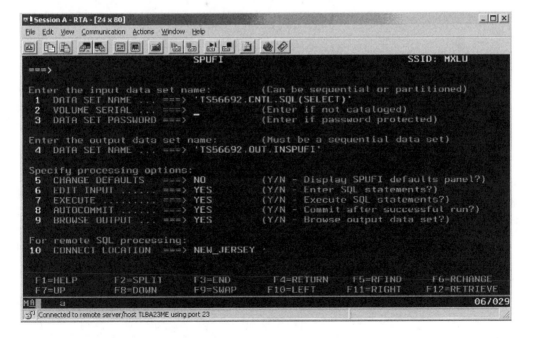

Figure A.29 Option 1 (SPUFI) from the DB2I primary option menu.

The output of this statement in the example is stored in dataset TS56692.OUT.INSPUFI. Figure A.30 shows the output.

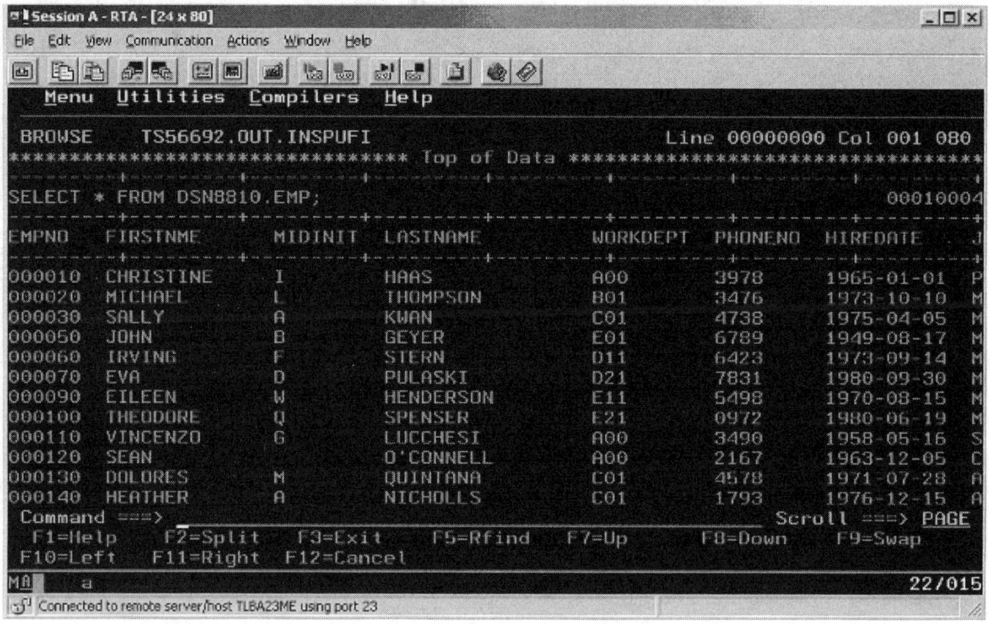

Figure A.30   Output of an SQL statement executed from SPUFI.

Option 7, DB2 Commands, is used to execute DB2 commands natively. Figure A.31 shows some commands previously executed from this option.

Other options in the DB2I primary option menu allow you to complete information specific to your environment for a specific task, which is then used to generate a Job Control Language (JCL) job that can be saved and reused in the future. For example, Option 8 Utilities allows you to generate a JCL job for several utilities such as RUNSTATS.

Using DB2 LUW Client Tools

To work with DB2 for zSeries, you can work with the DB2 LUW client tools—in particular, the CLP and the Control Center. Figure A.31 shows the Control Center with a connection to a DB2 for zSeries subsystem named NEW_JERS. Note that the Control Center folder, and options vary compared to a LUW database. For example, Figure A.32 shows a folder for Storage Groups that is specific to zSeries.

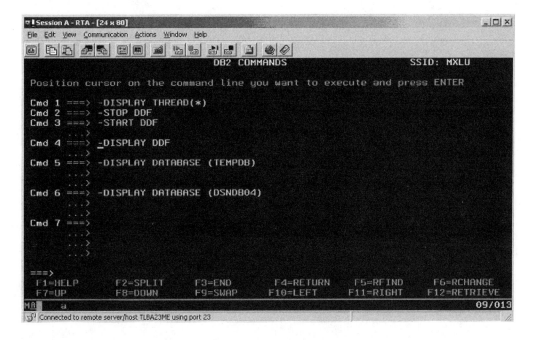

Figure A.31   The DB2 Commands option of the DB2I menu.

Figure A.33 shows how to connect to a DB2 for zSeries subsystem from the CLP and execute a query. The syntax of the connect statement is the same, just ensure you use a TSO ID and password that can access the DB2 subsystem. In addition, ensure that you have cataloged the connectivity information correctly in your system database directory, node directory, and DCS directory at your client machine.

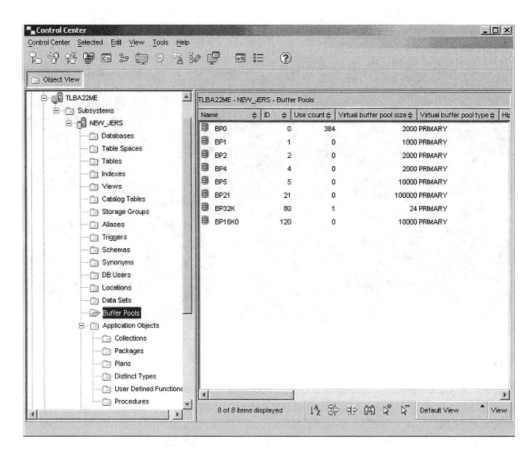

Figure A.32   The Control Center with a connection to a zSeries subsystem.

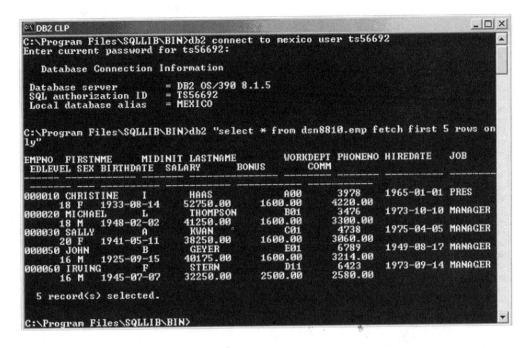

Figure A.33   The CLP used to connect to a zSeries subsystem and issue a query.

Note that in DB2 for zSeries, you connect to a subsystem, not to a specific database.

Summary

This appendix introduced some basic commands to get you started with a DB2 database. Creation and manipulation of DB2 instances, databases, buffer pools, table spaces, and tables were demonstrated. Some basic scripting and command options were also discussed. At this point, you should be able to set up a DB2 database to work with the examples shown in this book.

Inline SQL PL for DB2 UDB for Linux, UNIX, and Windows

From the very first chapter of this book, you have been learning the basics as well as the advanced elements of the SQL Procedural Language. Because this book is the *Essential Guide* to SQL PL, you will learn everything about SQL PL, including inline SQL PL.

Inline SQL PL is a procedural language that supports a subset of the SQL PL elements. The language is employed by dynamic compound SQL statements that are used in triggers, SQL user-defined functions (UDFs), SQL methods, and stand-alone code. Stand-alone code is also sometimes referred to as **SQL PL scripting**.

The concept of inline SQL PL is only supported in DB2 LUW for Linux, UNIX, and Windows. In DB2 LUW for iSeries and zSeries, stored procedures, functions, and triggers coded in SQL PL are all compiled into embedded C programs and bound into DB2 as packages.

Dynamic Compound Statement

Inline SQL PL is described as "inline" because the logic is expanded into and executed with the SQL statements that reference them. In this appendix, we look at statements and elements supported in inline SQL PL. For thorough discussions and examples of how it can be used, refer to Chapter 9, "User-Defined Functions and Triggers."

From the syntax diagram presented in Figure B.1, you can see that the dynamic compound statement must be wrapped inside a BEGIN ATOMIC ... END block. This ensures that either all or none of the statements inside the block will be committed to the database. Optionally, a label can be used to name the atomic block.

```
dynamic-compound-statement


>>-+-------------+--BEGIN ATOMIC-------------------------------->
   '-label:------'


>--+------------------------------------------+----------------->
   | .----------------------------------. |
   | v                                  | |
   '---+-| SQL-variable-declaration |-+---;-+-'
       '-| condition-declaration  |----'


   .-,------------------------.
   v                          |
>----SQL-procedure-statement--;-+--END--+-------+-------------><
                                        '-label-'


SQL-variable-declaration:


          .-,-----------------.
          v                   |
|--DECLARE----SQL-variable-name-+--data-type-------------------->

   .-DEFAULT NULL------------.
>--+------------------------+-----------------------------------|
   '-DEFAULT--default-values-'


condition-declaration:

|--DECLARE--condition-name--CONDITION--FOR--------------------->

               .-VALUE-.
   .-SQLSTATE--+-------+-.
>--+-------------------+--string-constant---------------------|
```

Figure B.1   Syntax diagram of a dynamic compound statement.

In the declaration section, only SQL variable and condition declarations are supported. This means that you cannot declare cursors and condition handlers. You may ask what good is it to declare conditions without the ability to declare handlers. In inline SQL PL, a condition will be useful when you want to raise an error with a SIGNAL statement using a named condition.

As for the SQL procedure statements supported in inline SQL PL, there are few restrictions. Refer to Figure B.2 for a complete list of supported SQL procedure statements.

CALL	IF
CASE	ITERATE
DECLARE <variable>	LEAVE
DECLARE <condition>	RETURN
FOR	SET
GET DIAGNOSTICS	SIGNAL
GOTO	WHILE

Figure B.2   SQL procedure statements supported in inline SQL PL.

Most of them are fairly straightforward, but a few statements warrant some discussion. The CALL statement enables the ability to CALL stored procedures from within triggers, SQL UDFs, SQL methods, and stand-alone code. This significantly extends the power of these objects and increases the reusability of stored procedures. For example, you can now indirectly handle conditions in an SQL UDF by calling a stored procedure that contains error-handling logic.

Because cursor declaration is not supported in inline SQL PL, cursor manipulations such as positioned updates and deletes are not possible. Rather than using cursors explicitly, you can alternatively use the FOR statement to loop through the result set returned from the specified SELECT statement. Here is an example extracted from Chapter 4, "Using Flow of Control Statements," that uses a FOR loop to iterate through all the rows returned from the SELECT statement. This method gives you the same result as declaring, opening, and fetching a cursor. In fact, a read-only cursor is declared under the cover when the following example is executed:

```
FOR v_row AS
    SELECT firstnme, midinit, lastname
      FROM employee
    DO
        SET v_fullname = v_row.lastname || ', ' ||
                         v_row.firstnme || ' ' || v_row.midinit;
        INSERT INTO tname VALUES (v_fullname);
END FOR
```

Figure B.3   An example of a *FOR* statement extracted from Chapter 4.

The SET statement support in inline SQL PL is slightly different from what it can do inside an SQL procedure. As you may already know, the SET statement is used to assign a value to a variable such as this:

```
SET v1 = 3;
```

You can also assign a result value from a SELECT statement to a variable:

```
SET v_salary = (SELECT salary FROM employee WHERE empno='000010');
```

Note that the SELECT statement must return only a single row; otherwise, the statement will raise an error. These statements are both valid in SQL procedures and inline SQL PL. In an SQL procedure, if you want to assign values to one or more variables, you must use the SELECT ... INTO ... statement—for example,

```
SELECT salary, bonus INTO v_salary, v_bonus FROM employee WHERE empno='000010';
```

However, in inline SQL PL, the SELECT … INTO … statement is *not* supported. You use the following SET statement to reach the same result instead. Remember that the SELECT statement shown previously must return only one row.

```
SET v_salary, v_bonus = (SELECT salary, bonus FROM employee WHERE empno='000010');
```

To summarize when to use which statement, refer to Table B.1.

Table B.1   Support SET and SELECT … INTO … Statements in SQL PL and Inline SQL PL

Sample SQL Statement	Supported in SQL PL	Supported in Inline SQL PL
`SET v1 = 3`	Y	Y

`SET v1 = (SELECT c1`
`FROM t1`
`        FETCH 1 ROW ONLY)`
	Y	

`        SET v1, v2 = (SELECT c1, c2`
`            FROM t1`
`            FETCH 1 ROW ONLY)`
	N	Y

`SELECT c1, c2`
`INTO v1, v2`
`FROM t1`
`FETCH 1 ROW ONLY`
	Y	N

Besides showing the list of supported statements allowed in inline SQL PL, Figure B.4 calls out the unsupported statements.

```
ALLOCATE CURSOR                    LOOP
ASSOCIATE LOCATORS                 REPEAT
DECLARE <cursor>                   RESIGNAL
DECLARE … HANDLER                  COMMIT
PREPARE                            ROLLBACK
EXECUTE
EXECUTE IMMEDIATE
```

Figure B.4   SQL procedure statements not supported in inline SQL PL.

Looking at Figure B.4, you already know the story about cursors and handlers. Therefore, any statements related to cursors and handlers are not supported.

Because the statements are dynamic, it is rational that the support of the PREPARE, EXECUTE, and EXECUTE IMMEDIATE statements are not needed. As for the LOOP and REPEAT statements, you can use the WHILE loop to implement the same logic. RESIGNAL is not supported because it can only be used within a condition handler for which it is not allowed in inline SQL PL.

Recall that a dynamic compound statement must be atomic so that all or none of the member statements commit successfully. Therefore, it does not make sense to commit or roll back any particular statement inside the block.

Stand-Alone Code

DB2 does support stand-alone codes, also known as **SQL PL scripting**. It is very straightforward to develop DB2 stand-alone codes because you have just learned about DB2 UDFs and triggers. DB2 stand-alone codes, which are the same as UDFs and triggers, are supported by DB2 inline SQL PL. Figure B.5 shows an example of the DB2 stand-alone code. The example requires a supporting table duplicate_empno, which is defined as the following:

```
CREATE TABLE duplicate_empno(empno CHAR(6))
```

The example in Figure B.5 is a utility script that can be used to quickly find out the duplicate employee number in the employee table. Assume that the data in the department table is found to be corrupted. For some reason, there are few cases of employees with the same employee ID. The code is used to quickly find the bad employee IDs for further investigation.

```
BEGIN ATOMIC                                        -- (1)
  DECLARE v_empno CHAR(6);
  DECLARE v_prev_empno CHAR(6);

  FOR c_emp AS                                      -- (2)
    SELECT empno FROM employee ORDER BY empno
```

```
DO

  SET v_empno = empno;


  IF (v_empno = v_prev_empno) THEN                       -- (3)
      INSERT INTO duplicate_empno VALUES (v_empno);
  END IF;


  SET v_prev_empno = v_empno;
  END FOR;
END                                                      -- (4)
@
```

Figure B.5   An example of DB2 stand-alone code.

A piece of stand-alone code must be encased within the BEGIN ATOMIC and END clause on Lines (1) and (4). An implicit cursor is used with a FOR loop on Line (2). The algorithm to find the duplicate IDs is to sort the IDs first and then compare each ID with the previous ID. All IDs matching their previous IDs are captured on Line (3) for further investigation.

The '@' character at the last line is the statement terminator. To execute the code, you need to save it to a file, say find_dup.db2. Then, execute the following at the command prompt:

```
db2 -td@ -f find_dup.db2
```

For more information on the statement terminator and on how to execute statements in files, refer to Appendix A, "Getting Started with DB2."

Please note that there are no duplicate employee numbers in the employee table. You need to manually insert a few rows of bad data in order to capture the duplicate employee numbers.

Choosing Between Dynamic Compound Statements and SQL Procedures

After knowing the differences between inline SQL PL and SQL PL, you are probably wondering when to choose dynamic compound statements as opposed to SQL procedures and vice versa.

First of all, both are compound statements if the SQL procedure contains more than one statement in the procedure body. Using compound statements usually improves performance because statements are grouped in one execution block. This minimizes network flow by sending only one request to DB2 for a set of statements versus one request for each statement.

At SQL procedure creation time, the procedure is compiled and a package is created. The package contains the execution path of how data will be accessed (also known as the **data access path**). In other words, the optimizer evaluates the best data access path when the procedure is being created. Depending on the query optimization class, the compile time or procedure creation time varies. On the other hand, dynamic compound statements are dynamic in nature, and data access plans are generated at execution time.

Other than understanding when dynamic compound statements and SQL procedures are being compiled, you should also take notice of the complexity of the logic you are implementing. If the logic is complex, we recommend you use SQL procedures because they support the comprehensive SQL PL with which you can easily implement efficient logic.

On other hand, if the logic is simple and the number of statements is relatively small, consider using inline SQL PL instead. With the power of SQL PL, SQL procedures can definitely handle simple logic but use of stored procedures incurs some overhead. In cases when only one or two SQL statements are wrapped inside a stored procedure, there might not be any performance gain. Sometimes it might actually negatively impact performance by using such a stored procedure. In such a case, you can probably obtain better performance results by using inline SQLs.

When inline SQLs are being executed, they are "inlined" into the calling SQL statements. These statements will be expanded to also contain the logic of the compound statements. Therefore, it is always a good practice to keep the inline SQL simple and short so that statement compilation and optimization can be performed efficiently.

Atomicity is also another area to think about. As highlighted in the previous section, commit and rollback are not allowed in dynamic compound statements because they must be atomic. If you need to implement transaction controls inside the compound statements, SQL procedures will be your only choice.

Summary

This appendix introduced you to a subset of SQL PL called inline SQL PL, which is only used by DB2 UDB for Linux, UNIX, and Windows. It is used in dynamic compound SQL statements that can be executed as stand-alone code. Dynamic compound SQL statements can also be used in triggers, SQL UDFs, and SQL methods. Because inline SQL PL does not contain all the SQL PL elements, supported as well as unsupported SQL statements were highlighted. Even though only simple logic is allowed in inline SQL PL, you can extend the power of stored procedures by calling them from within dynamic compound SQL statements.

The appendix explained that utilizing compound statements helps to improve performance. With dynamic compound statements and SQL stored procedures, there are few things to consider when choosing one over the other. First, it is crucial to understand when the data access plan is generated. Secondly, determine whether the complexity of the logic can be handled by dynamic compound statements. If so, pay attention to the size of the SQL statements that are going to be embedded. Use stored procedures if it is large and complex.

A simple example of how to use inline SQL PL in stand-alone code was demonstrated here. For more practical examples of the language usage in UDFs and triggers, Chapter 9, "User-Defined Functions and Triggers," is a must-read.

Building from the Command Line

This appendix aims to make building SQL procedures from the command line a breeze. The first part of the chapter focuses on building using LUW. Sections for iSeries and zSeries are toward the end.

Configuring the Build Environment

Because a C/C++ compiler is no longer a requirement for DB2 LUW, no configuration is needed before being able to build SQL procedures. However, you can specify options as to how DB2 builds the SQL procedure. These options can be configured at the instance level by setting the DB2_SQLROUTINE_PREOPTS DB2 registry variable or they can be configured at the SQL procedure level by calling the SET_ROUTINE_OPTS function.

To set the options at the instance level, use the DB2 registry variable

```
db2set DB2_SQLROUTINE_PREOPTS=<options>
```

where `<options>` lists the precompile options to be used. The following are the supported options:

```
BLOCKING {UNAMBIG | ALL | NO}
DATETIME {DEF | USA | EUR | ISO | JIS | LOC}
DEGREE {1 | degree-of-parallelism | ANY}
DYNAMICRULES {BIND | RUN}
EXPLAIN {NO | YES | ALL}
EXPLSNAP {NO | YES | ALL}
FEDERATED {NO | YES}
INSERT {DEF | BUF}
ISOLATION {CS |RR |UR |RS |NC}
QUERYOPT optimization-level
```

For example, to set the query optimization level to 2 and isolation level to RS for all SQL procedures to be created within the instance, you would issue the following command:

```
db2set DB2_SQLROUTINE_PREPOPTS="QUERYOPT 2 ISOLATION RS"
db2stop
db2start
```

Once you change the value of DB2_SQLROUTINE_PREOPTS, you need to restart the instance.

You can also specify the precompile options to use for the next SQL procedure compiled
from within your current session. The GET_ROUTINE_OPTS procedure can be used to return the
value of DB2_SQLROUTINE_PREOPTS. A SET_ROUTINE_OPTS procedure is used to specify the precompile options for the next compiled SQL procedure.

The following example builds on the previous example. Suppose you want to build an SQL
procedure with a query optimization level of 2, an isolation level of read stability, as well as the
ISO format for all date data types. First, you must be connected to the database. Then, issue the
following statements:

```
db2 CONNECT to sample
db2 CALL SET_ROUTINE_OPTS(GET_ROUTINE_OPTS() || ' DATETIME ISO')
db2 CREATE PROCEDURE NEWPREPOPTS RETURN 1
```

To override the value of DB2_SQLROUTINE_PREOPTS and specify particular precompile options,
use the SET_ROUTINE_OPTS procedure as demonstrated:

```
db2 CALL SET_ROUTINE_OPTS('DATETIME ISO')
```

or

```
db2 CALL SET_ROUTINE_OPTS('DATETIME ISO ISOLATION UR')
```

The SQL procedure created after the previous command will use only the precompile options
specified.

Finally, to clear the values set in either SET_ROUTINE_OPTS or DB2_SQLROUTINE_PREOPTS,
use the following technique:

```
db2 CALL SET_ROUTINE_OPTS(NULL)
```

or

```
db2set DB2_SQLROUTINE_PREPOPTS=""
db2stop
db2start
```

Building SQL Procedures

When SQL procedures are created outside of the Development Center, their definitions are typically stored in an ASCII flat file that will be sent to DB2 to process. When using this technique, you will have to change the default statement termination character by using one of the options in the DB2 command window. First, you will have to change the default statement termination by using a few options in the DB2 command window.

Options that you need to be familiar with are discussed in the following sections. All other supported options are covered briefly.

Creating a DB2 Command-Line Processor Script

The file extension does not affect how DB2 processes the file. However, the scripts used in this book end with an extension of .sql.

> **NOTE**
>
> It is important to note that the SQL procedures listed in the CLP script must be specified in an order that satisfies all dependencies. When the SQL procedure is created, the compiler will check for the existence of procedures being called at compilation time. If a calling procedure does not exist, DB2 will raise an error.

Type the complete CREATE PROCEDURE statement into the script file as you normally would. At the end of the statement, postfix it with a @ (or any other character not used in the code). This is the new statement termination character. Without it, DB2 would use the default character semicolon (;) as the statement terminator. However, because each statement inside the SQL procedure body already ends with a semicolon (;), this would cause each statement in the SQL procedure body to be executed separately as opposed to being part of the same statement. To tell DB2 to use a different statement terminator other than the default, use one of the DB2 CLP options (such as -td), which is demonstrated later in the chapter.

Before executing the script, connect to the database:

```
db2 CONNECT TO sample
```

Consider the script in Figure C.1.

```
CREATE PROCEDURE DB2ADMIN.CALC_EMP_RAISE ( IN p_EmpNum CHARACTER(6)
                                         , IN p_PerfReview INTEGER
                                         , OUT p_SugSalary DECIMAL(9,2) )
    DYNAMIC RESULT SETS 1
    LANGUAGE SQL
    SPECIFIC CALC_EMP_RAISE

P1: BEGIN
```

```
    -- Declare variables
    DECLARE v_SugSalary DECIMAL(9,2) DEFAULT 0.0;
    DECLARE v_prep_stmt VARCHAR(128) DEFAULT 'SELECT Rating, SuggestedSalary
    FROM SESSION.SalaryRange';
    -- Declare cursor
    DECLARE cursor1 CURSOR WITH RETURN FOR prep_stmt;
    -- Declare temporary table
    DECLARE GLOBAL TEMPORARY TABLE SESSION.SalaryRange
                   (Rating INT, SuggestedSalary DECIMAL(9,2));

    SELECT Salary INTO v_SugSalary
      FROM employee
     WHERE EMPNO = p_EmpNum;

    INSERT INTO SESSION.SalaryRange VALUES (1, v_SugSalary * 1.10);
    INSERT INTO SESSION.SalaryRange VALUES (2, v_SugSalary * 1.05);
    INSERT INTO SESSION.SalaryRange VALUES (3, v_SugSalary * 1.02);

    SELECT SuggestedSalary INTO p_SugSalary
      FROM SESSION.SalaryRange
     WHERE Rating = p_PerfReview;

    PREPARE prep_stmt FROM v_prep_stmt;
    -- Cursor left open for client application
    OPEN cursor1;
    RETURN 0;
END P1
@


CREATE PROCEDURE DB2ADMIN.EMP_LIST ()
    DYNAMIC RESULT SETS 1
    LANGUAGE SQL
    SPECIFIC EMP_LIST
BEGIN
    -- Declare cursor
    DECLARE cursor1 CURSOR WITH RETURN FOR
        SELECT Salary FROM employee;
    -- Cursor left open for client application
    OPEN cursor1;
END
@
```

```
CREATE PROCEDURE DB2ADMIN.PROC3 RETURN 3
@

CREATE PROCEDURE DB2ADMIN.PROC4 RETURN 4
@
```

Figure C.1   Sample DB2 CLP script containing SQL Procedure definitions.

To create the SQL procedures, issue the following command:

```
db2 -td@ -vf test_sprocs.sql
```

Now the SQL Procedure should be built and ready to use. Other options are available on the command line, see Table C.1 for their explanations.

Table C.1   CLP Options

Option Flag	Description
-a	Display SQLCA data.
-c	Automatically commit SQL statements.
-e{c|s}	Display SQLCODE or SQLSTATE. These options are mutually exclusive.
-f*filename*	Read command input from a file instead of from standard input.
-l*filename*	Log commands in a history file.
-n	Removes the newline character within a single delimited token. If this option is not specified, the newline character is replaced with a space. This option must be used with the -t option.
-o	Display output data and messages to standard output.
-p	Display a CLP prompt when in interactive input mode.
-r*filename*	Write the report generated by a command to a file.
-s	Stop execution if errors occur while executing commands in a batch file or in interactive mode.
-t	Specifies to use a semi colon (;) as the statement termination character.
-td*x*	Specifies to use *x* as the statement termination character.
-v	Echo command text to standard output.
-w	Display SQL statement warning messages.

Table C.1   CLP Options (continued)

Option Flag	Description
-x	Return data without any headers, including column names.
-zfilename	Redirect all output to a file (similar to the -r option, but includes any messages or error codes with the output).

Building SQL Procedures in DB2 UDB for iSeries

DB2 UDB for iSeries supports two basic types of procedures:

- External procedures
- SQL procedures

External procedures are programs or service programs written in a language such as C or COBOL. The supported languages are C, C++, CL, COBOL, COBOLLE, FORTRAN, Java, PLI, REXX, RPG, and RPGLE. The CREATE PROCEDURE statement corresponding to an external procedure is used basically to name the procedures, identify the parameters used by the procedures and their corresponding data types, and the location of where to find the compiled program. The statement will not compile the program for you.

SQL procedures are written entirely in SQL. SQL procedures are the focus of this book, and hence this section focuses on building SQL procedures. SQL is not just used for writing SQL procedures; it is also used to write functions and triggers. Although these routines (SQL procedures, functions, and triggers) are written entirely in SQL, when the CREATE statement for a SQL routine is issued a temporary C source file with embedded SQL statements is created. The source file is then prepared and compiled. All of this is done automatically for you. The iSeries integrated operating environment is packaged with an internal C compiler; hence, automatic compilation via the CREATE statement is possible.

The SET OPTION clause of the CREATE PROCEDURE statement (Chapter 2, "Basic SQL Procedure Structure") is used to specify processing options used to create the SQL procedure. Figure C.2 shows a syntax diagram of all the valid SET OPTION processing options when creating SQL procedures.

```
                   .-,------------------------------------.
                   V                                      |
>>-SET OPTION----+-ALWBLK = --alwblk-option---------+-+-------->< 
                 +-ALWCPYDTA = --alwcpydta-option---+
                 +-COMPILEOPT = --compile-option----+
                 +-COMMIT = --commit-option---------+
                 +-DATFMT = --datfmt-option---------+ *
                 +-DATSEP = --datsep-option---------+ *
```

```
+-DBGVIEW = --dbgview-option-------+
+-DECMPT = --decmpt-option---------+
+-DECRESULT = --decresult-option---+
+-DLYPRP = --dlyprp-option---------+
+-DYNUSRPRF = --dynusrprf-option---+
+-EVENTF = --eventf-option---------+
+-LANGID = --langid-option---------+
+-OPTLOB = --optlob-option---------+
+-OUTPUT = --output-option---------+
+-RDBCNNMTH = --rdbcnnmth-option---+
+-SQLCA = --sqlca-option-----------+
+-SQLCURRULE = --sqlcurrule-option-+
+-SQLPATH = --sqlpath-option-------+
+-SRTSEQ = --srtseq-option---------+
+-TGTRLS = --tgtrls-option---------+
+-TIMFMT = --timfmt-option---------+ *
+-TIMSEP = --timsep-option---------+ *
'-USRPRF = --usrprf-option---------'
```

Figure C.2   Simplified *SET OPTION* statement syntax diagram.

NOTE

Refer to the CREATE PROCEDURE and SET OPTION statements in the DB2 UDB for iSeries SQL Reference for a detailed description on each of the options. Some of the more commonly used ones are described here.

The options shown in Table C.2 are also valid for SQL user-defined functions and triggers, although with triggers, the DATFMT, DATSEP, TIMFMT, and TIMSEP options cannot be specified.

Table C.2   Processing Option Descriptions

Option	Valid Choices	Description
ALWBLK	*READ, *NONE, *ALLREAD	Specify if row blocking can be used and the degree to which it is used.
ALWCPYDTA	*YES, *NO, *OPTIMIZE	Specifies if a copy of the data can be used for SELECT statements.
COMMIT	*CHG, *NONE, *CS, *ALL, *RR	Specifies the isolation level to use.

Option	Valid Choices	Description
COMPILEOPT	*NONE, compile-string	Specifies additional parameters to use for the compiler command.
DATFMT	*JOB, *ISO, *EUR, *USA, *MDY, *DMY, *YMD, *JUL	Specifies format for date *JIS, columns.
DATSEP	*JOB, *SLASH, '/', *PERIOD, *COMMA, ',', *DASH, '-', *BLANK, ' '	Specifies separator for date columns.
DBGVIEW	*NONE, *SOURCE, *STMT, *LIST	Specifies to the compiler what type of debug information is required.
DECMPT	*PERIOD, *COMMA, *SYSVAL, *JOB	Specifies the format for the decimal point.
DECRESULT	(max precision, max scale, min divide scale)	Specifies the maximum precision to use for decimal operations.
DLYPRP	*YES, *NO	Specifies whether validation for dynamic statements is delayed.
DYNUSRPRF	*OWNER, *USER	Specifies which user profile to use for dynamic statements.
EVENTF	*YES, *NO	Specifies whether an event file is generated.
LANGID	*JOB, *JOBRUN, language-ID	Specifies the language identifier to use associated with SRTSEQ.
OPTLOB	*YES, *NO	Specifies whether or not to optimize LOB access through DRDA.
OUTPUT	*NONE, *PRINT	Specify whether or not to print precompiler and compiler listings.
RDBCNNMTH	*DUW, *RUW	Specifies whether to use distributed or remote unit of work for the connection.
SQLCA	*YES, *NO	Specifies whether or not to set fields in the SQLCA after each statement.
SQLCURRULE	*DB2, *STD	Specifies which SQL semantic option to use.
SLQPATH	*LIBL, path	Specifies function path for static SQL statements.

Option	Valid Choices	Description
SRTSEQ	*JOB, *HEX, *JOBRUN, *LANGIDUNQ, *LANGIDSHR, libname/startseq-table-name	Specifies which sort sequence to use for string comparisons.
TGTRLS	VxRxMx	Specifies the release on which the routine will be deployed.
TIMFMT	*HMS, *ISO, *EUR, *USA, *JIS	Specifies format for time data.
TIMSEP	*JOB, *COLON, ':', *PERIOS, '.', *COMMA, ',', *BLANK, ' '	Specifies separator for time data.
USRPRF	*OWNER, *USER, *NAMING	Specifies the user profile to implement at execution time.

If you have the DB2 CLP installed and remote access to a DB2 UDB iSeries database through DB2 CONNECT, you can use the CLP to issue commands against the database as described in he previous section.

For other methods of issuing SQL—for example, the CREATE PROCEDURE statements—see Appendix A, "Getting Started with DB2."

Building SQL Procedures in DB2 for zSeries

The DB2 UDB for z/OS V8 Application Programming and SQL Guide explains in detail how to build SQL procedures in DB2 for zSeries. In this section, the choices you have available areexplained. Note that you may need to contact your system programmer or DB2 for zSeries DBA to have him or her set up the environment required to build SQL procedures, because several levels of authorizations are involved in this process.

In DB2 for zSeries, a C/C++ compiler is required to build SQL procedures. Make sure these compilers are enabled via a parmlib member or dynamic enablement.

The Build Process

Building a SQL procedure involves three tasks:

1. Convert the SQL procedure source statements into a C language program with embedded SQL. This is performed by the SQL precompiler.
2. Create an executable load module and a DB2 package from the C language program by:
   - Precompiling the C language program to generate a DBRM and a modified C language program

- Binding the DBRM to generate a DB2 package. (Refer to the DB2 UDB for z/OS Command Reference Version 8 for the available `BIND` options.)

3. Define the SQL procedure to DB2 by executing the `CREATE PROCEDURE` statement. If you use the SQL procedure processor or the IBM DB2 Development Center to build a SQL procedure, this task is performed for you.

Methods to Build a DB2 for zSeries SQL Procedure

There are three methods available for building an SQL procedure:

- **IBM DB2 Development Center**.   Building DB2 for zSeries SQL procedures using the Development Center is similar to building SQL procedures for LUW. Behind the scenes in the case of zSeries, however, the Development Center invokes the SQL procedure processor DSNTPSMP to perform the build at the DB2 for zSeries server. Refer to Appendix D, "Using the DB2 Development Center," for more details.

- **DB2 for zSeries SQL procedure processor (DSNTPSMP)**.   The SQL procedure processor, DSNTPSMP, is a REXX-stored procedure that performs the three build process steps described in the previous section. As with any other stored procedure, it can be invoked using the SQL `CALL` statement. As mentioned earlier, the SQL procedure processor is also invoked from the Development Center.

NOTE
Before you can run DSNTPSMP, the following needs to be set up:

- Install DB2 UDB for z/OS REXX Language Support.

- Create a program that uses the SQL `CALL` statement.

- Set up a WLM environment in which to run DSNTPSMP.

The first and third tasks are commonly performed by your system's programmer or DBA.

- **JCL**. With this method, you manually have to code a JCL job using the three steps described earlier in the build process section. Your JCL job will need to do the following:

1. Preprocess the `CREATE PROCEDURE` statement by executing program DSNHPC, with the `HOST(SQL)` option. This process converts the SQL procedure source statements into a C language program.

2. Precompile the C language source program that was generated in Step 1.

3. Compile and link-edit the modified C source statements that were produced in Step 1. Ensure that the compiler options include the option `NOSEQ`.

4. Bind the DBRM that was produced in Step 1 into a package.

5. Define the SQL procedure to DB2 (puts the SQL procedure definition in the DB2 for zSeries Catalog) by executing the CREATE PROCEDURE statement for the SQL procedure.

As you can see, whereas in DB2 for LUW a CREATE PROCEDURE statement issued from the CLP is enough to build your SQL procedure, for DB2 for zSeries this is not the case. The recommended method to build your SQL procedure is to use the Development Center.

NOTE

Connecting to a DB2 for zSeries subsystem from a CLP client and issuing the CREATE PRO-CEDURE statement will give you syntax errors. To build a DB2 for zSeries SQL procedure from the CLP, you need to invoke the DSNTPSMP SQL procedure processor.

Summary

This appendix introduced the concept of building SQL procedures from the command line. The process, though slightly different on the various platforms, is fairly straightforward. By familiarizing yourself with the options on your platform, you can help ensure more efficient procedure execution and optimization.

Using the DB2 Development Center

The DB2 Development Center (DC) shown in Figure D.1 is an easy-to-use, integrated development environment (IDE) for building and debugging DB2 application objects.

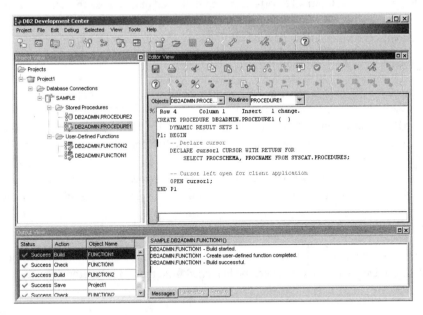

Figure D.1   The DB2 Development Center.

With the Development Center, you can:

- Create, build, and deploy Java and SQL stored procedures
- Debug SQL stored procedures using the integrated debugger
- Create, build, and deploy user-defined functions (UDFs)

TIP

A Microsoft .NET Visual Studio add-in is also available for DB2 which allows you to easily develop DB2 applications using a unified development environment.

Installing the DB2 Development Center

The Development Center is packaged with all DB2 UDB for Linux, UNIX, and Windows server installation CDs as well as with the DB2 Application Development Client CD. The CD that accompanies this book is a trial version of the server edition of the product.

For all new development efforts, it is recommended that you use the latest available FixPak to take advantage of performance enhancements and bug fixes. Be sure to apply the same FixPak level at both servers and clients (if separate).

TIP

DB2 v8.2 for LUW is the same as DB2 v8.1 for LUW with FixPak 7 applied.

DB2 FixPaks and client software are available for free download at `http://www.software`
`.ibm.com/data/db2/udb/support.html`. Follow the link for DB2 UDB Version 8 FixPaks and Clients.

In general, this chapter is written for an LUW user; however, iSeries and zSeries users can refer to the sections at the end of the chapter to obtain their platform-specific information.

DB2 for Windows

Before you do anything, check to ensure that the Development Center has not already been installed. The Development Center can be launched from the DB2 Development Tools menu (see Figure D.2).

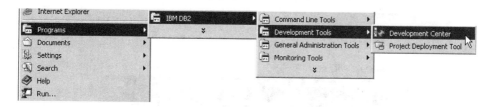

Figure D.2   The Development Center menu location in Windows.

Windows allows for three types of installation: Typical, Minimal, and Custom. When using a typical installation, Application Development Tools is included by default, and so is the DB2 Development Center.

If you perform a custom installation of DB2, ensure that the Development Center (under Application Development Tools) option is selected, as illustrated in Figure D.3.

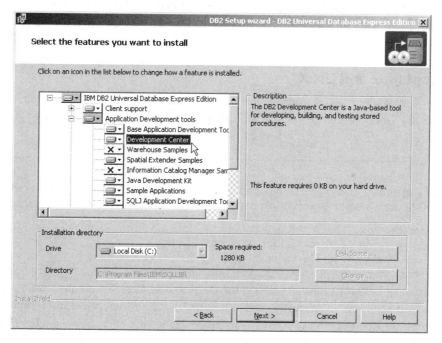

Figure D.3   Selecting the installation of DB2 Development Center during a custom installation.

If you have already installed DB2 but did not select Application Development Tools, you can change your existing installation from the Windows Control Panel (Add/Remove Programs).

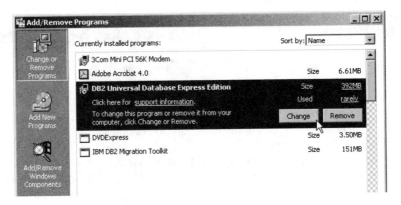

Figure D.4   Using Windows Control Panel to modify an existing DB2 installation.

The DB2 installer will look for the required files from previously known install locations. If the required files are not found, you will be prompted to provide the location of a DB2 installation image.

DB2 for Linux and UNIX

Before you do anything, check to ensure that the Development Center has already been installed. To launch the Development Center, log into the system as an instance user (such as db2inst1) and type db2dc.

TIP

The Development Center (db2dc) can also be run from a non-instance user that has sourced the DB2 instance environment script db2profile.

Here's an example:
- $ source /home/db2inst1/sqllib/db2profile
- $ /home/db2inst1/sqllib/db2profile

When installing DB2 for Linux and UNIX, the Development Center is not installed by default, because these platforms are typically used as servers. Be sure to select a custom install if you intend to use the Linux or UNIX system to run the Development Center. Select the Development Center (under Application Development Tools) option as illustrated in Figure D.5.

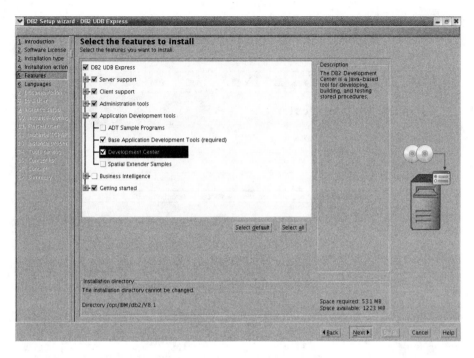

Figure D.5   Selecting the installation of the Development Center.

If you have already installed DB2 but did not select the Development Center, simply run the installation again using the same image. You do not have to uninstall. If you have applied a Fix-Pak since the original installation, you will have to reapply it before attempting to start DB2 again.

Using the Development Center for the First Time

The first time you launch the Development Center, you will be greeted with the Development Center Launchpad. Click the Create Project button at the top-left corner of the window to begin (see Figure D.6).

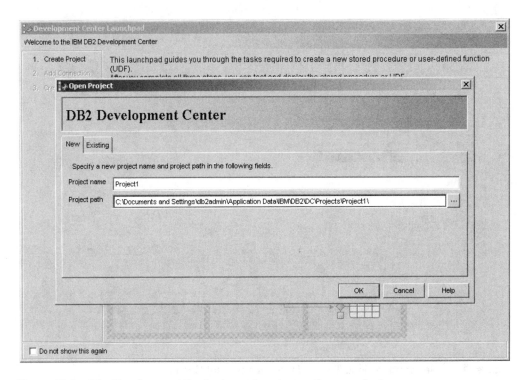

Figure D.6   The Development Center Launchpad—creating a project.

To start developing database application objects, you must first create a new project. A **project** is a logical grouping of related database application objects. The set of all objects in a project, however, may only be a subset of all database application objects already existing on a system.

For example, a single database may be shared by two different applications called Application A and B. Each application has its own unique set of stored procedures and functions stored in the same database. You might, then, define a project that contains only objects for Application A, and a separate project that only contains objects for Application B. In this way, you can limit your workspace to include only those objects related to the immediate task at hand. It is also possible to open and work with multiple projects at the same time. Projects will be discussed in more detail later.

The second step of the launchpad helps you define a connection for the project. Click Add Connection (see Figure D.7).

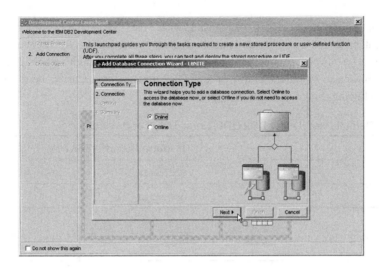

Figure D.7   Defining an online connection for a project.

An **online connection** means that the database is accessible immediately. Generally, this is what you want to do. You would create an **offline connection** if the database is not currently available for connection. Click Next to continue.

DB2 then prompts you to select the database connection from the pull-down menu (see Figure D.8). The SAMPLE database is selected in this case. If you want to access a remote database but is not configured on your client, you can click the Add button.

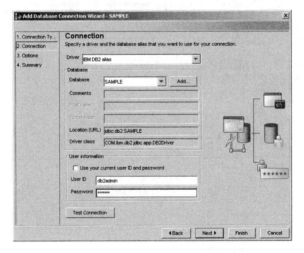

Figure D.8   Select a database and provide connection information.

Before you can move to the next step, you must provide a user ID and password for connecting to the selected database. You may provide a user ID and password explicitly, or use your current network user ID and password. Remember that DB2 uses operating system authentication services. If you do not have a solid understanding of how DB2 implements security, we recommend that you use the following shown in Table D.1.

Table D.1   Default User IDs for DB2 UDB Linux, UNIX, and Windows

Platform	Platform Default SYSADM
Windows	db2admin
UNIX/Linux	db2inst1

Before continuing, verify that the connection works by clicking the Test Connection button.

TIP

After the first two steps, you can usually accept the remaining defaults and click Finish without viewing the remaining steps of the wizard.

The final step displays a summary of the connection (see Figure D.9). Click Finish to create the connection. This will return you to the Development Center Launchpad.

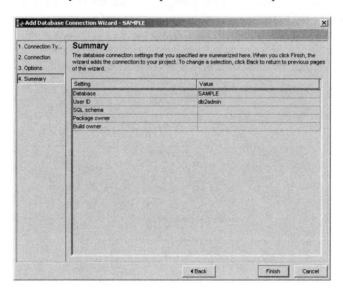

Figure D.9   The connection summary.

Now that you have a project (Project1) and a database connection object (to SAMPLE), the launchpad can help you create your first stored procedure. Click Create Object, and you will see the New Object dialog. Click OK to invoke the Create SQL Procedure Wizard (see Figure D.10.)

For the purposes of our example, however, you can directly click the Finish button to accept all defaults and create your first stored procedure (but feel free to step all the way through the wizard if you want). This will create a small sample procedure.

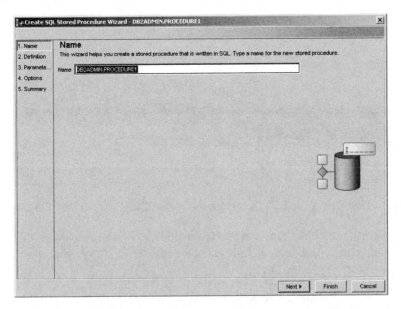

Figure D.10   Creating a sample stored procedure.

You can now close the launchpad to view the fruits of your labor in the Development Center interface.

TIP

The launchpad can be opened after the Development Center has started by selecting the Launchpad option from the Project menu.

The procedure created appears as PROCEDURE1 in the SAMPLE database's stored procedure folder. You can see in the Output view (bottom-left corner) that the build was successful (see Figure D.11).

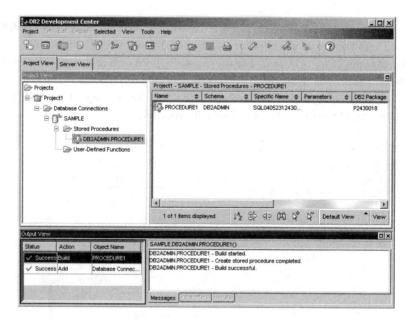

Figure D.11   First look at the DB2 Development Center IDE.

The source code for an object can be retrieved by double-clicking its icon, pressing CTRL-E while highlighting the object, or by right-clicking it and selecting the Edit menu item. This will open the Editor View (see Figure D.12).

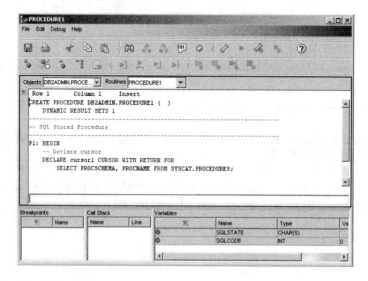

Figure D.12   The Editor View.

Development Center Views

The Development Center has four main views (as shown in Figure D.13):

- **Server view.** Allows you to look at objects that exist at the server, which may or not be part of your current project. From the Server view, you can import objects into your current project so that it also appears in your Project view.

- **Project view.** Allows you to navigate between projects. Currently, only one project is open (Project1). It is also possible to open multiple projects at the same time.

- **Output view.** Keeps a history of actions taken and resulting messages of each action.

- **Editor view.** Not opened by default, but you have seen it already (refer to Figure D.12). It is opened automatically if you edit or view source code for an object. When you launch the Editor view, you may notice that the Editor window is its own stand-alone window (by default). In some cases, it can be inefficient to switch between the main Development Center window and the Editor view. Therefore, in the next section, we show you how to customize Development Center to help you be more productive.

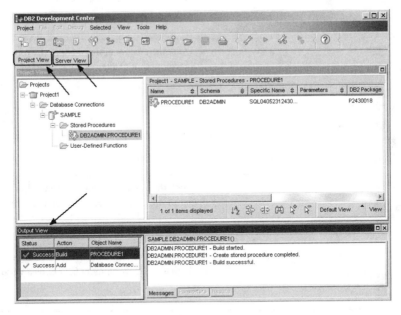

Figure D.13   The views of Development Center.

Customizing the Development Center

All the Development Center views are dockable and can be rearranged to your preferences. To rearrange a dockable component, simply use a mouse to grab the view's header and drag it to the desired location.

> **TIP**
>
> To identify dockable components in the Development Center, move the mouse icon around the screen until you see the hand icon.

When you click and hold the mouse on the component, the hand icon will change to the closed hand icon. While holding the mouse button, drag the icon to various parts of the screen to rearrange the component. By dragging the mouse to various parts of the Development Center interface, you will see a separate indicator appear indicating how to component will be docked if the mouse button was released.

Dozens of docking orientations are possible. A few of them are listed in Table D.2 as examples. The indicator that appears depends on where you drag a component.

Table D.2   Examples of Available Docking Orientations

Guide	Position
	Dock the current component to the top half of the Development Center as the first tab.
	Dock the current component to the top half of the Development Center as the second tab.
	Dock the current component to the lower-left corner of the Development Center as a window.
	Dock the current component to the lower-right corner of the Development Center as a window.
	Dock the current component to the right-hand window of the Development Center as a window.

To illustrate, let's walk through the process of re-arranging components as illustrated in Figure D.14. The following customizations will be made:

- The Editor view will be docked into the main the Development Center window.
- The debugging views will be hidden.

- The Server view will be closed.
- The Project view will be simplified.

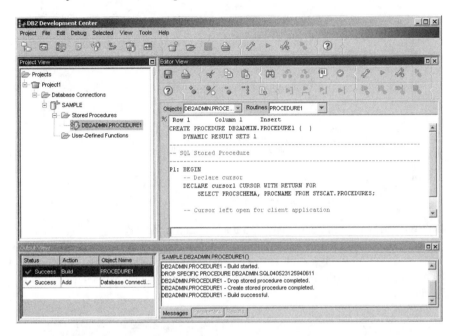

Figure D.14   A customized Development Center.

Open the Editor view on the procedure PROCEDURE1, as shown in Figure D.15.

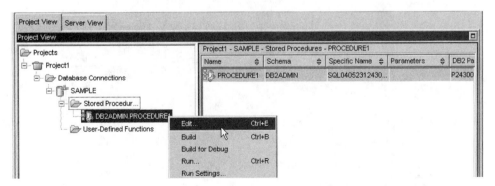

Figure D.15   Opening the Editor view on source code for PROCEDURE1.

The Editor view will be opened in its own window. Wave the mouse around the Editor window (near the top) until you see the white hand icon, as shown in Figure D.16.

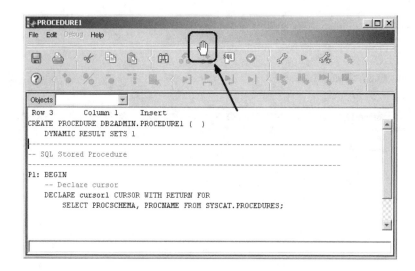

Figure D.16   Grabbing the Editor view as a docking component.

Click, hold, and drag to the top-right corner of Development Center. Look for a pop-up image like the one you see in Figure D.17, which indicates how the window will be docked in Development Center.

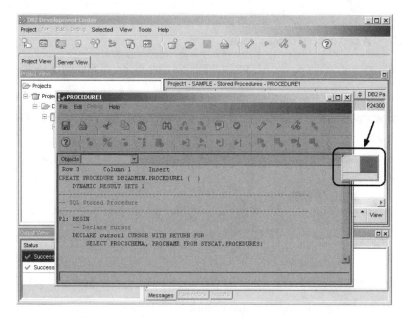

Figure D.17   Docking the Editor view into the main Development Center interface.

The Editor view then becomes docked within the main interface of the Development Center. After a docking operation, you may have to resize the Editor window so that the Editor view is of usable size. You can also hide the debugging views in the Editor to free up space by toggling the Show Debug Views button (see Figure D.18).

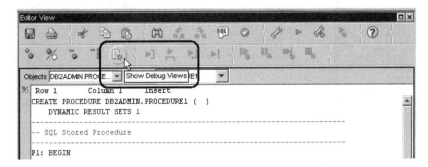

Figure D.18 Toggling Show/Hide Debug views.

You can also remove windows that you don't immediately need. Select the Server View tab, and close the window by clicking the Close Window button, as illustrated in Figure D.19.

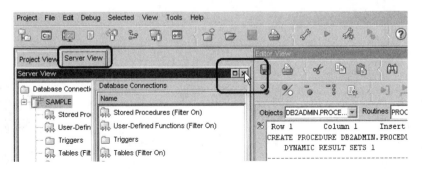

Figure D.19 Closing the Server view.

To bring back the Server view, you can always re-open it from the View menu.

The only remaining view in the top-left corner is the Project view. The Project view window is divided awkwardly, however. You can refine this layout by sliding the divider out of the way to the right (see Figure D.20).

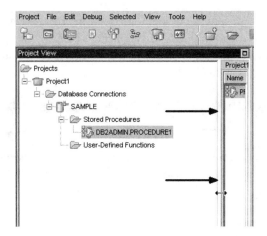

Figure D.20   Resizing the Project view panel.

The final layout should now look like Figure D.21.

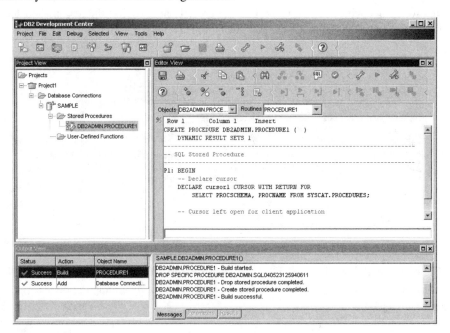

Figure D.21   The final customized Development Center.

Of course, this is just an example of what you can do. You should experiment with docking windows in different places to see which orientations make you most productive. If you ever get into a situation where the windows become severely disoriented, you can always start over by selecting Reset Views from the View menu.

Running Procedures

Continuing our example from the previous section, you can run procedure PROCEDURE1. Before a procedure can run, it must first successfully build on the database. Table D.3 contains the icons related to running procedures.

Table D.3 Icons for Building and Running Procedures and Functions

Icon		Description
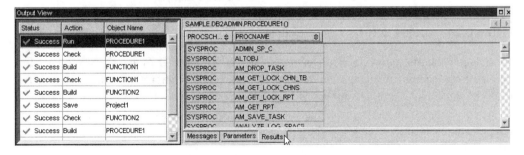	Build	Build the current object.
	Run	Runs the current procedure or function. If the object has not been built or has been updated since the last build, the Development Center can automatically (re)build it before running it.

PROCEDURE1 is fairly simple. It executes the following SQL statement:

```
SELECT PROCSCHEMA, PROCNAME FROM SYSCAT.PROCEDURES;
```

The resulting rows are returned to the application as a result set (the Development Center, in this case), where the rows in the cursor are fetched.

Select PROCEDURE1 and click the Run button. The Development Center detects that a cursor has been returned and automatically fetches rows back from it.

You will be able to see the rows fetched back in the Results tab of the Output view, as shown in Figure D.22.

Figure D.22 Viewing data returned by cursors in the Development Center.

If you are running a function or a procedure with OUT parameters, the results will appear in the Parameters tab of the Output view (see Figure D.23). PROCEDURE1 does not have any parameters. Therefore, no values are listed here.

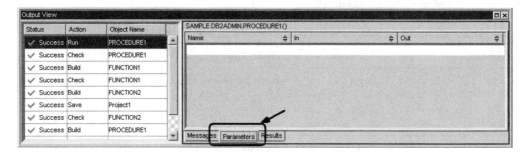

Figure D.23   Viewing input and output parameter values in the Development Center.

Stored Procedure Run Settings

Additional Run options are available in the Development Center (see Figure D.24).

Figure D.24   Setting stored procedure settings.

By changing the run settings of a procedure, as shown in Figures D.24 and D.25, you have the option of not having any changes committed. With this option, after a procedure has finished executing all changes will be automatically rolled back. This is useful for keeping the state of the database consistent while you debug your code. Scripts can also be set to run before or after the procedure executes. This gives you greater control over the testing environment of stored procedures.

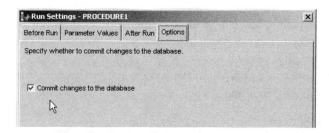

Figure D.25   Setting stored procedure Run options.

Debugging Stored Procedures

The Development Center offers a complete range of debugging tools for stepping through a procedure. The debugger is integrated into the Editor View. When a debug session is started, the Development Center will either open up a window for the current procedure or use an existing window if the procedure is already being edited.

The following icons shown in Table D.4 are used to initiate and terminate a debug session.

Table D.4   Debugger-Related Icons

Icon	Action	Description
	Build for debug	Builds a stored procedure in debug mode.
	Run with debug	Run a stored procedure in debug mode. This button is enabled only if the procedure was built for debug.
	Pause debug	Temporarily stop debugging.
	Resume debug	Resumes a paused debug.
	Terminate	Stop run in debug mode. Uncommitted changes will be rolled back.

A procedure must be built in debug mode in order for the debugging capabilities to be used. If a procedure is built in regular mode, attempts to run it in debug mode will result in the procedure simply being run normally.

Once a procedure is run in debug mode, you can use the stepping buttons shown in Table D.5 to walk though lines of code one by one.

Table D.5   Icons for Controlling Debugger Stepping

Icon	Action	Description
▷]	Step into	Trace through code one line at a time.
▷|	Step to cursor	Runs the procedure to the line of code where the cursor is currently placed or the next breakpoint.
▷⌐	Step over	Execute a block of code or a call to nested procedure without stepping through their sub steps. This allows you to avoid tracing entire blocks of code in which you are not interested.
▷▷	Run to completion	Run the procedure to the end ignoring all breakpoints.
▷⌐	Step return	Exit the procedure immediately from the current point in the code.

As you step through code in debug mode, you can view the state of all variables in the variables section of the Debug view (see Figure D.26).

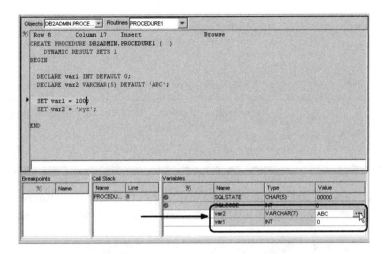

Figure D.26   Viewing and changing variable values in a debugging session.

TIP

When execution has paused in debug mode, variable values can be manually changed mid-flight if required (with the exception of SQLCODE and SQLSTATE).

A procedure can often be quite long, and having to step through many lines of code to reach the section of interest can be quite tedious. To alleviate this, a breakpoint can be added to the code which will halt the execution of a procedure when that point is reached by the debugger. Multiple breakpoints can be added to a procedure, and each breakpoint will be indicated by a red dot. A breakpoint is useful if you want to check the current values of a variable at a particular point in the code to ensure that the procedure is performing as expected.

The buttons shown in Table D.6 are used to manipulate breakpoints.

Table D.6   Icons for Setting and Manipulating Breakpoints in the Development Center

Icon	Action	Description
✛⬤	Add breakpoint	Adds a breakpoint at the current cursor position.
➖⬤	Remove breakpoint	Removes the breakpoint at the current cursor position.

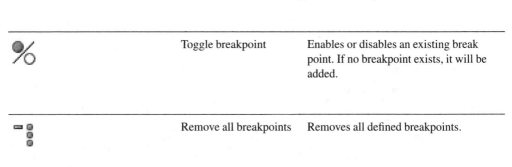

	Toggle breakpoint	Enables or disables an existing break point. If no breakpoint exists, it will be added.
	Remove all breakpoints	Removes all defined breakpoints.

A breakpoint can also be added, removed, and toggled by clicking in the leftmost column of the Editor view while the arrow is on the line of code where the break should occur (see Figure D.27).

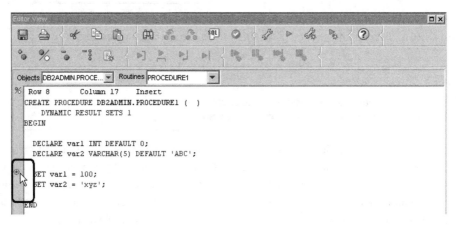

Figure D.27   Adding a breakpoint.

A breakpoint in a procedure can be reached by clicking the Step to Cursor icon. The code will execute until the current cursor position or the first breakpoint is reached.

Debugging Nested Stored Procedures

A stored procedure may call additional procedures as they execute, which can make debugging complicated. The Development Center Debugger has been designed to simplify this task. The parent stored procedure in which the debugger is initially started must be built in debug mode. When another procedure is called, at each nested level it is checked to see if it is also in debug mode. If the nested procedure has not been built in debug mode, it will be executed normally until it completes. If the nested procedure is also in debug mode, an edit window will be opened for it, and the debugger will begin to step through it. Consider the example shown in Table D.7.

Table D.7   Example of Debugging a Nested Stored Procedure

Procedure	Debug Mode	Procedure Called
Proc1	Debug	Proc2
Proc2	Debug	Proc3
Proc3	Normal	Proc4
Proc4	Debug	

Table D.7 represents a series of stored procedure calls: Proc1 calls Proc2 which calls Proc3 which calls Proc4. All are built-in debug mode except for Proc3. A developer initially debugs Proc1 by stepping through it. The debugger will execute the procedure one line at a time until the call to Proc2 is reached. An edit window for Proc2 will then be opened, and it will be stepped through because was built in debug mode. The debugger will stop when the call to Proc3 is reached and will run the procedure normally. The debugger will renew stepping through the code when the call by Proc3 to Proc4 is reached. Upon the completion of Proc4, the debugger will return to running Proc3 normally without any debugging options. At the completion of Proc3, the debugger will resume stepping through the procedure in Proc2's edit window. Upon completion of Proc2, the debugger will return to the original calling Proc1. Debugging will finish once Proc1 completes.

More complex debugging tasks can also be accomplished by adding breakpoints in nested procedures, as shown in Table D.8. The initial procedure will run normally until the breakpoint is reached in a nested procedure. The nested procedure with the breakpoint must be built in debug mode to allow the procedure to be stepped through once the breakpoint is reached. The nested break points can be reached by using the Step to Cursor icon. If multiple breakpoints are embedded in the procedures, then clicking on the icon again will cause the program to execute until the next breakpoint is reached.

Table D.8   Example of Debugging a Nested Stored Procedure Using Breakpoints

Procedure	DebugMode	Procedure Called
ProcA	Debug	ProcB
ProcB	Normal	ProcC
ProcC	Debug	(with breakpoint)

In Table D.8, procedure ProcA is run in debug mode. The Step to Cursor icon is then clicked. ProcA makes a call to ProcB, which will be executed normally, and the code will not be debugged. The execution will continue until ProcB calls ProcC and the breakpoint in ProcC is reached. You can then step through ProcC starting from the breakpoint. Upon completion of

ProcC, the debugger will return to executing ProcB normally until its completion. Finally, ProcA will be stepped through until it is completed.

Combining the mixture of debugged and non-debugged procedures with breakpoints allows problems that may be buried many levels down in a nested procedure to be found and tested easily. The procedures can be tested for correctness by ensuring that the top-level procedure is performing correctly until the first nested procedure call. A breakpoint can then be added just after the call so that earlier tested code does not have to be stepped through. As each layer of procedure is fully tested, the breakpoint can be moved or the procedure can be removed from being debugged completely by building it in normal mode. Stored procedures that call dozens of other procedures or are thousands of lines long can then be tested on a component or sectional basis without having to re-test code.

Working with Projects

The Development Center uses projects to logically group a set of related application objects for the developer. A project can even reference application objects from multiple databases. There can also be multiple and varying copies of the same procedure open in different projects. Each project will have its own local copy of all its procedures. This code can be saved, and it will not overwrite copies from other projects. The procedure code will be saved into the database when it is built. If a different copy of the procedure from another project is built, the new code from the second project will overwrite the code from the first project at the database server. Example 1 illustrates this concept.

Example 1:

Two projects, projectA and projectB, both contain a copy of procedure procTest from the same database.

User1 opens up projectA and edits its copy of procTest to have a return code of 4.

User2 opens up projectB and also edits its copy of procTest to have a return code of 3. There are now two versions of the procedure open.

User1 then builds procTest. If the procedure is now run, the return code will be 4. The code for procTest that User2 has open is not affected by User1's actions.

User2 then builds her copy of procTest. User2 will be asked if she wants to drop the old copy of the procedure (built by User1) and build a new one. If she chooses to build the procedure, then the return code of the procedure will be 3.

New projects can be created by selecting New Project from the Project pull-down menu. Multiple projects can be open in the Development Center at the same time. Projects can be opened from the Project pull-down menu by selecting the Open option. The Remove Project option will delete the project from memory but will not delete the application objects that were successfully built on the database. Be sure to save all your projects to ensure that all your changes to the project are kept. If you do not save the project and have not built the stored procedure, then your changes will be lost. Procedure changes will not take effect on the database until they are built, despite the project having been saved.

Importing Stored Procedures

Often, an SQL procedure that you want to work with has already been written by someone else or exists in another project. The Development Center allows you to quickly create a new procedure from code that is saved elsewhere.

Once you have opened up a project, you can import a procedure by right-clicking on the Stored Procedure folder icon and selecting Import, as illustrated in Figure D.28.

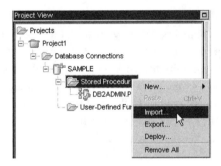

Figure D.28   Importing a stored procedure.

There are two sources from which a procedure can be imported: The procedure can be directly extracted from a database, or it can be read in from a file. The database import option allows you to use filters to limit the search for procedures that may exist in a database. The file system option will allow you to either import a procedure from a file or from another project. These two options are shown in Figure D.29.

Figure D.29   Import from a file or another database.

All SQL procedures used in this book are included in files on the book's CD, and are named based on chapter and figure numbers. When you import a procedure, a number of options are available that allow you to alter the properties and specifics of the procedure. These options should not be altered when you initially work with the sample procedures, but you are free to experiment with them as you become more comfortable with DB2 and SQL PL.

Another convenient way to import database application objects directly from a database is through the Server View in the Development Center. If your Server View is not open, open it from the View menu. In the Server View, you will see the procedures that currently exist on the database. Right-click on any object and select Add to Project (see Figure D.30).

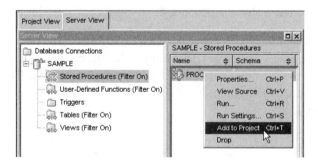

Figure D.30   Adding procedures to your project from the Server View.

> **TIP**
>
> If you want to add multiple objects to your project, use the Import feature from the Project View. If you want to quickly add only one or few objects, using Add to Project from the Server View is faster.

DB2 for iSeries Considerations

In order to connect to an iSeries server, the DB2 Development Center requires DB2 Connect for a connection that uses Distributed Relational Database Architecture (DRDA). Because the DB2 Development Center is a Java application, it also requires the iSeries Toolbox for Java JDBC driver for the JDBC connection. This driver can be downloaded at `http://www.ibm.com/servers/eserver/iseries/toolbox/`.

DB2 Enterprise Server Edition (ESE) for LUW comes packaged with DB2 Connect functionality, although if you are using the DB2 Application Development Client, then you will need DB2 Connect for a DRDA connection. (The CD packaged with this book is a trial server version of DB2 for LUW.)

Assuming you have access to the Development Center and connectivity through DB2 Connect, you will be able to use this environment for many development tasks available to DB2 for Linux, UNIX, and Windows, but not all. Specifically, the tasks that cannot be performed are debugging stored procedures and creating, building, and deploying user-defined functions (UDFs).

> **TIP**
>
> To debug stored procedures, you can use the IBM Toolbox for Java iSeries System Debugger, which is easily launched from the iSeries Navigator SQL Script window. A document showing how to accomplish this can be found at `http://www.ibm.com/servers/enable/site/education/abstracts/sqldebug_abs.html`.

The option to debug stored procedures natively always exists. By using the `SET OPTION DBGVIEW=*SOURCE` statement in the procedure declaration, the native debugger (`STRDBG`) or the GUI debugger (found under the Run pull-down menu on the Run SQL Scripts window) can be used.

For further reference on using the Development Center, a document showing the use of (a slightly older version) of the Development Center with iSeries can be found at `http://www.ibm.com/servers/enable/site/education/astracts/db2dev_abs.html`.

For developing UDFs', other interfaces—such as the Run SQL Scripts window of the iSeries Navigator—can be used, as well as native iSeries interfaces (`STRSQL`, `RUNSQLSTM`).

DB2 for zSeries Considerations

The Development Center can be obtained by ordering the DB2 Management Clients Package, a non-priced feature of DB2 for zSeries that is ordered separately. This package also includes DB2

Connect software that allows a DB2 LUW client to connect to DB2 for zSeries. If you have DB2 LUW Enterprise Server Edition (which comes with DB2 Connect capability) or have installed DB2 Connect software separately, you may not need to order the DB2 Management Clients Package to obtain the Development Center. Simply download the free DB2 LUW Application Development Client as mentioned in previous sections, and with DB2 Connect you will be able to connect to DB2 for zSeries.

Environment Settings

DB2 for zSeries has specific build options that can be specified in the Environment Settings window (see Figure D.31). To reach this window, choose Project > Environment Settings > Build Options.

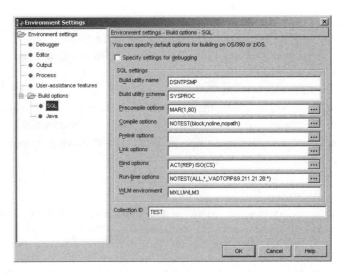

Figure D.31   DB2 for zSeries build options.

The only field you may want to change depending on your system settings is the WLM environment field. For the example, we chose MXLUWLM3 because this is the WLM environment created for stored procedures in the mainframe system where we tested our procedures. Other than this field, leaving the default values is normally good enough.

The build utility name field is where you specify the name of the SQL Procedure processor, which by default is DSNTPSMP. You may have multiple copies of the DSNTPSMP processor using different schema names. The reason you may do this is to support different datasets in the WLM proc used by DSNTPSMP. For example, you may use DEV.DSNTPSMP to create a development version of an SQL stored procedure that writes to dev.runlib.load. Then you might have PROD.DSNTPSP in order to create a production version of the same procedure that writes to prod.runlib.load. Different WLM environments and JCL procs would be needed to support this type of configuration.

Developing SQL Stored Procedures from the Development Center

When the launchpad is used to create a new project, the Options tab has information specific to DB2 for zSeries, as shown in Figure D.32.

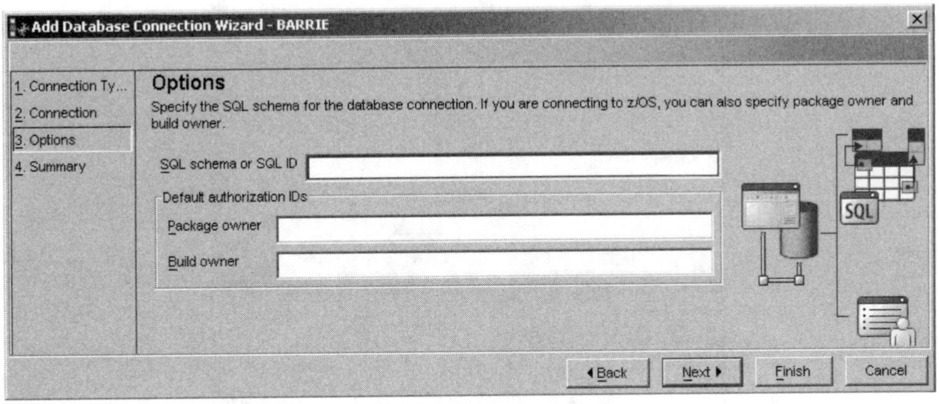

Figure D.32   Launchpad options specific to DB2 for zSeries.

In the Package Owner field, you can type the authorization ID of the owner of the DB2 package that will be stored in DB2 for zSeries containing the SQL of the stored procedure. This owner should have the appropriate privileges to execute the SQL in the stored procedure. If you leave this field blank, the ID used to connect to the database is used as the default.

In the Build Owner field, you can type the authorization ID of the person or group in charge of building, rebuilding, and dropping a stored procedure. You can type a secondary authorization ID or a group name if you want several users to share this responsibility. If you leave this field blank, the ID used to connect to the database is used as the default.

The Project and Server Views

Figure D.33 shows the project SQLPLBook containing a connection to the DB2 LUW SAMPLE database, and a connection to the DB2 for zSeries MEXICO subsystem from the Project View tab. Note that for DB2 for zSeries, there is only an option to develop stored procedures. DB2 for zSeries UDFs cannot be developed from this tool.

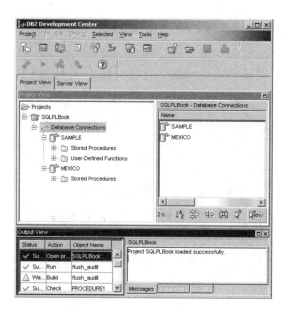

Figure D.33   DB2 for zSeries Project view.

Figure D.34 shows the Server view for both the DB2 LUW SAMPLE database and the DB2 for zSeries MEXICO subsystem. In this view, DB2 for zSeries stored procedures and triggers can be reviewed.

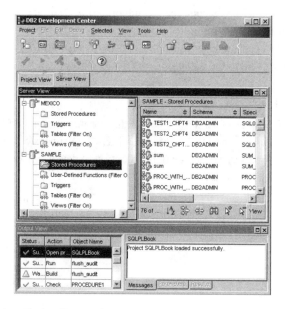

Figure D.34   DB2 for zSeries Server view.

Debugging DB2 for zSeries SQL Stored Procedures

DB2 for zSeries SQL stored procedures can be debugged from the Development Center using the integrated SQL debugger. A detailed discussion of the prerequisites, setup, and use of this tool can be obtained from the Redbook "DB2 for z/OS Stored Procedures: Through the CALL and Beyond" which can be found at this web site:

`http://www.redbooks.ibm.com/redbooks/pdfs/sg247083.pdf.`

Summary

The DB2 Development Center is a powerful IDE for developing stored procedures in all DB2 platforms. For DB2 LUW, user-defined functions can also be developed. By defining multiple projects (which may share the same database), you can manage related database application objects with ease. The integrated debugger allows you to debug complex SQL procedures, even if they make nested procedure calls. Debugging concepts and strategies were highlighted, and more help on the Development Center is available from the documentation provided with the product.

Security Considerations in SQL Procedures

Controlling access to the information stored in a database is a key requirement for almost all database implementations. DB2 offers database administrators a number of options on how they can control the access, creation, and manipulation of data in their systems. These privileges range from being allowed to read from a table using a SELECT statement to restricting users from creating new tables.

Stored procedures can perform a wide range of operations, including working with data and executing DDL. When building the procedures, it is important to consider who will need to be able to execute the procedures and what level of privileges they will need. It is also important to understand what is happening behind the scenes when a procedure is created.

This appendix provides an overview on security on each of the platforms. The platform-specifc documentation on security should be referenced for a more detailed view on security.

Privileges

When an SQL procedure is created, its procedure body is converted into DB2 bytecode and a corresponding package will be created. This bytecode is then executed by the database engine when the stored procedure is called. A **package** is an object in the database that contains the access method which DB2 will use for an application (or a procedure in this case). Privileges can be given to users to execute, bind, and control a package. This will be discussed in more detail later in the appendix.

Now that you understand that SQL procedures are actually database packages, let's talk about what privileges are required to create and execute them. There are basically two groups of users who need some kind of privileges to work with SQL procedures: developers and users.

Privileges Required by Developers

The first group is **development**, which includes developers who write and create the procedures. Developers need to have the privilege to create procedures.

Privileges Required by LUW Stored Procedure Developers

The developer, or group of developers, can be given the necessary privileges by using the DB2 GRANT command. In order to create a package, they need the CREATE_NOT_FENCED_ROUTINE privilege, a database-level privilege that allows them to add a procedure to a database. Refer to the SQL Reference Guide for the complete syntax of the GRANT statement. A user can be granted this privilege by issuing this command:

```
GRANT CREATE NOT_FENCED_ROUTINE ON DATABASE TO USER db2dev
```

The user will also need to have BINDADD privileges to allow him or her to create new packages in the database. Each procedure needs a package so the procedure cannot be created without this authority. Here is an example of how to grant the BINDADD privilege to a user:

```
GRANT CREATE_NOT_FENCED_ROUTINE ON DATABASE TO USER db2dev
```

Besides the BINDADD privilege, developers also need proper privileges to access database objects referenced within the procedures. Privileges can be granted to each developer individually or to the developer group—for example:

```
GRANT SELECT, DELETE ON TABLE employee TO USER db2dev
GRANT SELECT, UPDATE ON TABLE employee TO GROUP db2dgrp
```

In DB2, table privileges granted to groups only apply to dynamic statements. This means that if the procedure contains static SQL statements, table privileges must be granted to each developer individually or to PUBLIC. Otherwise, creation of such an SQL procedure will fail with insufficient privileges—for example:

```
GRANT SELECT, DELETE ON TABLE employee TO USER db2dev
GRANT SELECT, UPDATE ON TABLE employee TO PUBLIC
```

PUBLIC is not considered as a group but it instead represents every user who accesses the database.

If the underlying objects that the stored procedure references—such as a table or view—are dropped or are changed, then the package will have to be re-bound. The rebinding will occur implicitly when the package is next used. If, however, the package was dependent on a UDF that was dropped and re-created, an explicit REBIND command will have to issued for the package.

Privileges Required by iSeries Stored Procedure Developers

Figure E.1 shows what occurs when a create procedure is issued on iSeries. It will help you understand what privileges are required to create a stored procedure. Recall that a stored procedure is converted to C code, and compiled into an executable program.

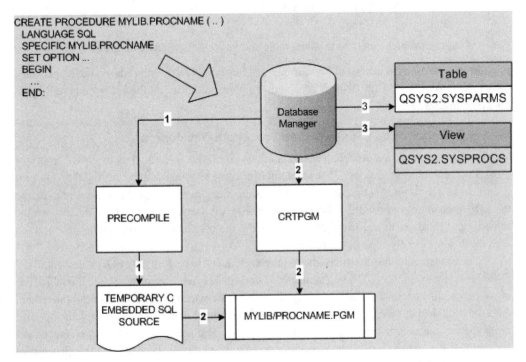

Figure E.1   Stored procedure creation on iSeries.

When a stored procedure is created, it is precompiled. The precompile step changes the SQL procedure into a C program, replacing the SQL statements in the original procedure with linkages to the iSeries system services which implement the statement (1). Directives to the compiler are passed via the SET OPTION clause of the CREATE PROCEDURE statement. A program object is then created using the CRTPGM command, taking the C source code as input (2). The system catalog tables and views are updated to register the stored procedure creation (3). In addition, the associated space for the program object is updated to include the same information that was added to the catalog tables. This information is used when invoking commands such as SAVOBJ/SAVLIB and RSTOBJ/RSTLIB.

In order for all the steps to complete without errors, the developer must have administrative authority or all of the following:

- *USE privilege on the CRTPGM command.
- Create in schema privileges for the target schema in which the proc is created. If the target schema (library) name is also the name of a user profile, then system authority *ADD is required on the library.
- INSERT privilege on the SYSPARMS table and *EXECUTE authority on the QSYS2 library.

In addition to the privileges listed here, if any distinct types are referenced, the developer must have USAGE privileges on the distinct type and *EXECUTE authority on the library where the distinct type resides.

Privileges Required by zSeries Stored Procedure Developers

The development of stored procedures and functions on zSeries is handled by two main groups of users, implementers and definers. The **implementer** is the user who will be writing the SQL procedure code. The **definer** is the user who will execute the CREATE PROCEDURE statement to define the SQL procedure in the DB2 subsystem. Normally, the implementer and the definer are the same user. A third group, the **invokers**, is covered in the user privileges section because it deals with those who actually execute the procedures.

The implementer needs to have the required privileges to perform any SQL statement in the procedure—for example, to update a table, UPDATE privilege is required on the particular table. The implementer also needs the BINDADD privilege to bind the package associated to the procedure. After binding the package, the implementer becomes the **package owner**. The implementer also needs to grant the EXECUTE privilege to the definer on the package containing the stored procedure.

When the definer issues the CREATE PROCEDURE statement, he becomes the **procedure owner**. Recall that the definer can execute the procedure because the EXECUTE privilege on the corresponding package is granted by the implementer.

In addition, for dynamic SQL in DB2 for zSeries, two main factors need to be considered: DYNAMICRULES bind/rebind options, and the runtime environment of the package. These are covered in the zSeries specific section at the end of the chapter.

Privileges Required by Users

The other group is the **user group**—those users who execute the procedure. The different privileges required in each environment are covered in the following sections.

Privileges Required by LUW Users

Users on LUW need the EXECUTE privilege on the procedure. EXECUTE is a procedure-level privilege that allows the grantee to run the stored procedure. GRANT EXECUTE requires the name of the stored procedure. Examples of granting execute privilege include the following:

```
GRANT EXECUTE ON PROCEDURE call_to_caller TO USER db2user
GRANT EXECUTE ON PROCEDURE  db2admin.test_proc TO GROUP db2ugrp
```

Notice that altering stored procedures is not mentioned in this book because stored procedures are one of the few database objects that cannot be altered. If a procedure requires code changes, it has to be dropped and re-created. In other words, if you rebuild a stored procedure, you will need to once again grant the EXECUTE privilege on the new procedure to the users and groups.

Privilege considerations for users on dynamic and static SQL statements coded in the SQL procedure are very straightforward. For static SQL statements, EXECUTE is the only privilege required by the users. With dynamic SQL statements, users also need appropriate access to each object referenced in the procedure, either explicitly to the user or implicitly to the user group:

```
GRANT SELECT, DELETE ON TABLE employee TO USER db2user
GRANT SELECT, DELETE ON TABLE employee TO GROUP db2ugrp
```

Privileges Required by iSeries Users

In order to be able to execute a stored procedure on iSeries, the authorization ID of the caller must have the EXECUTE privilege on the procedure being called and *EXECUTE authority on the library containing the stored procedure. The GRANT statement can be used to provide EXECUTE privilege on the procedure:

```
GRANT EXECUTE ON PROCEDURE MYLIB.PROCNAME TO PUBLIC
```

Additionally, as is the case in LUW, for dynamic SQL, the invoker must also have access to the individual objects referenced in the the dynamic SQL statement.

Privileges Required by zSeries Users

Typically, the invoker is the user who executes the SQL procedure. The definer needs to grant EXECUTE privilege for the procedure to the invoker. If anyone can be the invoker, the EXECUTE privilege can be given to PUBLIC as shown:

```
GRANT EXECUTE ON PROCEDURE MYSCHEMA.PROCNAME TO PUBLIC
```

Using Stored Procedures in a Production Environment

When you use stored procedures in a production environment, it is important to keep track of how the stored procedures are being used. Some applications use a single user, or a small group of users, to access the database. Often this access is performed using stored procedures. When a stored procedure is rebuilt, you will need to ensure that the user is again granted the privileges to execute the procedures that they use.

DB2 for zSeries Considerations

When working with procedures on DB2 for zSeries, there are two important things to consider.

DYNAMICRULES Bind/Rebind Option Value

The DYNAMICRULES option on the BIND or REBIND command determines what values apply at runtime for the following dynamic SQL attributes:

- The authorization ID that is used to check authorization
- The qualifier that is used for unqualified objects
- The source for application programming options that DB2 uses to parse and semantically verify dynamic SQL statements

The DYNAMICRULES option also determines whether dynamic SQL statements can include GRANT, REVOKE, ALTER, CREATE, DROP, and RENAME statements.

It is worth mentioning that the installation panel DSNTIP4 (Application Programming Defaults Panel 2) has the field USE FOR DYNAMICRULES that will determine from where the values for certain application programming defaults are taken:

- If USE FOR DYNAMIC RULES has a value of YES (default), the values of the following fields in panel DSNTIPF and DSNTIP4 will be used regardless of what is specified in the DYNAMICRULES bind/rebind option:

  ```
  DECIMAL POINT IS
  STRING DELIMITER
  SQL STRING DELIMITER
  MIXED DATA
  DECIMAL ARITHMETIC
  ```

- If USE FOR DYNAMIC RULES has a value of NO, the values specified in the DYNAMICRULES bind/rebind option will take effect.

The Package's Runtime Environment

In addition to the DYNAMICRULES value, the runtime environment of a package controls how dynamic SQL statements behave at runtime. The two possible runtime environments are

- The package runs as part of a stand-alone program (outside the scope of this book).
- The package runs as a stored procedure or user-defined function package, or is called by a stored procedure or user-defined function.

The combination of these two factors determine four dynamic SQL statement behaviors: RUN, BIND, DEFINE, and INVOKE. The two behaviors applicable to stored procedures are DEFINE and INVOKE; therefore, we will only describe these behaviors and the corresponding DYNAMICRULES values in this section.

The *DEFINE* Behavior

As mentioned earlier, the definer is the user who will initiate the CREATE PROCEDURE statement to define the stored procedure in the DB2 subsystem. Thus, the define behavior has these characteristics:

- DB2 uses the authorization ID of the user-defined function or stored procedure owner for authorization checking of dynamic SQL statements in the application package.

- The default qualifier for unqualified objects is the user-defined function or stored procedure owner.

The *INVOKE* Behavior

As mentioned earlier, the invoker is the user who will execute or invoke the procedure. Consider the following characteristics for invoking the procedures:

- DB2 uses the authorization ID of the user-defined function or stored procedure invoker for authorization checking of dynamic SQL statements in the application package. If the invoker is the primary authorization ID of the process or the CURRENT SQLID value, secondary authorization IDs are also checked if they are needed for the required authorization. Otherwise, only one ID—the ID of the invoker—is checked for the required authorization.

- The default qualifier for unqualified objects is the user-defined function or stored procedure invoker.

The corresponding DYNAMICRULES bind/rebind options for the define behavior are the following:

- **DEFINEBIND.** Processes dynamic SQL statements with the DEFINE behavior for stored procedures and functions, and with the BIND behavior when the package is run as a stand-alone program.

- **DEFINERUN.** Processes dynamic SQL statements with the DEFINE behavior for stored procedures and functions, and with the RUN behavior when the package is run as a stand-alone program.

- **INVOKEBIND.** Processes dynamic SQL statements with the INVOKE behavior for stored procedures and functions, and with the BIND behavior when the package is run as a stand-alone program.

- **INVOKERUN.** Processes dynamic SQL statements with the INVOKE behavior for stored procedures and functions, and with the RUN behavior when the package is run as a stand-alone program.

Common Attribute Values for the *DEFINE* and *INVOKE* Behaviors

The following attribute values apply to dynamic SQL statements in plans or packages that have the DEFINE, or INVOKE behavior:

- You can execute the statement SET CURRENT SQLID in a package or plan that is bound with any DYNAMICRULES value. However, DB2 does not use the current SQL ID as the authorization ID for dynamic SQL statements. DB2 always uses the current SQL ID as the qualifier for the EXPLAIN output PLAN_TABLE.

- As mentioned earlier, if the value of installation option USE FOR DYNAMICRULES is YES, DB2 uses the application programming default values that were specified during installation to parse and semantically verify dynamic SQL statements. If the value of USE for DYNAMICRULES is NO, DB2 uses the precompiler options to parse and semantically verify dynamic SQL statements.

- GRANT, REVOKE, CREATE, ALTER, DROP, and RENAME statements cannot be executed dynamically.

Simplifying Authorization

As you have seen throughout this appendix, there are many rules and considerations to take into account when setting up security in DB2 for zSeries. We would recommend you simplify security—as long as your installation standards allow it—following this simple strategy:

- The implementer should bind the procedure or user-defined function package using the DYNAMICRULES define behavior so that DB2 only checks the definer's ID to execute dynamic SQL statements in the routine. Otherwise, DB2 needs to check the many different IDs that invoke the user-defined function.

- If you have many different routines, group those routines into schemas and then grant EXECUTE on the procedures in the schema to the appropriate users. Users have EXECUTE authority on any functions that you add to that schema. For example, to grant the EXECUTE privilege on a schema to PUBLIC, issue the following statement:

```
GRANT EXECUTE ON PROCEDURE myschemaname.* TO PUBLIC;
```

Summary

Table E.1 summarizes the privileges required by the developers and users when different types of SQL statements are used in DB2 LUW, DB2 for iSeries and for zSeries.

Table E.1 Summary of Privileges

	GROUP	**DYNAMIC SQLs**	**STATIC SQLs**
LUW	Developers	BINDADD & Table privileges granted to individual developer or to developer group.	BINDADD & Table privileges granted to individual developer or to PUBLIC.
	Users	EXECUTE & Table privileges granted to individual developer or to developer group.	EXECUTE
iSeries	Developers	Administrative Authority or *USE privilege on the CRTPGM command, create in schema for the target schema, INSERT privilege on SYSPARMS, and *EXECUTE on QSYS2 &. Table privileges granted to individual developer or to PUBLIC.	Administrative Authority or *USE privilege on the CRTPGM command, create in schema for the target schema, INSERT privilege on SYSPARMS, and *EXECUTE on QSYS2 &. Table privileges granted to individual developer or to PUBLIC.
	Users	*EXECUTE on the procedure & Table privileges granted to individual developer or to PUBLIC.	*EXECUTE on the procedure.
zSeries (simplified)	Developers (implementers and definers)	BINDADD & Table privileges granted to individual developer or to developer group. & Depends on value of DYNAMICRULES: DEFINEBIND DEFINERUN INVOKEBIND INVOKERUN	BINDADD & Table privileges granted to individual developer or to developer group.
	Users (invokers)	EXECUTE & Table privileges granted to individual developer or to developer group.	EXECUTE

DDL

This appendix contains all the Data Definition Language (DDL) statements for the SAMPLE database and other database objects required to run the examples in this book. The first script is the DDL for the SAMPLE database, which can be created using the methods described in this appendix. The second script has the additional DDL required for the examples and you will have to create those objects manually.

Creating the SAMPLE Database on LUW

The SAMPLE database provided with DB2 on LUW can be created by using one of two methods:

- Create the database from the First Steps dialog, which launches automatically after installation.
- Create the database from the command line.

The default schema used for tables in the database will be the user ID you used to log in to the operating system (on Windows, this will be the user ID used to install DB2, and on UNIX, the instance user ID).

You can also create the SAMPLE database from the command line. Included with DB2 is a program called db2sampl that will create and populate the database for you. This program can be found in the bin subdirectory of the directory where db2 was installed. For the purpose of running the examples presented in this book, foreign key constraints are required. The db2sampl program can be executed with an option to also create the primary keys, such as this:

```
db2sampl -k
```

For reference, Figure F.2 shows the DDL for the SAMPLE database. You can use this DDL to create the tables for the SAMPLE database; however, they will not contain any data. Running the db2sampl program will also populate the tables with sample data.

In addition to the SAMPLE database tables, you still need to create a few other tables to ensure that you can run every example shown in this publication. Figure F.3 provides the DDL for the additional tables. You should create these tables using the same schema used to create the SAMPLE database tables.

Creating the SAMPLE Database on iSeries

DB2 UDB for iSeries comes with a stored procedure to create a SAMPLE database. You can create the SAMPLE database as follows:

```
CALL QSYS.CREATE_SQL_SAMPLE('SAMPLE');
```

The stored procedure creates the sample tables under the schema that is passed in as a parameter (in this case, SAMPLE) and populates them with some data as well. Although the tables created on iSeries are a superset of the tables created on LUW, the data with which they populate differ on the two platforms, and in some cases the tables on iSeries have additional columns. A few tables on iSeries have had aliases created for them to match the table name on LUW, because the table names are different but the table definitions are the same.

Other differences such as the creation of primary keys, foreign keys, and indexes also exist across the platforms. To make the iSeries database objects a complete superset of the LUW objects, you need to create additional objects, as shown in Figure F.1

```
-- DDL Statements for primary key on Table STAFF
ALTER TABLE ORG
   ADD PRIMARY KEY
         (DEPTNUMB);


--- DDL Statements for primary key on Table STAFF
ALTER TABLE STAFF
   ADD PRIMARY KEY
         (ID);
```

Figure F.1   Additional DDL for iSeries.

For reference, Figure F.2 shows the DDL for the SAMPLE database on LUW. You can use this DDL to create the tables for the SAMPLE database, however they will not contain any data. Running the CREATE_SQL_SAMPLE stored procedures will also populate the tables with sample data.

> **NOTE**
>
> The accompanying CD has the DDL creation script corresponding to the LUW database. It also contains the sample data as populated in the LUW platform. You can use the files if you want identical SAMPLE databases (definition and data) on both platforms.

In addition to the SAMPLE database tables, you still need to create a few other tables to ensure that you can run every example shown in this publication. Figure F.3 provides the DDL for the additional tables. You should create these tables using the same schema used to create the SAMPLE database tables.

Creating the SAMPLE Database on zSeries

DB2 UDB for zSeries comes with two installation jobs—DSNTEJ1 and DSNTEJ7—which are used to create sample objects, including a sample storage group, databases, table spaces, tables, views, and indexes. The sample tables are created and populated under the schema DSN8810.

Although the tables created on zSeries are similar to the tables created on LUW, their names and structure are slightly different. The data with which they populate differ as well on the two platforms.

For the examples used in the book, we suggest you create the tables using the script shown in Figure F.2. By using a DB2 LUW client and the DB2 Connect software, you can connect to a DB2 UDB for zSeries subsystem and run the script. The schema or table qualifier will be the TSO ID you use to connect to the DB2 for zSeries subsystem. Make sure the lines that are specific to zSeries are not commented out in the scripts.

> **NOTE**
>
> The accompanying CD contains the DDL creation script corresponding to the LUW SAMPLE database. It also contains the sample data as populated in the LUW platform. You can use the files if you want identical sample databases (definition and data) on both platforms.

In addition to the SAMPLE database tables, you still need to create a few other tables to ensure that you can run every example shown in this publication. Figure F.3 provides the DDL for the additional tables. You should create these tables using the same schema used to create the SAMPLE database tables.

SAMPLE Database DDL: Script 1 sampleDDL_1.db2

```
-------------------------------------------------
-- This DDL script is a common script for all
--   platforms.  For LUW, the tables will be
--   created in the default tablespace, which
```

```
--    is USERSPACE1 when defaults are used for
--    database creation.  For zSeries, the tables
--    will be created in the DSNDB04 default
--    database.  In addition, make sure to uncomment
--    the lines that are specific to zSeries.
--
-- DDL Statements for table ORG
 CREATE TABLE ORG  (
            DEPTNUMB SMALLINT NOT NULL ,
            DEPTNAME VARCHAR(14) ,
            MANAGER  SMALLINT ,
            DIVISION VARCHAR(10) ,
            LOCATION VARCHAR(13) )
              ;


-- DDL Statements for primary key on Table ORG

-- zSeries only
-- CREATE UNIQUE INDEX ORG_PK
--        ON ORG
--                (DEPTNUMB);

ALTER TABLE ORG
   ADD PRIMARY KEY
          (DEPTNUMB);



------------------------------------------------
-- DDL Statements for table STAFF
------------------------------------------------

 CREATE TABLE STAFF (
            ID      SMALLINT NOT NULL ,
            NAME    VARCHAR(9) ,
            DEPT    SMALLINT ,
            JOB     CHAR(5) ,
            YEARS   SMALLINT ,
            SALARY DECIMAL(7,2) ,
            COMM    DECIMAL(7,2) )
              ;
```

```
-- DDL Statements for primary key on Table STAFF


-- zSeries only
-- CREATE UNIQUE INDEX STAFF_PK
--         ON STAFF
--                 (ID);


ALTER TABLE STAFF
   ADD PRIMARY KEY
           (ID);




------------------------------------------------
-- DDL Statements for table DEPARTMENT
------------------------------------------------


 CREATE TABLE DEPARTMENT  (
             DEPTNO   CHAR(3) NOT NULL ,
             DEPTNAME VARCHAR(29) NOT NULL ,
             MGRNO    CHAR(6) ,
             ADMRDEPT CHAR(3) NOT NULL ,
             LOCATION CHAR(16) )
             ;


-- DDL Statements for primary key on Table DEPARTMENT


-- zSeries only
-- CREATE UNIQUE INDEX DEPARTMENT_PK
--         ON DEPARTMENT
--                 (DEPTNO);



ALTER TABLE DEPARTMENT
   ADD PRIMARY KEY
           (DEPTNO);




------------------------------------------------
-- DDL Statements for table EMPLOYEE
------------------------------------------------
```

```
CREATE TABLE EMPLOYEE  (
          EMPNO     CHAR(6) NOT NULL ,
          FIRSTNME  VARCHAR(12) NOT NULL ,
          MIDINIT   CHAR(1) NOT NULL ,
          LASTNAME  VARCHAR(15) NOT NULL ,
          WORKDEPT  CHAR(3) ,
          PHONENO   CHAR(4) ,
          HIREDATE  DATE ,
          JOB       CHAR(8) ,
          EDLEVEL   SMALLINT NOT NULL ,
          SEX       CHAR(1) ,
          BIRTHDATE DATE ,
          SALARY    DECIMAL(9,2) ,
          BONUS     DECIMAL(9,2) ,
          COMM      DECIMAL(9,2) )
          ;


-- DDL Statements for primary key on Table EMPLOYEE

-- zSeries only
-- CREATE UNIQUE INDEX EMPLOYEE_PK
--        ON EMPLOYEE
--                (EMPNO);

ALTER TABLE EMPLOYEE
   ADD PRIMARY KEY
          (EMPNO);



-------------------------------------------------
-- DDL Statements for table EMP_ACT
-------------------------------------------------


CREATE TABLE EMP_ACT  (
          EMPNO     CHAR(6) NOT NULL ,
          PROJNO    CHAR(6) NOT NULL ,
          ACTNO     SMALLINT NOT NULL ,
          EMPTIME   DECIMAL(5,2) ,
          EMSTDATE  DATE ,
          EMENDATE  DATE )
          ;
```

```
-------------------------------------------------
-- DDL Statements for table PROJECT
-------------------------------------------------


 CREATE TABLE PROJECT  (
             PROJNO    CHAR(6) NOT NULL ,
             PROJNAME VARCHAR(24) NOT NULL ,
             DEPTNO    CHAR(3) NOT NULL ,
             RESPEMP  CHAR(6) NOT NULL ,
             PRSTAFF  DECIMAL(5,2) ,
             PRSTDATE DATE ,
             PRENDATE DATE ,
             MAJPROJ  CHAR(6) )
                ;


-- DDL Statements for primary key on Table PROJECT


-- zSeries only
-- CREATE UNIQUE INDEX PROJECT_PK
--         ON PROJECT
--                 (PROJNO);


ALTER TABLE PROJECT
    ADD PRIMARY KEY
            (PROJNO);




-------------------------------------------------
-- DDL Statements for table EMP_PHOTO
-------------------------------------------------


-- zSeries only
-- CREATE LOB TABLESPACE PHOTOTS IN DSNDB04 LOG NO;
-- COMMIT;


 CREATE TABLE EMP_  PHOTO  (
             EMPNO    CHAR(6) NOT NULL ,
             PHOTO_  FORMAT VARCHAR(10) NOT NULL ,
             PICTURE BLOB(102400) )
                ;
```

```
-- DDL Statements for primary key on Table EMP_PHOTO

-- zSeries only
-- COMMIT;
-- CREATE UNIQUE INDEX EMP_PHOTO_PK
--         ON EMP_PHOTO
--                 (EMPNO,
--         PHOTO_FORMAT);

ALTER TABLE EMP_PHOTO
   ADD PRIMARY KEY
          (EMPNO,
           PHOTO_FORMAT);

-- zSeries only
-- CREATE AUXILIARY TABLE EMP_PHOTO_AUX
--         IN DSNDB04.PHOTOTS
--         STORES EMP_PHOTO
--         COLUMN PICTURE;

-- CREATE UNIQUE INDEX XEMP_PHOTO
--         ON EMP_PHOTO_AUX;

-- COMMIT;

-------------------------------------------------
-- DDL Statements for table EMP_RESUME
-------------------------------------------------

-- zSeries only
-- CREATE LOB TABLESPACE RESUMETS IN DSNDB04 LOG NO;
-- COMMIT;

 CREATE TABLE EMP_RESUME   (
            EMPNO          CHAR(6) NOT NULL ,
            RESUME_FORMAT VARCHAR(10) NOT NULL ,
            RESUME         CLOB(5120) )
          ;
```

```
-- DDL Statements for primary key on Table EMP_RESUME


-- zSeries only
-- COMMIT;
-- CREATE UNIQUE INDEX EMP_RESUME_PK
--          ON EMP_RESUME
--                 (EMPNO,
--                  RESUME_FORMAT);


ALTER TABLE EMP_RESUME
   ADD PRIMARY KEY
          (EMPNO,
           RESUME_FORMAT);


-- zSeries only
-- CREATE AUXILIARY TABLE EMP_RESUME_AUX
--          IN DSNDB04.RESUMETS
--          STORES EMP_RESUME
--          COLUMN RESUME;


-- CREATE UNIQUE INDEX XEMP_RESUME
--          ON EMP_RESUME_AUX;


-- COMMIT;

-------------------------------------------------
-- DDL Statements for table SALES
-------------------------------------------------


 CREATE TABLE SALES   (
           SALES_DATE   DATE ,
           SALES_PERSON VARCHAR(15) ,
           REGION       VARCHAR(15) ,
           SALES        INTEGER )
           ;



-------------------------------------------------
```

```
-- DDL Statements for table CL_SCHED
--------------------------------------------------

 CREATE TABLE CL_SCHED  (
          CLASS_CODE CHAR(7) ,
          DAY        SMALLINT ,
          STARTING   TIME ,
          ENDING     TIME )
          ;



--------------------------------------------------
-- DDL Statements for table IN_TRAY
--------------------------------------------------

 CREATE TABLE IN_TRAY  (
          RECEIVED TIMESTAMP ,
          SOURCE CHAR(8) ,
          SUBJECT CHAR(64) ,
          NOTE_TEXT VARCHAR(3000) )
          ;
```

Figure F.2   DDL for the SAMPLE database.

DDL for Additional Database Objects: Script #2 sampleDDL_2.db2

```
--------------------------------------------------
-- This DDL script is a common script for all
--    platforms.


--------------------------------------------------
-- DDL Statements for table tname
--------------------------------------------------
CREATE TABLE tname ( fullname VARCHAR(50) );


--------------------------------------------------
-- DDL Statements for table queue
--------------------------------------------------
    CREATE TABLE queue (data int);
```

```
-------------------------------------------------
-- DDL Statements for table identity_tab
-------------------------------------------------
CREATE TABLE identity_tab (
        id INT NOT NULL GENERATED ALWAYS AS IDENTITY,
        data VARCHAR(100)) ;


-------------------------------------------------
-- DDL Statements for table service_rq
-------------------------------------------------
CREATE TABLE service_rq(
   rqid SMALLINT NOT NULL
        CONSTRAINT rqid_pk PRIMARY KEY,

     status VARCHAR(10) NOT NULL
        WITH DEFAULT 'NEW'
        CHECK ( status IN ( 'NEW', 'ASSIGNED', 'Pending', 'CANCELLED' ) ),

     rq_desktop CHAR(1) NOT NULL
        WITH DEFAULT 'N'
        CHECK ( rq_desktop IN ( 'Y', 'N' ) ),

     rq_ipaddress CHAR(1) NOT NULL
        WITH DEFAULT 'N'
        CHECK ( rq_ipaddress IN ( 'Y', 'N' ) ),
     rq_unixid CHAR(1) NOT NULL
        WITH DEFAULT 'N'
        CHECK ( rq_unixid IN ( 'Y', 'N' ) ),

     staffid INTEGER NOT NULL,
     techid INTEGER,
     accum_rqnum INTEGER NOT NULL

        GENERATED ALWAYS AS IDENTITY
          ( START WITH 1,
          INCREMENT BY 1,
        CACHE 10 ),
   comment VARCHAR(100) );
-------------------------------------------------
-- DDL Statements for table svcrq_sw
-------------------------------------------------
```

```
CREATE TABLE svcrq_sw (
   rqid SMALLINT NOT NULL
            CONSTRAINT rwid_pk PRIMARY KEY,
   status VARCHAR(10) NOT NULL
         WITH DEFAULT 'NEW'
         CHECK (status IN ('NEW', 'ASSIGNED', 'Pending', 'CANCELLED')),
     ostype VARCHAR(50) NOT NULL
         WITH DEFAULT 'W2K',
     staffid INTEGER NOT NULL,
     techid INTEGER,
     accum_rqnum INTEGER NOT NULL
         GENERATED ALWAYS AS IDENTITY
           ( START WITH 1,
            INCREMENT BY 1,
            CACHE 10 ),
     comment VARCHAR(100) );


------------------------------------------------
-- DDL Statements for sequence service_rq_seq
------------------------------------------------
CREATE SEQUENCE service_rq_seq AS SMALLINT
     START WITH 1
     INCREMENT BY 1
     MAXVALUE 5000
     NO CYCLE
     CACHE 50;


------------------------------------------------
-- DDL Statements for sequence staff_seq
------------------------------------------------
CREATE SEQUENCE staff_seq AS INTEGER
      START WITH 360
      INCREMENT BY 10
      NO MAXVALUE
      NO CYCLE
      NO CACHE;


------------------------------------------------
-- DDL Statements for table audit
------------------------------------------------
```

```
CREATE TABLE AUDIT (
   event_time TIMESTAMP,
   desc VARCHAR(100));


-------------------------------------------------
-- DDL Statements for view emp_dep_v
-------------------------------------------------
CREATE VIEW emp_dep_v AS
   SELECT empno, firstnme, lastname, deptname
   FROM employee e LEFT OUTER JOIN department d
               ON e.empno=d.mgrno;


-------------------------------------------------
-- DDL Statements for table atomic_test
-------------------------------------------------
CREATE TABLE atomic_test(
   proc VARCHAR(20),
   res VARCHAR(20));


-------------------------------------------------
-- DDL Statements for sequence seq1
-------------------------------------------------
CREATE SEQUENCE seq1;


-------------------------------------------------
-- DDL Statements for table master_table
-------------------------------------------------
CREATE TABLE master_table (id INT NOT NULL, data VARCHAR(100));
----------------------------------------------------
-- DDL Statements for index ix1 on table master_table
----------------------------------------------------
CREATE UNIQUE INDEX ix1 ON master_table (id);


--------------------------------------------------------------
-- DDL Statements for adding constraint on table master_table
--------------------------------------------------------------
ALTER TABLE master_table ADD CONSTRAINT master_pk PRIMARY KEY (id);
----------------------------------------------------
-- DDL Statements for table stage_table
----------------------------------------------------
```

```
CREATE TABLE stage_table LIKE master_table;


------------------------------------------------------------------
-- DDL Statements for user temporary table space usertempspace
------------------------------------------------------------------
-- DB2/LUW
CREATE USER TEMPORARY TABLESPACE usertempspace
    MANAGED BY SYSTEM USING ('usertempspace')
    BUFFERPOOL ibmdefaultbp;


-- DB2/390
create database tempdb AS TEMP;
create tablespace temptbl in tempdb bufferpool BP0;
```

Figure F.3   DDL for additional tables.

APPENDIX G

Additional Resources

There are many ways to obtain additional information pertaining to DB2 and DB2 SQL stored procedures. This appendix attempts to serve as a comprehensive list of such resources. Note that some information can be found in more than one place.

IBM Redbooks

IBM Redbooks are developed and published by IBM's International Technical Support Organization, the ITSO. ITSO develops and delivers technical materials to technical professionals of IBM, business partners, customers, and the IT marketplace.

IBM Redbooks are ITSO's core product. They typically provide positioning and value guidance, installation and implementation experiences, typical solution scenarios, and step-by-step "how-to" guidelines. They often include sample code and other support materials that are also available as downloads from this site: www.redbooks.ibm.com.

Redbooks are available as hardcopy books and in IBM Redbook CD-ROM collections. Refer to the How to Buy page for order details.

The following Redbooks contain information about DB2 stored procedures.

LUW

"DB2 UDB V7.1 Performance Tuning Guide, SG24-6012-00." *Redbook*, December 17, 2000, www.redbooks.ibm.com/pubs/pdfs/redbooks/sg246012.pdf.

"DB2 UDB V7.1 Porting Guide, SG24-6128-00." *Redbook*, December 11, 2000, www.redbooks.ibm.com/pubs/pdfs/redbooks/sg246128.pdf.

"DB2 Java Stored Procedures Learning by Example, SG24-5945-00." *Redbook*, September 6, 2000, www.redbooks.ibm.com/pubs/pdfs/redbooks/sg245945.pdf.

iSeries

"Stored Procedures, Triggers, and User Defined Functions on DB2 Universal Database for
    iSeries, SF24-6503-01." *Redbook*, March 2004,
    www.redbooks.ibm.com/pubs/pdfs/redbooks/sg246503.pdf.

"Advanced Database Functions and Administration on DB2 UDB for iSeries, SG24-4249-
    03." Redbook, December 14, 2001,
    www.redbooks.ibm.com/pubs/pdfs/redbooks/sg244249.pdf.

"DB2 UDB for AS/400 Object Relational Support, SG24-5409-00." *Redbook*, February 14,
    2000. www.redbooks.ibm.com/pubs/pdfs/redbooks/sg245409.pdf.

zSeries

"DB2 for z/OS Stored Procedures: Through the CALL and Beyond, SG24-7083-00." *Redbook*,
    March 2004, www.redbooks.ibm.com/pubs/pdfs/redbooks/sg247083.pdf.

"DB2 for z/OS and OS/390: Squeezing the Most Out of Dynamic SQL, SG24-6418-00."
    Redbook, May 31, 2002, www.redbooks.ibm.com/pubs/pdfs/redbooks/sg24641800.pdf.

Cross-Platform

"Cross-Platform DB2 Stored Procedures: Building and Debugging, SG24-5485-01."
    Redbook, May 8, 2001, www.redbooks.ibm.com/pubs/pdfs/redbooks/sg245485.pdf.

"SQL Reference for Cross-Platform Development."ftp.software.ibm.com/ps/products
    /db2/info/vr7/pdf/letter/ibmsqlr.pdf.

Certification

Your DB2 skill set can be validated by completing the appropriate DB2 UDB Certifications. Here
are few popular certifications:

- IBM Certified Database Associate—DB2 Universal Database V8.1 Family
- IBM Certified Database Administrator—DB2 Universal Database V8.1 for Linux,
  UNIX, and Windows
- IBM Certified Application Developer—DB2 Universal Database V8.1 Family
- IBM Certified Advanced Database Administrator—DB2 Universal Database V8.1
  Linux, UNIX, and Windows
- IBM Certified Solutions Expert—DB2 Universal Database V7.1 Database Administra-
  tion for OS/390

Additional information on DB2 Certification can be obtained from www.ibm.com/certify.

Certification Guides

Baklarz, George, and Bill Wong, *DB2 Universal Database V8 for Linux, UNIX, Windows Database Administration Certification Guide*, 5th Edition. Indianapolis: Prentice Hall PTR, 2003.

Lawson, Susan. *DB2 Universal Database for OS/390 Version 7.1 Application Certification Guide*. 2003. Indianapolis: Prentice Hall PTR, 2003.

Sanders, Roger. *DB2 Universal Database V8.1 Certification Exam 700 Study Guide*. Indianapolis: Prentice Hall PTR, 2003.

Sanders, Roger. *DB2 Universal Database V8.1 Certification Exams 701 and 706 Study Guide*. Indianapolis: Prentice Hall PTR, 2003.

Sanyal, Steve, David Martineau, Kevin Gashyna, and Michael Kyprianou. *DB2 Universal Database Version 8.1 Application Development Certification Guide*, 2nd Edition. Indianapolis: Prentice Hall PTR, 2003.

Snow, Dwain, and Thomas Xuan Phan. *Advanced DBA Certification Guide and Reference for DB2 UDB V8 for Linux, UNIX, and Windows*. Indianapolis: Prentice Hall PTR, 2003.

Yevich, Richard and Susan Lawson. *DB2 Universal Database for OS/390 Version 7.1 Certification Guide*. Indianapolis: Prentice Hall PTR, 2001.

Tutorials

These three series of tutorials are designed to help you prepare for the DB2 Fundamentals Certification (Exam 700), DB2 DBA Certification (Exam 701), and DB2 Application Development Certification (Exam 703). These tutorials provide a solid base for each section of the exam. However, you should not rely solely on these tutorials as your only preparation for the exam. Each tutorial includes a link to a free DB2 Universal Database Enterprise Server Edition download.

www.ibm.com/developerworks/db2/library/tutorials/db2cert/db2cert_V8_tut.html

www.ibm.com/developerworks/db2/library/tutorials/db2cert/701_prep.html

www.ibm.com/developerworks/offers/lp/db2cert

Education

A variety of instructor-led and computer-based training is also available.

IBM Learning Services

IBM Learning Services offers a complete set of traditional classroom courses and workshops for both DB2 developers and database administrators. For additional offerings that are not listed here, turn to the IBM web site at www.ibm.com/software/data/education.html. To look for class schedules in Canada, consult the IBM Learning Services Canada site at www.can.ibm.com/ser-vices/learning/index.html. In the United States, consult the IBM Learning Services US - DB2 site at www.ibm.com/services/learning/spotlight/db2, or call 1-800-426-8322 for the latest course offerings and schedule information. Information about computer-based training (CBT) courses is also available from the sites.

The following lists highlight some of the traditional classroom and CBT courses for DB2, which are offered by IBM Learning Services.

Application Programming

DB2 UDB Programming Fundamentals (CF103)
DB2 UDB Fast Path to DB2 for Experiences DBAs (CF281) (Free offer—see the following section)
DB2 UDB Advanced Programming (CF113)
DB2 UDB Programming Using Java (CG112)
DB2 UDB Stored Procedures Programming Workshop (CF710)
Accessing DB2 UDB for iSeries with SQL (S6137)
Developing iSeries applications with SQL (S6138)
DB2 UDB for iSeries SQL Advanced Programming (S6139)
DB2 UDB for z/OS and OS/390 Programming using Java (CG140)

Database Administration

DB2 UDB Database Administration Workshop for Linux (CF201)
DB2 UDB Database Administration Workshop for UNIX (CF211)
DB2 UDB Database Administration Workshop for Windows NT (CF231)
DB2 UDB Programming Fastpath Course (CT10) (Free offer—see the following section)
DB2 UDB EEE for UNIX Administration Workshop (CF241)
DB2 UDB EEE for Windows NT Administration Workshop (CF261)
DB2 UDB Database Administration Workshop for Sun Solaris (CF271)
DB2 UDB Advanced Administration Workshop (CF451)
DB2 UDB Advanced Admin. For Experienced Relational DBAs (CF481)
DB2 UDB Advanced Recovery & High Availability Workshop (CF491)
DB2 UDB EEE for DB2 UDB EE DBAs (CG241)
DB2 UDB for z/OS and OS/390 Database Administration Workshop - Part 1 (CF830)
DB2 UDB for z/OS and OS/390 Database Administration Workshop - Part 2 (CF840)
DB2 UDB for z/OS and OS/390 System Administration (CF850)

Performance Tuning

DB2 UDB Performance Tuning and Monitoring Workshop (CF411)
DB2 UDB EEE for UNIX Performance Monitoring and Tuning Workshop (CF441)

DB2 UDB for iSeries SQL & Query Performance Workshop (www.ibm.com/servers/eserver/iseries/service/igs/db2performance.html)
DB2 UDB for OS/390 Application Performance and Tuning (CF960)

Free Self-Study Computer-Based Training Courses

- **DB2 UDB Self-Study for Experienced Relational DBA's (CF281)**. For a limited time the Fast Path to DB2 UDB for Experienced Relational DBAs is available for free download from www.ibm.com/software/data/db2/selfstudy/. The course is targeted toward the DBA who is already proficient in one or more non-IBM relational database products, but could use some help in getting up-to-speed with the DB2 Universal Database. This fast-path course can be completed in as little as eight hours.
- **DB2 UDB Programming Fast Path Course (CT10)**. A new, second offering—DB2 UDB Programming Fast Path—is designed to teach experienced relational database programmers how to create applications that access data in a DB2 Universal database system. It provides a fast path for acquiring the skills necessary to write programs against a DB2 UDB database, and is available free for download from www.ibm.com/software/data/db2/ct10crs/.

IBM Solution Partnership Centers (SPCs)

IBM SPCs provide various workshops that are free to members of PartnerWorld for Developers. Schedules are available at the PartnerWorld for Developers web site: www.developer.ibm.com.

Tutorials

DB2 Fundamentals Certification (Exam 512) Preparation:
www7b.software.ibm.com/dmdd/library/tutorials/db2cert/db2cert_tut.html
IBM DB2 Migration Series:
webevents.broadcast.com/ibm/db2migrate/home.asp
Developer Webcast on Demand:
webevents.broadcast.com/ibm/developer/on_demand.asp
DB2 Intelligent Miner Scoring online education:
www.ibmweblectureservices.ihost.com/ibm/imse/
Content Manager on Demand education:
www.ibm.com/software/data/ondemand/education.html
iSeries Navigator Tutorials:
www.ibm.com/servers/enable/sie/education/ibo/view.html?oc#db2
Visual Explain for DB2 for z/OS:
www.ibm.com/software/data/db2/os390/db2ve/

Books

Bauch, Tom, and Mark Wilding. *DB2 for Solaris: The Official Guide*. Indianapolis: Prentice Hall PTR, 2003.

Conte, Paul and Mike Cravitz. *SQL/400 Developer's Guide*. Loveland, CO: 29th Street Press.

Gunning, Philip. *DB2 UDB v8 Handbook for Windows and UNIX/Linux*. Indianapolis: Prentice Hall PTR, 2003.

Melnyk, Roman and Paul Zikopolous. *DB2: The Complete Reference*, 1st Edition. New York: McGraw-Hill, 2001.

Mullins, Craig. *DB2 Developer's Guide*, 4th Edition Indianapolis: SAMS, 2000.

Sanders, Roger. *DB2 Universal Database SQL Developer's Guide*. Emeryville, CA: Osborne McGraw-Hill, 1999.

Shirai, Tetsuya and Robert Harbus. *DB2 Universal Database in Application Environments*. Berkeley: Peachpit Press, 2000.

Sloan, Susan Graziano. *The Official Introduction to DB2 for the Z/OS: Version 8*. Indianapolis: Prentice Hall PTR, 2004.

Zikopolous, Paul and George Baklarz, Dirk deRoos, and Roman Melnyk. *DB2 Version 8: The Official Guide*, Indianapolis: Prentice Hall PTR, 2003.

Zikopolous, Paul and Jennifer Gibbs and Roman B. Melnyk. *DB2 Fundamentals Certification for Dummies* by. Indianapolis: John Wiley and Sons, 2001.

Additional Websites

DB2 home page: www.ibm.com/software/data/db2/

DB2 Technical Materials Library (books, white papers, brochures and specs, consultant reports and technology overviews, magazine articles and reviews, newsletters, and technical information and manuals): www.ibm.com/software/data/pubs/

DB2 application development: www.ibm.com/software/data/db2/udb/ad/

DB2 manuals: www.ibm.com/software/data/db2/library/

DB2 white papers: www.ibm.com/software/data/pubs/papers/#dbpapers or www.ibm.com/software/data/pubs/papers/#dbpapers

DB2 UDB for iSeries manuals: ibm.com/eserver/iseries/db2/books.html

DB2 UDB for iSeries white papers:
ibm.com/servers/enable/site/education/ibo/view.html?wp#db2
or ibm.com/iseries/db2/awp.html

DB2 UDB for iSeries online courses and presentations:
ibm.com/servers/enable/site/education/ibo/view.html?oc#db2

DB2 UDB for zSeries manuals:
www.ibm.com/software/data/db2/zos/v8books.html

DB2 UDB for zSeries courses: www.ibm.com/software/data/db2/zos/
education.html
IBM database and data management software home page:
www.ibm.com/software/data/
IBM support for data management products: www.ibm.com/software/data/support
DB2 Developer Works: www.ibm.com/developerworks/db2
IBM PartnerWorld for Developers home page: www.developer.ibm.com
IBM Redbooks: www.redbooks.ibm.com
DB2 professional certification program:
www.ibm.com/certify/certs/db_index.shtml
DB2 newsgroup: comp.databases.ibm-db2
iSeries newsgroup: comp.sys.ibm.as400.misc
DB2 on CompuServe: Go ibmdb2

DB2 FixPaks and Downloads

DB2 maintenance info:
www.software.ibm.com/data/db2/udb/winos2unix/support/
or www.ibm.com/iseries/db2/support.html
DB2 maintenance FTP site:
ftp.software.ibm.com/ps/products/db2/fixes/english-us/
DB2 software product downloads: www.ibm.com/software/data/db2/udb/
downloads.html

Email Services and Periodicals

DB2 UDB News: www.ibm.com/software/mailing-lists. Subscribe to receive notification of new FixPaks and other DB2 service news.

DB2 Today: www.ibm.com/software/data/db2today/. Each monthly issue will bring you the latest offers, downloads, events, web-based seminars, product news, and more. Subscribe to receive via email.

DB2 Magazine:- www.db2mag.com. Each issue contains a variety of features on technical and business-level topics for the DB2 community, plus tips and techniques in columns on data mining, programming, system administration, content management, and more. *DB2 Magazine* is available in print as well as on the web.

eServer iSeries Magazine. http://www.eservercomputing.com/iseries/. Regularly includes articles on DB2 UDB for iSeries technology.

iSeries NEWS. http://www.iseriesnetwork.com/. Regularly includes articles on DB2 UDB for iSeries technology.

User Groups and Conferences

International DB2 User Group (IDUG):   www.idug.org/

DB2 and Other IBM Technical Conferences: www.ibm.com/services/learning/conf/us/index.html

COMMON (iSeries Customer User Group): www.common.org.

Sample Application Code

This appendix provides supplementary examples of application code that is not SQL. In Chapter 5, "Understanding and Using Cursors and Result Sets," the notion of returning result sets to an application program from an SQL procedure was introduced. In Chapter 8, "Nested SQL Procedures," the notion of SQL stored procedures processing result sets was introduced.

This appendix discusses how an application program, written in C or Java, can process results sets that would be returned by a stored procedure. Additionally, examples of how Java stored procedures can process result sets are also provided. This information is particularly useful for the iSeries platform, where SQL stored procedures cannot process result sets.

Receiving Result Sets in Java

The following examples cover how Java can be used in conjunction with stored procedures.

Receiving Result Sets in a Java Application

Figure H.1 shows java application code, `TotalRaise.java`. It is a complete rewrite of the `total_raise()` SQL procedure of Figure 5.3. `TotalRaise.java` relies on calling the SQL procedure `read_emp()` (in Figure 5.22) to provide a cursor for data to be processed. The `Total-Raise.java` program and the `read_emp()` procedure together accomplish exactly the same task as the `total_raise()` SQL procedure, although the two approaches are fundamentally different in design. When implementing the logic inside the SQL procedure, less data is passed between the client and server, which results in less network traffic and better performance. Using SQL procedures to process the logic, therefore, is more suitable for transactions involving large result sets. There are, however, advantages to processing data in the application as well:

- You can implement more complex business logic on the client side because it can be integrated better with the client's application logic.

- SQL PL is not as powerful a programming language as C/C++ or Java. For example, with these languages on the client side, you can issue calls to the operating system, as well as have access to information about the client environment.

- You can build applications that can be portable across different RDBMs by using standard APIs.

Figure H.1   shows the code <for TotalRaise.java.

```
import java.lang.*;
import java.util.*;
import java.io.*;
import java.sql.*;
import COM.ibm.db2.jdbc.app.*;

class TotalRaise
{
    static
    {
        try
        {
            Class.forName ("COM.ibm.db2.jdbc.app.DB2Driver").newInstance ();
        }
        catch (Exception e)
        {
            System.out.println ("\n  Error loading DB2 Driver...\n");
            System.out.println (e);
            System.exit(1);
        }
    }

    public static void main (String argv[])
    {
        double v_min, v_max;

        Connection con = null;

        if (argv.length != 2)
        {
```

```
        System.out.println("Usage: java TotalRaise MinRaise MaxRaise");
        System.exit(1);
}

v_min = Double.parseDouble(argv[0]);
v_max = Double.parseDouble(argv[1]);

try
{
    // Connect to Sample database
    String url = "jdbc:db2:sample";
    con = DriverManager.getConnection(url);

    CallableStatement cs = con.prepareCall("CALL db2admin.read_emp()");

    cs.execute();
    ResultSet rs = cs.getResultSet();                            /*--(1)*/

    double v_total=0;
    double v_raise;
    double v_salary, v_bonus, v_comm;

    while ( rs.next() )                                          /*--(2)*/
    {
        v_raise = v_min;
        v_salary = rs.getDouble(1);                             /*--(3)*/
        v_bonus  = rs.getDouble(2);
        v_comm   = rs.getDouble(3);                             /*--(4)*/

        if ( v_bonus >= 600 ) { v_raise += 0.04; }

        if ( v_comm < 2000 )
        {
            v_raise += 0.03;
        }
        else if ( v_comm < 3000 )
        {
            v_raise += 0.02;
        }
        else
```

```
                {
                    v_raise += 0.01;
                }

                if ( v_raise > v_max ) { v_raise = v_max; }

                v_total += v_salary * v_raise;
            } /* while */

            System.out.println(v_total);

            rs.close();
            cs.close ();
            con.close ();

            System.out.println("Complete(0).");
        }
        catch (Exception e)
        {
            try
            {
                if( con != null )
                {
                    con.close();
                }
            }
            catch (Exception x)
            {   //ignore this exception
            }
            System.out.println (e);
        } /* try-catch block */
    } /* main() method */
} /* class TotalRaise */
import java.util.*;
import java.io.*;
import java.sql.*;
import COM.ibm.db2.jdbc.app.*;

class TotalRaise
{
```

```java
static
{
    try
    {
        Class.forName ("COM.ibm.db2.jdbc.app.DB2Driver").newInstance ();
    }
    catch (Exception e)
    {
        System.out.println ("\n  Error loading DB2 Driver...\n");
        System.out.println (e);
        System.exit(1);
    }
}

public static void main (String argv[])
{
    double v_min, v_max;

    Connection con = null;

    if (argv.length != 2)
    {
        System.out.println("Usage: java TotalRaise MinRaise MaxRaise");
        System.exit(1);
    }

    v_min = Double.parseDouble(argv[0]);
    v_max = Double.parseDouble(argv[1]);

    try
    {
        // Connect to Sample database
        String url = "jdbc:db2:sample";
        con = DriverManager.getConnection(url);

        CallableStatement cs = con.prepareCall("CALL db2admin.read_emp()");

        cs.execute();
        ResultSet rs = cs.getResultSet();                          /*--(1)*/
```

```
    double v_total=0;
    double v_raise;
    double v_salary, v_bonus, v_comm;

    while ( rs.next() )                                        /*--(2)*/
    {
        v_raise = v_min;
        v_salary = rs.getDouble(1);                            /*--(3)*/
        v_bonus  = rs.getDouble(2);
        v_comm   = rs.getDouble(3);                            /*--(4)*/

        if ( v_bonus >= 600 ) { v_raise += 0.04; }

        if ( v_comm < 2000 )
        {
            v_raise += 0.03;
        }
        else if ( v_comm < 3000 )
        {
            v_raise += 0.02;
        }
        else
        {
            v_raise += 0.01;
        }

        if ( v_raise > v_max ) { v_raise = v_max; }

        v_total += v_salary * v_raise;
    } /* while */

    System.out.println(v_total);

    rs.close();
    cs.close ();
    con.close ();

    System.out.println("Complete(0).");
}
catch (Exception e)
```

```
        {
            try
            {
                if( con != null )
                {
                    con.close();
                }
            }
            catch (Exception x)
            {   //ignore this exception
            }
            System.out.println (e);
        } /* try-catch block */
    } /* main() method */
} /* class TotalRaise */
```

Figure H.1   *TotalRaise.java*—An example of using Java *import java.lang* to receive a result set provided by an SQL procedure.

In Java, you need a `CallableStatement` object to invoke SQL procedures. The result sets will be returned when you invoke the `getResultSet()` method of the `Statement` interface in Line (1). To receive the result set, you will need to also declare a `ResultSet` object to hold the retrieved data. The `ResultSet` class has many `getXXX()` methods for all regular SQL data types. In this example, the `getDouble()` method is used on Lines (3) and (4). By calling the `getDouble()` method, data is fetched into a local variable. The `ResultSet` class has the `next()` method to advance the cursor and fetch the next row of data. The return value from the `next()` method on Line (2) indicates whether the end of result set is reached. If `next()` returns `false`, the cursor has reached the end of the result set.

For better performance, and as good programming practice, close all `ResultSet`, `CallableStatement`, and `Connection` objects when they are no longer needed.

There are other useful methods for the `Statement` and `ResultSet` interface. Some of them will be covered later in this appendix.

Receiving Result Sets in a Java Stored Procedure

Writing a Java stored procedure is very similar to writing a Java application program. Figure H.2 shows how the procedure `total_salary`, as shown in Figure 8.15, can be rewritten in Java.

```
/**
 * JDBC Stored Procedure DB2ADMIN.TotalSalary
 * @param p_dept
 * @param p_total
 */
package TotalSalary;

import java.sql.*;                    // JDBC classes

public class TotalSalary
{
    public static void totalSalary ( String p_dept,
                                     java.math.BigDecimal[] p_total ) throws
SQLException, Exception
    {
        // Get connection to the database
        Connection con =
DriverManager.getConnection("jdbc:default:connection");  /* --1 */
        CallableStatement cStmt = null;
        ResultSet rs = null;
        String sql;

        // parameters from procedures
        String v_fname, v_lname;
        java.math.BigDecimal  v_salary;

        // Set up the dynamic call to the procedure
        //   Setup input parameters
        //   Register output parameters
        //   Call the procedures
        sql = "CALL to_caller1(?)";
        cStmt = con.prepareCall(sql);
        cStmt.setString(1, p_dept);
        cStmt.execute();

        // Process the result set
        rs = cStmt.getResultSet();

        p_total[0] = new java.math.BigDecimal("0.00");
```

```
      while (rs.next()) {
        v_fname = rs.getString(1);
        v_lname = rs.getString(2);
        v_salary = rs.getBigDecimal(3).setScale(2);

        p_total[0] = p_total[0].add(v_salary);
      }

      // Close the result set and statement
      rs.close();
      cStmt.close();


   }
}
```

Figure H.2   Rewrite of *total_salary()* in Java.

In a Java stored procedure, because the calling application already has a connection to the database, you inherit the connection as shown on Line (1). The Java procedure calls the `to_caller` SQL procedure, and traverses through the employees in the department to return the sum of the salaries for the department. In addition to building the `java` package for the stored procedure in Figure H.2, you would also need to register the stored procedure using the CREATE PROCEDURE statement. Figure H.3 shows an example of this for the iSeries platform.

```
CREATE PROCEDURE TotalSalary ( IN p_dept CHARACTER(3),
                               OUT p_total DECIMAL(9,2) )
    SPECIFIC TOTAL_SALARY
    NOT DETERMINISTIC
    LANGUAGE Java
    EXTERNAL NAME 'DB2ADMIN.TOTAL_SALARY:TotalSalary.TotalSalary.totalSalary'
    FENCED
    PARAMETER STYLE JAVA
```

Figure H.3   Registering the *totalSalary* procedure on iSeries.

Receiving Result Sets in a C or C++ Application

When writing a database application using C or C++ to process the result sets from SQL procedures, you have to use DB2 Call Level Interface (CLI) instead of embedded SQL. Figure H.4
performs the equivalent data processing logic as the previous Java sample.

```c
#include <stdio.h>

#include <string.h>

#include <stdlib.h>

#include <sqlcli1.h>

#include <sqlca.h>


#define MAX_SERVER_LENGTH     10

#define MAX_UID_LENGTH        10

#define MAX_PWD_LENGTH        10

#define MAX_STMT_LENGTH      200


int main(int argc, char *argv[])
{
    SQLRETURN      sqlrc = SQL_SUCCESS;
    SQLHANDLE      henv;  /* environment handle */
    SQLHANDLE      hdbc;  /* connection handle */
    SQLHANDLE      hstmt;  /* statement handle */
    SQLCHAR        server[MAX_SERVER_LENGTH + 1] ;
    SQLCHAR        uid[MAX_UID_LENGTH + 1] ;
    SQLCHAR        pwd[MAX_PWD_LENGTH + 1] ;
    SQLCHAR        stmt[MAX_STMT_LENGTH + 1];
    SQLDOUBLE      salary, bonus, comm;
    double         raise, totalRaise;
    double         min_raise, max_raise;

    /* process the input parameters */
    if ( argc != 3 )
    {
        printf("Usage: TotalRaise Min_Raise_Percentage
Max_Raise_Percentage\n");
        printf("        Both percentages have to be integers.\n");
        return -1;
    }

    min_raise = atoi(argv[1])/100.0;
```

```
max_raise = atoi(argv[2])/100.0;


/* allocate an environment handle */
sqlrc = SQLAllocHandle( SQL_HANDLE_ENV, SQL_NULL_HANDLE, &henv );
if ( sqlrc != SQL_SUCCESS )
    printf( "\n--ERROR while allocating the environment handle.\n" );


/* allocate a database connection handle */
sqlrc = SQLAllocHandle( SQL_HANDLE_DBC, henv, &hdbc );
if ( sqlrc != SQL_SUCCESS )
    printf( "\n--ERROR while allocating the connection handle.\n" );


/* connect to sample database */
strcpy( (char *)server, "sample" );
strcpy( (char *)uid, "db2admin" );
strcpy( (char *)pwd, "db2admin" );

sqlrc = SQLConnect( hdbc,
                    server, SQL_NTS,
                    uid,    SQL_NTS,
                    pwd,    SQL_NTS
                  );
if ( sqlrc != SQL_SUCCESS )
    printf( "\n--ERROR while connecting to database.\n" );


/* allocate a statement handle */
sqlrc = SQLAllocHandle(SQL_HANDLE_STMT, hdbc, &hstmt);            /*--(1)*/
if ( sqlrc != SQL_SUCCESS )
    printf( "\n--ERROR while allocating the statement handle.\n" );


/* calling the SQL procedure */
strcpy( (char *)stmt, "CALL DB2ADMIN.READ_EMP()" );

sqlrc = SQLExecDirect( hstmt, stmt, SQL_NTS );                   /*--(2)*/
if ( sqlrc != SQL_SUCCESS )
```

```
            printf( "\n--ERROR while calling the SQL procedure.\n" );


    /* bind columns to variables */
    sqlrc = SQLBindCol(hstmt, 1, SQL_C_DOUBLE, &salary, 0, NULL);        /*--(3)*/
    if ( sqlrc != SQL_SUCCESS )
        printf( "\n--ERROR while binding salary column.\n" );

    sqlrc = SQLBindCol(hstmt, 2, SQL_C_DOUBLE, &bonus, 0, NULL);
    if ( sqlrc != SQL_SUCCESS )
        printf( "\n--ERROR while binding bonus column.\n" );

    sqlrc = SQLBindCol(hstmt, 3, SQL_C_DOUBLE, &comm, 0, NULL);
    if ( sqlrc != SQL_SUCCESS )
        printf( "\n--ERROR while binding comm column.\n" );


    /* fetch result set returned from SQL procedure */
    sqlrc = SQLFetch(hstmt);                                             /*--(4)*/
    if ( sqlrc != SQL_SUCCESS && sqlrc != SQL_NO_DATA_FOUND )
        printf( "\n--ERROR while fetching the result set.\n" );

    totalRaise = 0;
    while (sqlrc != SQL_NO_DATA_FOUND)
    {
        raise = min_raise;

        /* calculate raise */
        if ( bonus >= 600 )
            raise += 0.04;

        if ( comm < 2000 )
            raise += 0.03;
        else if ( comm < 3000 )
            raise += 0.02;
        else
            raise += 0.01;

        if ( raise > max_raise )
            raise = max_raise;
```

```
        totalRaise += salary * raise;

        sqlrc = SQLFetch(hstmt);
        if ( sqlrc != SQL_SUCCESS && sqlrc != SQL_NO_DATA_FOUND )
            printf( "\n--ERROR while fetching the result set.\n" );
    }

    printf("The total cost of the raise is: %.2f\n", totalRaise);



    /* free the statement handle */
    sqlrc = SQLFreeHandle(SQL_HANDLE_STMT, hstmt);
    if ( sqlrc != SQL_SUCCESS )
        printf( "\n--ERROR while freeing the statement handle.\n" );



    /* disconnect from the database */
    sqlrc = SQLDisconnect( hdbc ) ;
    if ( sqlrc != SQL_SUCCESS )
        printf( "\n--ERROR while disconnecting from database.\n" );



    /* free the connection handle */
    sqlrc = SQLFreeHandle( SQL_HANDLE_DBC, hdbc ) ;
    if ( sqlrc != SQL_SUCCESS )
        printf( "\n--ERROR while freeing the connection handle.\n" );



    /* free the environment handle */
    sqlrc = SQLFreeHandle( SQL_HANDLE_ENV, henv );
    if ( sqlrc != SQL_SUCCESS )
        printf( "\n--ERROR while freeing the environment handle.\n" );



    printf("Completed(0).\n");
    return( 0 );
} /* main */
```

Figure H.4 *TotalRaise.c*—An example of receiving single result set from the CLI application.

In DB2 CLI, you need to allocate a statement handle before you can invoke SQL procedures (or execute any SQL statement, for that matter). The function is `SQLAllocHandle()` on Line (1) with appropriate parameters. In this case, because the SQL procedure requires no input parameters, you can invoke the procedure by calling the `SQLExecDirect()` function on Line (2) without going through `SQLPrepare()` and `SQLBindParameter()` calls, which would allow you to bind the host variables with input and output parameters.

After execution, the result sets are returned through the statement handle. To access the data, you need to bind the host variables to the result set columns using the `SQLBindCol()` function on Line (3). Another useful function, `SQLNumResultCols()` (which is not used in our example), allows you to check the number of columns returned by the cursor. This function would be useful if you need to write more dynamic code to deal with cases in which the result set columns are unknown. Once the variables are bound, you can fetch one row at a time using the `SQLFetch()` function on Line (4) in a `while` loop. The condition of the loop checks the return code of `SQLFetch()` against a defined constant `SQL_NO_DATA_FOUND`.

For more information on CLI/ODBC programming, refer to DB2 Call Level Interface Guide and Reference.

When finished with the cursor, don't forget to free all your allocated handles.

Receiving Multiple Result Sets in Java

Receiving multiple result sets from a procedure in Java is an easy process as long as the outputs from a stored procedure are clearly documented. The following sections detail how multiple result sets can be receive in both a Java Application and in a Java Stored Procedure.

Receiving Multiple Result Sets in a Java Application

Receiving multiple result sets is similar to receiving a single result set discussed in the previous section. The question you would want to ask yourself when you write your client code is whether you want to process the result sets in parallel.

Processing result sets in sequence means you access each result set one at a time. The current result set will be closed before the next result set is opened. Processing result sets in parallel means you can have more than one result set open at the same time.

If the calling application is an SQL procedure, you have the option of processing the result sets in sequence or in parallel. This is covered in Chapter 8, "Nested SQL Procedures." Similarly, if the calling application is a DB2 CLI program, you will have the same options. If the calling application is a Java program, however, the result sets must be processed in sequence.

In JDBC, you can move to the next result set by calling the `getMoreResults()` method of the `Statement` interface. According to the JDBC standard, this method implicitly closes any existing `ResultSet` objects obtained with the method `getResultSet()`.

Figure H.5 shows the complete Java client code for receiving and using all three returned result sets. The program simply prints all data received from each cursor, in sequence, without saving retrieved data in local variables. The program can only process a result set after the previous result set has been processed.

```java
import java.lang.*;
import java.util.*;
import java.io.*;
import java.sql.*;
import COM.ibm.db2.jdbc.app.*;

class PrintSalary
{
    static
    {
        try
        {
            Class.forName ("COM.ibm.db2.jdbc.app.DB2Driver").newInstance ();
        }
        catch (Exception e)
        {
            System.out.println ("\n  Error loading DB2 Driver...\n");
            System.out.println (e);
            System.exit(1);
        }
    }

    public static void main (String argv[])
    {
        Connection con = null;

        try
        {
            double v_salary, v_bonus, v_comm;

            // Connect to Sample database
            String url = "jdbc:db2:sample";
            con = DriverManager.getConnection(url);

            CallableStatement cs = con.prepareCall("CALL
db2admin.read_emp_multi()");

            cs.execute();
```

```
        ResultSet rs1 = cs.getResultSet();

        while ( rs1.next() )                            /*--(1)*/
        {
            v_salary = rs1.getDouble(1);
            System.out.println(v_salary);
        }                                               /*--(2)*/

        cs.getMoreResults();                            /*--(3)*/
        ResultSet rs2 = cs.getResultSet();

        while ( rs2.next() )
        {
            v_bonus = rs2.getDouble(1);
            System.out.println(v_bonus);
        }

        cs.getMoreResults();
        ResultSet rs3 = cs.getResultSet();

        while ( rs3.next() )
        {
            v_comm = rs3.getDouble(1);
            System.out.println(v_comm);
        }

        rs1.close();
        rs2.close();
        rs3.close();
        cs.close ();
        con.close ();

        System.out.println("Complete(0).");
    }
    catch (Exception e)
    {
        try
        {
            if( con != null )
            {
```

```
                    con.close();
                }
            }
            catch (Exception x)
            {   //ignore this exception
            }
            System.out.println (e);
        }
    }
}
```

Figure H.5   *PrintSalary.Java*—An example of receiving multiple result sets from a Java
application.

Even though three different `ResultSet` object variables were declared and used for each result
set, you still cannot process all result sets at the same time. If you moved the block of code processing the first result set between Lines (1) and (2) to after the invocation of the `getMoreRe-`
`sults()` method on Line (3), you would not be able to access the first result set anymore. If you
wanted to work with the first and the second result set at the same time, you will have to declare
an array to hold the first result set.

Receiving Multiple Result Sets in a Java Stored Procedure

As mentioned earlier, Java cannot process multiple result sets from the same procedure in parallel. If you wanted to rewrite the `receive_multi` procedure shown in Figure 8.18 in Java, you
would not be able to because it processes two results sets in parallel from the `emp_multi` procedure. To receive equivalent functionality, you would need to split the `emp_multi` procedure into
two procedures that return result sets. In this case, the two result sets can be processed in parallel
because they are not returned from the same procedure. Figure H.6 shows the `emp_multi` procedure broken out into two procedures `emp_mult1` and `emp_multi2`.

```
CREATE PROCEDURE emp_multi1 ( IN  p_dept CHAR(3) )
    LANGUAGE SQL
    SPECIFIC emp_multi1                           -- applies to LUW and iSeries
-- WLM ENVIRONMENT <env>                          -- applies to zSeries

    DYNAMIC RESULT SETS 1
em1: BEGIN
    -- Procedure logic
    -- Selects firstname
    DECLARE v_cur1 CURSOR WITH RETURN TO CALLER
        FOR SELECT firstnme
```

```
            FROM    employee
            WHERE   workdept = p_dept;
    OPEN v_cur1;
END em1


CREATE PROCEDURE emp_multi2 ( IN  p_dept CHAR(3) )
    LANGUAGE SQL
    SPECIFIC emp_multi2                          -- applies to LUW and iSeries
-- WLM ENVIRONMENT <env>                         -- applies to zSeries

    DYNAMIC RESULT SETS 2
em2: BEGIN
    -- Procedure logic
    -- Selects lastname
    DECLARE v_cur2 CURSOR WITH RETURN TO CALLER
        FOR SELECT lastname
            FROM    employee
            WHERE   workdept = p_dept;
    -- Selects salary
    DECLARE v_cur3 CURSOR WITH RETURN TO CALLER
        FOR SELECT salary
            FROM    employee
            WHERE   workdept = p_dept;
    OPEN v_cur2;
    OPEN v_cur3;
END em2
```

Figure H.6   Procedure *emp_multi()* separated into two procedures.

With the two procedures `emp_multi1` and `emp_multi2`, you can now rewrite the procedure `receive_multi` as a Java stored procedure, as shown in Figure H.7.

```
/**
 * JDBC Stored Procedure DB2ADMIN.ReceiveMulti
 * @param p_dept
 * @param p_names
 * @param p_total
 */
package ReceiveMulti;

import java.sql.*;                    // JDBC classes
```

```java
public class ReceiveMulti
{
    public static void receiveMulti ( String p_dept,
                                       String[] p_names,
                                       java.math.BigDecimal[] p_total ) throws
SQLException, Exception
    {
        // Get connection to the database
        Connection con =
DriverManager.getConnection("jdbc:default:connection");
        CallableStatement cStmt1 = null;
        CallableStatement cStmt2 = null;
        ResultSet rs1 = null;
        ResultSet rs2 = null;
        String sql;

        // parameters from procedures
        String v_fname = "";
        String v_lname = "";
        java.math.BigDecimal  v_salary = new java.math.BigDecimal("0.00");

        // Set up the dynamic call to the first procedure
        //   Setup input parameters
        //   Register output parameters
        //   Call the procedures
        sql = "CALL emp_multi1(?)";
        cStmt1 = con.prepareCall(sql);
        cStmt1.setString(1, p_dept);
        cStmt1.execute();                                       /* --1 */

        // Set up the dynamic call to the second procedure
        //   Setup input parameters
        //   Register output parameters
        //   Call the procedures
        sql = "CALL emp_multi2(?)";
        cStmt2 = con.prepareCall(sql);
        cStmt2.setString(1, p_dept);
        cStmt2.execute();                                       /* --2 */

        // The first proc has 1 result set, the second has two
```

```
    // Process the first result set of each proc in parallel
    // Then process the second result set of the second proc
    rs1 = cStmt1.getResultSet();                              /* --3 */
    rs2 = cStmt2.getResultSet();                              /* --4 */

    p_names[0] = "The employees are: ";
    while (rs1.next()) {                                      /* --5 */
       rs2.next();
       v_fname = rs1.getString(1);
       v_lname = rs2.getString(1);
       p_names[0] = p_names[0] + v_fname + " " + v_lname + " ";
    }
    rs2.next();

    // Close the resources associated with the first proc
    rs1.close();
    cStmt1.close();

    // Continue processing result sets from the second proc
    cStmt2.getMoreResults();                                  /* --6 */
    rs2 = cStmt2.getResultSet();

    p_total[0] = new java.math.BigDecimal("0.00");            /* --7 */
    while (rs2.next()) {
       v_salary = rs2.getBigDecimal(1).setScale(2);
       p_total[0] = p_total[0].add(v_salary);
    }

    // Close the result set and statement
    rs2.close();
    cStmt2.close();

   }
}
```

Figure H.7   Rewrite of *receive_multi()* in Java.

The two procedures `emp_multi1` and `emp_multi2` are called on Lines (1) and (2), respectively. The result set from `emp_multi1` is received in object `rs1` on Line (3), and the result set from `emp_multi2` is received in object `rs2` on Line (4). The `while` loop on Line (5) processes the two result sets in parallel. `emp_multi2` has a second result set that is accessed on Line (6), and the `while` loop on Line (7) processes the result set.

Figure H.8 shows an example of how the procedure can be registered on the iSeries platform.

```
CREATE PROCEDURE ReceiveMulti ( IN p_dept CHARACTER(3),
                                OUT p_names VARCHAR(100),
                                OUT p_total DECIMAL(9,2) )
    SPECIFIC RECEIVE_MULTI
    NOT DETERMINISTIC
    LANGUAGE Java
    EXTERNAL NAME
'DB2ADMIN.RECEIVE_MULTI:ReceiveMulti.ReceiveMulti.receiveMulti'
    FENCED
    PARAMETER STYLE JAVA
```

Figure H.8   Registering the *empMulti* procedure on iSeries.

Receiving Multiple Result Sets in a C or C++ Application

DB2 CLI has a similar function as the `getMoreResults()` JDBC method for sequential result set processing. The function is `SQLMoreResults()`. Additionally, DB2 CLI supports another function called `SQLNextResult()` that allows you to access and process more than one result set at the same time. Both functions are demonstrated in Figure H.9.

```c
#include <stdio.h>
#include <string.h>
#include <stdlib.h>
#include <sqlcli1.h>
#include <sqlca.h>

#define MAX_SERVER_LENGTH   10
#define MAX_UID_LENGTH      10
#define MAX_PWD_LENGTH      10
#define MAX_STMT_LENGTH     200

int main(int argc, char *argv[])
{
    SQLRETURN    sqlrc = SQL_SUCCESS;
    SQLHANDLE    henv;  /* environment handle */
    SQLHANDLE    hdbc;  /* connection handle */
```

```
SQLHANDLE      hstmt1;  /* statement handle */
SQLHANDLE      hstmt2;  /* statement handle */
SQLCHAR        server[MAX_SERVER_LENGTH + 1] ;
SQLCHAR        uid[MAX_UID_LENGTH + 1] ;
SQLCHAR        pwd[MAX_PWD_LENGTH + 1] ;
SQLCHAR        stmt[MAX_STMT_LENGTH + 1];
SQLDOUBLE      salary, bonus, comm;

/* allocate an environment handle */
sqlrc = SQLAllocHandle( SQL_HANDLE_ENV, SQL_NULL_HANDLE, &henv );
if ( sqlrc != SQL_SUCCESS )
    printf( "\n--ERROR while allocating the environment handle.\n" );


/* allocate a database connection handle */
sqlrc = SQLAllocHandle( SQL_HANDLE_DBC, henv, &hdbc );
if ( sqlrc != SQL_SUCCESS )
    printf( "\n--ERROR while allocating the connection handle.\n" );


/* connect to sample database */
strcpy( (char *)server, "sample" );
strcpy( (char *)uid, "db2admin" );
strcpy( (char *)pwd, "db2admin" );

sqlrc = SQLConnect( hdbc,
                    server, SQL_NTS,
                    uid,    SQL_NTS,
                    pwd,    SQL_NTS
                  );
if ( sqlrc != SQL_SUCCESS )
    printf( "\n--ERROR while connecting to database.\n" );


/* allocate statement handles */
sqlrc = SQLAllocHandle(SQL_HANDLE_STMT, hdbc, &hstmt1);
if ( sqlrc != SQL_SUCCESS )
    printf( "\n--ERROR while allocating the statement handle1.\n" );
```

```
sqlrc = SQLAllocHandle(SQL_HANDLE_STMT, hdbc, &hstmt2);
if ( sqlrc != SQL_SUCCESS )
    printf( "\n--ERROR while allocating the statement handle2.\n" );



/* calling the SQL procedure */
strcpy( (char *)stmt, "CALL DB2ADMIN.READ_EMP_MULTI()" );

sqlrc = SQLExecDirect( hstmt1, stmt, SQL_NTS );
if ( sqlrc != SQL_SUCCESS )
    printf( "\n--ERROR while calling the SQL procedure.\n" );



/* fetch first two result sets */
sqlrc = SQLBindCol(hstmt1, 1, SQL_C_DOUBLE, &salary, 0, NULL);
if ( sqlrc != SQL_SUCCESS )
    printf( "\n--ERROR while binding salary column.\n" );

sqlrc = SQLNextResult(hstmt1, hstmt2);                          /*--(1)*/
if ( sqlrc != SQL_SUCCESS )
    printf( "\n--ERROR while opening the second result set.\n" );

sqlrc = SQLBindCol(hstmt2, 1, SQL_C_DOUBLE, &bonus, 0, NULL);
if ( sqlrc != SQL_SUCCESS )
    printf( "\n--ERROR while binding bonus column.\n" );

sqlrc = SQLFetch(hstmt1);
if ( sqlrc != SQL_SUCCESS && sqlrc != SQL_NO_DATA_FOUND )
    printf( "\n--ERROR while fetching the result set.\n" );

sqlrc = SQLFetch(hstmt2);
if ( sqlrc != SQL_SUCCESS && sqlrc != SQL_NO_DATA_FOUND )
    printf( "\n--ERROR while fetching the result set.\n" );

while (sqlrc != SQL_NO_DATA_FOUND)
{

    printf("%.2f, %.2f\n", salary, bonus);
```

```
    sqlrc = SQLFetch(hstmt1);
    if ( sqlrc != SQL_SUCCESS && sqlrc != SQL_NO_DATA_FOUND )
        printf( "\n--ERROR while fetching the result set.\n" );

    sqlrc = SQLFetch(hstmt2);
    if ( sqlrc != SQL_SUCCESS && sqlrc != SQL_NO_DATA_FOUND )
        printf( "\n--ERROR while fetching the result set.\n" );
}


/* fetch the third result set */
sqlrc = SQLMoreResults(hstmt1);                                          /*--(2)*/

sqlrc = SQLBindCol(hstmt1, 1, SQL_C_DOUBLE, &comm, 0, NULL);
if ( sqlrc != SQL_SUCCESS )
    printf( "\n--ERROR while binding comm column.\n" );

sqlrc = SQLFetch(hstmt1);
printf("\nThe comissions are:\n");
while (sqlrc != SQL_NO_DATA_FOUND)
{
    printf("%.2f\n", comm);

    sqlrc = SQLFetch(hstmt1);
    if ( sqlrc != SQL_SUCCESS && sqlrc != SQL_NO_DATA_FOUND )
        printf( "\n--ERROR while fetching the result set.\n" );
}


/* free the statement handles */
sqlrc = SQLFreeHandle(SQL_HANDLE_STMT, hstmt1);
if ( sqlrc != SQL_SUCCESS )
    printf( "\n--ERROR while freeing the statement handle1.\n" );

sqlrc = SQLFreeHandle(SQL_HANDLE_STMT, hstmt2);
if ( sqlrc != SQL_SUCCESS )
    printf( "\n--ERROR while freeing the statement handle2.\n" );
```

```
    /* disconnect from the database */
    sqlrc = SQLDisconnect( hdbc ) ;
    if ( sqlrc != SQL_SUCCESS )
        printf( "\n--ERROR while disconnecting from database.\n" );


    /* free the connection handle */
    sqlrc = SQLFreeHandle( SQL_HANDLE_DBC, hdbc ) ;
    if ( sqlrc != SQL_SUCCESS )
        printf( "\n--ERROR while freeing the connection handle.\n" );


    /* free the environment handle */
    sqlrc = SQLFreeHandle( SQL_HANDLE_ENV, henv );
    if ( sqlrc != SQL_SUCCESS )
        printf( "\n--ERROR while freeing the environment handle.\n" );


    printf("Completed(0).\n");
    return( 0 );
} /* main */
```

Figure H.9   *PrintSalary.c*—An example of receiving multiple result sets from the CLI application.

The C/CLI version of the `PrintSalary.c` program is similar to its Java version. However, because of the `SQLNextResult()` function, data from different result sets can be accessed at the same time. The example in Figure H.6 prints the salary and bonus columns on the same line.

In order to use `SQLNextResult()`, you need to declare and allocate an additional statement handle. With the `SQLMoreResults()` function on Line (2), the first result set is closed to allow the next result set to be accessed. With the `SQLNextResult()` function on Line (1), the additional statement handle is associated with the next result set without closing the first result set, allowing access to both result sets at the same time. Once the result sets are associated with different statement handles, you can fetch and use the result sets in any order you want.

`SQLMoreResults()` and `SQLNextResult()` can be used together in any order. When either function is called, a result set from the SQL procedure is transferred to a statement handle at the client and is removed from the queue of remaining result sets to be processed by that procedure, so you do not have to worry about accessing the same data twice.

Index

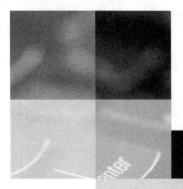

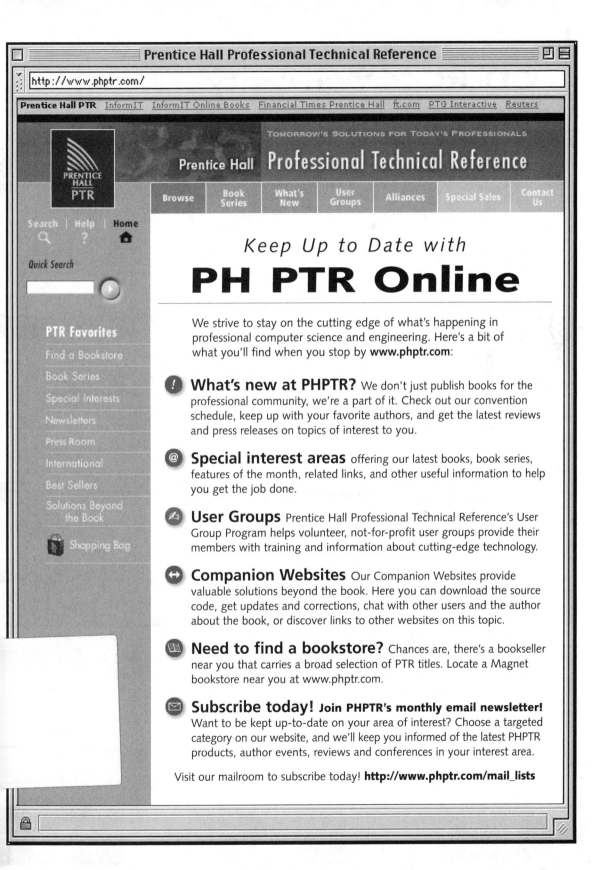

CD-ROM Warranty _____